MEDIEVAL DUBLIN

Medieval Dublin XII

*Proceedings of the Friends of Medieval Dublin
Symposium 2010*

Seán Duffy

EDITOR

FOUR COURTS PRESS

Typeset in 10.5 pt on 12.5 pt Ehrhardt by
Carrigboy Typesetting Services for
FOUR COURTS PRESS LTD
7 Malpas Street, Dublin 8, Ireland
www.fourcourtspress.ie
and in North America for
FOUR COURTS PRESS
c/o ISBS, 920 NE 58th Avenue, Suite 300, Portland, OR 97213.

A catalogue record for this title is available
from the British Library.

ISBN 978–1–84682–334–3 hbk
ISBN 978–1–84682–335–0 pbk

This book is published with the active support of
Dublin City Council/Comhairle Chathair Átha Cliath.

Dublin City
Baile Átha Cliath

Printed in England
by Anthony Rowe Ltd, Chippenham, Wilts.

Contents

Contributors

JUDITH CARROLL is an archaeological consultant and director of Judith Carroll & Co.

ÁINE FOLEY holds a PhD in medieval history from Trinity College Dublin.

ALAN R. HAYDEN is an archaeological consultant and director of Archaeological Projects Ltd.

COLM LENNON is a member of the Royal Irish Academy and emeritus professor of history in NUI Maynooth.

ROSANNE MEENAN is a freelance archaeological consultant.

EDMOND O'DONOVAN is an archaeological consultant with Edmond O'Donovan & Associates.

ELLEN O'FLAHERTY is assistant librarian (College Archives), Manuscripts and Archives Research Library, Trinity College Dublin.

LINZI SIMPSON is an archaeological consultant and project manager.

GERALDINE STOUT is an archaeologist with the Archaeological Survey of Ireland.

CLAIRE WALSH is a director of Archaeological Projects Ltd.

Editor's preface

The twelfth annual symposium on medieval Dublin was held by the Friends of Medieval Dublin in Trinity College Dublin on Saturday 22 May 2010 and this volume presents revised versions of some of the papers delivered on the day, and others that are now ready for the press, including unsolicited material submitted to us. We are always anxious to receive and publish good-quality scholarly studies relating to medieval Dublin (to 1610), so do feel free to contact the editor (sduffy@tcd.ie).

Those interested in learning more about the activities of the Friends of Medieval Dublin – activities which include, besides our free annual symposium and this annual volume, a free monthly lunchtime lecture-series (in conjunction with Dublin City Council), and free guided walking-tours of medieval Dublin in Heritage Week – can find out more by keeping in touch with us on Facebook: there you will find regular updates on our activities and news of events and developments that may be of appeal if you are interested in the history of Dublin or are involved in Irish archaeology or just like anything medieval.

None of this would be possible without the support of our sponsors, as it were. The annual symposium is free of charge to any member of the public who wishes to attend but there are expenses involved in the hire of facilities, etc. which are met by the Department of History at Trinity College, for which we remain grateful. As for this volume of proceedings, it is expensive to produce, and we have only managed to keep it afloat because it has the full backing of our colleagues in Dublin City Council who have managed, even in these straitened times, to provide a small sum towards keeping the price of this book affordable to ordinary Dubliners. We are thankful, therefore, to Dublin's City Manager, John Tierney, to the City Heritage Officer, Charles Duggan, and the City Archaeologist, Ruth Johnson, who have been great partners in this ongoing project.

As ever, we owe a great debt of gratitude to the staff of Four Courts Press (especially Martin Fanning who has lost a few more hairs with this one) for their commitment to the series.

Seán Duffy
Chairman
Friends of Medieval Dublin

Early Christian and medieval excavations at Teach Naithí: the changing morphology of a church site in Dundrum, County Dublin

EDMOND O'DONOVAN

INTRODUCTION

This contribution describes the findings of an archaeological excavation where substantial remains of the early medieval defences around St Nahi's church (Teach Naithí) were uncovered in the former grounds of Notre Dame School off the Churchtown Road, Dundrum, Co. Dublin. The site later developed into a medieval farm. The site (National Grid Reference 316820/228400) is located in Churchtown Upper townland, immediately west of and adjacent to the upstanding ecclesiastical remains of St Nahi's church and graveyard. It lies on a flat promontory or ridge to the north-west of the village of Dundrum and overlooks the meandering course of the river Slang (now mostly culverted). The excavation site was formerly a grass hockey pitch measuring 100m south–north by 90m east–west. The base of the excavation (surface of natural boulder clay) varied from 50.37m OD to the north to 48.28m OD to the south of the site.

The archaeological excavations revealed three ecclesiastical enclosures (figs 1.1, 1.2 and 1.3), two of which functioned as defensive ramparts dating from the Early Christian period (AD600–1100). These enclosures or ditched defensive boundaries defined the outer precinct around St Nahi's church. The enclosures are likely to have surrounded the priest's house and other settlement-related structures. This contrasts with the activity within the inner enclosure at the core of the church site where the church and graveyard are still located today (beyond the area excavated).

The first phase of the enclosure at the site comprised a 44.7m-long palisade enclosing an excavated area of 25m by 25m. The second phase started when the site was defended by a large earth-cut ditch measuring 2.8m (9ft) wide and 1.6m (5ft) deep. This defensive ditch would have been further protected by a large bank (likely to have been topped by a stout timber fence). These defensive earthworks or enclosures were expanded and altered (phases III and IV) later in the early medieval period, resulting in a ditch measuring 4m (13ft) wide and 3m (10ft) deep. It is suggested that the ditches are not only an indication of the importance of the site, but reflect the proximity of the church site to the Viking powerbase in Dublin, which provides the context for such

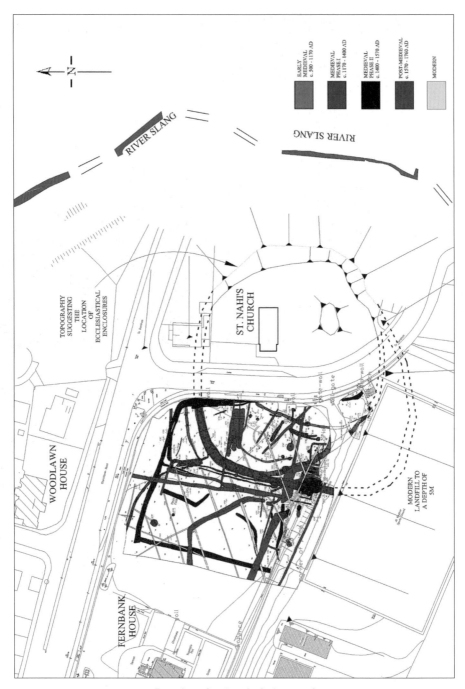

1.1 Location of archaeological excavations

1.2 Aerial view of site looking SE

1.3 Aerial view of enclosure ditches looking N

sizeable defences. The phases II and III/IV enclosure ditches identified during the excavation were so substantial that they must have been constructed in response to a period of change when the territory and site were under threat.

Later settlement remains indicate that the church was the administrative centre for a farm in the later medieval period (AD1200–1500). A significant number of artefacts were uncovered on the site, including an almost complete Flemish redware jug (thirteenth century); these artifacts are typical of the later medieval period and are illustrative of the wealth of the site at that time.

ARCHAEOLOGICAL AND HISTORICAL BACKGROUND

Edmond O'Donovan and Teresa Bolger

Early medieval period (c.AD500–1100)

Origins of Dundrum The name Dundrum (Dún Droma), meaning the 'fort on the ridge', has its origins in the early medieval period (*c.*AD500–1100). The location of the 'fort' has not been established, but the place-name suggests that the site lies on higher ground overlooking the present village. The present site of Dundrum Castle has always been thought to be the site of the original Dún Droma. However, research excavations at Dundrum Castle between 1988 and 1991 have not uncovered any earlier phases of activity consistent with a pre-existing fort predating the Anglo-Norman castle, although the director of the excavations has pointed out that the scope of the excavations was limited to an area adjacent to the surviving castle walls and that an earlier site in that location cannot be ruled out (Elizabeth O'Brien, pers. comm.).

Taney, from Tech Nath Í (later, Teach Naithí), meaning '[St] Nathi's house' or '[St] Nathi's church', was located within the over-kingdom of Leinster (Laigin), close to the north-western limit of the territory controlled by the Uí Briúin Chualann, a dynasty with close genealogical ties to the Uí Dúnlainge, who controlled the north of Laigin (Laigin Tuathgabair) from the seventh century. Though the river Liffey marks the northern border of the over-kingdom of Laigin for most of the early medieval period, it appears that in the fifth century (and indeed earlier) the territory of Laigin extended much further north, most likely demarcated by the river Boyne (Smyth 1974; Smyth 1982).

Dundrum and the surrounding area of south County Dublin was occupied in the fifth century by the Dál Messin Corb, an early Leinster lineage from whom a number of early saints in the locality, including St Nath Í, claimed descent. The most acclaimed Dál Messin Corb saint is Cóemgen (Kevin) of Glendalough. By the seventh century the principal lineage of the Dál Messin Corb (Uí Garrchon) was restricted to the east of the Wicklow Mountains, along the coast in the area where Wicklow town was later established, with smaller collateral dynasties further north along the coast (within the territory of Uí Briúin Chualann) at Delgany (Uí Bráen Deilgni) and Shankill (Uí Amsáin). However, analysis of the annals, the saints' Lives (in particular the seventh-century Vitae of Patrick) and the location of ecclesiastical sites founded or associated with members of the Dál Messin Corb, clearly indicates that originally they were based in the plains of Kildare, dominating the politics of Laigin in the fifth and sixth centuries (Smyth 1974).

In the seventh century, these lands south of river Liffey were known as Cualu and, as the power of the Dál Messin Corb declined in the latter part of the seventh century, Cualu came under the control of two lineages, the Uí Chellaig Chualann and the Uí Briúin Chualann. From the eighth century the area around Dundrum lay within territory controlled by the Uí Briúin Chualann dynasty (Stout and Stout 1992, 19). The river Liffey separated Cualu from the over-kingdom of Brega (comprising, approximately north Dublin, Meath and south Louth) to the north. Historical sources suggest that tillage crops were important at this time and tell us that the ale of Cualu was renowned for its quality and was consumed from vessels made from horns of wild ox. According to one early text, 'He is not king over glorious Ireland who does not consume the ale of Cualu' (Corlett 1999, 34).

Further upheavals in the late ninth and tenth centuries occurred with the establishment of the Norse settlement of Dublin, whose rulers extended control over large tracts of modern County Dublin both north and south, creating a hinterland (Dyflinarskiri or Fine Gall). This impacted on the territories of the Uí Dúnchada branch of Uí Dúnlainge in south-west Co. Dublin and the land of Uí Briúin Chualann in south-east Co. Dublin and north-east Co. Wicklow. The initial Anglo-Norman documentation in relation to this latter area indicates that the main overlords, the Harolds and Meic Torcaill, were of Norse extraction.

Taney church/St Nahi's church Taney church had its origins in the Early Christian period. The place-name Taney is derived from Tech Nath Í (or Teach Naithí), the house or church of Naithí, its patron saint. This saint is thought to have been a bishop, who probably lived in the sixth century. A significant number of Laigin saints are drawn from the ranks of the Dál Messin Corb, primarily from the branches of the dynasty which formed the forsluinte hUa Náir (CGH 120 b 25–46), clearly reflecting the political importance of the dynasty during the missionary period (fifth-sixth centuries AD). Other saints of Dál Messin Corb include Coégem of Glendalough (†622), Étcheán of Clonfad (†578) and Conláed, bishop of Kildare, a contemporary of St Brigit, who is closely associated with her. A commentator (O'Brien 1988, 519) has argued for the sixth-century date for the saint, having connected Nath Í to Conláed on the basis of a passage within the genealogies of the forsluinte hUa Náir, in Rawlinson B502 which reads 'Da hūa Emri Conlaed 7 epscop Nathí' (CGH

120b 45). This passage simply translates 'Of the Uí Emri, Conlaed and bishop Nath Í', i.e. that Conláed and Nath Í were members of the Uí Emri. Significantly, this appears to be a conflation or a misreading of his source material by the compiler of the manuscript. Though Conláed was of the Uí Emri (CGSH 252.1–3), Nath Í, in both the secular and ecclesiastical genealogies, is clearly descended though Fergus Láebderc, a brother of Eimre; further evidence for this scribal error or conflation can be found in a section of the ecclesiastical genealogies (CGSH 254.1–3). A much more interesting passage in this context occurs within another section of these genealogical tables:

> '*Epscop Domungin 7 Epscop Nathí, – .i. duo fratres – is é dobered grada for clerchib 7 callechaib la Brigit …*' (Bishop Domungin and Bishop Nath Í, two brothers, it is he who confers [ecclesiastical] offices on clerics and nuns with Brigit …) (CGSH 670.86–7).

This description would more immediately be associated with Conláed, who is recorded in a variety of sources (including the various lives of St Brigit) as a contemporary of hers and co-administrator of Kildare. The source and validity of this association between Brigit and Nath Í is not clear. Overall though the placement of Nath Í within the genealogies of the Dál Messin Corb does suggest that he belongs in the latter half of the fifth to sixth centuries AD, coinciding with the period when Dál Messin Corb control was exercised over a much greater proportion of northern Laigin (Leinster). In most of the genealogical tables and also the martyrologies, Nath Í is accorded the title of bishop (*epscop*) and associated with a church called Cuil Foirthirbi and occasionally with a foundation called Cuil Sacaille, which may, or may not, be the same site. A footnote in the *Book of Lecan* places Cuil Foithirbi in Dál nAraide (generally south County Antrim); more recently a location in south County Dublin has also been suggested (O'Brien 1988, 519). Later medieval sources appear to name the river Slack, which flows to the east of Taney church as the Sadoyle or Saeoyle; in a footnote to the *Liber Niger*, Archbishop Alen equates it with Oinnehy (MacNeill 1950, 87), possibly a derivation of Abhainn Naithí. There is a possibility that Sadoyle/Saeoyle could derive from Sacaille, which would indicate that Taney was the site of Cuil Sacaille.

There are no specific pre-Anglo-Norman references to Tech Nath Í by that name, but it has been suggested that the site was an early medieval bishopric, eliminated during the twelfth century reform of the Irish church, specifically on foot of the Synod of Kells-Mellifont in 1152 (Harkin 2005). Certainly, if it was the primary foundation of St Nath Í, then it is likely that it was indeed an episcopal church. However, while the place-name Tech Nath Í clearly associates the site with him either as founder or patron saint, it cannot be identified definitively with Cuil Foithirbi or Cuil Sacaille, the primary sites

1.4 St Nahi's church with bell-cote, looking N

associated with him, with absolute certainty. He is included in the saints of Uí Náir and is also believed to be the patron of Tobernea near Blackrock (Chris Corlett, pers. comm.). According to parish records, a church was built on the site about AD800, probably on the ruins of a still older building. Taney parish records indicate that the church at St Nahi's was rebuilt in 950, 1650, 1750 and in 1910, when the latest restoration was completed.

Viking influence on the church at St Nahi's is attested to by the discovery of two grave-slabs in the graveyard at St Nahi's. These slabs are part of a group of grave-slabs known as the Rathdown Slabs, which are only recorded in the barony of Rathdown and feature abstract designs of Viking origin (Corlett 1999, 42). Examples have been found at Rathmichael, Rathfarnham, Tully, Ballyman, Dalkey, Kilgobbin, Killegar, Kiltiernan and Whitechurch as well as St Nahi's in Dundrum. The example discovered at St Nahi's in 2003 features a saltire cross, formed by elongated X-shaped lines, with a small cupmark at the intersection of the lines. The slab is of local granite and originally would have been 1.64 metres high by 0.46 metres wide and 0.12 metres thick; the second slab is fragmentary but has a large dot and circle decoration with a suggestion of radiating lines (Harkin 2005, 180).

The landscape in and around the early medieval church site at St Nahi's has altered radically since its foundation over a thousand years ago. According to Swan (1985), in almost all cases of known early monastic enclosures, the surviving elements comprise a church and graveyard of mostly late medieval or post-medieval date. The present Church of Ireland church on Upper Churchtown Road was rebuilt between 1750 and 1760. It is likely to be located on the site of an earlier church within the original monastery. A bell-cote present in the gable end of the existing church appears to have been retained from the earlier medieval church and the granite wall fabric indicates that it is likely that the earlier structure was remodelled rather than completely rebuilt in 1750/60 (fig. 1.4). Thus elements of the present eighteenth-century church incorporate earlier phases of an older medieval or late medieval church. Swan (ibid.) also indicates that the pattern of present-day streets, roads or field fences invariably provides an indication of the outline and dimensions of an earlier enclosure, and at times constitutes the only evidence for the existence of an early monastic site. The curving arc of the Upper Churchtown Road represents the alignment of an enclosure at the site. This is likely to have been the inner enclosure surrounding the church and graveyard. The enclosing ditch or outer enclosure found during the archaeological excavations in the grounds north of the proposed convent site suggests that the early ecclesiastical settlement extended west of the Lower Churchtown Road which separates the inner enclosure from the outer enclosure at the site.

Later medieval period (c.AD1100–1600)
At the time of the Anglo-Norman invasion, the whole area had come into the control of an Irish lord, Domnall Mac Gilla Mo-Cholmóc, who married the daughter of the then king of Leinster, the notorious Diarmait Mac Murchada. Around 1170, the lands around Dundrum were granted to John de Clahella and, between 1180 and 1197, the same John granted the tenement of Thacney (Taney), 'a moiety [or half] of Tignai with the church of that vill … to Holy Trinity church, the Archbishop of Dublin and his successors' (MacNeill 1950, 8). However, there is good evidence to suggest that this grant was either the re-confirmation of an existing landholding or the expansion of that landholding. Various records outlining the possessions of Holy Trinity (Christ Church) in 1178–9 include either Taney or a moiety (i.e., half the lands) of Taney with its church (MacNeill 1950, 3; White 1957, 2; McEnery and Refaussé 2001, 102). Further to this, a later confirmation of the landholding of Holy Trinity by King John, in 1202, includes the moiety, adding that it was originally granted by 'Marmacruadin' (MacNeill 1950, 28; McEnery and Refaussé 2001, 103). Clearly this reflects a pre-Anglo-Norman donation to Holy Trinity.

Though the see of Dublin already had a cathedral church in Holy Trinity, its canons were Arroasians, in holy orders, rather than secular canons as was more common during this period. For this reason, sometime in the 1190s, the then parish church of St Patrick's was raised to collegiate and cathedral status. The original intention was probably that St Patrick's would supplant Holy

Trinity, but the prior and canons of the older foundation were quite tenacious and ensured that it not only retained its cathedral status, but was accorded primary status.

Associated with the establishment of the new cathedral was the establishment of a series of new prebendaries, which included Taney. Despite some conflict with Holy Trinity, the prebendary of Taney was assigned to the archdeacon of Dublin from the late thirteenth century until 1851 (Lawlor 1930, 75), except for a brief hiatus in the mid-sixteenth century on foot of the dissolution of the monasteries. The composition of parochial churches assigned to the deanery varied over the course of the medieval period, including at various points, Lucan Clonshaugh, Palmerstown, Chapelizod, Coolock, Kilgobbin, Donnybrook, Whitechurch, Saggart, Clondalkin, Clontarf, Glasnevin. The exact landholding, within Taney, associated with the prebendary is only clearly identified in an extent of 1547, prepared for Henry VIII when the deanery of St Patrick's was surrendered to him. It outlines the archdeacon's possession in Taney as a messuage, nine acres of land and a stang of meadow (RCB C2.1.22.8.15; Harkin 2005, 173). Post-medieval accounts of the glebe lands (see below) suggest that they did not include the excavation site, instead extending east from the church and graveyard. After the surrender of the deanery to the king, St Patrick's was downgraded to a parish church, though its cathedral status was later restored under Philip and Mary. The prebendaries also appear to have been restored; a record of the instatement of Henry Ussher as archdeacon in 1580 lists the rectories of Taney, Rathfarnham, Donnybrook and Kilgobbin as part of the dignity of the office (Gillespie 1997, 37).

The main lands of Taney, however, formed part of the archiepiscopal manor of St Sepulchre's. The manorial centre was adjacent to St Patrick's cathedral at St Sepulchre's palace (now Kevin Street Garda Station) and its lands extended south from there and included Rathmines, Cullenswood, Milltown and Roebuck as well as Taney. A manorial extent of 1326 describes the extent of the archbishop's landholding at Taney and Milltown as 'four score acres ... 40 acres waste and untilled for want of tenants ... four cottages now waste for want of tenants' (MacNeill 1950, 171) with an additional five score acres let to Adam de Bertynes. Leases or grants of sections of the lands of Taney are recorded in Archbishop Alen's Register (MacNeill 1950, 8; 86; 204; 237; 295; 302–3). Some of these leases can clearly be identified with the modern townland of Churchtown Lower, and it is likely that lands in Churchtown Upper (perhaps including the site of the present excavation) were also part of the manor.

Post-medieval period (AD1600–1800)
The parish of Taney is illustrated on the 1656 Down Survey map as consisting of the townlands of Dondrom, Ballintery, Rabuck, Owenstown, Kilmacudd,

Ballowley, Tyberstowne, Moltanstowne, and Militowne. Dondrom and Ballintery
are represented by the modern Townlands of Ballinteer (i.e., *Baile an tsaoir*, or
the town of the carpenter), Drummartin, and Dundrum.

Unlike the individual churches, the archbishopric of Dublin appears to have
maintained and retained much of its medieval property and landholding
during the sixteenth century. A document of 1602 details leases and grants by
the archbishop of lands located in most of the medieval archiepiscopal manors
including: 'the Towne and village of Thanahie within the L[ordshi]pp of St
Sepulchre's and all other Lands and hereditaments near Dondrome, commonlie
called the bushups Lands' to Patrick Hearring (Gillespie 1997, 115). A calendar
of leases from the period 1576–1776 notes a lease of 'the T and L of Thanahy
and all the lands near Dundrum ... belonging to the Abpric' to Arthur
Sheppard in 1679 (RCB C2.1.27.14). The Civil Survey of 1654–56 (Simington
1945, 262–3) records a moiety of Churchtowne (60 acres) held by Sr William
Ussher 'as his inheritance'; the boundaries listed for this suggest it may
correspond to the modern townland of Churchtown Lower. The survey also
records a second landholding (88 acres), Churchtown alias Taunee held by
John Kempe 'by Vertue of a Lease from the Bishop of Dublin'. The boundaries
cited for this second landholding are identical to an earlier entry for Kilmacud
(Simington 1945, 162) and are likely to be erroneous; comparison with modern
townland mapping as well as historic mapping (Down Survey; John Rocque)
supports this viewpoint. A number of seventeenth- and eighteenth-century
rent rolls for the lands of the archbishopric survive; an example from 1704
for St Sepulchre's includes 'lands in churchtowne' (RCB C.2.1.27). Other
landholdings listed can be clearly equated with properties listed in medieval
land grants, for example St John's Leyes (MacNeill 1950, 234).

Early in the seventeenth century, the church was returned in good repair
and provided with books, but some years later it was stated to be in ruin. No
curate is recorded for the period 1641–78 (Leslie and Wallace 2001, 247) and
for the rest of the seventeenth and most of the eighteenth century it shared a
curate with at least one other parish (usually Kilgobbin) (Leslie and Wallace
2001, 247–8). The curacy in 1647 was returned as vacant and probably the
church became quite unfit for use during the Commonwealth (Ball 1903).
After the Restoration, Taney parish was generally placed in charge of the
curate appointed to Donnybrook and the church was allowed to remain in a
state of dilapidation. It was not until the middle of the eighteenth century that
the structure, now known as the old church of Taney, was erected (rebuilt) by
Dr Mann, who was in 1757 appointed archdeacon of Dublin, and his curate
Reverend Jeremy Walsh, who was nominated in 1758 to the parishes of
Killgobbin and Taney (Ball 1903). The Record of Monuments and Places
describes the site as currently being occupied by a plain Church of Ireland
church built in 1760 by William Monk Gibbon on the site of an earlier church,

1.5 Location of archaeological
features set onto 2nd edition
OS Map 1871

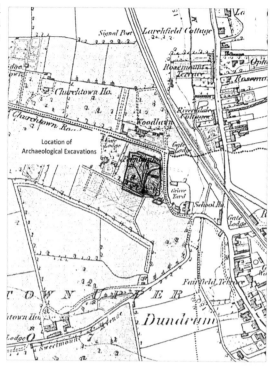

the precise location of which has not been established, but which is likely to coincide with the site of the present building. The presence of a bell-cote, or bell-tower, at the gable end of the church suggests it may even have incorporated part of an earlier structure. However, within fifty years parish record indicate that the congregation had increased to the level at which it was necessary to build a new church (RCB, Vestry Minute Book 1792–1812). The new church was opened in 1818 at a site on Drumar Lane, although it was not fully consecrated until 1872. Nineteenth-century maps and parish records record St Nahi's as a mortuary chapel.

The church and rectory of Taney retained a landholding, initially controlled by the archdeacon, but after 1851 passing to the appointed rector; a lease of 1781, from the archdeacon to Alexander Castell, describes the glebe lands of the archdeacon in Taney as comprising 6 acres, 2 roods and 37 perches. A survey of the glebe lands, in 1871, shows them extending east from the church and graveyard, across the river Slack and also the main road to Dundrum. Allowing for the loss of lands to the new railway line, the extent of the property (6 acres, 1 rood and 12 perches) seems to be the same as the lease a century earlier and not too greatly reduced from the 9 acres recorded in 1547.

The present graveyard boundary curves on the south and the west (Churchtown Road Lower) of the site (fig. 1.5), suggesting that it follows the curvature of the supposed Early Christian enclosure. The graveyard to the south of the church is raised above the level of the ground outside the boundary and falls away steeply by approximately three to five metres.

Churchtown, which most likely derives its name from the presence of St Nahi's (Pearson 1998), covers the townlands of Churchtown Upper and Whitehall. The area, as much of the environs of Dundrum, remained a principally rural one into the twentieth century. It is situated beneath the Dublin and Wicklow mountains and the quality of its land ensured that the area was principally characterized by demesne lands in the nineteenth century. As Lewis (1837, 594), in his *Topographical dictionary*, writes of Taney 'the surrounding scenery is richly diversified, and the parish thickly studded with handsome seats and pleasing villas.' The rural character of the Churchtown area is evident on Rocque's mid-eighteenth-century map of County Dublin, where only four structures, including St Nahi's, are indicated, surrounded by green fields west of the river Slang. Two of these were accessible off Upper Churchtown Road, in the area now occupied by the Notre Dame des Missions Convent. The easternmost structure, opposite St Nahi's church, appears to have an associated garden. In the first quarter of the nineteenth century there were still very few houses in the district, but a few houses did develop around the junction of Beaumont Avenue and Upper Churchtown Road, the closest Churchtown came to ever being a town. The houses, as shown by Taylor, included Belfield and Churchtown, as well as Taney Lodge on the north side of Upper Churchtown Road and Taney on the south side of Upper Churchtown Road. The latter, Taney, may be the unnamed structure indicated by Rocque within the western grounds of the Notre Dame des Missions Convent. Taylor also depicts a stand of trees on the eastern grounds of the convent, opposite St Nahi's church.

Greatest detail regarding the development history of the Notre Dame des Missions Convent is provided by the Ordnance Survey series maps, and the first edition, which was published in 1843, clearly illustrates the concentration of big houses and landscaped demesnes that characterized the Churchtown area in the nineteenth century. The map first shows the early Victorian Wood Ville in the grounds of the Notre Dame des Missions Convent and school, which may be a successor of the structure indicated as Taney by Taylor. Fernbank, which the Notre Dame Sisters purchased shortly after the end of the Second World War (a date of 1953 is indicated above the door to the sisters' residence), dates from the mid-nineteenth century, and is shown on the 1871 Ordnance Survey revision map to the east of Wood Ville. The area of land originally associated with the house extended to 8 acres 1 rood and 22 perches. Representatives of Michael Nolan owned both properties. Fernbank House at that time comprised a 'house, office, gate lodge and land' and had a rateable value of £80 (£58 for the buildings and £22 for the land). The first occupier of the property was John Webb. In 1871 John M. Greene took over the lease. By 1875 a second house with a separate yard was constructed on the property. A walled garden at Fernbank is also shown on this map, but no trace of associated structures, such as the gate lodges, survive above ground level. The ground to the rear, south and south-east of both Fernbank and Wood Ville, incorporates the area of this development. The 1871 Ordnance Survey revision depicts this area at a lower level than the land to the north and is shown largely as gardens. The ground to the east of Fernbank is shown as open green space, much as it appears today prior to the development of the site.

ARCHAEOLOGICAL EXCAVATION RESULTS

Edmond O'Donovan

The full excavation report on the archaeological excavations at the site is *c.*400 pages long. The descriptions of the excavated sites herein (and summary of the small finds) is a significant summary and does not include a full account or description of the findings.

Early medieval period (c.AD600–c.AD1170)

The earliest phase of archaeological activity identified on the excavation consists of outer boundaries that were successively built around the site (fig. 1.6). The boundary or outer enclosure began as a simple fence feature defining the western side of the church site (Phase I), but later developed into sizeable fortifications (Phases II, III and IV) and are illustrated as a series of expanding enclosing features. The radiocarbon dates obtained from these features are early medieval. Additionally, several perforated bone pins from the inner boundary ditch are typical for the early medieval to Viking period and are comparable in date and type to finds from other Dublin excavations (O'Donovan 2008). Datable finds from the latest fills of the large enclosure ditch (Phase III) and its recut (Phase IV) suggest that it was still partially open (albeit substantially filled up) in the high to later medieval period (*c.*AD1200).

Enclosure phase I: palisade enclosure and associated activity
A sub-circular enclosure (F118 and F187) was located on the western side of the church site (fig. 1.7). The western remains (F118) measured 24.5m in length, although it was truncated by later activity to the south and north-east. The feature varied from 0.6m to 0.8m in width with an average depth of 0.26–0.42m and a U-shaped profile. The main fill (F119) of the ditch was composed of orange-brown compact clay with large packing-stones at the base throughout the ditch; little or no charcoal was present in the feature. The

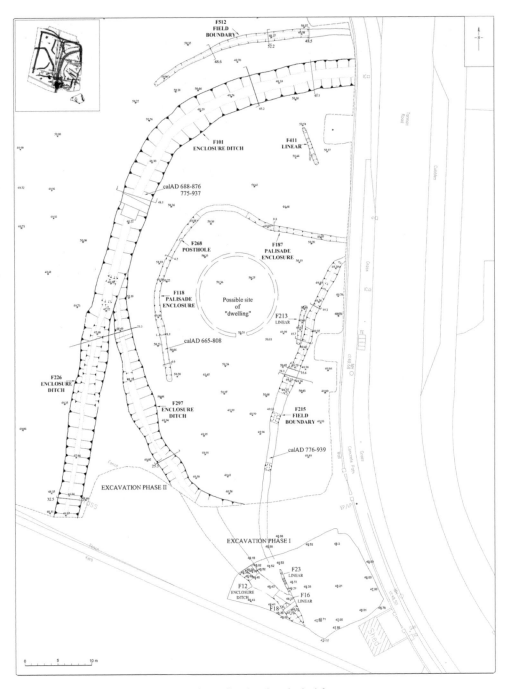

1.6 Early medieval archaeological features

1.7 Early palisade enclosure F118, looking SE

packing-stones suggest that the trench supported a palisade/timber fence. An animal bone (cow horn) from the fill was dated to AD665–808 (2 sigma cal C14 date, 94.5% probability); the bone was retrieved from the base of the feature. No pottery was recovered from the feature. Several disintegrated pieces of animal bone and three flint-flakes (*119:1–3*) were discovered from the lower part of the fill.

The northern side of the palisade trench (F187) was also U-shaped in profile and was recorded over a 15.05m long stretch. The ditch was 0.76m wide and 0.46m deep. The single fill (F188) was composed of yellowish mid-brown silty clay with occasional mid-sized limestone boulders present. Pieces of animal bone were found in the fill. The ditch was completely truncated, to the north-west by a pit (F179) and to the east by two medieval ditches (F413 and F464). Two sherds of medieval pottery (Leinster cooking ware: *188:1–2*) were recovered from the upper fill, although these were interpreted as being intrusive.

Enclosure phase II: the V-shaped ditch
The next phase of activity at the site is represented by a circular defensive rampart constructed outside the earlier (Phase I) palisade trench (fig. 1.8). The ditch appears to have encircled the church site and was between 2.26m and 2.8m wide and up to 1.6m deep and had a pronounced V-shaped profile and a narrow flat base between 0.4m to 0.55m wide. The ditch was recorded over a

1.8 Working shot showing V-shaped ditch F297 (*left*) and U-shaped ditch F101 (*right*), looking S under excavation

1.9 Aerial view of site showing large enclosure ditch F101/F226 cutting earlier ditch F297

41.84m section (fig. 1.9). The ditch extended to the east beyond the limit of the excavation and was entirely cut away by the later (Phase III) ditch (F101) to the north. It was clear that the V-shaped ditch (F297) originally partially shared its alignment with the later U-shaped ditch (F101) where it was completely removed by the latter's (F101) construction.

The basal fill of the V-shaped ditch (northern end) was composed of compact yellowish-brown clay with occasional limestone gravel (F298). Further to the south, the basal fills contained dark grey (F338) to greyish-brown (F339 and

F355) silty clay. The middle fills (F315, 340, F341 and F342) and the upper fills (F316 and F343) consisted of orange-brown (F316, F340, F341 and F343) to mid-greyish brown (F315 and F342) silty clay with occasional dark brown to greyish (F315 and F340) and brown (F316) mottling. Small pieces of animal bone (F338) were recovered from the basal fill. Medieval pottery (Leinster cooking ware: *343:1* and Dublin-type ware: *343:2–3*) was retrieved from the upper fills. The V-shaped enclosure ditch (F297) was cut by several medieval features.

Enclosure phase III: the U-shaped ditch
The third phase of enclosure at the site consists of a large U-shaped ditch (F101/F226, figs 1.10 and 1.11). This curvilinear enclosure ditch was located surrounding the western half of the site. The ditch (F101) runs to the east beyond the eastern limit of the excavation under the existing boundary wall of Churchtown Road Upper.

Throughout the north-western to eastern part of the ditch (F101), the enclosure ditch was from 3.65m to 4.36m wide and from 1.85m to 2.2m deep (figs 1.11 and 1.12). The ground level into which the ditch was cut dropped from 50.5m OD at the north-eastern end to 49.5m OD around the middle section. The exposed length was 59m and the ditch had a slightly U-shaped profile and a flat base. The average width at the base of the feature was 1.3m.

The sequence of the excavated fills was similar throughout the ditch. The bottom of the ditch appeared to be affected by the groundwater; the fill was composed of blackish-dark grey sterile clay (F497/F295), a mixed oxidized natural boulder clay. A local deposit (F294) in the southern third of the ditch lay above that layer at the sides of the base. It was composed of dark greyish-black sandy silt. The deposit, lying above these lowest local fills, was composed of mottled yellow dark grey sandy silt (F471) in the northern part of the ditch and of black sandy silt (F112/F250/F434) to the south. Small pieces of animal bone (F471 and F112) and slag-like material (*112:1*) were found in these fills. A local fill to the south (F435) was composed of mid-grey sandy clay and occasional snail shells, which would suggest that his section of the ditch contained pools of open water, prior to subsequent infilling. The next layer (F104/F474/F436/251) above the basal fills was composed of highly organic dark brown-blackish clay/silt with numerous snail shells present, as well as some animal bone (F104 and F474). According to the character of the fills of the ditch as described above, the presence of snail shells throughout represents the base of the infilling ditch in moderately wet conditions as the ditch slowly silted up.

Enclosure phase IV: the recut of the enclosure ditch (defensive renovation)
The large U-shaped ditch (F101/F226) silted up and was recut (F106) and rebuilt in Phase IV. The defences were reconstructed along the entire length of

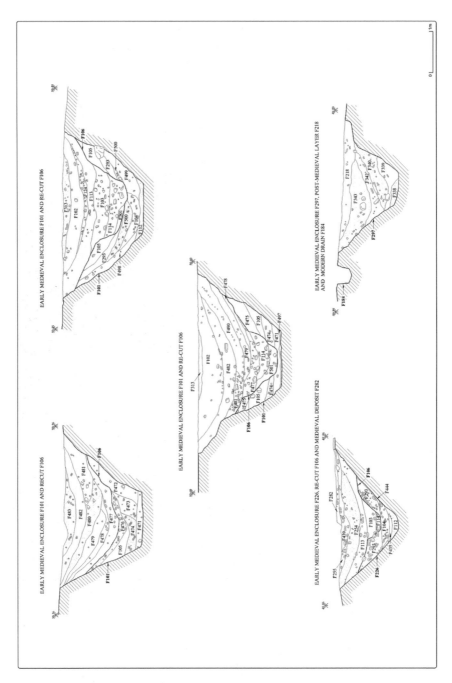

1.10 Section through early medieval enclosure ditch F101 and recut F106 and through
early medieval enclosure ditch F226 and F297

1.11 Post-excavation view of ditch F101, showing stepped 'pockets'

1.12 Section through southern portion of ditch F101/F226, looking N

1.13 Section showing recut F106 in ditch F101, looking W

the ditch that was investigated (fig. 1.13). The cut penetrated into the lower, middle and upper fills (F104/F474 and F105/F475) of the enclosure and was irregular in shape. The newly recut ditch had varying base profiles which changed from uneven to flat and concave, with varying section forms alternating between V-shaped to almost concave along the sides. This reflects the fact that the new ditch was recut into the older softer primary fill. It appears that the ditch (F101) had significantly silted up when the recut took place from the surface of the upper middle fills (F105 and F475). The width of the ditch, measured from the breaking slopes, was between 1.4m and 2m; though it was much wider at the eastern end where it widened to 2.7m. The average depth, depending on the OD of the surface, dropped from 1.95m to the north-east to 1.4m to the south. The average base level of the recut was 48.68m OD in the northern and north-eastern section, but dropped from 48.68m OD north of the steps mentioned above to 47.46m OD at its southern end.

The basal fill (F114/F476) was composed of dark brown to greyish mid-brown silty clay with snail shells and charcoal flecks. Several large pieces of animal bone and an alabaster stick pin (possibly late twelfth to early fourteenth century: *114:1*), were recovered from the fill. A local basal fill (F501) was situated in the north-western part of the ditch and consisted of yellowish mottled mid-brown silty clay. The main middle fill (F477/F103/F438 = F485) was composed of yellowish-brown silty clay with very frequent snail shells and charcoal flecks present. Fragments of a human skullcap (F485), animal bone (F103 and F485), a piece of slag (*103:1*) and two medieval potsherds (Dublin-type ware: *103:1–2*) were recovered from the fill. A local fill (F314) was located at the eastern side of the middle section, composed of mid-brown silty clay and snail shells. At the eastern end of the ditch the middle fills were composed of very silty greyish (F478 and F481), yellowish (F479) or mid-brown (F480) clay with frequent middle-sized limestone boulders present. The upper fills are represented by F482/F113/F253 and F483/F102 /F111/F255 = F484. The first (F482/F113/F253) was composed of mid-brown yellowish mottled silty clay, containing large animal bones (F113). A local fill (F126) between these upper fills, located in the middle section of the ditch, was composed of yellowish-grey clay. A similar local fill (F254) was located further south. The second and uppermost fill (F483/F102/F255) was composed of blackish-dark brown sandy silt with inclusions of charcoal throughout. Animal bone (F102/F111 and F483), several metal objects (fragment of strap-hinge: *102:1*, penannular iron-loop: *102:2*, nails: *102:3–4*, bone handle and iron tang: *484:1*) and medieval pottery (Dublin-type coarse ware: *102:5*, Dublin-type ware: *102:6, 11–13*; *111:1*, Leinster cooking ware: *102:7–10*; *484:2–7* and Saintonge motted green glaze: *484:8*) were discovered from this fill. The post-medieval finds (clay-pipe: *484:12*, fragment of paint palette: *484:13*, pottery/eighteenth–nineteenth century: *484:8–11*) from the top of the fills appeared to be intrusive. Three local upper fills (F124, F125 and F313), located in the middle section as well, were part of the upper-most fills and composed of greyish (F124) to orangey (F125) or yellowish (F313) brown sandy clay, with some animal bone recovered from F124.

The recut was clearly visible throughout the northern and middle part of the ditch but rather blurred and partly indistinguishable from the fills of the original cut (F101/F226) to the south.

An inner subdivision

A smaller V-shaped ditch (F215) was located in the eastern and south-eastern part of the excavation (fig. 1.14). It was located roughly parallel and *c.*27m to the east of the enclosure ditch (F101/F106). It ran from the eastern boundary wall, where it was cut by the foundation-trench (F273/F275), to the south-eastern limit of the excavation. A narrow ditch (F23) located in the Phase I area to the south is likely to be the continuation of the feature. A 36m length of the feature was uncovered. A slight kink was recorded along the feature adjacent to a shallow linear trench (F213). The ditch (F215) was 1m wide and 0.66m deep at its northern end. It widened along its length to the south. At the southern end of the ditch the very shallow upper part of the cut was 2.3m wide and the entire ditch 0.8m deep. The irregular V-shaped profile of the northern half was slightly stepped in some places and was narrow with a base measuring 0.1m wide.

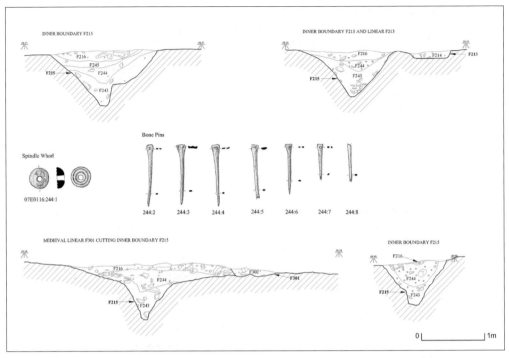

1.14 Sections through medieval inner boundary F215

The waterlogged basal fill (F243) was composed of light orangey-brown sandy clay which was evident on either edge. Large pieces of animal bone and limestone boulders were frequently present in the base of the ditch, particularly at the northern end where several cow skulls were recovered with distinctive compression fractures on the temple. A possible shank of an iron nail (*243:1*) and a piece of animal bone with inscribed designs (*243:2*) were recovered from the fill. The middle fill (F244) was composed of light greyish-brown charcoal-rich silty clay. It contained large amounts of animal bone. The upper fill (F245) was composed of light greyish-brown orange mottled sandy-silty clay, with occasional charcoal flecks and limestone pebbles present. Several bone-pins (*244:2–8*) and a spindle whorl (*244:1*) were recovered from the upper fill. A fill (F216) that was only present in the southern end of the feature and included soils mixed from later deposit was composed of mid-greyish-brown sandy clay (F216) with occasional limestone pebbles and boulders. Animal bone, a ferrous object (unidentified: *216:1*), several fragments of granite stone-querns and hone-stones (*216:1–4*), medieval (Dublin-type ware: *216:16–17* and Leinster cooking ware: *216:10–15*) and post-medieval pottery (seventeenth–eighteenth century: *216:9*, eighteenth–nineteenth century: *216:5–6* and nineteenth–twentieth century: *216:7–8*) were recovered from the fill. The date of the pottery in contrast to the date of the bone pins suggests a later medieval or post-medieval event that finally filled or sealed the ditch. Several medieval features cut the ditch in the middle third: a medieval channel (F301), running west–east from a well (F207) to its pit-like terminus, and two large storage pits (F299 and F366) to the south of the area. Later post-medieval activity represented by several ditches (F135, F193 and F189) disturbed the area as well. Clearly the northern end of the ditch (F213) was substantially truncated, most likely during the landscaping associated with the construction of the hockey pitch. The southern end of the feature survived largely intact, where the ground sloped away.

Discussion
Phase I –The palisade enclosure adjoining the church and graveyard
A simple small curvilinear palisade fence (F118 and F187) was constructed adjoining the main church and graveyard during the first phase of activity recorded during the excavation (Phase I). This has been interpreted as being contemporary with a small number of other partially truncated linear features. There is a suggestion of a separate larger outer concentric ditch (F512) to the north-west, although no trace of the feature survived to the west or south.

The palisade trenches (F118 and F187) have been interpreted as an enclosure or boundary around a small number of dwellings. No evidence for these dwellings was uncovered during the excavation; however, significant truncation of the boulder clay surface occurred in these locations and therefore it is argued that these more ephemeral archaeological structures (post-holes and hearths, etc.) were removed during subsequent landscaping, especially during the construction of the hockey pitch in the mid-twentieth century.

The arc of the palisade trenches (F118 and F187) encloses an area measuring *c*.20–25m in diameter or up to *c*.625 sq. m. This space would easily accommodate a small number of circular dwellings (*c*.12m in diameter). It is tempting to suggest that the distinct kink in the palisade enclosure, where F118 and F187 meet, reflects the location of one such building. The location of a 12m diameter circular house is tentatively suggested, with a suggested entrance in the south-east corner. A small north–south-running linear channel (F411) is probably contemporary and has been interpreted as a possible division between houses located within the dwelling area. The palisade enclosure was open to the south and this and the boundary's small scale indicates that its function was not defensive. A palisade such as this would augment the site's protection from the prevailing elements.

The layout, nature and function of early medieval ecclesiastical sites have been matters for debate and discussion for some time (Swan 1983; Edwards 1990). A model of church development was envisioned by F.H.A. Aalen and is illustrated within the *Atlas of Irish rural landscape* (Stout and Stout 1997, 50). This suggests a sequential evolution of ecclesiastical sites commencing around the most sacred element, the cemetery. The burial place of the site's founder, in some instances, became a particular place of worship. This is followed, but not exclusively, by the establishment of a church at the core of the site, all within the inner enclosure and cemetery. The establishment of enclosures and boundaries, often concentric, beyond this is a later development and distinguishes the core area associated with burial and the church from areas where dwelling and other secular activities took place. These outer enclosures were not necessarily exclusively associated with secular activities and were clearly constructed to adjoin the focal 'spiritual' core of the church site.

The palisade trench uncovered at St Nahi's church site has been interpreted as evidence for an outer adjoining enclosure to the west of the pre-existing church and burial site. It is argued above that this was likely to have enclosed a dwelling, such as the priest's house for him or his retinue. The radiocarbon date from the palisade enclosure (F119) dates to 687–808 cal AD (2 sigma). This strongly suggests that the palisade enclosure was eighth-century AD in date; this dating sequence is supported by the stratigraphic and artefactual evidence from the excavated horizons.

Phase II – The fortification of the church site The site was substantially extended with the construction of a new defensive enclosure around the site. This involved the construction of a substantial V-shaped ditch (F279). The ditch was substantial and measured on average between 2.8m wide and 1.6m deep. Such a ditch would have had a defensive bank of roughly similar proportion, most likely surmounted with a palisade fence. Therefore the defensive earthwork is likely to have been at least 3.2m tall with the addition of a fence (palisade) of *c.*1.5m. This defensive earthwork stands in stark contrast to the earlier palisade fence (Phase I) that surrounded the site. The palisade enclosure is a boundary type which was not constructed with defence as the primary criterion or function. The new V-shaped ditched enclosure appeared to be concentric around the entire church site and measured *c.*70m in diameter.

V-shaped ditches have been built on many contemporary defended sites in Britain and Ireland. Parallels include the site at Repton in Derbyshire where a substantial defensive earthwork was added to the Saxon church site in the ninth century by the Vikings (Biddle and Kjølbye, 1992). There are also rural and urban parallels in Ireland for early medieval sites with V-shaped ditches. Most significantly, defensives ditches were recently recorded adjacent to the site of St Michan's church in Dublin during archaeological excavations at Church Street and Mary Street (Meenan 2004, 97). The Church Street site revealed the presence of a V-shaped ditch cut into underlying sands and gravels measuring *c.*4m wide and 2m deep. The remains of ten burials were recovered from the ditch, six of which were intact and were clearly buried and placed within the line of the ditch. These were orientated east–west, with heads to the west and were radiocarbon dated to AD980–1160 (95.4% probability) and AD890–1030 (95.4% probability). The biggest issue for dating at the Church Street site was the presence of medieval pottery from the ditch (ibid., 97); however, a Viking-Age date was suggested by the excavator. The outer (Phase I) enclose at Millockstown in Co. Louth was also V-shaped in profile. The ditch was associated with settlement remains that suggest an early date straddling the late Iron Age/early medieval period (Manning 1986, 163).

Clearly, V-shaped ditches are widespread at this time and have been used on sites directly associated with Viking campaigns in Britain, as at Repton and at the Hiberno-Norse settlement (Oxmantown) on Church Street. They are also present on sites such as Millockstown in Co. Louth, which is presumably from the Gaelic tradition and is an example of a rural settlement site. Other examples of non-ecclesiastical Gaelic early medieval sites surrounded with V-shaped ditches include Killickaweenny, Co. Westmeath (Walsh and Harrison 2003) and Killedardadrum, Co. Tipperary (Manning 1984).

The scale of the ditch (Phase II) indicates its defensive function, its construction with a V-shaped section adds to its defensive character. A U-shaped ditch has a flat bottom and is easier to construct and easier to move around in. However, it is difficult to pass an obstacle or person in a V-shaped ditch. Wide V-shaped ditches are hazardous to domesticated animals and prevented horse-mounted assaults on ramparts. Both U-shaped and V-shaped ditches are extremely difficult to get out of when wet, especially if they have been constructed with steeply sloping sides. The deliberate or natural (weather-related) retention of a wet base within a ditch would augment its defensive characteristics. These characteristics of the Phase II ditch at St Nahi's are discussed later in the paper.

The radiocarbon date obtained from the lower fill (F104) of the U-shaped ditch (F101) of AD681–890 cal (2 sigma) indicates that the earlier V-shaped ditch (F297) predates this period. The V-shaped ditch is interpreted as being later than the palisade enclosure (F118), based upon the fact that an internal bank (inside the V-shaped ditch) would have covered the southern end of the palisade enclosure. Therefore, a date in the early to mid-ninth century is proposed. The radiocarbon sample from the ditch sent to the C14 laboratory failed to give a determination.

Phases III and IV The next major phase uncovered during the archaeological investigations occurred with the construction of a large U-shaped ditch (F101/F226) surrounding the site. There was evidence for at least two major episodes of repair of the defensive ditch. The construction of the U-shaped ditch was a further significant expansion of the defences at the site from the earlier V-shaped ditch. The U-shaped ditch measured between *c*.3.7m to 4.4m wide and from 1.9m to 2.2m deep. Such a ditch would have had a defensive bank of roughly similar proportion. It also would have been most likely surmounted with a palisade fence. Therefore the defensive earthwork is likely to have been at least 4.5m high, 9m wide with the addition of a fence (palisade) of *c*.1.5m at the top. The U-shaped enclosure appears to have been concentric around the church site and was estimated to be *c*.100m in diameter. This defensive earthwork is not consistent with the scale of an enclosure one would expect at a locally important church or ecclesiastical site. Excavated church sites such as Drumkay in Co. Wicklow had enclosure ditches that were not over 1m deep (O'Donovan 2009) and other church sites such as the church of St Michael le Pole in Dublin had no visible enclosure (O'Donovan 2008, 45). Three ditches were uncovered at the contemporary early medieval church site at Kilgobbin in Dublin (Bolger 2008). These ditches are likely to have formed part of the enclosing element around the church site and measured *c*.1m deep and 1m wide and dated between AD600 and AD950 (ibid., 103).

The size of the Phase II, III and IV defences at St Nahi's are comparable with the size of the defences at the great ecclesiastical centre at Clonmacnoise (Murphy 2003). The outer enclosure ditch at Clonmacnoise had a V-shaped profile and measured 6.2m wide at the top, 1m wide at the base and was 3.7m deep. The enclosure ditch was dated to AD714–873 (ibid., 13). However, these major ecclesiastical church sites, described as 'monastic cities' by Swan (1994), such as Glendalough, Clonmacnoise, Kells, etc., all had substantially larger enclosures measuring *c*.400m in diameter (Swan 1994, 55) which reflects the regional importance of these sites as ecclesiastical centres. The site at Taney (St Nahi's) is smaller (*c*.100m in diameter). Two radiocarbon dates were obtained from the basal fill of the primary U-shaped ditch (F114) and from the recut ditch (F106), dating AD688–876 cal and AD775–937 cal (both 2 sigma) respectively. They indicate that the defences of the site were physically expanded, enlarged and repaired after being erected during Phase II. An alabaster stick-pin (*114:1*) was found in the lower fill of the recut ditch. Its suggested date differs from the radiocarbon determination. Scully dates the artefact to the late twelfth to early fourteenth centuries AD. The dating of the pin is on the basis of stylistic comparison. The pin was found very close to the edge of a large medieval pit (F317) cutting the ditch and may be intrusive.

The enclosed area was divided by an inner boundary ditch (F215) parallel to the large enclosure. The radiocarbon date from the basal fill (F243) of the inner boundary dates the feature to between AD776–939 (cal, 2 sigma), which matches the date obtained from the Phase IV recut/repair to the large U-shaped enclosure. The finds from the feature (bone pins and spindle whorl, described above) are typical of the period and would be consistent with discoveries on Viking-Age sites from Dublin (O'Donovan 2008, 97) and

Waterford (Hurley 1997a, 670). However, these find types have also been found on 'Irish' sites throughout the country such as at Lagore (Edwards 1990, 85) and point to the exchange of (at the very least) artefacts and styles from neighbouring communities, demonstrating the difficulty in ascribing an ethnic background to material culture.

High medieval period (c.AD1170–c.AD1400)

Archaeological features and deposits dating to the high medieval period were located throughout the excavated area (figs 1.15, 1.16 and 1.17). These were made up of rectilinear field-boundaries that developed around and over the early medieval field enclosures. Direct evidence for settlement was characterized by the presence of large storage or refuse pits, a well with related water-management activity and evidence for house structures located in the south-west of the site.

Settlement

Rectangular slot-trench / building foundation (F211) The earliest remains of settlement activity post-dating the enclosure was a slot-trench (F211). It was located adjacent to contemporary medieval pits and other linear features in the south-eastern corner of the excavated area. The northern side of the L-shaped slot-trench was orientated west–east with its surviving eastern side running south. It was exposed over a length of 12m. The western end of the slot-trench had been truncated by a later rectangular ditch (F326). The trench was 0.55m wide and between 0.15 and 0.2m deep. The fill (F212) was composed of greyish-brown silty clay with occasional limestone pebbles. Animal bone, a decorated stone object (lignite, possible bracelet fragment or gaming piece (*212:1*)), a flint flake (*212:2*) and medieval pottery (Leinster cooking ware: *212:3–12*) were recovered from the features.

Pits Most of the medieval pits from this phase were located in the south-eastern corner of the excavation area; the pits relate to the settlement activity that was concentrated in this portion of the site. They were partially aligned in a west–east row (F317 (fig. 1.18), F204 and F299) and were sited to the east and west of the large well (F207). Two pits (F375 and F366) were located to the south of the well. Not all of the pits contained dateable finds, but their physical relationship and general appearance suggest that they were medieval in date (fig. 1.19). The finds recovered from the pits (pottery and other dateable artefacts) range from early twelfth to the fourteenth century in date. The finds from the pits were comparable, and hence the pits have been subdivided into groups based on size, shape in plan and depth.

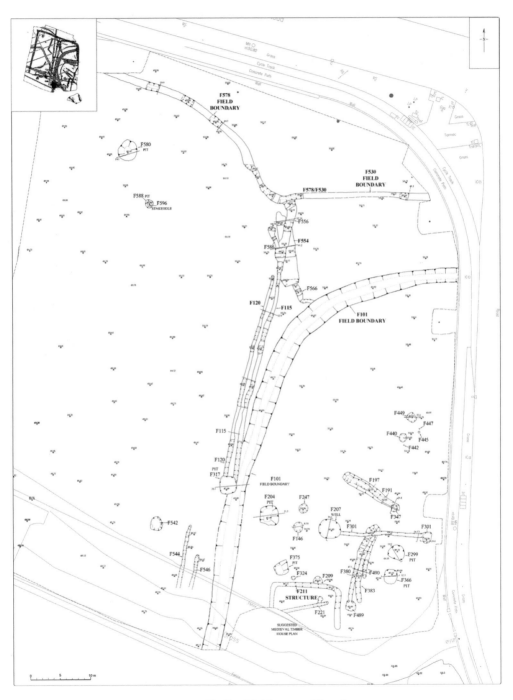

1.15 Medieval field systems Phase I

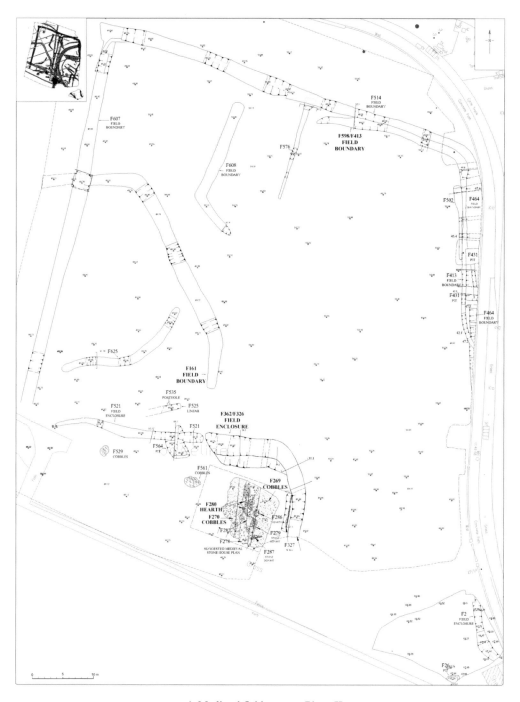

1.16 Medieval field systems Phase II

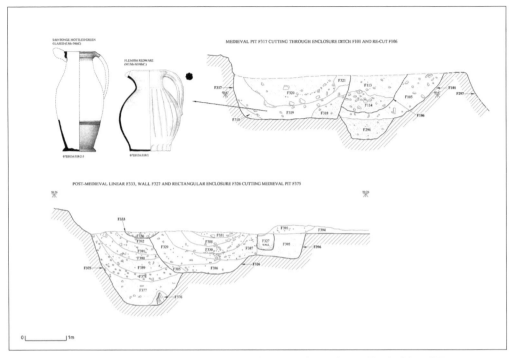

1.17 Section through medieval pit F317 and rectangular enclosure F326 with wall F327

1.18 Pit F317 cutting enclosure ditch F101, looking N

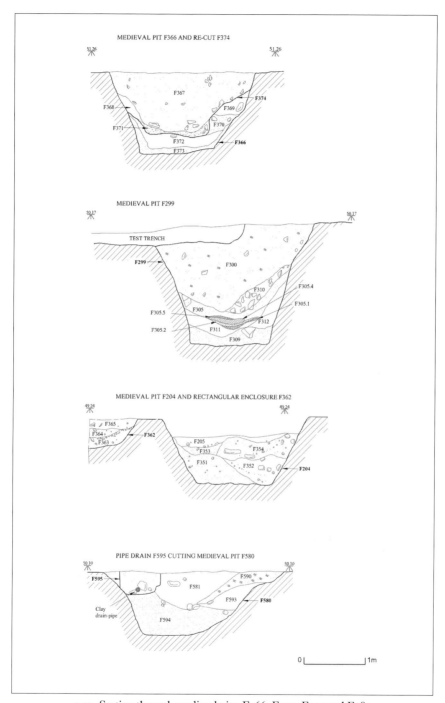

1.19 Section through medieval pits, F366, F299, F204 and F580

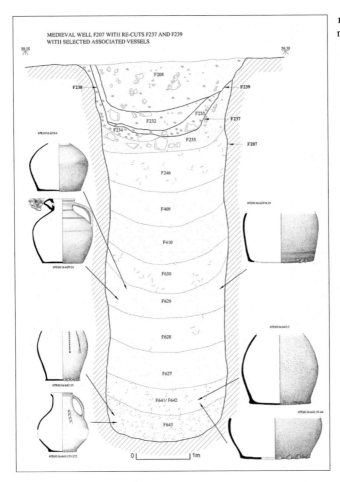

1.20 Section through medieval well

Group 1 – small pits: The first group consisted of nine small, mainly circular shaped pits (F209, F146, F247, F449, F588, F440, F347, F489 and F301) with concave profiles, gradual sloping sites and concave or flat bases. Only one pit (F301) was rectangular in shape and had vertical sides and a flat base. The majority measured between 1.05 and 1.6m in diameter with an average depth between 0.2 and 0.3m. About half of these pits (F449, F440, F347, F489 and F301) contained medieval pottery. Two pits (F301 and F489) were linked by a contemporary linear feature.

Group 2 – large sub-circular and sub-rectangular pits: The second group consisted of eight large sub-circular/-rectangular pits (F299, F366, F207, F204, F317, F375, F580 and F542) measuring in diameter between 1.4m and 3m on average with one larger exception. This group includes the recut (F237, F238, F239) medieval well (F207). Its shape and size suggests that the well was

1.21 Medieval pit (F431) cutting F464 and F413, looking S

reused as a rubbish pit. Six of these pits were very similar, with conical funnel-shaped sides and a rather sharp break of slope to a flat base. They were much deeper rather than wider in comparison to the smaller circular pits described above. Some of these large pits contained dateable finds with only a few sherds being recovered. There were two exceptions to this, the pit (F317) that contained two almost complete medieval jugs, both imported from continental Europe, together with pieces of local pottery-wares and the triangle-shaped base of a stone-pillar and recut well (F207) that contained several pieces of pottery (local Dublin and Leinster cooking wares) together with imported pottery from England (fig. 1.20). Unlike the primary fills of the well, where several vessels of local Dublin ware and imported English wares were recovered, no Leinster cooking ware was recovered from the base of the well. Two pits (F580 and F542) of the second group were of the same size and shape in plan, but different in profile. Rather concave in section, the pits had slightly irregular sides and were not as deep as the funnel-shaped pits alluded to above.

Group 3 – irregular large pits: The third group comprised two large rectangular medieval pits of unknown function in the eastern and south-western parts of the excavation. The first pit (F431) was a 7–9m long pit, box-shaped in section with a flat base (fig. 1.21). It cut the medieval field-boundary but was cut itself by a second medieval recut of the same field-boundary. The second pit (F564)

Edmond O'Donovan

had irregular sloping sides and a concave base. It cut two medieval ditches in the area (F520 and F521).

An overview of the three groups is given in Table 1.

Table 1. Medieval pits – Groups 1, 2 and 3

No.	Grp.	Plan	Section	Break at Base	Base	Sides	Length	Width	Depth
209	1	circular	concave	gradual	concave	shallow sloped	1.5	1.35	0.18
146	1	circular	concave	gradual	concave	shallow sloped	1.24	1.26	0.28
247	1	circular	concave	rounded	flat	gradual sloped	1.5	1.48	0.2
449	1	circular	concave	rounded	irreg. flat	gradual sloped	1.6	1.6	0.43
588	1	circular	concave	gradual	concave	shallow sloped	1.32	1.28	0.12
440	1	sub-circular	concave	rounded	irregular	gradual sloped	1.7	1.2	0.12
347	1	sub-rectang.	concave	rounded	flat	gradual sloped	1.06	0.9	0.25
489	1	sub-rectang.	concave	gradual	concave	shallow sloped	1.75	1.75	0.26
301	1	rectang.	box-shaped	sharp	flat	vertical	1.6	1.1	0.8
No.	Grp.	Plan	Section	Break at Base	Base	Sides	Length	Width	Depth
299	2	circular	funnel-shaped	sharp	flat	conical	2.6	2.6	1.99
366	2	circular	funnel-shaped	sharp	flat	conical	2.4	2.4	1.3
(207)	2	sub-circ.	funnel-shaped	sharp	flat	conical	3	2.85	1.3
204	2	sub-rectang.	funnel-shaped	sharp	flat	conical	3	2.5	2.12
317	2	sub-rectang.	funnel-shaped	sharp	flat	conical	2.85	2.6	1.5
375	2	sub-rectang.	funnel-shaped	sharp	flat	conical	2.5	2	2.2
580	2	sub-circ.	concave	rounded	flat	irregular sloped	4.3	3.4	1
542	2	sub-circ.	concave	gradual	concave	gradual sloped	2.5	2–2.5	1
No.	Grp.	Plan	Section	Break at Base	Base	Sides	Length	Width	Depth
564	3	sub-rectang.	concave	rounded	concave	irregular sloped	5.6	3.69	0.8
431	3	sub-rectang.	box-shaped	sharp	flat	gradual sloped	7–9	min 1.7	0.7

Discussion

St Nahi's or Taney church is known to have been an important rural church site. After the Anglo-Norman invasion of 1170 the church and its surrounding lands were assigned to the see of Dublin and became a prebend of St Patrick's cathedral with the establishment of the archiepiscopal manor of St Sepulchre's shortly afterwards. By the mid-twelfth century it had become the rural deanery of Taney. The medieval features uncovered on the site reflect these changes and the 'downgrading' of the church which took place during the later medieval period. The large Early Christian enclosure ditch (F101/F226) was already abandoned and only visible as a shallow depression when the first building, indicated by the slot-trench (F211), was constructed to the south-east of the site. It was probably part of a farm (possibly an ecclesiastical manor) that now occupied the land to the west of St Nahi's church. A curvilinear field-system (F578/F530) limited the site to the north and divided it in the centre (F554), its linear boundary ditches (F115 and F120) following the remains of the older enclosure. Several large pits, a well and other features close to the building were the last remains of the settlement related to that activity. A later rectangular field system replaced the former and split the area up into two equally sized north/south oriented rectangular fields, both measuring roughly 6om by 3om. A C14 date (1040-1223 cal AD, 2 sigma) obtained from the lower middle fill (F495) of the eastern side (F464) is consistent with the preliminary date based on the pottery found in the fills (Leinster cooking ware, twelfth–fourteenth century AD). The eastern side (F464 and F2) probably followed an older inner enclosure ditch surrounding the church and the graveyard, indicated by the present curving Upper Churchtown Road. The finds from the boundary ditches and stratigraphy indicate that this field-system remained in use during the late-medieval period.

Late-medieval period (c.late 14th century–c.1540)

Introduction: 'House-complex' phase I

The farmyard mentioned above experienced substantial alterations in the ensuing late-medieval period, indicated by the construction of a house ('House-complex' F266) to the south of the site, enclosed by a rectangular ditch (F362/F326), and adjacent boundary ditches (figs 1.22, 1.23 and 1.24).

The large rectangular ditch

A large L-shaped ditch (F362/F326) was located to the south of the excavation (fig. 10). The northern branch (F362) followed the alignment of the southern boundary (F520) further to the east and curved after 13.5m right-angled southwards (F326) where it extended beyond the limit of excavation. Fragments of an earlier cut (F428) of the same ditch and its fill (F429),

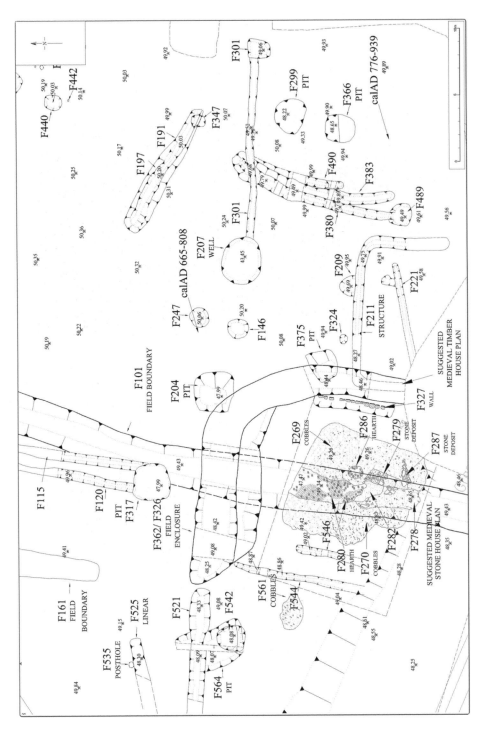

I.22 Plan of medieval structures and associated cobbled surfaces to south of site

1.23 Pit F375 cut by L-shaped ditch F326, looking S

1.24 Revetment wall F327 and ditch F326 cutting ditch F297 and pit F375, looking NW

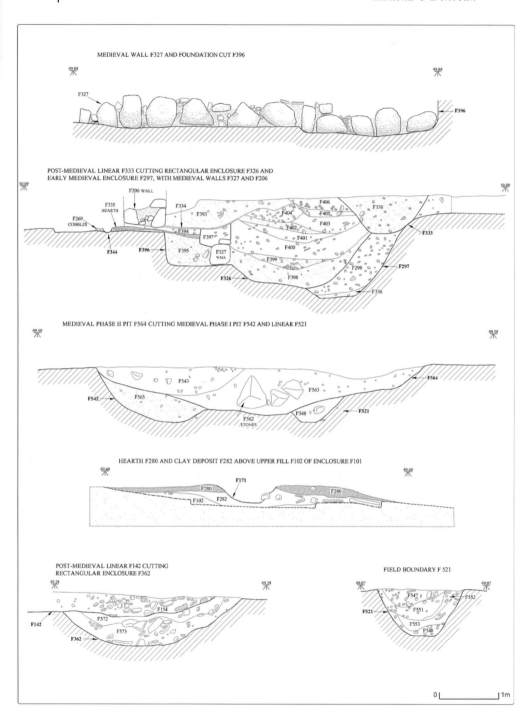

1.25 Elevation and section through medieval wall F327, medieval pit (Phase II) F564,
hearth F280 and post-medieval ditch

composed of yellowish-grey mottled mid-brown silty clay, were visible only in the section at the southern limit of excavation. It contained animal bone. The exposed length of the whole ditch (F326/F362) was 28.5m. The ditch was concave in profile and *c.*2.5m to 2.6m wide with an average depth of 1.2m to 1.35m. The western side of the eastern branch (F326) abutted the foundation trench (F396) for a revetment-like wall (F327). The lower and middle fills were abutting the wall (F327) as well, indicating that both the ditch and the revetment existed contemporaneously. The ditch was filled with a sequence of clay fills (F398/F379, F385, F386, F356, F363 and F573) and medieval finds of all types.

The revetment wall and cobbled surface and associated activity
As mentioned above, the remains of a wall (F327) and its foundation-cut (F396) were contemporary with the rectangular ditch (F326/F362) and reinforced its inner side (figs 1.24 and 1.25). It was constructed from large, roughly hewn granite blocks (measuring 0.5m by 0.5m by 0.3m), forming an east face, with limestone and granite stones packed in between and behind. Little of the wall structure survived. Cobbled/metalled surfaces (F269, 240/264, F270 and F561) were located to the south of the L-shaped rectangular ditch (F326/362).

Related field enclosures
A south-west–north-east running curvilinear boundary ditch (F625) was located in the south-western corner of the site. It was cut by the later southern boundary ditch (F520). The 20m-long ditch curved from its southern limit to the east and then to the north-east. It was 1.4m wide, from 0.2 to 0.5m deep and concave in profile. Its single fill (F626) was composed of grey-brown silty clay, limestone pebbles present. Medieval pottery (Leinster cooking ware: *626:1*) was recovered from the fill. The ditch might have marked the original entrance to the field system in the north, its southern part running slightly parallel to another boundary (F525). Other field systems are clearly active and in use during this period.

Discussion
The large enclosure ditch (F101 and F106) and the inner boundary ditch to the east (F215) were finally filled up during the later medieval period, indicated by contemporary medieval deposits sealing the original fills. The fills of the large enclosure ditch were still subsiding at the time of the construction of a building to the south of the site (probably a farm building) causing substantial levelling activity prior to a cobbled surface (F269/F270), now covering the area. A large rectangular ditch (F326/F362) is likely to have enclosed the farm building, of which little remains. The rectangular ditch was

reinforced by a revetment wall (F327) at its 'inner' sides, although this wall only survived at the eastern side of the enclosed area. The medieval field-system remained in use through the late-medieval period and minor alterations to the boundary ditches took place: the surrounding rectangular boundary (F607/F514/F464) has been recut (F413) and the entrance from the 'farmyard' at the southern boundary to the western field, indicated by a north-east curving ditch (F625), experienced some alterations as well. Rocque's map, although published much later (1760), seems to reflect the field system since it shows a north–south-running boundary, probably the same as the eastern boundary ditch (F607).

Early post-medieval period (c.1540–c.1760)

Introduction: 'House-complex' phase II
Several wall-fragments and related levelling activity attest to a stone building or remodelled farm building built over the medieval cobbled surface described above. Several layers of levelling material and a mortar layer or surface were later constructed inside the building. Other alterations in the area included a large boundary ditch to the south-west of the site. These structures included medieval and significant post-medieval finds, including tightly dateable post-medieval pottery (seventeenth-century 'Westerwald' pottery).

Discussion
The fact that the stone building (F266) was built directly on top of the medieval cobbled surface (F269/F270) indicates an early date in the post-medieval period for the construction of this building (fig. 1.26); it indicates the likely re-use of the existing medieval farm buildings rather than a separate new and unrelated habitation episode. The enclosing ditch (F326/ F362) was still in use in that time and the gap between the rectangular ditch and the boundary ditch to the west (F520) indicates that the entrance to the field to the north – originally located in the south-western corner of the site – had been moved directly to the north of the farm building. Only fragments of a cobbled surface (F529) in that area survived. The deposited layers (F278, F277 and F281) and the mortar surface (F219) show that the ground inside the house has been levelled and renewed several times during the post-medieval period. Disarticulated human bones and related finds from these layers (F277 and F281) and in the uppermost fill (F186) of the rectangular ditch were possibly related to the construction of the present building of St Nahi's church that took place in the mid-eighteenth century. The church was consecrated in 1760 and Rocque's map from the same year refers to it as the 'New church'. The finds from the mortar surface (F219) and related deposits date mainly from the seventeenth to the nineteenth century, suggesting that the building, which is not shown on Rocque's map, had been refurbished in the nineteenth century

1.26 House structure F266 with cobbled surface F269/F270, looking W

for the last time before it was abandoned and destructed. The robber-trenches (F228 and F241) and related finds indicate the deliberate removal of the building. This took place at the latest in the first half of the nineteenth century, since the first edition of the OS maps, published in 1843, does not illustrate a building at the site.

Later post-medieval and modern period (seventeenth–twentieth century)

Several renewed boundary ditches indicate that the medieval field-partitioning was maintained during the post-medieval period into modern times, with new boundary ditches to the south-east and west of the site. A large sub-rectangular pit complex (possibly associated with flax production) to the east of the site with a related drain running to the north–south oriented inner boundary attests to activity in that area. Later post-medieval activity includes several drains running across the former farm site to the south and the last southern boundary ditch.

The character of the archaeological features/deposits (field boundaries, house site and limited occupation) identified during this period illustrate the continued use of the land as a farm. It is clear that the field systems laid out *c.*AD1200 were maintained and recut and the field boundaries remained in place for *c.*700 years. The field pattern and size did not alter significantly in the period. The large pit complex (F179) was possibly associated with the production of flax and may suggest that this crop became important prior to the suburbanization of Taney. The farm buildings or 'manor house' established within the medieval rectilinear enclosure were rebuilt and reconstructed in the post-medieval period. This farm building complex appears to have gone out of use by the mid-eighteenth century but was certainly in use in the late seventeenth and early eighteenth century. No buildings are illustrated within the excavation footprint on Rocque's map. It is possible that Rocque did not illustrate smaller, less important dwellings on his map, however, the reorganization of the site with the construction of Woodbrook House in the eighteenth century and Fernbank House in the nineteenth century changed the site's character from that of a rural farm; it was now part of the expansion of the eighteenth- and nineteenth-century suburbs of Dublin, which saw the construction in the area of large houses associated with wealthy mercantile families from the city.

CONCLUSIONS

The excavation of the lands to the west of St Nahi's within the former grounds of Notre Dame School in the townland of Taney, Co. Dublin uncovered evidence of multi-period settlement on the site; from the earliest medieval occupation, in the seventh or early eighth century, up to post-medieval times (AD1700).

Late seventh to early tenth century
The first evidence of occupation came from the western part of the site; it revealed a settlement first enclosed within a simple palisade and later defended by concentric defensive ditches. The deep defensive ditches survived but there was little evidence of the settlement itself inside the enclosure. It should, of course, be kept in mind that these ditches may have been only an outer ring of defences, where the main settlement itself may have existed under the road and in the modern church grounds and graveyard to the east. The ground level was truncated within the enclosure.

The defences
The earliest defences, represented by a curvilinear ditch (F118 and F187) to the west and a concentric ditch (F512) to the north-west, would have enclosed an area of *c.*625 sq. m. The enclosing ditch was up to 1.1m in width and was probably augmented by a palisade fence, though all that was left of the fence were the packing stones used to hold the posts in place. The C14 date obtained from the ditch fill (F119) dates the construction of the enclosure to 687–808

cal AD (2 sigma). The first enclosing defences were substantially altered with the construction of a large V-shaped ditch (F279). This ditch was larger and up to 2.8m in width. The V-shaped ditch was likely constructed shortly after the palisade enclosure (F118) and both ditches may well have been in contemporary use.

The earlier defences were replaced with the construction of a large U-shaped ditch (F101/F226) surrounding a slightly expanded enclosed settlement. This ditch was in use and was maintained over a considerable period; there was evidence for at least one major renovation of this ditch with the recut (F106). The original ditch was up to 4.3m in width. The excavated area, within this enclosure, measured 35m E/W by over 70m N/S. The C14 date obtained from the lower fill (F104) dated the U-shaped ditch (F101) to 681–890 cal AD (2 sigma) while two C14 dates from the basal fill (F114) of the recut (F106) date the recut to 688–876 cal AD and 775–937 cal AD (both 2 sigma).

There is no evidence for defensive banks around the site but they could well have been removed over the centuries by land improvement schemes; it would certainly be unusual for such large ditches not to have internal banks adding to the defensive strength of the site. From the time the settlement was first established, probably sometime in the late seventh century, to the last major renovation of the outer ditch, probably in late ninth or early tenth century, the defences undoubtedly grew in substance and this does not take into account the existence of a contemporary inner defensive ditch to the east. The threat, from native warring Irish dynasties and later from the Viking raiding parties, was real but this raises the question of what was being defended that required such large, three to four metre wide, ditches. The location, close to the top of a ridge overlooking a valley and an important north–south routeway, suggests an important strategic site, possibly even the site of the original *Dún Droma* ('fort of the ridge') from which Dundrum gets its name. The hinterland of Viking Dublin was under the control of its Viking kings. Dundrum is located so close to the Viking town that it must have come under their influence and control. The presence of Vikings in the area is attested to in a local townland name: Balally (from *Baile Amlaíb*, later *Baile Amhlaoibh*) is named after an Olaf, perhaps even the first king of Viking Dublin, who is reputed to have built a fort in the locality. Clearly the Vikings in Dublin would not have allowed a fortification of the scale and size of Taney to have existed if it was not in their control or in the control of one of their allies.

There is no clear evidence for the existence of structures or for the usual signs of domestic activity, e.g. refuse and storage pits, kilns or fires, etc., from within the enclosure. What did survive was a number of enigmatic linear cuts. The largest of these (F215) ran parallel to and between 25m–27m east of the large enclosure ditch. The C14 date from the basal fill (F243) puts this event in the same period (776–939 cal AD, 2 sigma) as the later recut activity of the

U-shaped enclosure. The bone pins found in the fills are also consistent with this date. Allowing for the fact that many features may not have survived the course of time, the absence of features might also suggest that a second internal defensive system existed further east, possibly along the line of what is now the Upper Churchtown Road and that the main early medieval settlement existed behind this fortification.

The appearance of the enclosure changed dramatically from a simple palisade to a large defensive ditch. The two events within the latest enclosure-ditch suggest that it was recut and extended to the south in the last phase of the enclosure. As mentioned above, it is probable that the curving arc of the Upper Churchtown Road represents the alignment of another enclosure ditch or inner subdivision, likely to have been the inner enclosure surrounding the church and graveyard. The large ditch (F101/F226) and its predecessor (F279) could therefore represent the second, outer enclosure. The outer enclosure in its later manifestation also represented a substantial defensive feature surrounding the early medieval ecclesiastical site.

Early tenth to early twelfth century

There is an absence of evidence for any major new activity on the site from this period. One explanation for this could be the increasing influence on the area of the Viking settlement in Dublin. Viking, and later Hiberno-Norse, hegemony over the area, from its first beginning in the mid-ninth century, covered a period of almost three hundred years. This new force would have broken down many of the old boundaries and divisions between the Irish kingdoms around Dublin and, as a result, the site may have lost much of its strategic importance: control of the routeway from this site may have become indefensible or simply redundant as the Hiberno-Norse domain expanded and contracted over this period of time.

The historical record (see section 2 above) is unclear as to whether this precise area was one of the earliest sites associated with a church dedicated to St Naithí; the presence of two Rathdown grave slabs in the church graveyard, assuming they have not been moved from another location, would suggest that there was a church and graveyard on the site in the mid-tenth century. However, it seems unlikely that the Vikings, a pagan people in the first century of their occupation, would have allowed a monastic stronghold to remain untouched so close to their territory; all monastic sites in the area were attacked and those closest to Dublin, such as Dublin and Kilmainham, were destroyed in the ninth century.

The evidence strongly suggests that the site was used primarily as a strong fortification before the coming of the Vikings. Whether it was a monastic settlement or the site of the original *Dún Droma* is not clear, as there was no evidence from this excavation for the type of settlement within the enclosure.

It would appear more likely, however, that the church site was established, or possibly re-established, once the Norse settlement in Dublin became more Christianized towards the latter end of the tenth century. The site may well have continued as a strong fortification that included a new episcopal, or even a new monastic, settlement, particularly if it was, as some suggest, also the site of a bishop's residence in the eleventh century. However, by the mid-twelfth century and before the coming of the Anglo-Normans the site appears to have lost its original fortified status and the last of the ditches had been greatly reduced. These events may coincide with the postulated loss of the bishopric after the reorganization of the Irish church following the Synod of Kells-Mellifont in 1152 (Harkin 2005).

Early twelfth to late fourteenth century
By the time pottery comes into extensive use in the twelfth century the earlier defensive system is depleted. The final recut of the U-shaped ditch had occurred no later than the first decades of the tenth century and it was only in the very upper fills of this recut that dumped sherds of pottery are introduced. The lower fills suggest that the ditch had gradually silted up over time and that the ditch only remained as a shallow hollow prone to subsidence. However, the perimeter ditch may well have continued to exert some influence on the settlement, particularly in the early stages, as the majority of features are concentrated within the exposed internal area of the old enclosure. There were a range of features from within the area of the old enclosure, including a possible timber build structure, a well and numerous refuse and storage pits, as well as occasional post and stake holes. The first building, indicated by the slot-trench (F211), was constructed to the south-east of the site and extended beyond its southern limits. It was a small building measuring ten metres east–west in external width. The well, the pits and other small features stood close to the building. This building and its ancillary activity probably constitute a small tenant farmhouse or serf holding belonging to the newly established field system. The curvilinear ditch (F2), located in the south-east corner of the preliminary excavation and extending beyond that area, contained a large amount of broken pottery sherds and pockets of dumped domestic refuse, and would suggest that there was probably another enclosed residence to the east of the ditch; the number of pottery sherds would indicate that this was a larger and/or longer-lived residence.

A curvilinear field system (F578/F530) limited the site to the north and divided it in the centre (F554); its linear boundary ditches (F115 and F120) partially respected the remains of the older enclosure ditch. A later rectangular field system replaced the former and split the area up into two equally sized north–south-oriented rectangular fields, both measuring roughly 60m by 30m. A C14 date (1040–1223 cal AD, 2 sigma) obtained from the lower middle fill

(F495) of the eastern side (F464) is consistent with an earlier date for the types of pottery found in the fills; e.g., Leinster cooking ware which was produced in various styles from the twelfth to sixteenth century. Finds from the boundary ditches and the stratigraphical relationships indicate that this field system remained in use up to the end of the medieval period. As with any excavation that achieves only a partial view of the overall monument and surrounding landscape it is difficult to establish what was the dominant influence effecting the changes on the site. The unexcavated area under the road, church and graveyard to the east probably holds the key to these changes. The historical record does show that after the coming of the Anglo-Normans the lands were taken over as a prebend first by Holy Trinity and later by St Patrick's. The development of the new rectangular field system and its contemporary small farm building probably occurred under the new landownership; Anglo-Norman land divisions had a great propensity for straight lines and grid systems whereas the earlier Gaelic divisions were far more varied in form.

Late fourteenth to mid-sixteenth century
The most notable development in this period is the indication that a new building was built to the west of the earlier timber structure. A large rectangular ditch (F326/F362), reinforced by a revetment wall (F327) at its 'inner' sides, probably enclosed the area around the building, though the structural remains of the building itself have not survived. However, a large cobbled surface (F269/F270) survived within the north–east elbow of the ditch enclosure. The builders of the cobbled surface must have been aware of the possibility of subsidence, caused by the underlying large enclosure ditch from the earlier fortifications, and introduced clays to level and compact the ground prior to the cobbled surface being laid. There was also evidence for two hearths within the cobbled area. The earlier field system remained in use throughout this time with only minor alterations to the boundary ditches. The surrounding rectangular boundary (F607/F514/F464) has been recut (F413) and the entrance from the 'farmyard' at the southern boundary to the western field, indicated by a north–east curving ditch (F625), experienced some alterations as well. Rocque's map, although published much later (1760), seems to reflect the field system since it shows a north–south-running boundary, probably the same as the eastern boundary ditch (F607).

Mid-sixteenth to mid-eighteenth century
There was some evidence for a stone building, partially built directly on top of the earlier cobbled surface (F269/F270), replacing the late medieval structure mentioned above. The main structural elements of the new building to survive were three small sections of masonry wall, F541 to the west, F206 to the east and F265 to the south. Based on the location of these walls the building would

have measured 16m east–west by 8m north–south. The internal area was heavily disturbed but contained evidence for consistent renewal of the floor surfaces with spreads of mortar, a new hearth (F280) and spreads of ash. While there was certainly enough evidence for the existence of a new building in this location, so little survived that the configuration of the structure or structures can be no more than a guess. The new building respected the enclosing ditch (F326/F362), which suggests that it continued in use in that time; fragments of a cobbled surface (F529) survived in the enclosed farmyard area. The gap between the ditch and the boundary ditch to the west (F520) indicates that the entrance to the field to the north, originally located in the south-western corner of the site, had been moved directly to the north, possibly at the same time as the stone building was constructed. The fields to the north and west of the farm building continued as before. The stone building was the last of the farm structures, first established in the late twelfth century, to be built in this general location. When it finally went out of use the area returned to agricultural use sometime before 1760 and Rocque's survey of Co. Dublin.

The balance of historic evidence suggests that the lands under excavation were not part of St Patrick's Taney prebend or, if included in the glebe lands originally, had changed hands at a later date. The exact landholding, within Taney, associated with the prebend is only clearly identified in an extent of 1547, prepared for Henry VIII when the deanery of St Patrick's was surrendered to him. It outlines the archdeacon's possession in Taney as a messuage, nine acres of land and a stang of meadow (RCB C2.1.22.8.15; Harkin 2005, 173). Post-medieval accounts of the glebe lands suggest that they did not include the excavation site, instead extending east from the church and graveyard (Section 2 above). The excavation evidence shows a gradual evolution, both in the location of the farm buildings and the changes to the field system, consistent with a constant land usage from the early twelfth century – in which case it would suggest that the site of St Nahi's church was physically separated from the lands to the west throughout the medieval period, much as it is today. This is in marked contrast to the early medieval period when the defensive ditches found in the excavated area must have enveloped the present site of St Nahi's church and graveyard.

Mid-eighteenth century to modern times

From at least the mid-point of the eighteenth century the lands were used for agricultural purposes or as a part of landscaped gardens. The topography was drastically altered when the valley to the south of the site was culverted and reduced to a gentle downward slope. There are no buildings recorded on the land from the maps of this period, except for a building illustrated in the very north-east corner of the site on Rocque's map. There was no evidence for this building but as the road was widened in the twentieth century it may well lie under the path and road just outside the excavated area.

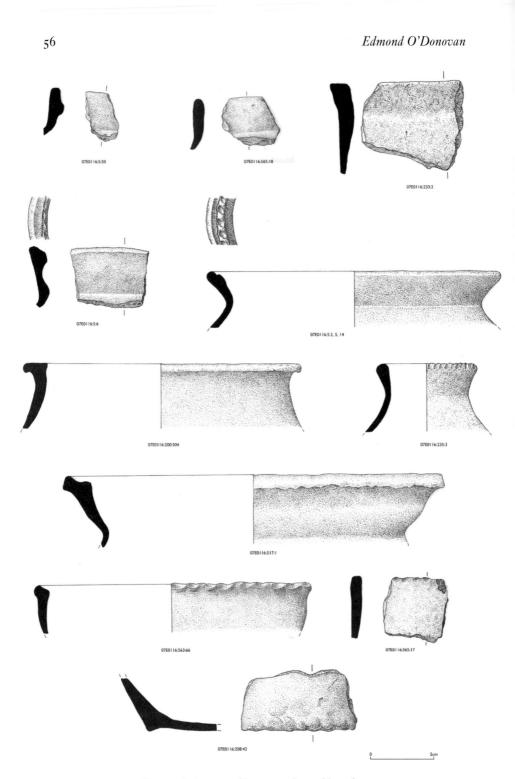

1.27 Pottery: Leinster cooking ware, rim and base fragments

SMALL FINDS REPORTS

Siobhán Scully

Medieval and post-medieval pottery

A total of 2350 sherds of pottery were recovered from the archaeological excavations at St Nahi's. The pottery ranged in date from the late eleventh century to the twentieth century. The majority of this pottery (62%), however, was medieval in date and most of this was locally produced, with only small amounts of pottery imported from England, France and the Flemish territories. The post-medieval wares on the other hand tended to be mostly imported wares, the majority of which were English, with only a small number imported from Germany, Holland, Wales and Scotland and very small quantities of Irish-made pottery. The descriptions and typologies herein are based upon McCutcheon's work (2000 and 2006).

Medieval pottery
The vast majority (98%) of the medieval pottery was locally-made ware, such as Leinster cooking wares (figs 1.27, 1.28 and 1.29) and various Dublin-type wares. The imported medieval wares make up only 2% of the pottery assemblage; 1% imported from England and 1% imported from the Continent.

	MNV	*MNR*	*Sherds*	*% of assemblage*
English	0	2	16	1%
Continental	2	6	18	1%
Irish	17	66	1414	98%
TOTALS	19	74	1448	100%

The medieval pottery assemblage ranges in date between the late eleventh and fourteenth century. The local wares date from the late twelfth to the fourteenth century. The English imported pottery is from south-east Wiltshire, dating from the late eleventh century to the thirteenth century and slightly later pottery from Chester dating to the thirteenth to mid-fourteenth century. The French imported wares are mostly from the Saintonge and date to the thirteenth and fourteenth centuries, with one sherd of 'Miscellaneous French' ware, provisionally dated to the late twelfth to thirteenth century. One complete jug (fig. 1.30), one small body sherd of medieval pottery were imported from the Flemish territories and date between the mid-thirteenth and the mid-fourteenth century. The table below shows the medieval pottery by type, form, date and origin as well as quantifying how much of each type of pottery was recovered:

Type	Sherds	MNV	MNR	Form	Date Range	Origin
Southeast Wiltshire ware	2	0	1	Pitcher/jug?	L11th–13thC	English
Chester-type ware	14	0	1	Jugs?	13thC–mid-14thC	English
Misc. French: unidentified	1	0	1	Jug	L12th–E13thC??	French
Saintonge mottled green glazed	15	1	3	Jugs	13thC–14thC	French
Flemish redware	2	1	2	Jugs	mid13thC–	Flemish
Leinster cooking ware	811	9	25	cooking pots; jugs; shallow dishes; platters	mid14thC L12thC–14thC	Irish
Dublin-type coarse ware	17	2	4	Jugs; cooking pot	L12thC– c.mid13thC	Irish
Dublin-type ware	399	5	22	Jugs; storage jars	13thC onwards	Irish
Dublin-type cooking ware	53	0	5	cooking pots	L12thC–14thC	Irish
Dublin-type fine ware	139	1	10	Jugs	L13thC–14thC	Irish

Post-medieval pottery

There are 902 sherds of post-medieval pottery from the St Nahi's site which represents 38% of the pottery assemblage and has a MNV of 90. The majority of the sherds are from vessels imported from England, with a small number of sherds from Germany, Wales, Scotland and Holland. A wide range of ceramic forms were represented within the post-medieval pottery assemblage and these are listed in the table below by pottery type, date and origin; the table also quatifies each type of pottery found.

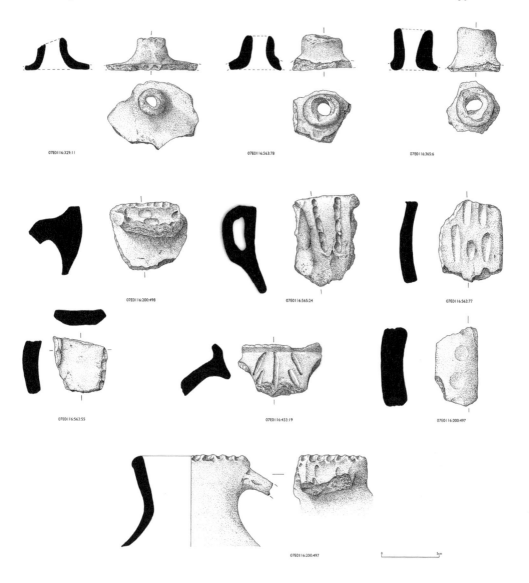

1.28 Pottery: Leinster cooking ware, handles

1.29 *(opposite page, left)* Leinster cooking ware jug (12th–14th century) from F198 from pit F317
1.30 *(opposite page, right)* Flemish redware jug (mid-13th–mid-14th century)

Type	Sherds	MNV	MNR	Form	Date Range	Origin
Frechen	4	2	4	Jug/Mug	L16th–E18thC	German
Westerwald	4		1	Jugs	E17th–L18thC	German
North Holland slipware	2		2	Plates/Dishes	L16th–18thC	Dutch
Fine Black glazed red earthenware	17	3	3	Small jugs	15th–E17thC	English
North Devon gravel-tempered ware	66	1	5	Storage vessels/jug	17thC	English
North Devon gravel-free ware	125	4	7	Storage vessels/jugs	17thC	English
North Devon Sgraffito	26	3	4	Plates/Jug?	17thC	English
Slip-trailed red earthenware	10	2	2	Plates/Dishes	17thC–18thC	English/Irish
Donyatt slipware	1	1	1	Plate/Dish	17thC–18thC	English
Staffordshire-Bristol slipware	19	3	6	Ointment pot/plates/mugs/jugs	mid17thC–mid18thC	English
Slip-coated red earthenware	10	1	1	Plate/Dish	L17thC–19thC	English/Irish
Manganese mottled ware	7	1	2	Candlestick/storage vessel/tankards/cups/mugs	L17thC–mid18thC	English
Tin-glazed earthenware	22	3	7	Plates/hollow vessels	16th–18thC	Dutch/English/Irish
Salt-glazed ware	13	1	3	Plates/cup?	18thC	English
Debased scratch blue	1		1	Chamber pot?	L18thC	English
English stoneware	16	2	7	Vessel unknown	18thC–19thC	English/Irish (1)
Black glazed red earthenware – imported	167	23	23	Storage jars	mid18thC–19thC	English/Welsh
Black glazed red earthenware – local	25	3	3	Storage jars	18thC–19thC	Irish
Glazed red earthenware	15	4	5	Storage jars	18thC–19thC	Irish/English
Unglazed red earthenware	82	4	6	Flowerpots	19thC	Irish/English
Redware	1		1	teapot/mug/jug??	1760s–1780s	English
Creamware	106	6	10	Bowls/plates/cups/jugs/serving dish	mid-18thC–E19thC	English
Pearlware	16	5	6	Plates/cups/jars	L18th–19thC	English
Over-painted pearlware	15	2	2	Plates/cups	L18th–19thC	English
Shell-edged ware	3	3	3	Plates	L18thC–19thC	English
Transfer printed ware, blue	16	3	8	Plates	Mid18th–20thC	English
Transfer printed ware, grey	7		2	Cup/plates	19th–20thC	English
Transfer printed ware, brown	4	2	4	Cup/plates	19th–20thC	English
Transfer printed ware, green	3	1	1	Plates/Dishes	19th–20thC	English

Type	Sherds	MNV	MNR	Form	Date Range	Origin
Transfer printed ware, purple	2		1	Plate?/Cup?	19th–20thC	English
Transfer printed ware, red	1		1	Saucer?	19th–20thC	English
Over-painted transfer printed ware	1		1	Cup	19th–20thC	English
Drabware	1	1	1	Bowl	19th Century	English
Mochaware	4	1	1	Cup/Mugs	19th Century	English
Yellow ware	2		2	Plate?	L19thC	English
Spongeware	5		1	Cups/Mugs	L19th–E20thC	Scottish
Semi-porcelain	36	3	13	Mugs; cups; plates; saucers	19th/20thC	English
White glazed earthenware	45			Plates/cups/ mugs/serving dish/paint pan	19th/20thC	English
20thC black glazed red earthenware	1	1	1	Teapot/jug?	20thC	English
Cornish stoneware	1	1	1	Jug?/mug?	E20thC	English

The post-medieval pottery ranges in date from the late sixteenth to the twentieth century and the detailed descriptions below have been divided into smaller date brackets for convenience. The following table shows the MNV and number of sherds present by date brackets, as well as the percentage of each age range within the post-medieval assemblage.

Date Range	MNV	No. of Sherds	% of post-medieval assemblage
16th–18th Century	24	313	35%
18th–19th Century	53	460	51%
19th–20th Century	13	129	14%

It can be seen by this table that over half of the post-medieval wares date to the eighteenth and nineteenth century and they also have the highest MNV. While the sixteenth- to eighteenth-century wares are well represented there is only a very small amount of nineteenth-century and modern wares.

Ceramic building materials

A small quantity of ceramic building materials was recovered from the excavations at St Nahi's. These included two medieval floor tiles, five post-medieval floor tiles and two post-medieval wall tiles. The medieval floor tiles both came from F365 which was the middle fill of the large medieval/post-medieval ditch F362. The remaining floor tiles and wall tiles were all from post-medieval features. Two of the post-medieval floor tiles were from post-

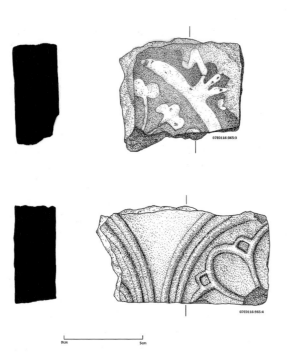

1.31 Medieval floor tiles

medieval pit fills; one from pit F107 and one from pit F623. Two floor tiles were from post-medieval post-hole fills, one each from F177 and F195, and one floor tile came from the upper fill of the post-medieval ditch F223. The tin-glazed wall tile came from the upper fill of the post-medieval ditch F142 and the green-glazed wall tile was recovered from the mortar deposit inside the walls of structure 266.

Medieval floor tiles

Two medieval floor tiles were recovered from the excavations at St Nahi's (fig. 1.31). One is a two-colour tile (*365:3*) and one is a raised relief tile (*365:4*). They are both from the same context. Two-coloured tiles were decorated with white clay and were the most popular type of floor tile from the mid-thirteenth century to the mid-sixteenth century (Eames and Fanning 1988, 17). Relief decorated tiles were decorated using stamps on which the areas to be left flat had been hollowed out (ibid., 43). Some relief decorated tiles date to the fourteenth century, but most date to the fifteenth and sixteenth centuries (ibid., 44–6).

Two-colour tile: T192 circular band with stiff-leaf foliage The fragment of a two-colour tile (*365:3*) from St Nahi's has a 4-tile design, consisting of a circular band with stiff-leaf foliage. This was a very popular design and appears in a number of variations at a number of different sites (Eames and Fanning 1988, 29). The T192 design is also found at Downpatrick cathedral and its variants at St Patrick's cathedral and Christ Church cathedral in Dublin, Great Connell priory, Mellifont abbey and Graiguenamanagh abbey (ibid., 84). Tiles with foliate sprays with trefoil terminations were a popular motif during the thirteenth century (ibid., 24).

Raised relief tile: unidentified design with circular band and floral motif
This fragment of tile (*365:4*) has decoration in raised relief. It was probably one part of a multi-tile design, possibly having more than four tiles as each edge of this tile probably joined another to the side. Tile designs such as R4, from the Deanery Yard in Waterford and R5 from Christ Church, Dublin and Mellifont abbey were based on 16-tile designs with large circular bands and date to the fifteenth or sixteenth century (Eames and Fanning 1988, 44).

Post-medieval floor tiles
Five post-medieval floor tiles were recovered from St Nahi's. Two (*108:4, 224:3*) are small fragments of North Devon gravel-tempered tiles. Tiles with this type of fabric were imported into Ireland from the North Devon area during the seventeenth and eighteenth centuries. The other three post-medieval tile fragments (*178:1, 196:2, 624:1*) all have the same red earthenware fabric with frequent inclusions of small stone. They are thick tiles with sandy bases.

Artefacts of skeletal material

Fifteen artefacts of skeletal material were recovered from the excavations at St Nahi's. These included seven bone pins, a spindle whorl, a pin-beater, two bone handles, a possible parchment pricker, a modified antler tine and a 'motif piece' (fig. 1.32). All the bone pins and the 'motif piece' came from the medieval ditch F215; the pins from the middle fill and the 'motif piece' came from the bottom fill. The parchment pricker was recovered from the medieval deposit F504. The pin-beater was found in the fill of the post-medieval pit F139 and the modified antler tine was recovered from the upper fill of another post-medieval pit F259. The two bone handles and the comb teeth were all retrieved from the topsoil. The raw material for the artefacts came from a number of different types of animal. The bone pins were all made from pig fibulae. The spindle whorl and 'motif piece' were both from cattle femurs and the modified antler tine was from a deer. The remaining artefacts of skeletal material were so altered that it was not possible to say what animal they came from. I am grateful to Jonny Geber for the animal bone identifications.

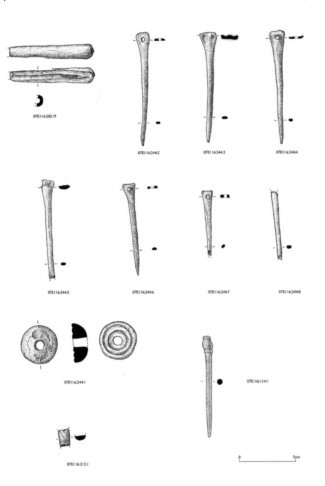

1.32 Medieval artefacts of skeletal material and small finds

Bone pins

Seven bone pins (*244:2–8*) were recovered from F244, the middle fill of the medieval ditch F215. All these pins are made from modified pig fibulae, although two (*244:3, 5*) appear to be unfinished and two (*244:7–8*) are broken. The distal end of the bone has been shaped to form the head and the shaft has been cut and then formed into a pointed shank. Four of the pins have circular or sub-circular perforations in the head. These pins could have been used as dress pins, needles or weaving tools. The modified pig fibulae from York were separated into groups according to how they had been worked and the variety of different shapes present suggested that the pins could have been used for a number of different functions (MacGregor, Mainman and Rogers 1999, 1950). Some may have been used as needles. These are more likely to be those which have been trimmed at the perforated end rather than those that are splayed (ibid., 1951) and the tops of the heads are usually cut straight across (Keene 1990, 232). As they are quite large needles they would only have been used for sewing coarse materials (ibid.). It is unlikely that the St Nahi's modified pig fibulae were used as needles as the six examples which have heads all have splayed heads.

Many of the bone pins found in York were thought to have been dress pins and it was suggested that the pins that were perforated would have been held in place by a cord strung through the perforation (MacGregor, Mainman and Rogers 1999, 1950). Five pins made from modified pig fibulae were found during excavations in Waterford and it was suggested that they may have been used as dress pins (Hurley 1997a, 671). Large numbers have been found on early Christian sites in Ireland such as Lagore Crannog, Ballinderry Crannog no. 2 and Cahercommaun (ibid.). It is quite feasible that the St Nahi's modified pig fibulae could have been used as dress pins, especially given the two unperforated examples, although it is also possible that these are unfinished. The other possibility is that modified pig fibulae were used as weaving implements. Those found in Winchester were thought to have been used in weaving due to the fabrication marks and their highly polished surface (Keene 1990, 232). They were probably used to lift groups of threads while weaving and the perforations may have been used to attach the pins to the weaver so they would not get lost (ibid.). The pins from St Nahi's could have been used for this purpose. They all have highly polished surfaces. As all the pins were found together it is possible that they formed part of a weaver's toolkit. Groups of pins have been found in other places such as the three modified pig fibulae with perforated heads which were found together in the corner of a tenement building dating to the late tenth century at 16–22 Coppergate, York (MacGregor, Mainman and Rogers 1999, 1880, fig. 861) or the five pins found together in a pit at Golden Lane, Dublin 8 (Scully 2008). Similar pins were also found from excavations in Cork, although they tended to be almost twice the length. Two were recovered from Skiddy's Castle (E130:11908–9) and seven from Christ Church; four with eyes (E146:6121, 6599, 8115, 25273) and three without eyes (E146:27075, 27081, 27124) and they were all thought to be weaving tools (Hurley 1997b, 256–7).

Spindle whorl

A spindle whorl (*244:1*) made from the head of a bovine femur was also recovered from the middle fill (F244) of the medieval ditch F215. The spindle whorl is dome-shaped with a circular perforation through the centre and is decorated with two concentric grooves on the flat surface of the spindle whorl. Spindle whorls helped maintain the momentum of the spindle during spinning and could be made from a variety of materials including bone, stone, lead, ceramics or any other suitable material (Woodland 1990, 216). Spindle whorls made from bovine femur heads were first used in the Iron Age but were particularly common in the medieval period (MacGregor 1985, 187). Four bone spindle whorls were recovered from excavations at Christ Church, Cork. One was unstratified but the other three were from thirteenth-century contexts and they weighed between 10.2g and 14.2g (Hurley 1997b, 254–6). All of the 46 bone spindle whorls from excavations in Waterford were made from the femur heads of large mammals and they had an average weight of 10.4g. It is thought that the weight of a spindle was reflective of its function but they tend to range widely in weight. The bone spindle whorl from St Nahi's weights 7.6g, which is a little lighter than those found in Cork or Waterford.

Pin-beater

There is one possible pin-beater (*140:4*) from St Nahi's. It may be a type of pin-beater which is flat and single-ended, sometimes called a 'picker-cum-beater' (MacGregor, Mainman and Rogers 1999, 1967). Unfortunately the example from St Nahi's is incomplete. Flat pin-beaters tend to be polished all over, as the St Nahi's one is and its working end has a wide point. Pin-beaters had a number of uses such as evening out the warp threads of an upright loom, picking up misplaced threads and pushing weft threads into position. Flat pin-beaters were used from the late ninth or tenth century until the thirteenth or fourteenth century (Rogers, 1997). Twelve pin-beaters of this type were recovered from excavations at Coppergate, York which came from contexts dating between the tenth and the twelfth century (MacGregor, Mainman and Rogers 1999, 1967).

Bone handles

Two bone handles were found at St Nahi's. Both were for whittle-tangs. One (*200:50*) is a small fragment of handle which is sub-rectangular in section and splays slightly towards the butt. The butt has a small circular hole drilled in it which possibly held a rivet that kept the tang in place. The other handle (*200:19*) is cylindrical in shape, although it widens slightly towards the butt, which has a decorative knop. Both handles are probably post-medieval in date. An iron fork (*143:1*) and two iron handles (*292:1, 543:1*) from St Nahi's also have bone scales (see metal report).

Parchment pricker

A fragment of a possible parchment pricker (*504:1*) was found at St Nahi's. Only the moulded head with a collar remains, so it could also possibly represent the remains of a pin but the shape of the terminal is very like that commonly found on parchment prickers. These were implements that were used in the production of manuscripts. The page layout was controlled by a series of ruled lines and pairs of holes on either side of the page ensured that the ruled lines were evenly spaced (Biddle and Brown 1990, 733–4). Five examples were recovered from excavations at Winchester dating from the late twelfth to the sixteenth century (ibid.). Thirty-five were recovered from excavations in York (MacGregor, Mainman and Rogers 1999, 1974). Two parchment prickers came from excavations at St Peter's church, Waterford, one of which still had its metal point. They were both turned on a lathe and had spherical heads (Hurley 1997a, 698). Three parchment prickers were found on various excavations in Cork city; at Christ Church (Hurley 1997b, 269), Grattan Street (Hurley 2003, 332) and Kyrl's Quay (Hurley 1996, 31–2).

Comb teeth
Four teeth (*200:32, 47–9*) from a comb were found in the topsoil. They are all wide and flat teeth of the same size and shape and possibly came from the same comb but are no longer joined together.

Modified antler tine
One modified antler tine (*262:3*) was found in the upper fill of the post-medieval pit F259. The surface of the tine has been planed to form six flat sides around the tine and a small quantity of cancellous tissue appears to have been removed, possibly to form a crude type of notch. Similar modified antler tines have been found in excavations in Waterford (Hurley 1997a, 681–684), Cork (Hurley 1997b, 268; Hurley 1997c, 112) and Dublin (Hurley 1997a, 681). They vary greatly in appearance and a number of functions have been suggested for them. As large numbers of modified antler tines were found associated with comb-making waste at High Street, Dublin, they were suggested as having been clamps used in comb-making. They were found associated with other antler waste in Waterford (ibid.). They are also suggested to be linchpins or stave pegs, pegs for tanning or for use as braiding or matting needles (Hurley 1997a, 681; Hurley 1997b, 268; Hurley 1997c, 112). A function for the St Nahi's modified antler tine cannot be readily attributed; it seems too blunt to be a peg and the 'notch' is not very convincing so it is doubtful that it was used as a type of clamp and neither is it the hollow type of modified antler tine found at Waterford which were used as phials (Hurley 1997a, 678).

'Motif piece'
A possible 'motif piece' (*243:2*) was found in the bottom fill of the medieval ditch F215 (fig. 1.33). The distal end of a cattle femur has drawing scratched into the surface. On the patellar articular surface are a series of eight parallel lines with a diagonal struck through them and a rectangular box divided into four. On the medial surface of the distal diaphysis is a box divided into four with an 'x' in each box, two spiral decorations and some other scratching. This artefact cannot be accurately described as a 'motif piece', which are bones on

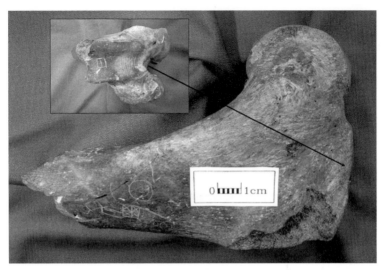

1.33 Distal end of cattle femur from ditch F215, showing etched decoration

which decorative schemes have been 'tried out' before being finalized on some other piece or on other materials. The drawings on the St Nahi's bone do not really represent a design but could be considered instead to be the equivalent of 'doodling'.

Metal finds

One-hundred-and-seventy-seven metal artefacts were recovered from the excavations at St Nahi's. The vast majority of these artefacts (91%) were made from ferrous metal with only a small amount of non-ferrous artefacts (figs 1.34 and 1.35). The metal finds display a variety of functions and allude to a number of activities taking place on site. Many of the finds are personal possessions, such as the dress accessories and fragments of musical instruments, while others are domestic in nature, such as the cutlery and household pins and the lightening equipment represented by the candleholder and strike-a-light. There is also a small assemblage of security equipment and horse equipment. A small number of tools indicate several activities taking place on site including a number of iron punches which may have been used in metalworking and the possible comb teeth which were used for processing textiles. There is a large collection of structural iron, representing 59% of the total metal assemblage, which include not only a considerable amount of nails but also hinges, staples, spikes, hooks, bands from buckets and other miscellaneous pieces of structural iron. The majority of the metal finds cannot be dated to a specific period as they are types which were used for hundreds of years, particularly the structural iron, but most of the metal finds probably date to the post-medieval period. There

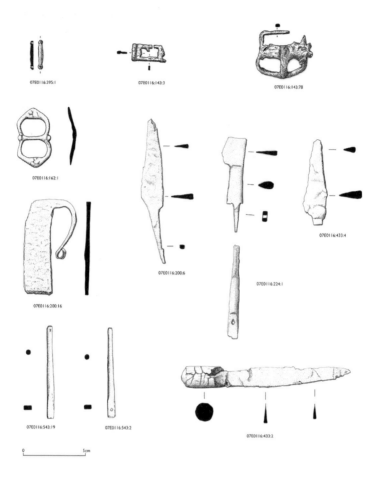

1.34 Metal finds I

are a number of notable metal finds which date to the medieval period, such as the two spurs (*190:1, 330:1*) which both date to the fourteenth or fifteenth century, and the candleholder (*563:1*) and strike-a-light (*200:16*) which are also medieval in date. The two bronze tuning pegs (*543:12, 19*) could be medieval or early post-medieval in date. Two of the buckles can be closely dated to the early post-medieval period; one (*162:1*) dating *c.*1550–1600 and one (*143:78*) *c.*1575–1700. The single coin (*194:1*) from St Nahi's dates to *c.*1680 and the 'pistol'-grip fork (*143:1*) dates to the early eighteenth century.

The metal finds are discussed below according to function and a full catalogue of the metal finds is presented in the catalogue at the end of the report. The following table summarizes the finds by function group and by ferrous and non-ferrous metal.

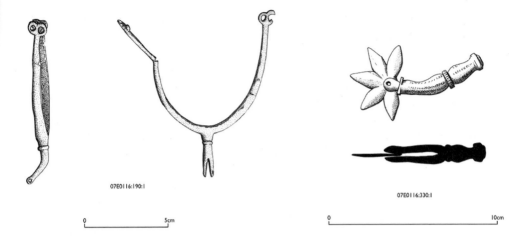

07E0116:190:1

07E0116:330:1

0   5cm   0   10cm

1.35 Metal finds II

Function	Total no. of Finds	Ferrous	Non-Ferrous
Trade & exchange	1	0	1
Dress accessories	11	7	4
Musical instruments	2	0	2
Domestic equipment	27	23	4
Security equipment	2	2	0
Horse equipment	5	4	1
Tools	11	11	0
Structural iron	105	105	0
Misc. & unidentified	13	9	4

Trade and exchange: coin

There is one coin (*194:1*) from St Nahi's. It is a Charles II halfpenny, possibly from 1680. In 1680 Irish regal halfpennies were issued in an attempt to replace the unofficial trade tokens that were in general use at the time because of a lack of good copper coinage. On one side these had the bust of the king with a laurel wreath and the legend 'CAROLVS II DEI GRATIA' and a crowned harp on the reverse with the legend 'MAG BR FRA ET HIB REX'. This halfpenny was issued in 1680, 1681 and 1682 (Colgan 2003, 133–4).

Dress accessories

Buckles There are six buckles from St Nahi's; four are made of iron and two are made of copper alloy. Two of the buckles could be dated. One is a copper alloy spectacle buckle (*162:1*) with a cast double-loop angled frame. It has a knop at either end of the strap bar and has moulded roundels on the surface of the buckle which possibly represent rosettes at the outer edge of each loop. This buckle can be dated to *c.*1550–1650 (Whitehead 2003, 60). The other dateable buckle is a double-loop D-shaped iron buckle (*143:78*) which appears to have two small protrusions at one end of the strap bar. The buckle has the remains of white metal plating on parts of the frame and pin and can be dated to *c.*1575–1700. The remaining buckles are incomplete. One iron buckle (*143:3*) has one rectangular loop remaining and one end of the frame is rolled. There is a partial double-loop iron buckle (*190:5*) which was probably originally rectangular in shape and a possible partial iron buckle (*200:40*) which has a rectangular frame which has a D-shaped plate at one end. There is also a possible fragment of a copper alloy buckle frame (*486:2*) which is sub-rectangular in shape and has a series of grooves decorating the front.

Belt loop

There is one possible belt loop (*200:44*) from St Nahi's. It is an iron loop, oval in shape which possibly has an iron pin looped through the slit.

Button and snap fastener

One brass button (*200:22*) and a partial snap fastener (*200:24*) were found at St Nahi's. The button is a copper alloy dished suspender button with four central perforations. It has the name of the maker 'KENNY & OWENS DAME ST' on the front. Only the perforated receiver half of the copper alloy snap fastener remains.

Shoe cleats

Two possible shoe cleats (*200:20–21*) were found at St Nahi's. They are both small horseshoe-shaped iron objects. One (*200:20*) has straight heels and five nail holes are visible in the x-ray and the heels of the other (*200:21*) point slightly inwards and four nail holes are visible in the x-ray. Despite their horseshoe-shaped appearance they are too small to be horseshoes but are instead toe-irons or heel-guards for shoes. A 'heel-guard' of such shape was recovered from the excavations at St James's church, Galway, which dated to the late nineteenth or twentieth century (Higgins 1996, 72). A toe iron from a boot or shoe was found during excavations of the falling mill at Ardingly, Sussex (Goodall 1976, 64) and a heel iron was found at Tilbury Fort, Essex which dated to the late seventeenth or early eighteenth century (Moore 2000, 70).

Musical instruments

Tuning pegs Two copper alloy tuning pegs (*543:12*, *19*) were recovered from
F543 at St Nahi's. They both have a circular shank with a small circular
perforation at one end and an expanded rectangular head at the other. Many
tuning pegs have been found from medieval and post-medieval sites in Ireland
and Britain and their variations in size would suggest that they were used for a
number of different instruments. While many tuning pegs are known in bone,
they are also known in bronze, although they are possibly later in date and
are possibly associated with the development of large Irish harps (Hurley
1997a, 665). A bronze harp peg was recovered from excavations prior to the
construction of Shannon Airport but it was not closely dated (Rynne 1964,
268, 271, fig. 11.39).

Domestic equipment

Blades and knives There are 17 iron knifes and blades or possible blades
from St Nahi's. These include four whittle-tang knives, one scale-tang knife,
three folding knives, eight partial blades and one tang probably from a knife.
Three of the whittle-tang knives are comparable with blades from Goodall's
(1990a) typology of knives from Winchester. There is one Type A blade (*518:1*)
which has a blade back which rises and then angles down to the tip and has a
curved cutting edge. Blades of this type from Winchester were found in
contexts dating no later than the thirteenth century (ibid., 838). One Goodall
Type C blade (*433:2*) was found at St Nahi's. This type of blade has a blade
back and cutting edge that are parallel and taper to the tip. Blades of this type
from Winchester were found in contexts dating throughout the medieval
period and occasionally in the post-medieval period (ibid.). The St Nahi's
blade has the burnt remains of a wooden handle which is circular in section
and there is also a separate wooden handle fragment (*433:3*) which is probably
from the same knife. There is one Goodall Type D blade (*200:6*) from St
Nahi's which has a blade back and cutting edge which taper from the junction
with the tang to the tip. The Winchester blades of this type occurred in both
medieval and post-medieval contexts (ibid.). There is one whittle-tang blade
from St Nahi's which has a bolster (*224:1*), which is a thickened expansion
between the blade and the tang. The bolster on the St Nahi's blade is sub-
rectangular in shape and oval in section. Bolsters began to be used during the
sixteenth century (ibid., 839). The shape of the bolster on the St Nahi's blade
is similar to one found at Basing House, Hampshire (Moorehouse and Goodall
1971, fig. 17.5) which was dated to the mid-seventeenth century (ibid., 36).
There is one scale-tang knife from St Nahi's (*484:1*) which has two wooden
scales. The blade has a parallel blade black and cutting edge. The tang is
rectangular in section and widens towards the butt. The wooden scales are held
in place by three copper alloy rivets. Three folding knives were found at St
Nahi's and they are probably all post-medieval in date. One of the folding

knives (*180:1*) has iron scales but also appears to have had a whittle-tang handle. One of the other folding knives (*200:7[1]*) also has iron scales but these are decorated with a white metal, possibly silver and the other folding knife (*200:7[2]*) has tortoise shell blades. There is one small knife blade (*433:4*) which has only a very small section of the tang remaining, so it is uncertain if it is a whittle-tang or scale-tang blade. The blade back is straight and in line with the tang and the cutting edge is angled. One other blade (*292:9*) has a blade back and cutting edge which curve towards the tip. Only the junction between the blade and the tang of another blade (*563:2*) survives. The blade back and cutting edge were possibly parallel. There are four other blade fragments (*138:2, 200:41, 205:5, 456:2*), all of which have a triangular section, one possible blade from a folding knife (*200:534*) and one possible fragment of a tang (*565:1*).

Fork There is one fork (*143:1*) from St Nahi's. It is a two-pronged iron fork with a scale-tang, 'pistol-grip' bone handle. This type of handle can be dated to the early eighteenth century (Hume 1969, 180).

Spoon One incomplete pewter spoon (*200:10*) was found at St Nahi's. Only a very small section of the bowl survives where it joins with the handle, which is hexagonal in section. This spoon could possibly be medieval or early post-medieval in date. It is at least pre-eighteenth century in date.

Handles In addition to the handles attached to the items above there are also three other handles. One is an iron scale-tang handle (*292:1*) which has a bolster before the tang and two bone scales. The handle splays towards the butt. Another handle (*543:1*) is also made of iron with bone scales but has a copper alloy plate on the butt. The handle widens towards the butt and has a projection at the back. There is also a perforation near the butt, which is lined with copper alloy, and this would have allowed the object to be suspended by the handle. There is one other possible handle (*292:2*) which is very heavily corroded and encrusted but appears to be a handle with scales in the x-ray, with a collar at one end and a rounded butt at the other.

Household pins Three small copper alloy household pins (*206:7, 316:1, 393:1*) were found at St Nahi's. They all have wire-wound heads and circular shanks. Only one (*393:1*) is complete and the other two have their points broken off. They are probably post-medieval in date and were used in dress-making or for general household purposes.

Scissors There is a single arm of a scissors (*281:1*) from St Nahi's which has a circular loop. Shears were more commonly used than scissors during the

medieval period (Ward-Perkins 1993, 151). Three are known from thirteenth-
or fourteenth-century contexts from London (De Neergaard 2000, 60). The
partial scissors from St Nahi's, however, is probably post-medieval in date.

Candleholder One iron docketed candleholder (*563:1*) was recovered from St
Nahi's. It has a simple straight stem with curved flanges which form the socket
or cup. The earliest known example of this type of candleholder was found in
Winchester and dates to the late eleventh or twelfth century (Goodall 1990b,
983). They have been found from excavations in London from the late
thirteenth century to the early fourteenth century (Egan 1998, 134).

Strike-a-light A partial strike-a-light (*200:16*) was found at St Nahi's. The
striking plate is rectangular in section and it has one handle remaining which
terminates in a decorative scroll. Two perforated strike-a-lights with a single
hooked handle are known from Winchester dating from eleventh- to twelfth-
century contexts (Goodall 1990b, 983) and a similar one from London, which
came from a late thirteenth- to mid-fourteenth-century context (Egan 1998,
121). These are all single-handled strike-a-lights. The strike-a-light from St
Nahi's is incomplete and was probably double-handed. The handle is also
more decorative and is comparable with the strike-a-light from Charlesland,
Wicklow (04E0387:91:1). A similar strike-a-light from St John's Lane
(E173:510), held in the National Museum of Ireland, dates to the ninth or
tenth century.

Security equipment

Keys Two keys for mounted locks were recovered from the excavations at St
Nahi's. One (*364:1*) has a kidney-shaped bow and a solid circular moulded
stem. The bit of this key is in line with the stem and has three wards cut
parallel to the stem. Keys found during excavations in Winchester with the
kidney-shaped bow form came from contexts dating to the fourteenth or
fifteenth centuries (Goodall 1990c, 1007) but those from excavations in York
tended to be from post-medieval contexts (Ottaway and Rogers 2002, 2876).
Keys with moulded stems are more common in the post-medieval period
(Moorhouse and Goodall 1971, 39–41). The other key (*200:1*) has an oval bow
and a solid circular moulded stem which projects beyond the bit, which has
wards cut parallel to the stem. Keys with oval bows were found throughout the
medieval and post-medieval periods. This key also has a knop at the end of the
stem which is often a feature associated with post-medieval keys, for example, a
key from Basing House, Hampshire, which was occupied during the sixteenth
and seventeenth centuries (ibid., no. 29, fig. 18.29), but is occasionally found
on medieval keys, for example, a number of knopped keys from excavations in
London were from medieval contexts (Ward-Perkins 1993, Pl. XXXI 49 and

56; Egan 1998, 115, fig. 90.326) and two knopped keys from Fishergate in York came from fifteenth/sixteenth-century contexts (Ottaway and Rogers 2002, 3142, 2874, fig. 1452, 15096–7).

Horse equipment

Spurs There is one iron rowel spur (*190:1*) and one neck fragment of a copper alloy rowel spur (*330:1*), figs 1.34 and 1.35. Rowel spurs began to be used in the thirteenth century and almost completely replaced the earlier prick spurs (Ellis 1995, 129). The almost complete spur (*190:1*) is just missing its rowel. It has a curving neck with a bifurcated rowel box which has a decorative collar where it meets the sides. The sides are straight and terminate in two figure-of-eight perforations. The remains of a white metal plating, possibly sliver, can be seen on the surface of the spur. The curving neck fragment (*330:1*) representing the other spur is made of copper alloy and is decorated with lines of half circles which have the remains of gilding. The neck has a bulbous moulding and a collar before the bifurcated rowel box. The rowel, which was originally a six-pointed flower-shaped rowel but has only five points remaining, is still held in the rowel box but is no longer secured by a pin. Both spurs probably date to the fourteenth or fifteenth centuries.

Horseshoes Three incomplete horseshoes were recovered from St Nahi's. The right-hand side of one horseshoe remains (*140:3*). It is part of a U-shaped horseshoe which probably dates to the nineteenth century. The heel has a calkin formed by the thickening of the heel (Clark 1995, 81 Type a). There are four nail holes visible in the x-ray. There are two other heel fragments (*277:1*, *365:1*) from St Nahi's, both of which have Type a calkins.

Tools

Comb teeth Three thin incomplete shanks of iron (*304:1*) were recovered from the same feature. These terminate in points and one has a flat head only slightly wider than the shank. It is possible that these may have been teeth from a wool comb. They are comparable with the remains of a wool comb found at York where the iron teeth were held together by a wooden binding plate (Ottaway 1992, 538, fig. 212.2273). After the wool was cleaned it was then combed to remove any foreign material. A similar comb, called a heckle, was used in the production of flax, where the flax is passed through combs to break up the stalks after scotching (ibid.).

Punches Five possible iron punches (*190:2*, *194:2*, *200:533*, *217:1*, *219:1*) were found at St Nahi's. They all have flat heads which are unitary with their shanks. Two heads (*190:2*, *194:2*) are slightly burred, caused by repeating striking and one head is slightly angled (*200:533*). Three of the punches have expanded points (*190:2*, *194:2*, *217:1*). These punches could have been used in metalworking, the pointed ones from making holes in hot iron and the ones with expanded points for cutting metal strips or plate or making decorative channels in the metal (Ottaway 1992, 517).

File/rasp This is a long flat iron bar (*200:45*), slightly waisted one third of the way along the bar, which was possibly used as a file or rasp for metal-working or woodworking, although there is no evidence for teeth.

Sickle An iron sickle (*200:46*) was found in the topsoil. It has a curved blade, triangular in section and a tang which would have received a wooden handle. This is a small hand-held tool which was used for harvesting grain crops or for gardening.

Stone artefacts

Twenty-six artefacts of worked stone were recovered from the excavations at St Nahi's. These included an alabaster pin, seven querns, three hones, a bullaun stone, a spud stone, a pot lid, a handle from a stone vessel, a plough pebble, a decorated lignite object, three pieces of architectural stone, four roofing slates and two pieces of possibly worked stone that were too fragmentary to identify.

Alabaster pin
An alabaster stick pin (*114:1*) was recovered from the bottom fill of the recut (F106) of the enclosure ditch F101. It is a spatulate-headed pin; the head is rounded with a flat circular top and a collar below the base. It is slightly different to forms of spatulate-headed pins classified by O'Rahilly (1998, 29–30) and has more in common with spatulate-headed pins found in Cork (Carroll and Quinn 2003, 271–4; fig. 5.8:13). These types of stick pins are towards the end of the dating sequence for stick pins; in Cork they were found in contexts from the late twelfth to the early fourteenth century (ibid.).

Querns
There are two types of querns from St Nahi's; rotary querns and a saddle quern. There is one small granite fragment (*200:59*) which may be from a quern but it is too small to say for sure. **Saddle quern:** There is one saddle quern (*543:3*) from St Nahi's. It is made of fine-grained sandstone, is trapezoidal in shape and has a slightly concave upper surface. Saddle querns were introduced into Ireland around 3000 BC. The grain was placed on a stone with a slightly concave surface, the saddle stone, and an oval stone (the 'rubber') was moved back and forward over the surface to grind the grain. Anne Connolly has studied the morphology and distribution of saddle querns

in Ireland. From those she studied she found that they were rare finds on Neolithic sites and were much more common from Middle and Late Bronze Age contexts. There is a lack of secure dates for those found on Iron Age sites and they are rare finds on medieval settlement sites (Connolly 1994; quoted in Cotter 1999, 60–1). *Rotary querns:* Rotary querns are handmills where the flat surfaces of two stones are in contact. Grain is poured into the central hole and the upper stone is rotated. The grain is ground between the two stones and is forced out between the stones (Caulfield 1983, 59). There are three main classes of rotary quern (disc, beehive and pot), two of which are represented in the St Nahi's stone assemblage; there are four fragments of disc rotary querns (*117:1, 200:60, 361:1–3, 361:4*) and one fragment of a beehive quern (*200:61*). *Beehive quern:* Beehive querns were used in Ireland from the first century AD until about the sixth century. The beehive querns have two domed stones with flat grinding surfaces. The fragment of a beehive quern (*200:61*) from St Nahi's is domed and has a flat grinding surface and is made from coarse-grained sandstone. A reference find from the area was found in Terenure (O'Donovan 1996). *Disc querns:* Disc querns were introduced into Ireland around about the same time as the beehive querns but they survived in use up until the middle of the twentieth century. The disc querns are made up of two stones which not only have a flat grinding surface but also have flat upper and lower surfaces. The disc querns from St Nahi's are all made of granite. Two (*200:60, 361:4*) have small inclusions of mica and quartz, while the other two (*117:1, 361:1–3*) have large plates of mica. One of the stones (*361:4*) is obviously the upper stone and has a circular depression to take the spindle.

Hones

There are two fragments of small hones from St Nahi's as well as a large rectangular stone that may be an unfinished hone. Hones or whetstones were used for sharpening blades, not just while they were being made but also in the upkeep of the blade (Mainman and Rogers 2000, 2484). The coarseness and size of a hone was related to the function it was intended for and MacGregor suggests that the coarse-grained hones were used for preliminary sharpening, while the fine-grained ones were used for finishing (ibid., 2497). One (*495:2*) of the small hones is rectangular in section, broken at each end and is made from fine-grained limestone. The other small hone fragment (*143:6*) is made of fine-grained sandstone and is circular in section with one rounded end and the other end is broken off. There is a large rectangular piece of coarse-grained granite (*216:1–2*), which may be an unfinished hone.

Bullaun stone

There is one possible bullaun stone (*585:1*) from St Nahi's. It is roughly triangular in shape with a rounded base and a flattish top with a small circular depression in it. Bullaun stones are found at many early Christian sites around Ireland. Their purpose is unknown but many have been re-used as fonts.

Spud stone

The spud stone from St Nahi's (*282:1*) is a large, irregularly-shaped stone made of fine-grained limestone. It has a circular depression in the top of the stone which would have been the socket for a post on which a door swung. The top end of the door would have swung on a 'creak' or hook (Brooks, Adcock and Agate 1999, ch. 9). This method of hanging a swing gate or door, known as the 'harrhanging' method was used throughout Ireland, as well as Scotland, the Lake District, Cornwall and Brittany (ibid.). The spud stone would probably have been set into the ground or formed part of the threshold stone of the doorway. There is mortar present on the base and along one side.

Pot lid

A flat worked piece of limestone (*494:1*), roughly octagonal in shape, from St Nahi's was probably a pot lid. A number of stone discs found during excavations in York were suggested to have been lids for wooden or ceramic vessels. These all dated from the late ninth to the mid-eleventh century (Mainman and Rogers 2000, 2565). These were all between 64mm to 90mm in diameter. The St Nahi's stone is only slightly larger at 101mm.

Handle

A handle fragment (*200:62*) from a straight-sided vessel was found at St Nahi's. The handle is sub-rectangular in shape. The vessel may have been a rectangular stone box.

Plough pebble

There is one plough pebble (*200:57*) from St Nahi's. Wooden plough-soles were studded with pebbles to make them more hard-wearing. This gives the pebbles a convexly worn face with striations across it. The plough pebble from St Nahi's has a convexly worn face but does not have any visible striations. Plough pebbles are found throughout Scandinavia as well as Britain and Ireland. They were used in the medieval and post-medieval periods (Fenton 1963, 277–8).

Decorated lignite object

A small fragment of decorated stone (*212:1*), possibly lignite, was found in the fill of the medieval ditch F211. The stone is D-shaped in section but the back is rough and may be broken and so the object may originally have been circular in section, or perhaps this side was just left unworked as it was not meant to be seen. It has a black, shiny surface which is incised with pairs of parallel lines

1.36 Limestone
clustered
pillar-base
(Romanesque?)
from medieval
pit F317

which intersect. It is slightly wider at one end and here there is evidence of a
possible perforation. Lignite was used to manufacture bracelets, pendants and
rings and was used for these objects from the Bronze Age into the medieval
period. Lignite bracelets dating to the early medieval period often have a D-
shaped section. A possible gaming piece of lignite was also found at Lagore
(Edwards 1996, 96) and this is a possibility for the St Nahi's lignite fragment.

Architectural stone
A moulded base of a pillar or arch (*318:1–2*) and two other pieces of architectural
stone (*563:3, 565:3*) were recovered from St Nahi's. The pillar/arch base is a
flat triangular stone with three roll mouldings (fig. 1.36). The triangular base
and the mouldings are carved out of the same stone. There is a hollow chamfer
at each point of the triangle. There is a projection off one of the roll mouldings
but it is broken. The other two possible architectural stones are a fragment of a
possible sill (*565:3*) and a fragment of building stone (*563:3*).

Leather finds

A small assemblage of leather artefacts were recovered from the excavation of
the well F207 at the site. The leather was in contexts from the middle to the

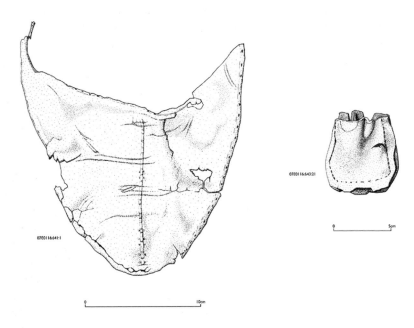

1.37 Leather: purse and shoe upper

bottom of the well (F630, F629, F628, F627 F641 and F643) and is all
medieval in date. The majority of the leather finds represented shoe leather
but a small leather pouch (fig. 1.37) and perforated disc as well as one off-cut
and two leather fragments were also recovered.

Footwear
There are approximately thirteen items of footwear from the well, although
some of these also have some small associated fragments. Medieval shoes were
manufactured using the 'turn-shoe' technique. The leather was cut to shape
and then moulded on a wooden last. The shoe was stitched inside out and then
turned out (Grew and de Neergaard 2001). There are examples of at least three
different types of shoe from St Nahi's. The earliest type of shoe represented,
where the method of fastening is apparent, is a quarter from a side-laced shoe
(*628:9*). It has four perforations at the front of the quarter where the shoe
would have been laced. The quarter folded around the back of the heel and
there is still a triangular heel stiffener in place. There is also one rand fragment
associated with the quarter. Side-laced shoes found from excavations in
London dated to the early to mid-thirteenth century, although they did not
become the 'standard' form until the early/mid-fifteenth century (Grew and
de Neergaard 2001, 18). In York, side-laced shoes were found in contexts
dating from the fourteenth to the sixteenth centuries with the exception of

one shoe from an eleventh-/twelfth-century context (Mould, Carlisle and Cameron 2003, 3329–30). These shoes are of two-piece construction with a separate vamp and quarters, such as the one from St Nahi's. Two-piece construction became more common in the late fourteenth century, replacing the earlier 'wrap-around' style (Grew and de Neergaard 2001, 31–2).

There are two toggle fastening shoes from St Nahi's. They are both quarters with an extended flap at the front of the quarter with two slits in it for fastening over the instep. One (*628:1–7*) has three inserts/heel stiffeners and three rand fragments associated with it. The other (*628:11*) has one associated rand fragment. Shoes fastened with toggles date from the late thirteenth to the early fourteenth century (Grew and de Neergaard 2001, 21). Five front toggle-fastened shoes were recovered from excavations in York but this was a common type found through Britain and Europe (Mould, Carlisle and Cameron 2003, 3322). Another quarter fragment (*630:2*) from St Nahi's has a front latchet-fastener. This type of shoe has narrow latchets at the front of each quarter with slits in them through which a leather thong was passed through and secured. Front latchet-fastened shoes became popular in the late fourteenth century and continued into the fifteenth century (Grew and de Neergaard 2001, 3, 32). Two front latchet-fastened shoes were found at 16–22 Coppergate in York, one dated to the late fourteenth century and the other to the early fifteenth century (Mould, Carlisle and Cameron 2003, 3333). The quarter from St Nahi's also has a rand fragment associated with it. Two vamp fragments (*641:1, 629:3*) with central vamp stripes running from the vamp throat to the toe were also found. The vamp stripe was produced by making two incised lines using a small awl with an S-shaped blade. The incisions were made on the grain side and did not pass through to the flesh side of the leather. A decorative thread could then be woven through the holes. Vamp stripes with two lines appeared in the late eleventh century but were most popular during the twelfth century (Grew and de Neergaard 2001, 77–9). The vamps from St Nahi's have rounded two and wide vamp wings but the decoration is worn on one (*629:3*) of the vamps. This vamp also has three rand fragments associated with it. A fragment of a rounded toe (*643:8–18b*) and three very worn leather fragments (*643:8–18c*) and six rand fragments also represent the uppers of a shoe. Five complete shoe soles and one sole fragment (*630:1*) were recovered from the well. The soles are all from late thirteenth-century shoes which have rounded heels, narrow waists and pointed toes. These are all separate soles and are from shoes made from two-piece construction. The five complete soles could be measured for shoe size with a 10% allowance for shrinkage, which would have occurred due to their deposition and subsequent conservation (Thornton 1990, 595). One sole (*628:8*) is size 3–4, one (*628:10*) is size 5, one (*629:1*) is size 7 and two (*627:1, 643:19*) are size 8. All but one (*627:1*) are right-sided soles.

Pouch
A small pouch (*643:21*) was recovered from F643 in the well. It has rounded
corners at the base and narrows slightly towards the top of the pouch. The
front of the pouch has two V-shaped slits cut into it. The stitching is still *in situ*
but the two pieces of leather are no longer attached. Three small leather
pouches were recovered from excavations carried out by the Department of
Urban Archaeology in London. These were all closed with drawstrings and
came from contexts ranging in date between the late twelfth century and the
late fourteenth century (Egan and Pritchard 1991, 342, 344). The pouch from
St Nahi's probably had a cord passed through the V-shaped notches although
this probably didn't act as a drawstring.

Disc
The leather disc (*643:20*) from F643 has roughly cut edges and a central
perforation. These have been found on a number of excavations, usually in
medieval contexts and often associated with leather-working or tanning,
although there is no evidence of these activities from St Nahi's. Four leather
discs were found during excavations in Waterford, six from Cork and twenty-
three from excavations in York. Although their function is unknown a number
of uses have been suggested for these leather discs such as fasteners, washers,
gaming pieces, tags for tanned hides and handle-grips (O'Rourke 1997 a and b;
Mould, Carlisle and Cameron 2003, 3411).

Off-cut
Only one leather off-cut (*641:2*) was recovered from the well. It is a small
narrow strip of leather which is cut on all sides, apart for one narrow end
which is torn.

THE FAUNAL REMAINS

Jonny Geber

Introduction
Three main phases of occupation were indicated: an early medieval phase (*c.*
AD500–1100) represented by substantial ditch enclosures associated with the
nearby St Nahi's church; a later medieval phase (*c.*AD1100–1600) with
indications of a large farm settlement related to the same church, and a post-
medieval phase (*c.*AD1600–1800) with a continuing occupation indicated by
ditches, pits and also walls. The assemblage comprised of mammal, bird, fish,
amphibian bones and mollusc shells at a total amount of 4806 fragments at an
overall weight of 132kg. The preservation was excellent, with solid cortices and
only minimal post-depositional fragmentation was noted. The assemblage was

hand-collected during the archaeological excavation, which inevitably would have led to a bias towards bones from medium and large sized mammals. A total of 63% of the fragments and 92% of the weight could be identified to species. Twenty-two species were identified (Table 1): the main domesticates (cattle, sheep, goat, pig, horse, dog, cat, goose and fowl) and also wild fauna (red deer, woodcock, barn owl, raven, amphibian, fish and shell fish). The widest range of species was found in the medieval and post-medieval phases, which were also the phases from which the majority of the bone assemblage dated from.

Table 1. Identified animal species by number of identified fragments (NISP) from St Nahi's. Abbreviations: LM = large sized mammal; MM = medium sized mammal

Species	Early medieval	Medieval	Post-medieval	Total
Mammals				
Cattle (*Bos taurus*)	79	878	421	1378
Caprovine (*Ovis aries/Capra hircus*)	20	355	190	565
Pig (*Sus sp.*)	7	224	51	282
Horse (*Equus caballus*)	31	182	135	348
Red deer (*Cervus elaphus*)	1	2	5	8
Dog (*Canis familiaris*)		98	14	112
Cat (*Felis catus*)	7	29	11	47
LM	97	576	337	1010
MM	24	420	135	579
Mammals indet. (*Mammalia sp.*)	1	73	60	134
Birds				
Goose (*Anser anser*)		5	2	12
Fowl (*Gallus gallus*)		154	4	158
Woodcock (*Scolopax rusticola*)		1		1
Barn owl (*Tyto alba*)		19		19
Raven (*Corvus corax*)		8		8
Bird indet. (*Aves sp.*)		5	6	6
Amphibians				
Amphibian indet. (*Amphibia sp.*)		1		1
Fish				
Fish indet. (*Pisces sp.*)		1		1

Species	Early medieval	Medieval	Post-medieval	Total
Molluscs				
Common European Oyster (*Ostrea edulis*)	1	38	4	43
Common European Edible Cockle (*Cardium edule*)	1	13	8	22
European Prickly Cockle (*Cardium echinatum*)		5	1	6
Common Limpet (*Patella vulgata*)		6		6
Venus Clam (*Venerupis decussata*)		8		8
Common Whelk (*Baccinum undatum*)		3	1	4
Mussle indet. (*Mytlius sp.*)		13	6	19
Razor Shell indet. (*Solenacea sp.*)		17		17
Molluscs indet. (*Mullusca sp.*)		12		12
Total	269	3146	1391	4806

Discussion

Based on fragment count, cattle dominate over caprovines and pigs in all periods. The early phase at St Nahi's is in closest correlation with Killeen Caste Demesne, which appears to reflect a rural economy focusing mainly on cattle with very little dependency on pigs. In the medieval period, lesser reliance on cattle is shown which continues at a similar distribution into the post-medieval period.

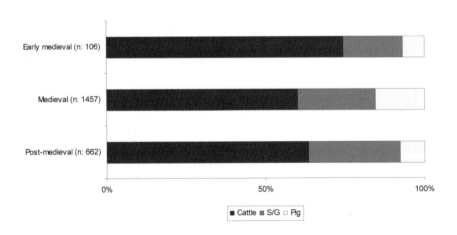

The relative prevalence in identified bone fragments (NISP) among the main domesticates at St Nahi's

It is not possible to determine whether the early medieval cattle were reared within a dairy-based economy or if they were primarily kept for meat production. McCormick has suggested, on the basis of zooarchaeological evidence in consensus with surviving written records from the period, that cows' milk was not intensively used at the time. Instead, he suggested that the main purpose for cattle was for the use of labour and meat (McCormick 1992). Cattle in pre-Anglo-Norman Ireland were very important as a means of wealth and were used as a currency standard, but this sense of value was beginning to lose its importance in the years prior to the Viking invasion (Edwards 1990, 56–60; Kelly 1997, 27; McCormick and Murray 2007, 111–115). Cattle bone fragments constituted the majority in the medieval remains, but less so than in the preceding period. The osteological analysis suggest that cattle were reared, slaughtered, butchered and consumed within the vicinity of St Nahi's church within a dairy-based production economy in the medieval period. Although not directly proven, cattle hides were likely utilized in tanneries elsewhere which would explain the under-representation of skeletal elements such as skulls, metapodials and phalanges. The same trend continued into the post-medieval period.

Other than being used as a medium of currency alongside cattle, early Irish texts emphasize the importance of sheep as wool producers (Kelly 1997, 67), and it is likely that the wool of early medieval sheep at St Nahi's was utilized although the osteological evidence is too scarce to prove that assumption. A wool-producing economy did, however, evidently take place in the medieval period, and probably in the post-medieval phase as well. A clear majority of the caprovine remains derive from sheep, which is expected from a rural economy and is not surprising. Previous research has noted that goat-keeping in Ireland during the early medieval period was largely an urban phenomenon (McCormick and Murphy 2007, 202). The same result was seen in the analysis of the faunal assemblage from Killeen Castle demesne where no goat bones were identified.

Pigs are believed not to have been traded as a form of currency in early-medieval Ireland (Kelly 1997, 86), which could explain the relatively small amount of pig bones present at St Nahi's. With a dressing percentage of 70–75%, the only purpose of pig-rearing would be for the meat yield (Van Wijngaarden-Bakker 1986, 71). There are, however, secondary uses of pigs, such as using the bones for artefact crafting and skins for leather goods, but any indications of these could not be proven osteologically. In comparison with other contemporary medieval sites, a much larger proportion of pigs at St Nahi's were slaughtered young. This could reflect that a higher proportion of pigs were reared at St Nahi's than in the other locations. A seventeenth-century English account describes how the pork from 9–12-month-old pigs was the 'daintiest' and that bacon was recommended from animals aged 12–18 months (Albarella and Davis 1996, 38).

Horse bones constituted 12% of all mammal bone fragments in the early-medieval phase, 6% in the medieval and 10% in the post-medieval phase. Horses were used for riding and for labour (work-ponies); however, the main work animals in Ireland up until the fourteenth to fifteenth centuries were draught oxen (Kelly 1997, 21; McCormick 2005, 25). Consumption of horse flesh, so-called hippophagy, became a Christian taboo after a ban was issued by the European churches from at least the fourth century and onwards (Vretemark 1997, 144). There is, however, a possibility that horse-flesh consumption was accepted in Ireland up until at least the eighth century, which was the period when a papal prohibition was issued (McCormick 2005). This prohibition came into place, despite no known verses in the Bible which condemn the eating of horse meat, and it is likely that these regulations were simply an expression to distance the Christian church from surviving pagan traditions and rituals in which the horse as a magical animal often played a significant role (Sanmark 2004, 218–19). One of the consequences for breaking this taboo is mentioned in the Irish Canons (*Canones Hibernenses*, *c.*AD665) where a punishment of four years on bread and water was to be laid upon the wrongdoer (McCormick 2005, 23; Sanmark 2004, 218–19).

The presence of cats in the assemblage reflects the importance these animals would have had in farming societies. Cats keep the rodent population under control, which otherwise can potentially cause serious destruction and contamination of grain and other food stuffs. The cat was likely introduced to Ireland during the first centuries AD from Roman Britain (Kelly 1997, 121).

Shell fish were primarily exploited during the later medieval period. Only a few shells were found in early medieval and post-medieval features, and it is possible that these were originally medieval deposits which have either contaminated earlier features or been re-deposited in later features. The shell fish species identified are commonly occurring in the Irish Sea. Oysters and cockles were of primary importance. Not enough well preserved shells were present to discuss season exploitation.

The complete lack of bird bones from early medieval features is interesting. This could just be a reflection of the excavation methodology; however, the presence of bird bones in later medieval and post-medieval features would contradict that suggestion. Perhaps no domestic birds were housed at St Nahi's during the early medieval phase of occupation?

RADIOCARBON DATING

Chrono Centre QUB

Eight bone-samples (Sample-Numbers 8, 41, 164, 173, 119, 174, 184, 142) were sent to and processed by the [14]CHRONO-Centre at the Queens

LIST OF BONE-SAMPLES TAKEN FOR C14 DATING

Sample	Context	Type of feature	Type of bone	Weight	C14 Age	1 sigma Cal (68.35%)	2 sigma Cal (95.4%)	δ13C
8	F119	Fill of palisade enclosure F118	Cattle horncore	108,12g	BP 1271±28	AD687–771	AD665–808	-22.3
41	F104	Lower fill of large enclosure ditch F101	Dog nasal bones	2,80g	BP 1227±42	AD716–870	AD681–890	-20.4
164	F114	Basal fill of 'recut' F106 of large enclosure ditch F101	Scapula fragment of dog	4,11g	BP 1235±26	AD 694–859	AD688–876	-20.2
173	F114	Basal fill of 'recut' F106 of large enclosure ditch F101	Large mammal rib fragment	36,14g	BP 1183±24	AD782–886	AD775–937	-20.4
119	F243	Basal fill of inner boundary ditch F215	Cattle maxilla fragment	5,69g	BP 1178±23	AD782–889	AD776–939	-23.6
174	F495	Lower middle fill of medieval boundary ditch F464	Cattle mandible fragment	7,15g	BP 879±34	AD1053–1215	AD1040–1223	-31.6

Successfully dated samples and radiocarbon dates from St Nahi's, calibration data set: intcalo4.14c # (Reimer et al. 2004)

| 184 | F513 | Main fill of inner boundary ditch F215 | Indet. animal bone | 8,62g | Failed | | | |
| 142 | F465 | Basal fill of medieval boundary ditch F464 | Large mammal rib fragment | 26,10g | Failed | | | |

Failed samples from St Nahi's

University Belfast, 42 Fitzwilliam Street, Belfast BT9 6 AX, for radiocarbon-dating. Two samples (184 and 142) failed due to a low Nitrogen signal (this signal helps to determine the probable amount of useable and dateable collagen remaining within the bone matrix). The six radiocarbon dates obtained from St Nahi's reflect the general sequence of phases derived from the physical relationships between the features (see excavation results for further information). The above table shows the dated samples in their chronological order, based upon the two sigma (95.4 % certainty) radiocarbon date shown in the right-hand column.

ACKNOWLEDGMENTS AND DEDICATION

This paper is dedicated to the memory of Simon Dick (1965–2008). Simon was a key figure in the archaeological excavation at St Nahi's church site, where he worked as the principal surveyor and as one of the site supervisors in his last professional dig. Tragically, Simon was taken ill after completing the dig in December 2007 and died less than a year later in September 2008. His obituary has been published in an earlier volume in this series (Simpson 2010). These notes are intended partly as an insight to his talent as an archaeological excavator, but more particularly as a testament to his friendships with those with whom he worked on the archaeology of medieval Dublin over the last two decades.

Simon brought all of his skills to the excavations at St Nahi's and this is reflected in the success of the project. However, Simon's contribution to the professional archaeological record is only part of his offering: he was a teacher whose gentle guidance of site staff was always conducive to a happy working day. He was a hard worker, which was to his detriment as he dismissed as the all too familiar digging twinges what was in hindsight the onset of his illness. He was shy, yet paradoxically wonderfully social and loved a pint, a laugh and a cigarette. He had a very strong social conscience and teabreaks would involve an analysis of the *Guardian* and his engagement in lively debates on where Tony Blair had gone wrong. He always took the side of the underdog. Simon's friendships at work, with Peter Kerins, Kevin Weldon, Bill Frazer, Franc Myles, Linzi Simpson, Mags Gowen, Melanie McQuade, the author and so many others, are testament to the gentleman he is remembered as being.

The excavation took place over five months from 9 July to 14 December 2007. The dig was managed by Margaret Gowen and Co. for Park Developments Ltd. The site crew (fig. 1.38) was made up of Simon Dick (†), Stephan Bueck, Deirdre Collins, Ciara Burke, Antoine Arekian, Michael Moran, Ian O'Leary, Finbar Dwyer, Rachel Flynn, Laura O'Flynn, Victor Rodriguez, Clifford Nolan, Philip Melia, Steve P. Doyle, Garry Bedford, Jack Whelan and Eoin Ó Liatháin. Simon Dick, Stephan Bueck and Deirdre Collins supervised the work on site. Siobhán Scully managed the small finds on site and also later in post-excavation. The finds were illustrated by Simon Dick and Alva McGowan and photographed by Kevin Weldon; the site plans were digitized by Deirdre Collins, Stephan Bueck, and Lindsay Delahunty. Peter Kerins and particularly Stefan Bueck assisted in the preparation of the final site report. A final thanks to Kieron Goucher who stepped in at the last minute to convert CADs to JPGs – bribery with beer goes a long way – and to Dr Seán Duffy whose patience was surely tested (he has triumphed the editor's nightmare, trial by archaeologists). The author (Edmond O'Donovan) directed the excavations, all credit belongs to the above, errors and omission are all too often my own.

1.38 Some of the excavation crew.
(*left to right*) Simon Dick (inset), Michael Moran, Finbar Dwyer, Stephen Doyle (hidden),
Ian O'Leary, Deirdre Collins, Edmond O'Donovan, Rachael Burke, Stephan Bueck,
Antoine Arekian, Laura O'Flynn and Rachael Flynn.

ABBREVIATIONS

CGH   O'Brien, M.A. 1962 *Corpus genealogiarum Hiberniae*. Dublin. Dublin Institute for
       Advanced Studies.
CGSH   Ó Riain, P. 1985 *Corpus genealogiarum sanctorum Hiberniae*. Dublin. Dublin
       Institute for Advanced Studies.
RCB   Representative Church Body Library.

BIBLIOGRAPHY

Albarella, U. and Davis, S.J.M. 1996 Mammals and birds from Launceston Castle,
    Cornwall: decline in status and rise in agriculture. *Circaea* 12, 1–156.
Ball, F. E. 1903 (reprinted in idem ed. 1995) *A history of County Dublin*, Vol. II. Dublin. The
    H.S.P. Library.
Biddle, M. and Brown, D. 1990 Writing equipment. In M. Biddle, *Object and economy in
    Medieval Winchester*, 729–47. Oxford. Clarendon Press.

Biddle, M. and Kjølbye, B. 1992 Repton and the Vikings. *Antiquity* 66, 36–51.

Bolger, T. 2008 Excavations at Kilgobbin church, Co. Dublin. *Journal of Irish Archaeology* 17, 85–112.

Carroll, M. and Quinn, A. 2003 Ferrous and non-ferrous artefacts. In R.M. Cleary and M.F. Hurley (eds), *Excavations in Cork City, 1984–2000*, 257–98. Cork. Cork City Council.

Clark, J. 1995 Horseshoes. In J. Clark (ed.), *The medieval horse and its equipment*, 75–123. London. HMSO.

Colgan, E. 2003 *For want of good money: the story of Ireland's coinage.* Bray. Wordwell.

Corlett, C. 1999 *Antiquities of Old Rathdown: The archaeology of south County Dublin and north County Wicklow.* Bray. Wordwell.

Cotter, C. 1999 *Cahercommaun Fort, Co. Clare: a reassessment of its cultural context.* Western Stone Forts Project. Discovery Programme Reports 5. Dublin. Royal Irish Academy/ Discovery Programme.

De Neergaard, M. 2000 The use of knives, shears, scissors and scabbards. In J. Cowgill, M. de Neergaard and N. Griffiths (eds), *Knives and scabbards.* 2nd ed. Woodbridge. Boydell.

Eames, E.S. and Fanning, T. 1988 *Irish medieval tiles.* Dublin. Royal Irish Academy.

Edwards, N. 1990 *The archaeology of early medieval Ireland.* London. Batsford.

Egan, G. and Pritchard, F. 1991 *Dress accessories, 1150–1450.* London. Museum of London.

Egan, G. 1998 *The Medieval household: medieval finds from excavations in London.* London. The Stationary Office.

Ellis, B.M.A. 1995 Spurs and spur fittings. In J. Clark (ed.), *The medieval horse and its equipment*, 124–56. London. HMSO.

Fenton, A. 1963 Early and traditional cultivating implements in Scotland. *Proceedings of the Society of Antiquaries of Scotland* 96, 264–317.

Gillespie, R. 1997 *The first chapter act book of Christ Church Cathedral, Dublin 1574–1634.* Dublin. Four Courts Press.

Goodall, I.H. 1976 The metalwork. In O. Bedwin, The excavation of Ardingly fulling mill and forge, 1975–76. *Post-medieval Archaeology* 10, 60–64.

Goodall, I.H. 1990a Knives. In M. Biddle (ed.), *Object and economy in medieval Winchester*, 835–60. Oxford. Clarendon Press.

Goodall, I.H. 1990b Iron fittings for lights. In M. Biddle (ed.), *Object and economy in medieval Winchester*, 981–983. Oxford. Clarendon Press.

Goodall, I.H. 1990c Locks and keys. In M. Biddle (ed.), *Object and economy in medieval Winchester*, 1001–1036. Oxford. Clarendon Press.

Harkin, M. 2005 St Nathi's church and graveyard, Dundrum, Co. Dublin. In T. Condit, and C. Corlett (eds), *Above and beyond: essays in memory of Leo Swan*, 171–86. Bray. Wordwell.

Higgins, J. 1996 *Excavations at St James' church and Cemetery, Gleninagh Heights, Galway.* Galway. Rock Crow's Press.

Hume, I.N. 1969 *A guide to artifacts of Colonial America.* Philadelphia. University of Pennsylvania Press.

Hurley, M.F. 1996 Excavations in Cork City Kryl's Quay/North Main Street (Part 2). *Journal of the Cork Archaeological and Historical Society* 101, 39–41.

Hurley, M.F. 1997a Artefacts of skeletal material. In M.F. Hurley and O.M.B. Scully (eds), *Late Viking Age and medieval Waterford: excavations, 1986–1992*, 650–702. Waterford. Waterford Corporation.

Hurley, M.F. 1997b Artefacts of skeletal material. In R.M. Cleary, M.F. Hurley and E. Shee Twohig (eds), *Skiddy's Caste and Christ Church Cork: Excavations 1974–77*, 239–73. Cork. Cork Corporation.

Hurley, M.F. 1997c The bone and antler artefacts. In M.F. Hurley and C.M. Sheehan (eds), *Excavations at the Dominican priory, St Mary's of the Isle, Cork*, 112–15. Cork. Cork Corporation.

Hurley, M.F. 2003 Artefacts of skeletal material. In R.M. Cleary and M.F. Hurley (eds), *Excavations in Cork City 1984–2000*. Cork. Cork City Council.

Keene, S. 1990 Eyed weaving implements. In M. Biddle, *Object and economy in medieval Winchester*, 232–4. Oxford. Clarendon Press.

Kelly, F. 1997 *Early Irish farming*. Early Irish Law Series Vol. IV. Dublin. Dublin Institute for Advanced Studies.

Lawlor, H.J. 1930 *The fasti of St Patrick's, Dublin*. Dundalk. Tempest.

Leslie, J.B. and Wallace, W.J.R. 2001 *Clergy of Dublin and Glendalough: biographical succession lists*. Dublin. Diocesan Councils of Dublin and Glendalough.

Lewis, S. 1837 (reprinted 1970) *A topographical dictionary of Ireland comprising the several counties, cities [etc.]*. New York. Kennikat Press.

MacGregor, A. 1985 Bone, antler, ivory and horn. In *The technology of skeletal materials since the Roman period*. London and Sydney. Croom Helm.

MacGregor, A., Mainman, A.J. and Rogers, N.S.H. 1999 *Craft, industry and everyday life: bone, antler, ivory and horn from Anglo-Scandinavian and medieval York*. York. Council for British Archaeology.

Mainman, A.J. and Rogers, N.S.H. 2000 *Craft, industry and everyday life: finds from Anglo-Scandinavian York*. York. Council for British Archaeology.

Manning, C. 1984 The excavation of the Early Christian enclosure of Killederdadrum in Lackenavorna, Co. Tipperary. *Proceedings of the Royal Irish Academy* 84 C, 237–68.

Manning, C. 1986 Archaeological excavations at Millocktown, Co. Louth *Proceedings of the Royal Irish Academy* 86 C, 133–81.

MacNeill, C. 1950 *Calendar of Archbishop Alen's register, c.1172–1534*. Dublin. Royal Society of Antiquaries of Ireland.

McCormick, F. 1992 Early faunal evidence for dairying. *Oxford Journal of Archaeology* 11(2), 201–209.

McCormick, F. 2005 Archaeology: the horse in early Ireland. In M. McGrath and J.C. Griffith (eds), *The Irish draught horse: a history*, 17–29. Cork. Collins Press.

McCormick, F. and Murray, E. 2007 *Knowth and the zooarchaeology of Early Christian Ireland*. Excavations at Knowth, 3. Dublin. Royal Irish Academy.

McCutcheon, C. 2000 Medieval pottery in Dublin: new names and some dates. In S. Duffy (ed.), *Medieval Dublin I*, 117–25. Dublin. Four Courts Press.

McCutcheon, C. 2006 *Medieval pottery from Wood Quay, Dublin*. Dublin. Royal Irish Academy.

McEnery, M.J. and Refaussé, R. 2001 *Christ Church deeds*. Dublin. Four Courts Press.

Meenan, R. 2004 The excavation of pre-burials and ditch near St Michan's church. In S. Duffy (ed.), *Medieval Dublin V*, 91–110. Dublin. Four Courts Press.

Moore, P. 2000 Tilbury Fort: a post-medieval fort and its inhabitants. *Post-medieval Archaeology* 34, 3–104.

Moorhouse, S. and Goodall, I. 1971 Finds from Basing House, Hampshire (*c*.1540–1645): Part Two. *Post-medieval Archaeology* 5, 35–76.

Mould, Q., Carlisle, I. and Cameron, E. 2003 *Craft, industry and everyday life: leather and leatherworking in Anglo-Scandinavian and medieval York*. York. Council for British Archaeology.

Murphy, D. 2003 Excavation of an early monastic enclosure at Clonmacnoise. In H.A. King (ed.), *Clonmacnoise Studies: Seminar Papers 1998*. Vol. 2. Dublin. Stationary Office.

O'Brien, E. 1988 Churches of south-east County Dublin, seventh to twelfth centuries. In G. Mac Niocaill and P.F. Wallace (eds), *Keimelia, studies in medieval archaeology and history in memory of Tom Delaney*, 504–24. Galway. Galway University Press.

O'Donovan, E. 1996 A beehive quernstone at Terenure, Co. Dublin. Journal of the Royal Society of Antiquaries of Ireland 126, 183.

O'Donovan, E. 2008 The Irish, the Vikings and the English: new archaeological evidence from excavations at Golden Lane, Dublin. In S. Duffy (ed.), *Medieval Dublin VIII*, 36–130. Dublin. Four Courts Press.

O'Donovan, E. 2009 Excavations at Drumkay on the Wicklow Port Access Town Relief Road. In I. Bennett (ed.), *Excavations 2006: summary accounts of archaeological excavations in Ireland*. Bray. Wordwell.

O'Rahilly, C. 1998 A Classification of bronze stick-pins from the Dublin Excavations 1962–1972. In C. Manning (ed.), *Dublin and Beyond the Pale: Studies in Honour of Patrick Healy*, 23–33. Bray. Wordwell.

O'Rourke, D. 1997a Leather artefacts. In M.F. Hurley, O.M.B. Scully and S.W.J. McCutcheon (eds), *Late Viking Age and medieval Waterford: Excavations 1986–1992*, 703–36. Waterford. Waterford Corporation.

O'Rourke, D. 1997b Leather artefacts. In M.F. Hurley, O.M.B. Scully and S.W.J. McCutcheon (eds), *Skiddy's Castle and Christ Church Cork: Excavations 1974–77*, 311–39. Cork. Cork Corporation.

Ottaway, P. and Rogers, N. 2002 *Craft, industry and everyday life: finds from medieval York*. York. Council for British Archaeology.

Ottaway, P. 1992 *Anglo-Scandinavian ironwork from Coppergate*. London. Council for British Archaeology.

Pearson, P. 1998 *Between the mountains and the sea: Dun Laoghaire–Rathdown*. Dublin. O'Brien Press.

Reimer, P.J. et al. 2004 IntCal04 Atmospheric radiocarbon age calibration, 26–0 ka BP. *Radiocarbon* 46:1026–58

Rogers, P.W. 1997 *Textile production at 16–22 Coppergate*. York. Council for British Archaeology.

Rynne, E. 1964 Some destroyed sites at Shannon Airport, Co. Clare. *Proceedings of the Royal Irish Academy* 63C, 245–77.

Sanmark, A. 2004 Power and conversion. A comparative study of Christianization in Scandinavia. *Occasional Papers in Archaeology* 34. Uppsala.

Scully, S. 2008 The medieval small finds from Golden Lane. In E. O'Donovan, The Irish, the Vikings and the English, excavations at Golden Lane, Dublin. In S. Duffy (ed.), *Medieval Dublin VIII*, 71–99. Dublin. Four Courts Press.

Simington, R.C. 1945 *The Civil Survey A.D. 1654–1656: Volume VII*. Dublin. Stationery Office.

Simpson, L. 2010 Simon Dick: an appreciation. In S. Duffy (ed.), *Medieval Dublin X*, 11–12. Dublin. Four Courts Press.

Smyth, A.P. 1974 The Uí Néill and the Leinstermen in the annals of Ulster, 413–516 AD. *Études Celtique* 14 (i), 121–43.

Smyth, A.P. 1982 *Celtic Leinster: towards an historical geography of early Irish civilisation AD500–1600*. Dublin. Irish Academic Press.

Stout, M. and Stout, G. 1997 Early Landscapes: from prehistory to plantation. In F.H.A. Aalen, K. Whelan and M. Stout (eds) *Atlas of the Irish rural landscape*, 31–63. Cork. Cork University Press.

Stout, M. and Stout, G. 1992 Patterns in the past: County Dublin 5000BC–1000AD. In F.H.A. Aalen and K. Whelan (eds), *Dublin City and County from prehistory to present*, 5–14. Dublin. Geography Publications.

Swan, L. 1983 Enclosed ecclesiastical sites and their relevance to settlement patterns of the first millennium AD. In T. Reeves-Smyth and F. Hamond (eds) *Landscape archaeology in Ireland*, 269–94. BAR British Series 116.

Swan, L. 1985 Monastic proto-towns in early medieval Ireland: the evidence of aerial photography, plan analysis and survey. In H.B. Clarke and A. Simms (eds) *Comparative history of urban origins in non-Roman Europe*, 77–101. Oxford.

Swan, L. 1994 Ecclesiastical settlement in Ireland in the early medieval period. In M. Fixot and É. Zadorio-Rio (eds), *L'environnement des églises et la topographie religieuse des campagnes médiévales: congrès international d'archéologie médiévale, Aix-en-Provence, 28–30 sept. 1989*. Maison des Sciences de L'homme. Paris.

Thornton, J.H. 1990 Shoes, boots, and shoe repairs. In M. Biddle (ed.), *Object and economy in medieval Winchester*, 591–621. Oxford. Clarendon Press.

Van Wijngaarden-Bakker, L.H. 1986 The animal remains from the beaker settlement at Newgrange, Co. Meath. *Proceedings of the Royal Irish Academy* 86 C, 313–83.

Vretemark, M. 1997 *Från ben till boskap. Kosthåll och djurhållning med utgångspunkt i medeltida benmaterial från Skara*. Skrifter från Länsmuseet Skara 25. Skara: Skaraborgs länsmuseum.

Walsh, F. and Harrison, J. 2003 Early medieval enclosure at Killickaweeny, Co. Kildare. *Archaeology Ireland* 17(1), 33–6.

Ward-Perkins, J.B. 1993 *London Museum medieval catalogue 1940*. Ipswich. Anglia Publishing.

White, N.B. (ed.) 1957 *The 'Dignitas decani' of St Patrick's Cathedral, Dublin*. Dublin. Stationery Office.

Whitehead, R. 2003 *Buckles 1250–1800*. Witham. Greenlight Publishing.

Woodland, M. 1990 Spindle-whorls. In M. Biddle (ed.), *Object and economy in medieval Winchester*, 216–25. Oxford. Clarendon Press.

WEBSITES

'Stone-Walls'. In A. Brooks, S. Adcock, and E. Agate (eds), *Dry stone walling: a practical handbook*, British Trust for Conservation Volunteers (1999), available at: http://www.handbooks.btcv.org.uk/handbooks/content/section/1637.

The *longphort* of Dublin: lessons from Woodstown, County Waterford and Annagassan, County Louth

LINZI SIMPSON

INTRODUCTION

The recent archaeological discoveries of two ninth-century Viking *longphuirt* or 'ship camps' in Ireland, at Woodstown, Co. Waterford, and, Annagassan, Co. Louth, have considerable implications for our understanding of the first Viking settlement at Dublin, at the mouth of the Liffey. While the existence of at least twenty such camps has been charted in the monastic annals, the lack of positive identification of these sites has, until now, stymied research on what was clearly a very important part of the successful military strategy employed by the Viking invaders.

The discoveries followed on from scholarship in the field, which had begun to identify potential *longphuirt* by focussing on specific topographical criteria, and locations for which there was little pre-existing archaeological evidence (Kelly and Maas 1995, 30–2; Kelly and O'Donovan 1998, 12–16; Ó Floinn 1998, 137–8; Sheehan 2008, 282–95) (fig. 2.1). The unexpected find at Woodstown in 2003, followed by the more recent discovery at Annagassan in 2010, however, must now – and rather spectacularly – support the hypothesis that there is a morphological 'type', as proposed by Kelly, a specific kind of earthwork or monument in Ireland, which can be identified in the field and associated with the Scandinavian invasions of Ireland from the late eighth century onwards. Obviously, as with any monument type, there are likely to have been variations in morphology. While some of the raiding camps mentioned in the annals must have been transitory in nature, created literally just for a matter of days, it now seems clear that there were also 'super-camps', established on a much more permanent basis, with evidence of diversification of activity from the earliest levels.

This proposed new site-form has been well defined in the literature to date on the subject and a number of criteria have been laid down. Such 'ship-camps' or 'ship-landings', as the name suggests (Bhreathnach 1998, 36) are accessible by water, usually located on a major navigable river, and perhaps at a bend or crook formed with a tributary, creating a naturally-defended space. The bases are enclosed or defined by some form of earthen defences, such as banks, ditches or palisades, or a combination of all three, and some may have had a naturally-defended area or citadel within the main enclosure. The presence of a pool, or marshy ground denoting the site of a former pool, can

2.1 Possible *longphort*
sites (after Kelly and
O'Donovan 1998)

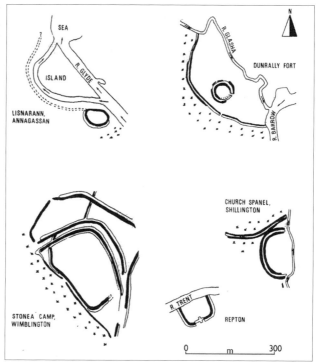

also be considered a significant indicator, the pool being exploited for moorage, especially important for an invading army whose mobility was dependant on ships (Kelly and O'Donovan 1998, 12–16). This, then, was the type of campaign-base the annalists struggled to describe when they used the term *longphort* for the invaders' camp at the mouth of the Liffey at Dublin in 841.

DUBLIN

Much has been written on the subject of the search for the *longphort* established at Dublin in 841 but until recently there was little actual physical evidence for what must have been a very extensive settlement, despite substantial excavations within the historic core, in and around the Christ Church and Wood Quay area (Clarke 2002; Wallace 2010). These internationally renowned excavations did, as is well known, pinpoint the exact location of the somewhat later defended Viking town, on a prominent ridge on the south bank of the Liffey but the earliest levels were dated to the tenth rather than the ninth century, prompting the conclusion that this settlement might relate to a later Viking incursion into Dublin, described in the annals for 917, after they had been forced out (so the annals tell us) in 902 (Wallace 1990).

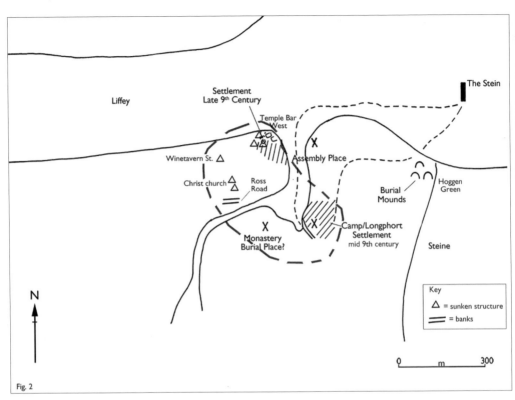

2.2 Dublin in the ninth century

Subsequent excavations, however, within the north-east angle of this settlement, at Parliament Street and Temple Bar West, finally identified evidence of pre-tenth-century domestic occupation, suggesting that the riverbank, if not the ridge, was occupied in and around the late ninth century, i.e., within the *longphort* years (841–902) (Gowen with Scally 1996; Simpson 1999; Simpson 2010, 80–2) (fig. 2.2). But the evidence of domestic houses and formal layout appeared at this early date to be confined to the eastern side of the settlement, along the west bank of the Poddle river, and did not extend westwards towards Fishamble Street, suggesting a focus of activity along the Poddle river-channel rather than the Liffey (Simpson 2010, 86–7) (fig. 2.3).

The most significant recent advance in the quest for ninth-century Viking levels in Dublin was made in 2003 when, finally, early evidence of occupation and burial was found at South Great George's Street but this site lay off the ridge entirely, in the low-lying Poddle valley to the south (Simpson 2005; Simpson 2010, 75–9; Simpson 2011, 28–32) (fig. 2.2). The discovery of this settlement, on the southern side of a tidal pool on the Poddle, was somewhat unexpected and, perversely, the lowest levels produced very early dates, the

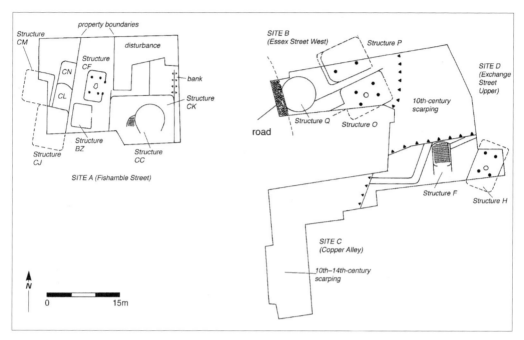

2.3 The internal layout of Temple Bar West, Dublin

C14 determinations suggesting a date from the early 800s onwards. While permanent occupation here is likely to have dated to after 837, when the Vikings are first mentioned as 'taking' Dublin (Downham 2010, 98), the discovery of four Viking warrior burials does suggest that this settlement formed part of the elusive early *longphort* phase, established sometime in the first half of the ninth century. In any event, the evidence suggested that the site certainly predated the settlement along the southern bank of the Liffey at Parliament Street and Temple Bar West further north.

New evidence: morphology and size
While it is evident that the South Great George's Street site must be considered part of the *longphort* settlement of Dublin, the new evidence about typology coming on-stream now suggests that this might not be the full picture (Simpson 2010, 72–88). The recent research has established two main elements which can be applied to Dublin, namely, the identification of a morphological 'type' and new insights into the potential size of *longphuirt* in Ireland. The Poddle Valley site does tick some of the newly defined 'morphology' boxes (figs 2.2 and 2.4). It lies within a bend of the Poddle river, a curve that was certainly in existence in the tenth century, and the site has produced evidence of ninth-century Viking activity. This area was flanked by a large tidal pool on the eastern side (which may in fact have been the very

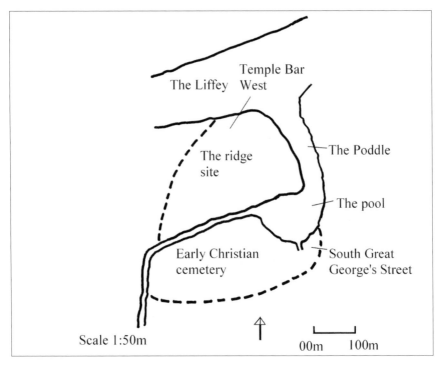

2.4 The *longphort* of Dublin

'Black Pool' or *Dubh-linn* that gave the settlement its name), and to the south
the land was low-lying and marshy, potentially creating a defined space that
measured roughly 320m east–west by 300m north–south, delineated, perhaps,
in the curving street pattern of South Great George's Street and Golden Lane.

But a glance at the topographical map of the mouth of the Liffey
immediately highlights a far more likely site, based on the new morphology:
the ridge to the north, also in the bend of the river Poddle and defended on
three sides by water, suggesting a space potentially measuring 440m east–west
by 240m north–south, the site, in fact, of the tenth-century Viking town, or
dún, as it was called from the mid-tenth century (Clarke 2002, 3). This
hypothesis is certainly nothing new and has been proposed many years ago but
speculation has tended to suggest that the *longphort* was confined to the eastern
half of the subsequent *dún* or even to within the confines of the later Dublin
Castle, which highlights the other major advance made in *longphort* studies to
date, the question of the potential size of some of the ship-camps, especially
those mentioned frequently in the annals.

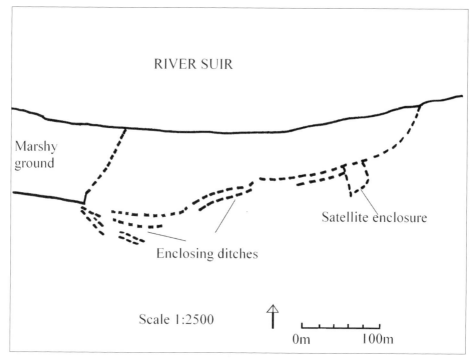

RIVER SUIR

Marshy
ground

Satellite enclosure

Enclosing ditches

Scale 1:2500

↑

0m   100m

2.5 The *longphort* at Woodstown, Co. Waterford

WOODSTOWN, CO. WATERFORD

Evidence as to the potential size of some of these sites has come dramatically to light from the spectacular Viking *longphort* found during road works by the National Roads Authority, in 2003, at Woodstown, Co. Waterford, on the river Suir, just 6km west of Waterford (O'Brien and Russell 2005; Russell et al., 2007) (fig. 2.5). The site was comprehensively tested and the investigations revealed a massive D- or B-shaped enclosure, fronting onto the river Suir and defended by a series of banks and ditches along the landward side. A marsh, possibly the remains of a pool, flanked the earthwork on the northern side (Russell et al., 2007, 32). The site has been dated from the mid-ninth to the early to mid-tenth century, as might be expected, and has produced an extensive collection of over 4,500 artefacts, including a large collection of lead weights and some hack silver, the latter clearly the spoils of raiding and plunder. In addition to this evidence, the presence of actual Viking warriors has been confirmed by a single furnished warrior grave lying just 20m outside the enclosure. While the skeletal remains were non-existent, this man was evidently originally of high status, as he was buried with a plethora of grave-goods, which included a sword, spear-head, shield-boss and axe, along with his whetstone.

The potential size of Dublin and Woodstown

But what was most critical for anyone interested in the site of the *longphort* at Dublin was the ground-breaking information revealed at Woodstown about the size and scale of the encampment there, as the enclosure measures an astounding half a kilometre in length by at least 120m wide at its widest point (Simpson 2010, 83–4) (fig. 2.5). In addition to this, research excavations established that the area in use extended even further, beyond the enclosure, into the immediate environs. What Woodstown had finally provided for anyone interested in *longphuirt* in Ireland was a measurement of scale, which had been entirely lacking hitherto.

This 'measurement of scale', when applied to Dublin now suggests that the possible locations for the *longphort* cited to date, including the ridge site, are most probably far too small to have accommodated the numbers likely to have been living there, based on the Woodstown model (fig. 2.4). Dublin, in contrast to Woodstown, figures very prominently in the annals and was clearly the point of entry for many of the warriors flooding into Ireland in this period, the strong possibility being that it was a primary base responsible for founding daughter camps elsewhere, at Rosnaree on the Boyne, for instance, and Cluain Andobair, Co. Offaly (Downham 2010, 108).

Camps, by their nature, suggest transience and the likelihood that the Viking population at Dublin fluctuated but a figure of between 3,000 and 4,000 warriors may be suggested, based on the annalistic references of over 1,000 men from there killed in battles around the country in a single year (Duffy 1993, 4). While previously these figures might have been thought to have been greatly exaggerated, the size of Woodstown adds credence to such estimates, at the least, if one bears in mind the additional population that must have resided here, non-warriors and captives alike. The likelihood is, therefore, that Dublin was at least as big if not bigger than Woodstown, and this suggests that it was likely to have occupied a space measuring at least 500m in length.

It now seems extraordinary to contemplate that the gravel ridge would have been ignored by the Vikings when founding their base, in the light of the research by Kelly et al. The inclusion of this swathe of land would satisfy the compelling topographical criteria of the ridge site, within the crook of a major river and its tributary – a now familiar morphology – and place in context the evidence from Temple Bar West in the north-east corner, bringing it inside the main enclosure rather than consigning it to the status of associated sprawl along the river (fig. 2.4). It would also considerably expand the size of the ninth-century settlement, suggesting an area measuring approximately 550m north-south by 220m in width, stretching from South Great George's Street in the south as far north as the Liffey but divided by the Poddle river.

THE ARCHAEOLOGICAL EVIDENCE

The sunken structures There is some fragmented evidence which may support the hypothesis that the ridge site did form part of the *longphort*, based on the type of buildings found in the earliest levels at Christ Church Place and Winetavern Street (Murray 1983) (fig. 2.2). A comparison of these levels with Temple Bar West reveals a striking similarity in the presence of small domestic buildings, which are well-preserved on all three sites, as their floors were sunk deep into the boulder clay. Two sunken structures were found at Christ Church Place with a third at Winetavern Street and all three were dated roughly to the mid-tenth century by Murray who published a very useful catalogue of the buildings (Murray 1983, 169–75). However, the dating was based purely on the general sequence of the site rather than any scientific means, and there was no presentation of supporting artefactual evidence, as Murray points out. In fact, the sunken structures are listed independently by Murray and appear to have had no relationship with the buildings that followed. What is clear, however, is that all three sunken structures were primary features, being cut directly into boulder clay, which must raise the possibility that they were earlier than the general time frame proposed for the site, from the mid-tenth century onwards.

The significance of these buildings is that an additional three well-preserved examples were also found at Temple Bar West, clustered together on the bank of the Liffey (Simpson 1999, 14–18). These were clearly the same type of structure and were also cut into sterile boulder clay but had the benefit of being scientifically dated, which suggested a date in the late ninth century for their construction. Thus this specific type of small sunken structure, which does not appear again in the archaeological record of Dublin, is likely to have been a pre-tenth-century type, associated with the *longphort* phase only and not introduced again in that particular form when the Vikings returned to Dublin in 917. A fourth sunken structure was also found at Fishamble Street/Wood Quay, immediately west of the Temple Bar West group, which may help provide a link between the riverside examples at Temple Bar West and Winetavern Street (pers. comm., Adrienne Corless). If all the sunken buildings form part of the same settlement pattern and are dated similarly, their distribution is certainly suggestive of some form of scattered occupation along the top of the ridge by the late ninth century in tandem with what was occurring along the Liffey riverbank, at Temple Bar West.

The southern bank The presence of some form of occupation along the ridge in the late ninth century may also help explain the location of a pre-tenth-century earthen bank or rampart along the southern side of the ridge, which may have stretched from Ross Road as far west as Werburgh Street, a distance of approximately 200m (Walsh 2001, 106; Hayden 2002, 66) (fig. 2.2). The bank, halfway down the southern flank of the ridge, closely mirrors the alignment of the tenth-century ramparts, which were found just 10m to the south, hinting that, at this side at least, the boundaries of the later settlement followed those of the earlier. It also highlights the fact that there are two sequential alignments on this side, suggesting a general expansion on this side from the late ninth to the mid- to late tenth century, despite the documented 'expulsion' of the Vikings in 902. This, of course, correlates with the sequence at Temple Bar West which suggests continued occupation during the purported exile-period, between 902 and 917 (Simpson 1999, 4).

The western boundary While it is known that the Liffey and Poddle rivers defined the northern, eastern and southern boundaries of the tenth-century *dún*, there is no indication of the likely western boundary in the archaeological record, compounded by the fact that there is no defining natural topographical feature on this side (fig. 2.2). Thus the western limit of the dense occupation found within the historic core is not known. However, the dates of the various archaeological deposits in and around Christ Church suggest that High Street, to the west of Christ Church, lay outside the tenth-century settlement, the earliest houses and properties in this location being dated, by a sequence of coin evidence, to the early to mid-eleventh century (Murray 1983, 43). In tentative support of this, the first indications of western defences along the ridge are as far west as Back Lane and Cornmarket, a distance of approximately 300m just above the site of the bridge (Simpson 2011, 44–5). At Back Lane these were represented by a series of large postholes and a clay bank that were dated tentatively to the early twelfth century (although not scientifically), while at Cornmaket the two large ditches that were found were similarly dated to the late eleventh/early twelfth century (Coughlan 2000, 205; Hayden 2000, 86).

This combination of evidence to date infers that the tenth-century western boundary might well have run along the western side of Christ Church and down Nicholas Street to join with the stretch found at Ross Road, suggesting an oval shape for the settlement at this date, wider at the southern end than the northern end (Halpin 2005, 102; Simpson 2010a) (fig. 2.2). If the correlation between the ninth- and tenth-century defences at the southern side of the settlement at Ross Road and Werburgh Street can be paralleled on the western side, this may suggest that this alignment formed the western boundary of the ninth-century settlement also.

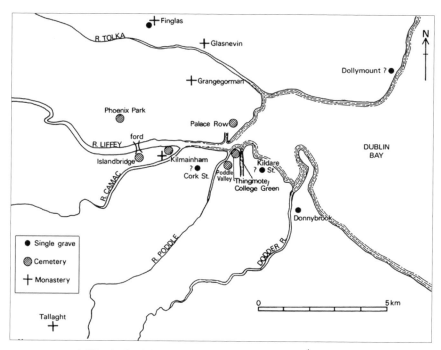

2.6 Warrior burials in the Dublin region (based on Ó Floinn 1998)

But despite the fact that the High Street end of the ridge appears to have been relatively sterile until the eleventh century at the earliest, it is most likely that this entire area was utilized from the earliest stages of the Viking occupation, perhaps under cultivation and perhaps even enclosed, the defences simply not having been located to date (Simpson 2010, 87–8). What is certain is that there is most likely to have been a major route running along the ridge in the ninth century linking the settlement with the great Viking warrior cemeteries at Kilmainham and Islandbridge (O'Brien 1998) (fig. 2.6).

Defences: Temple Bar West and Woodstown
There are other analogies that can be drawn between Temple Bar West and Woodstown, which may help support the hypothesis that the ridge formed part of the main *longphort* site in the mid-ninth century (Simpson 2010, 79, 83–4). The lack of defences at Temple Bar West was considered an impediment to this area forming part of the early *longphort*, yet the fortifications at Woodstown were not substantial either, comprising two successive ditches (Simpson 1999, 27–8). The ditches measured between 2.2m and 3m in width, suggesting they were not very elaborate, also indicated by the fact that the outer, larger ditch was allowed to silt up very rapidly (Harrison 2007, 31–2). This can be compared to Temple Bar West where the only suggestion of

enclosure was the southern flank of clay bank which was found running along
the Liffey but which was presumed to be a flood bank, similar to those found
further east at Parliament Street, although very low, surviving to 0.80m in
height by 2m in width (probably originally 3.70m at its widest) (Simpson 2011,
33; Gowen with Scally 1996, 11). In addition to this, the remains of an earlier
slot-trench were also found running parallel with the Liffey further west,
which is likely to have held some sort of a palisade, positioned just above the
high-water mark (Simpson 2010, 81).

Industrial activity: Temple Bar West and Woodstown
A comparison between the early levels found at Woodstown and Temple Bar
West also highlights the similarities between both sites as, at Temple Bar West,
a section of the site was identified as an industrial quarter, containing hearths,
surfaces, and producing copious evidence of burning associated with metal-
working over a significant period of time. This industrial quarter was a defined
space within a residential area, and this can be paralleled at Woodstown where
one of the most unexpected discoveries was the amount of metal-working
taking place within the actual enclosure, where occupation was occurring
(Harrison 2007, 36–7). Thus at Woodstown and Temple Bar West industrial
manufacturing was identified as a core function, emphasizing the commercial
over the trading aspect of these *longphort* sites, the inhabitants clearly not
simply warriors but a far more mixed population, including commercial
traders and industrial manufacturers and food providers. Furthermore, ironworking was identified as the dominant metal-working activity at Woodstown
and this was directly paralleled at Temple Bar West where iron-smelting was
suggested by the identification of the natural ore, hematite, presumably mined
from the nearest source, thought to be the Wicklow mountains (Harrison 2007,
36; Simpson 2011, 30–1).

The findings from Woodstown do have implications for how we perceive the
functions of these massive sites. While it is certainly the case that large armies
of warriors on the move did not need infrastructure, the longevity of
settlement at both Woodstown and Dublin clearly suggests that at least some of
the *longphuirt* were not just campaign bases but the beginnings of permanent
independent trading centres, where manufacturing and industrial activity was
taking place and where, in the case of Woodstown, at least three generations of
Vikings were raised.

The artefacts: Temple Bar West and Woodstown
Finally, parallels can also be made between the artefactual evidence from the
early levels on both sites: the Woodstown assemblage, although mostly
retrieved from plough-soil, can be dated to a narrow period from between
c.850 and c.920 (Harrison 2007, 25). The most striking aspect of this was the

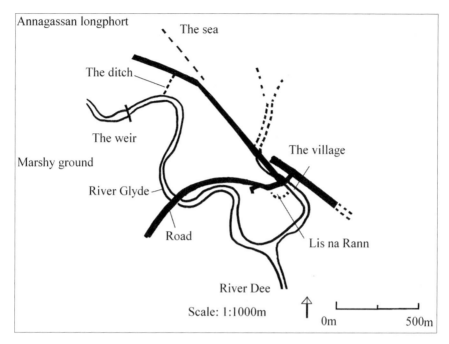

Annagassan longphort
The sea
The ditch
The weir
Marshy ground
River Glyde
Road
The village
Lis na Rann
River Dee
Scale: 1:1000m
0m
500m

2.7 The *longphort* of Annagassan, Co. Louth

collection over 200 lead weights, physical proof of the importance of trading hack silver and other bullion, in numbers not matched in the Scandinavian countries of origin. But this collection can be matched at Dublin, from the excavations at Wood Quay, west of Temple Bar West, which produced a similar number, although evidently of a slightly later date (Harrison 2007, 25). In addition to this, the earliest levels at Temple Bar West also produced a collection of artefacts that can be compared to the Woodstown assemblage, including copper alloy rings, silver finger rings, weighing scales, a miniature hammer, probably used in delicate metal-working, iron bars and links. Other items, perhaps booty from raids, consisted of a copper harness mount and a hollow boss of gilded gold. Strangely, and unlike Woodstown, silver is not well represented in the artefactual record in Dublin.

LINN DUACHAILL, AT ANNAGASSAN, CO. LOUTH

The hypothesis that the ridge site formed part of the original *longphort* suggests a sequential development for Dublin, the earliest evidence coming from the site at South Great George's Street in the Poddle Valley, which was possibly pre–841 in date. This must have rapidly expanded northwards to

include the ridge, the latter certainly occupied and defended by the late ninth
century. A similar progression has been suggested for the B-shaped enclosure
at Woodstown, both enclosures possibly sequential also, indicative of a general
expansion, presumably to accommodate growing numbers (Harrison 2007, 16).
But the northerly progression at Dublin is somewhat puzzling and unsatisfactory,
the body of evidence usually pointing to riverside locations that then expanded
into the interior, away from the major river, rather than the other way around.

The factors influencing the Vikings' initial choice at Dublin must have been
very specific and possibly had a close parallel in the second major *longphort* site
recently identified in Ireland, at Annagassan, Co. Louth, in 2010 (fig. 2.7).
This coastal site lies approximately 70km north of Dublin and, like Dublin, it
figures very prominently in the annals under the place-name Linn Duachaill,
the *linn* element referring to a pool, as it does in *Dubh-linn* (see website:
www.linnduachaill.ie). The two settlements compare well historically, both
established as permanent encampments in the very same year, 841, possibly
even by the same great army. In any event, the activities of the inhabitants of
both camps were intertwined from earliest times, the annals recording that a
combined force from both camps was involved in a campaign against the Ui
Néill in 841 (Downham 2010, 108).

The site at Annagassan fronts onto the sea and is bounded by the Glyde
river and its confluence with the river Dee, creating a long, steep-sided natural
enclosure with a distinctive rectangular bend in the river at the southern end
(fig. 2.7). At the south-eastern end, on the high ground above the confluence
of the rivers, lies a prominent earthwork known as Lis na Rann which, since
the eighteenth century, has been traditionally identified as a possible site for
Linn Duachaill but it is now considered to be on too high a prominence and
far too small. It may, however, have functioned as a citadel within a larger
enclosure, which is certainly a strong possibility (pers. comm., Eamon Kelly).

In 2004, following the discovery of Woodstown, a research group was
established at Annagassan to try and advance the search for the *longphort*,
expanding it from the Lis na Rann earthwork (www.linnduachaill.ie). After a
series of investigations, selected excavation was carried out by Kelly, Clinton
and McKeown, which identified an artificial ditch, used to cut off the headland
at it narrowest point but some distance north from Lis na Rann. The site of the
ditch was identified in a very innovative way. The research group, realizing that
access to water was restricted along the coastal side of the earthwork due to the
high ground, simply sailed up the river Glyde and identified the first point
where it was possible to land a boat while staying within the tidal reaches of the
river. This landing stage was found to be located just below a modern weir,
1.18km north of Lis na Rann. The results from just three trenches finally
proved beyond doubt what the research team had long suspected, that this was
the long-lost *longphort* of Linn Duachaill, subsequently confirmed by C14

determinations, which produced a ninth-century date. The trenches revealed significant evidence of occupation in and around the general area, the features including mettled surfaces, evidence of burning and postholes, which can be directly paralleled in the earliest levels at both Woodstown and South Great George's Street. In addition, evidence of occupation was also found 'outside' the enclosure, indicative of a general sprawl, similar to Woodstown.

The implications of the findings at Annagassan are considerable for the potential size of *longphuirt* in Ireland, as, if it can be established that the entire landmass enclosed by the river was occupied, the settlement would have measured at least 1.18km (from the ditch to Lis na Rann), over twice the size of the enclosure at Woodstown. What is certain is that the size was dictated by the topography of the river, the concentration of activity at the northern end presumably being related to the landing stage for ships, as it was at South Great George's Street.

The pool: Annagassan and South Great George's Street
The numbers of ships in a single Viking fleet obviously varied greatly but could be very substantial: in 849 the Annals of Ulster record a fleet of 140 ships sent to Ireland by 'the king of the foreigners (*rígh Gall*)' to 'exact obedience' from those Vikings already in Ireland (Duffy 1993, 4). Such a fleet, while probably at the extreme end of the spectrum, would take considerable management and would require either space to be pulled up out of the water or a body of water where they could be moored, most likely a combination of both. A recent estimate suggests that at least 300m is required to accommodate approximately sixty ships (Gibbons and Gibbons 2008, 27), and the size of both Annagassan and Woodstown was probably dictated by this need alone. At Annagassan the site is flanked by marshy ground on the north-western side, presumably the remnants of a pool or *linn*, preserved to this day in the modern place-name Linns. This can be compared directly with the site at South Great George's Street and perhaps holds the key to unravelling the Vikings' curious choice for their initial settlement at Dublin at South Great George's Street.

The requirement to land ships is likely to have been just as important at Dublin and this was no doubt possible along the Liffey frontage, as the sloping contours of the northern side of the gravel ridge suggest. But the presence of the 'Black Pool' or *Dubh-linn* on the southern side of the ridge was presumably equally important, being a safe haven where ships could be moored without being beached by the tidal waters. While clearly neither pool at Dublin or Annagassan is likely to have been able to accommodate vast numbers of ships, they provided handy moorage for storage or for carrying out repairs. At Dublin the pool was at least 6m in depth and was indeed used for this purpose as ship rivets were found deep in the gravel deposits of an inlet at South Great George's Street (Simpson 2011, 13–14) (fig. 2.4).

The monastery: Annagassan and South Great George's Street
But this may not have been the only attraction in the Poddle Valley at Dublin.
The second major comparison that can be drawn between Annagassan and
South Great George's Street is that both had pre-Viking monastic origins and
were therefore not virgin sites. Although the ecclesiastical site at Linn
Duachaill has not been located in the field to date, it is referred to in annalistic
sources and is thought to lie to the east of the site, on the other side of the river
(Griffiths 2010, 31). At Dublin, however, research has always identified the
Poddle Valley as the likely site of the ecclesiastical settlement and this was
supported by the discovery of an early Christian cemetery at the later church
of St Michael le Pole, a short distance to the west of South Great George's
Street. Flanking this cemetery to the west again, the excavations at Chancery
Lane revealed extraordinary evidence of street layout, probably pre-Viking in
date and certainly laid down sometime between the late seventh and late ninth
centuries (Walsh 2009). The flimsy remains of some sort of plots or properties
were found, respecting or aligned to at least one major stone road (and possibly
two), indicative of formal layout and land division at Dublin, even at this early
date (Walsh 2009, 14).

The Vikings at South Great George's Street occupied the ground immediately
east of this and initially both communities may have coexisted, although this is
very difficult to establish (Simpson 2010, 58–60; Simpson 2011, 19–20). But
the invading Vikings, while not adopting the existing infrastructure at
Chancery Lane (suggested by the fact that the road had silted over by the mid-
ninth century), were exposed to a form of nucleated settlement, of land
division and organization, which was very different from their traditional
settlement in their homelands and which may well have provided the blueprint
for the similar spatial organization that was to occur at Temple Bar West not
long afterwards.

Whatever influences may have been absorbed by the invaders, the benefits
of conquering existing monastic settlements were likely to be very considerable,
now that the evidence of how some of these large *longphuirt* functioned is
starting to come to light. Stereotypically, monasteries were their main targets
for portable plunder, the metal artefacts and the gathering of slaves, which
could be transported quickly offsite. But the redefinition of at least some of the
bases, as industrial and manufacturing centres, brings to the fore other
advantages of major ecclesiastical settlements, which may have influenced the
Vikings' choice of site at both Annagassan and Dublin. At monastic settlements
the invaders could expect infrastructure, for instance, established route-ways,
fords, bridges perhaps, buildings, stores of food, fresh water, waterfront
structures and local trade networks. In addition to this, there was a population
that could be exploited: the excavations in the Christian cemetery at Golden
Lane suggest that burial continued uninterrupted throughout the Viking

period and thus there was an Irish community which continued to live in Dublin, their social status as yet undetermined (O'Donovan 2008, 46). From 841 onwards both Annagassan and Dublin must have been in a position to secure enough foodstuffs and other necessities of life to carry the inhabitants through the winter, and this must have involved exploitation of the hinterland, whether by trade or direct management, to ensure a guaranteed food supply.

CONCLUSIONS

The discovery of the *longphuirt* sites at Woodstown and Annagassan has provided a vital – indeed, terrifying – insight into the scale of the invasions the Irish faced from the 840s onwards, the sheer scale of both sites pointing to a rapid change from transitory camps, designed to support raiding, to more enduring commercial, industrial and trading centres at Dublin, Annagassan and Woodstown. The dates of all three sites combine to demonstrate that by the mid-ninth century, if not sooner, the Vikings had already developed a military strategy that demonstrated immense organizational and operational skill, of a type that must have developed 'on the hoof' as the lucrative economic potential of the Irish Sea region was realized.

At Dublin, we get a glimpse of what these *longphuirt* must have looked like, the settlement that developed presumably as alien to the Scandinavians as it was to the Irish they encountered there. There were initial defences, exploitation of the pool as moorage for large fleets, and defended occupation on the prominent ridge site, to the north of the monastic settlement, outside the previously occupied area. Within this new settlement by the late ninth century there was a street network and a grid of property plots, some of which included workshops and animal pens. The interior was probably divided into different sectors, as is suggested at Woodstown, and at least one area was a designated iron-working area, an indication of the diversification of activities that were taking place. There was too evidence of collective activity, in communal dumping and the construction of at least one stone road, which cut through a previously occupied plot, perhaps indicative of some sort of central authority by the late ninth century. It is certainly the case that inhabitants were constantly manipulating their environment, infilling and reclaiming land along the frontage of both rivers and trying to control the tidal Liffey by means of flood defence systems, again presumably under some collective control. There may even have been 'sea-control defences', which have not survived the modern dredging of the Liffey (Gibbons and Gibbons 2008, 17).

Woodstown, by way of contrast, provides details of morphological layout and scale (preserved there because the site was later abandoned but lacking from Dublin since the early settlement evolved into a capital city). Woodstown, although as yet without the benefit of large-scale excavation, has enormous potential to provide vital detail about the early layout of such *longphuirt* sites, preserved in the boulder clay (despite considerable damage to the site by later ploughing). This may produce evidence of early street layout, plot divisions and partition of space within the enclosure, which can be paralleled at Dublin. The artefactual assemblage from this site has and will continue to produce a wealth of information in the future.

But it is the final site at Annagassan that is causing the most excitement among scholars interested in this subject. Sealed beneath re-deposited clays, the early levels are intact and have huge potential to produce very significant archaeological remains, undisturbed, unlike the previous two sites. In addition to this, future work may be able to establish that this settlement stretched from Lis na Rann to the northern ditch, a distance of 1.18km, an extraordinary size. While it is not clear how much of the interior was actually occupied, it may preserve details of cultivation or animal husbandry within this almost ready-made enclosure, providing crucial detail about how the *longphort* made the transition from short-term camp to medium-term settlement.

It may also help explain the puzzling concentration of Viking burials up the Liffey estuary, which implies that the Vikings' sphere of influence at Dublin extended well beyond the limits of any defended base at the mouth of the Liffey, extending at least 1.5km upstream to the massive grave-fields of Kilmainham/Islandbridge, where a minimum of fifty-two burials have been found, between the nineteenth and early twentieth centuries (Harrison 2010, 127). Clusters of other burial grounds, at Hoggen Green, just east of the *longphort* and on the north side of the Liffey at the Phoenix Park and Parnell Square/Granby Row, extending east to Mountjoy Square, attest to control if not settlement up the Liffey estuary (Ó Floinn 1998, 134–6), the size of which may be backed up in the future if the size of the site at Annagassan, Co. Louth can finally be established.

BIBLIOGRAPHY

Bhreathnach, E. 1998 Saint Patrick, Vikings and *Inber Dée – longphort* in the early Irish literary tradition. *Wicklow Archaeology and History* 1, 36–40.
Clarke, H.B. 2002 *Dublin Part 1, to 1610. Irish historic town atlas no. 11*. Dublin. Royal Irish Academy.
Coughlan, T. 2000 The Anglo-Norman houses of Dublin: evidence from Back Lane. in S. Duffy (ed.), *Medieval Dublin I*, 203–33. Dublin. Four Courts Press.
Downham, C. 2010 Viking camps in ninth-century Ireland: sources, locations and interactions. In S. Duffy (ed.), *Medieval Dublin X*, 93–125. Dublin. Four Courts Press.
Duffy, S. 1993 The political narrative. Historical background, in G. Scally, 'Archaeological excavation at 33–34 Parliament Street/Exchange Street Upper'. Stratigraphic report lodged with the former *Dúchas*: the Heritage Service and the National Museum.

–1996 Historical Background. In M. Gowen with G. Scally (eds), *A summary report on excavations at Exchange Street Upper/Parliament Street, Dublin*. Temple Bar Archaeological Report 4, 4–9. Dublin. Wordwell.

–2000 (ed.), *Medieval Dublin I–XII* (12 vols). Dublin. Four Courts Press.

Gibbons, M. and Gibbons, M. 2008 The search for the ninth-century *longphort*: early Viking-age Norse fortifications and the origins of urbanizations in Ireland. In S. Duffy (ed.), *Medieval Dublin VIII*, 9–20. Dublin. Four Courts Press.

Gowen, M. with G. Scally 1996 *A summary report on excavations at Exchange Street Upper/Parliament Street*, Dublin. Temple Bar Archaeological Report 4. Dublin. Wordwell.

Griffiths, D. 2010 *Vikings on the Irish Sea*. Stroud. Tempus.

Halpin, A. 2005 Development phases in Hiberno-Norse Dublin: a tale of two cities. In S. Duffy (ed.), *Medieval Dublin VI*, 94–113. Dublin. Four Courts Press.

Harrison, Stephen 2007 Woodstown 6, Supplementary Research Project, July 2007, Chapter 1 Academic Review, 3–95. Archaeological Consultancy Services Ltd.

–2010 Bride Street revisited – Viking burial in Dublin and beyond. In S. Duffy (ed.), *Medieval Dublin X*, 126–52. Dublin. Four Courts Press.

Hayden, A. 2000 West side story: archaeological excavations at Cornmarket and Bridge Street Upper, Dublin – a summary account. In S. Duffy (ed.), *Medieval Dublin I*, 84–125. Dublin. Four Courts Press.

Kelly, E. and Maas, J. 1995 Vikings on the Barrow, *Archaeology Ireland* 9, no. 3, 30–32.

Kelly, E. and O'Donovan, E. 1998 A Viking *longphort* near Athlunkard, Co. Clare, *Archaeology Ireland*, 12, no. 4, 13–16.

Murray, H. 1983 *Viking and early medieval buildings in Dublin*, British Archaeological Reports Series, 119. Oxford.

O'Brien, E. 1998 A reconsideration of the location and context of Viking burials at Kilmainham/Islandbridge, Dublin. In C. Manning (ed.), *Dublin beyond the Pale: studies in honour of Paddy Healy*, 35–44. Bray. Wordwell.

O'Brien, R. and Russell, I. 2005 The Hiberno-Scandinavian site of Woodstown 6, Co. Waterford. In J. O'Sullivan and M. Stanley (eds), *Recent archaeological discoveries on the National Road scheme 2004. Archaeology and National Roads Authority Series 2*. 111–29. Dublin.

O'Donovan E. 2008 The Irish, the Vikings, and the English: new archaeological evidence from excavations at Golden Lane, Dublin. In S. Duffy (ed.), *Medieval Dublin VIII*, 36–130. Dublin. Four Courts Press.

Ó Floinn, R. 1998 The archaeology of early Viking Age in Ireland. In H. Clarke, M. Ní Mhaonaigh and R. Ó Floinn (eds), *Ireland and Scandinavia in the early Viking Age*, 132–65. Dublin. Four Courts Press.

Sheehan, J. and Ó Corráin, D. (eds) 2010 *The Viking Age: Ireland and the west*. Dublin. Four Courts Press.

Sheehan, J. 2008 The *longphort* in Viking-Age Ireland, *Acta Archaelogica*, 79, 282–95.

Simpson L. 1999 *Director's findings: Temple Bar West*, Temple Bar Archaeological Report. 5. Dublin. Wordwell.

– 2000 Forty years a-digging: a preliminary synthesis of archaeological investigations in medieval Dublin. In S. Duffy (ed.), *Medieval Dublin I*, 11–68. Dublin. Four Courts Press.

– 2005 Viking warrior burials in Dublin: is this the *longphort*? In S. Duffy (ed.), *Medieval Dublin VI*, 11–62. Dublin. Four Courts Press.

– 2010 Pre-Viking and Early Viking-age Dublin: research questions. In S. Duffy (ed.), *Medieval Dublin X*, 49–92. Dublin. Four Courts Press.

– 2010a The first phase of Viking activity in Ireland: archaeological evidence from Dublin. In J. Sheehan and Ó Corráin, D. (eds), *The Viking Age: Ireland and the West*, 418–29. Dublin. Four Courts Press.

– 2011 Fifty years a-digging: a synthesis of medieval archaeological investigations in Dublin city and suburbs. In S. Duffy (ed.), *Medieval Dublin XI*, 9–112. Dublin. Four Courts Press.

Wallace, P. 1990 The origins of Dublin. In H.B. Clarke (ed.), *Medieval Dublin: the making of a metropolis*, 70–97. Dublin. Irish Academic Press.

– 2008 Archaeological evidence for the different expressions of Scandinavian settlement in Ireland: 840–1100. In Stephan Brink and Neil Price (eds), *The Viking world*, 434–438. Abington.

Walsh, C. 2001 Dublin's southern defences, ten to the fourteenth century: the evidence from Ross Road. In S. Duffy (ed.), *Medieval Dublin II*, 88–127. Dublin. Four Courts Press.

– 2009 An early medieval Roadway at Chancery Lane; from Duibhlinn to Áth Cliath? In S. Duffy (ed.), *Medieval Dublin IX*, 9–37. Dublin. Four Courts Press.

The excavation of an early roadway and Hiberno–Norse houses at the Coombe

CLAIRE WALSH

INTRODUCTION

Full archaeological excavation of the large site at 118–23, The Coombe, Dublin 8 was undertaken in 2008 and January 2009. The proposed redevelopment of the site entailed a full basement. The new development was to be stepped in from the present eighteenth- and nineteenth-century building line along the Coombe, which street had been widened in the late eighteenth century. This meant that for much of the medieval period, and into the post-medieval period, the full groundplan of the buildings on the site was not uncovered.

This article consists primarily of a catalogue of the pre-Anglo-Norman houses and earlier levels excavated on the site. The first buildings on the site overlay a roadway and accompanying ditch. At the time of writing (April 2012) the development continues to be stalled, and there has been no funding for post-excavation work. Recognizing the importance of the site, dating of two samples by C14 was provided through the kind offices of Dublin City Council via the City Archaeologist, Dr Ruth Johnson.

ARCHAEOLOGICAL AND HISTORICAL BACKGROUND

The site is located to the south-west of the Hiberno-Norse and medieval walled town of Dublin, on the south-sloping bank of the Coombe stream (fig. 3.1). This minor watercourse, a tributary of the river Poddle, rises in Drimnagh. It crosses to the north of the site, to meet the diverted Poddle east of the site, at a junction known as Cross Poddle. Cross Poddle also seems to lie at an intersection of three of the five 'great roads of early Ireland' (Simpson 1997, 18). A section of roadway, which may possibly be part of one of them, *Slige Dála*, was uncovered on the site.

Ó Lochlainn (1940, 465) states that roads are mentioned in the law tracts of early medieval Ireland, 'to enumerate the advantage and worth of roads and the penalties for their neglect' and he defines a *slige* as a highway (possibly originally a way cut through woodlands). The line of the Commons water or Coombe stream has been identified as the route of the Slige Dála meic Umóir (or Belach Mór Maige Dála). This route is said to have marked one of the

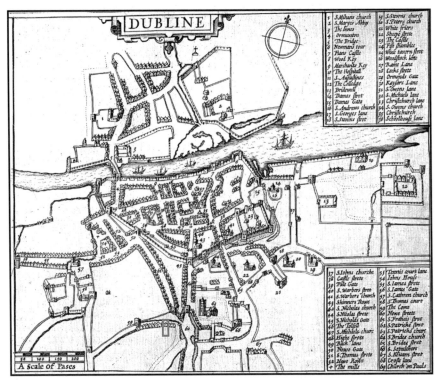

3.1 Site location on Speed's 1610 map of Dublin

boundaries of north Munster, and to have run from west Munster to Tara.
Ó Lochlainn states that part of it ran from Dublin via Drimnagh to
Clondalkin, and from there to Kildare, and thence south to Limerick. The
junction of the Slige Dála with the Slige Cualann is considered by Clarke
(2002) to extend northwards up Francis Street, thereby skirting the enclosed
medieval town to the west.

At 4m in width, the section of roadway described below is probably the
widest roadway yet uncovered in the vicinity of the medieval town. The eighth-/
ninth-century roadway excavated by the writer at Chancery Lane, in contrast,
had a maximum width of 2.35m (Walsh 2009, 15). Doran (2004) notes that
Irish medieval routes, unlike Roman roads, were not essentially physical
entities, thin strips of land with physical boundaries; rather they were rights of
way, sometimes with legal and traditional status. The Coombe stream, and
probably the Slige Dála, later formed the boundary between the Liberty of St
Sepulchre (lands held by the archbishop of Dublin) and the Liberty of Donore
(under the control of the abbey of St Thomas). There are few previously
recorded finds of pre-Anglo-Norman date from this part of the city, south-

3.2 Site location on
Rocque's 1756 map of
Dublin

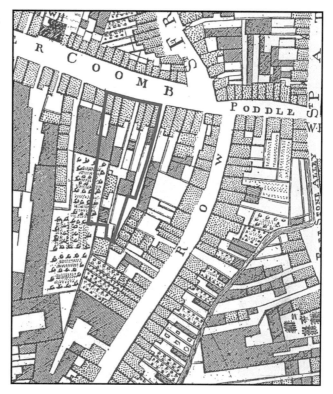

west of the pre-Anglo-Norman foundation of St Patrick's *in Insula* (later, St Patrick's cathedral). An iron sword of Viking type (NMI Wk. 26) from Cork Street is included in the list of stray finds in the files of the National Museum of Ireland (Bradley and King n.d., 157), while the excavations at the south end of Patrick St in 1990 recovered three bracteates, coins or tokens of early to mid-twelfth-century date, from lower levels of river silts of the Poddle river (Walsh 1997, 77).

PHASE I ROADWAY

The natural topography of the site slopes quite steeply from the southern part of the site towards the north, with a marked break in slope, reflecting the contour created by the Coombe stream. The site also sloped less discernably from west to east, towards the original Poddle valley that lay along New Street, east of the site. Due to the sloping ground, and the successive buildings of post-medieval date (figs 3.2, 3.3 and 3.4), coupled with probable tillage in the medieval period, no deposits that could be dated to the pre-Anglo-Norman era were identified on the southern side of the site.

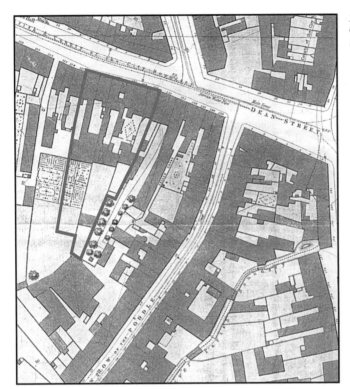

3.3 Site location on 1847 Ordnance Survey map

The earliest feature on the site was a metalled roadway, F154, which extended east–west across the entire width of the site, a distance of some 30m (figs 3.4, 3.5). The road measured a maximum of 4m in width; this appears to be its original width, as only a part of the original southern edge of the structure was intact. The roadway was level, and composed of both rounded and subangular fist-sized stones and smaller pebbles, which were bedded directly onto subsoil. The road was flanked on its southern edge by a shallow gully, which showed as a linear darker silt staining in the pale yellow-brown subsoil. This gully was visible for a length of 4,000mm along the original surviving line of the road, and measured 500mm in width.

The surface of the roadway was remarkably intact, although in one area stones had slipped onto the edge of a flanking ditch, F132, on the northern side of the road. This ditch extended east–west across the entire width of the site. It had a maximum width of 4,000mm (as did the road), and a depth of appproximately 600mm. The sides of the ditch sloped gently to a flat base. A constriction in the width of the ditch was apparent towards the eastern end, where later deposits of brushwood and stones had been deposited into the ditch, forming a crossing-point.

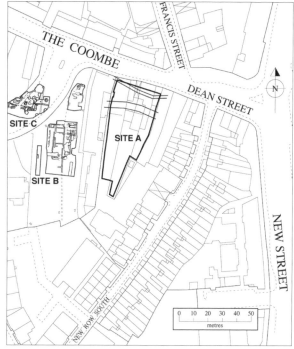

3.4 Site (A) on modern streetscape, showing roadway and ditch of Phase I, also nearby excavations at St Brigid's School (02E1780, B and C), Coombe Relief Road Site 1 (Hayden, this vol., below)

For part of its length, the northern side of the road and the southern edge of the ditch were bounded by a post-and-wattle fence, F125. This was quite strongly built and, apart from kerbing the stones and preventing slippage into the ditch, may have prevented livestock from eroding the sites of the ditch. The post-and-wattle fence did not continue along the line of the road at the crossing-point.

Primary ditch fills and crossing-point
The primary fill of the ditch was a gritty black silt, F133/207, which was naturally deposited by what appears to have been fairly low-level stagnant water. There were no finds in this deposit, which was composed of micro-lenses of fine gravel, interspersed with lenses of sod-like silt. Towards the eastern end of the site, bundles of brushwood had been cast into the ditch over an area almost 8m in width. While sections of the brushwood, F204, were evidently interwoven, and had originated as panels or screens, much of the material consisted of stacks of cut branches. Bundles of leaves, still identifiable as hazel, were also present, indicating that the material forming the crossing-point was removed from scrub growing along the bank of the Coombe stream, which lay to the north of the road and ditch.

The crossing-point over the ditch was bolstered by the addition of large flattish stones, F158, which were set in grey marly clay. This formed a

3.5 Roadway and ditch of Phase 1, ditch 115 of Phase 2, property boundaries on Rocque's
1756 map superimposed

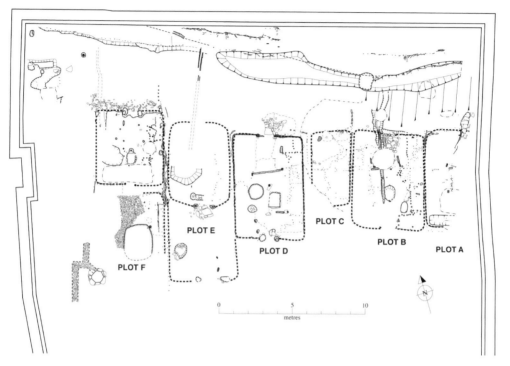

3.6 Plots, level 1

reasonable causeway across the ditch, with most of the stones having been tipped in from the south, the road side. A clean pale brown silt, F149, interpreted as sod, accumulated over the stones in the ditch; this was continuous with a layer of sod which overlay the metalling of the road. No finds were recovered from this level of activity on the site.

PHASE 2

The roadway and associated ditch of Phase 1 became obsolete, and six adjacent plots were created on the site (figs 3.6, 3.7). The archaeological evidence indicates that the road and associated ditch were moved further north towards the edge of the Coombe stream. The watercourse may have been channelled, contained, or otherwise embanked to facilitate the roadway; however, the evidence from excavations further west on the Coombe indicates that this occurred only in the thirteenth century (McQuade 2005). Phase 2, however, appears to pre-date by some significant period the water diversions carried out by the monks of St Thomas's abbey, established in 1177, and the construction of mills at Kevin Street and at Patrick Street (Simpson 1997). The suggested

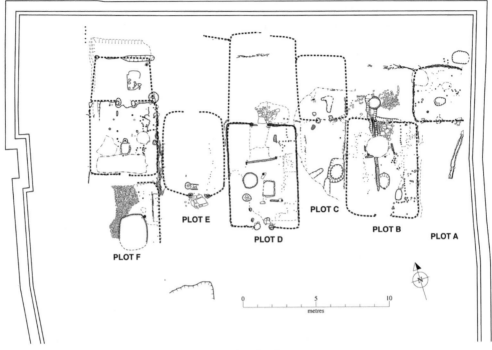

3.7 Plots, level 2

dating for the creation of the plots and the construction of the houses here is some time shortly after the late eleventh to early twelfth century.

Ditch F132 was deliberately infilled with stiff marly clays. The variation in the nature of the fills across the site from plot to plot would suggest that the infilling was carried out on a plot-by-plot basis by the builders of the houses. At the west end of the site, the main infilling of the ditch was stiff grey clay, overlain by mottled yellow/brown redeposited boulder clay. The mid-section of the ditch was infilled by a 600mm-thick deposit of grey/brown clay silt, while the infill over the easternmost plot was largely of compacted coarse gravel bedded in yellow/brown boulder clay, F203. No finds or other dating material was recovered from the ditch infill.

There appears to have been little or no interval between the infilling of ditch F132 and the construction of buildings on top of it. The choice of materials for the ditch fill was clearly dictated by what was available to hand, and boulder clay was the main choice. This suggests that a concerted effort to colonize this area for building meant the Coombe stream was contained, possibly channelled and deepened and some evidence of this was recovered from the northern part of the site. Additionally, the gap between the (northern) front door of the buildings and the new water channel, F117, formed the new line of the roadway. This road, formed of yellow/brown coarse gravel with an upper surface of compacted metalling (F113), had a width of 4,000mm from the door of the structure in Plot G to the edge of the waterchannel. The width of the roadway appears to have narrowed to approximately 3,000mm towards the eastern end of the site (Plot A); it is difficult to be certain, however, as sections of the early ground level were removed by later activity.

The river channel
The southern side of a channel, F117, which may be a flanking ditch to the repositioned roadway, F113, extended into the northern side of the site for a maximum width of approximately 3m. The footprint of the new development lies 3m south of the eighteenth-century streetfront, and the present culvert for the stream is beneath the street. As time progressed, the wide shallow route of the watercourse was contained and narrowed as settlement encroached on this area. Such a pattern was evident from Melanie Mc Quade's excavation further west along the Coombe (03E207) and from other excavations at rivers and streams around the medieval city (Walsh 1997).

The earliest channel, F117, clearly cut the earliest road level, F113, at the west end of the site in Plot F. The side of the channel sloped steeply with a depth of 700mm at the eastern end of the site (fig. 3.7) and was lined with a post-and-wattle fence, F115. At the western end the fence stood to less than 250mm in height, and was poorly preserved, but the more organic deposits at the east end of the site ensured that the fence here stood to a height of almost 500mm. The river channel had been later infilled with compacted yellow/brown clay and gravel, presumably as the water channel had been pushed out further to the north.

Plot divisions
Seven medieval plots, labelled A to G, were identified at the earliest level of Phase 2.[1] The dating of the construction of the first house on the site is based on the absence of pottery from the early levels, coupled with the information from C14 dating of two samples (see below). This is consistent across the entire site, and suggests that this phase dates to the late eleventh or early twelfth century. As is characteristic in Hiberno-Norse and Anglo-Norman Dublin, the plots were long and narrow, and accessed from the roadway on the north. The houses formed the width of the plots with a doorway at opposing ends, and tended to be placed towards the roadway. One structure in Plot F had a cobbled pathway leading from the rear door southwards, and a cess pit in a convenient location, probably associated with the later use of the structure. No other plots had evidence for pits and general yard levels.

The plots, however, were not of consistent width. From east to west, at the earliest level widths are as follows:

---

1 I tend towards the use of 'plot', although I interchange it with 'property', trusting this is found acceptable (Wallace 2000, 262).

A: greater than 3,000mm, plot not fully available for excavation.

B: full width 4,800mm.

C: smaller plot, 2,500mm in width, later moved. It may be significant that the crossing over the early ditch of Phase 1 was located here-and this existing, possibly older, boundary may have been intended as a laneway through the new plots. A laneway, however, did not continue in the same location, and the small plot was colonized.

D: full width 5,000mm, slight gap between properties to either side.

E: full width 4,200mm.

F: full width 4,500mm.

G: full width averages 5,000mm.

Characteristics of the earliest houses

The similarity in the size, materials, and internal layout of the houses at the earliest level indicates that they shared the same builders. As in the majority of the Fishamble Street structures of Types 1–3, which date to the tenth and mid-eleventh centuries, they tend towards single post-and-wattle walls (Wallace 1992, 31). The Coombe houses have remarkably squared corners, and are smaller: most of the Fishamble Street Type 1 houses were well over 30m2 in floor area. However, the houses of the later period are noted as being smaller than the tenth-century structures.[2]

The structural uprights were of two types, either whole timbers in the round, as in the matching jambs of structures F112 and F136, or tapered trapezoidal jambs as employed in structure F182 and F193. This enabled the ends of the post-and-wattle wall better to be tied into the jambs. The front and rear door jambs were neatly paired along the structure, with the internal roof supports tending to be sited in a classic four-post pattern, as at Fishamble Street. Two of the structures, D1 and and B2, had timbers placed horizontally between the internal uprights, as frequently found at Fishamble Street and elsewhere in Dublin.

Internally, there was a tendancy to single benches, compartments or other internal fittings, located on the east side of the structure; one structure had a corner compartment which had been floored with boards (structure 136). They all had hearths placed central to the short axis, but in each case located towards the rear door. There was variety in the form of the hearth, from the classic fully stone-kerbed hearth (F104) of structure F112, to the round clay pad in a pit of structure F182. In contrast, rectangular stone-kerbed hearths were the norm in the Fishamble Street structures, and these 'were usually located at the centre of the house, midway between the end walls' (Wallace 1992, 40). Only one structure, a smaller ancillary type structure, F196, appears to have burnt down.

All of the houses had successive flooring of thick clean quarried clay silt or marl, which was banked up inside the post-and-wattle walls. The thick clay silt

2 Murray 1983, Hayden 2002.

3.8 Road and ditch of Phase 1, view south

would have helped to prevent the upward seepage of groundwater within the houses, although water was always going to present a problem in this location. Several of the structures had drains, one of post-and-wattle, two of timber, and one of the earlier structures had a stone-lined and capped drain. One structure, B1, had a paved area within the front doorway.

Post-and-wattle wall construction was well preserved towards the eastern end of the site. The lower end of wall 192 had three rods used in a bunch, in a zone on the wall where strength was not an imperative. This resulted in a marked 'wailing' of the ends of the rods. This was noticeable also in the base of the exterior of the wall of structure 136. An outer wall to bolster only the corners appears to have been used in several of the structures.

There was a remarkable absence of artefacts from the floors and deposits between them, with no evidence for industrial or specific craft function within any of the structures.

CATALOGUE OF STRUCTURES

Plot A, level 1, structure 193 (fig. 3.9)
This was the first structure on this plot, and is probably contemporary with structure 182, Plot B (fig. 3.10).

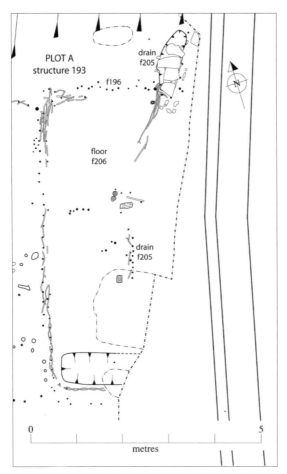

3.9 Plot A, level 1, structure 193

PLOT A
structure 193

drain
f205

f196

floor
f206

drain
f205

0   5

metres

Plan: rectangular, width incomplete, excess 3000mm, full length 6,500mm.

Wall: single post-and-wattle, rounded corners.

Doorway: part only of northern threshold survives.

Internal layout: two posts, located 1,500mm from west wall and 2,250mm from north wall, indicate roof supports at the north-west of the building. Both are posts in the round, measuring 200mm in diameter. Part of a decayed plank lies on the primary floor surface next to the posts. The south-west roof support is a squared timber.

An internal division on the west side of the structure is indicated by a row of post-holes which leads south and west of the roof support.

Primary flooring was of thick grey quarried clay marl F206, up to 500mm thick in parts, and contained within the post-and-wattle wall of the structure.

A wattle lined channel F205 led northwards through the doorway, and was filled with organic silt. This continued into a stone-lined and stone capped drain outside the structure, which extended beyond the area of excavation.

3.10 Plot B, level 1, structure 182

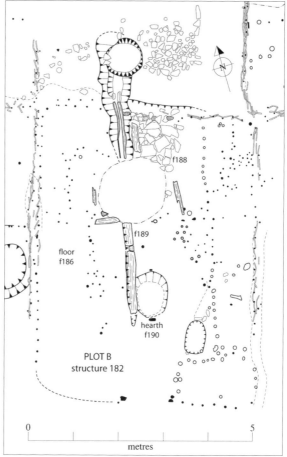

Plot A, level 2, structure 196 (fig. 3.7)
When structure 193 went out of use, a smaller hut, F196, was constructed to the north of the earlier structure. Structure 182 in the neighbouring plot to the west, B, however, appears to have continued in use during the lifespan of the smaller hut 196 in Plot A. Structure 196 is the only structure which appears to have burnt down.

Structure 196 was constructed on the original roadway which extended east–west to the north of the first structures on the Coombe. The north wall of each of the first structures maintained more or less the same alignment, and the road surface was located across the site from Plots A to F. Over time, however, the plots extended northwards, indicating that the Coombe stream was contained in a deeper channel, and flooding probably alleviated to some extent.

The north wall of structure 196 was built on the silts F200 which filled the edge of the river channel.

Plan: probably approximating to square, full extent not recovered. Full length: 3,500mm north–south, width in excess of 3,600mm.

Walls: single post-and-wattle/rods, tops charred on the south side. Standing to a height of 400mm, highest at the north wall, due to the slope here. The rods of the west wall had prominent 'wailing', with the ends protruding markedly on the inside of the wall, all in the one direction. The base of the north wall had groups of three rods used as a single unit, to construct with speed. The entrance appears to have been on the south side, with none evident on the north wall, but the structure extended beyond the excavated area. A single charred jamb remained *in situ*, while a pit along the line of the wall probably indicates where the other jamb was located.

Internal layout: random scatters of post-holes were present across the floor. A single squared post remains on the west wall; however, as this was set on the clay flooring, it does not appear to have been load bearing.

Floors: a thick deposit of quarried, sterile yellow grey clay and silt, F197, was placed within the walls of the structure. This was up to 350mm at minimum in depth. This was overlain by a smooth greasy silt and ash, and an ovoid hearth placed opposite the door. The occupation floors of the hut were compacted laminated ash and clay, F192, with twiglets and hazelnut shells present. A pit was dug into the floor.

To the north of the hut, a stone filled pit F195 appears to have functioned as a sump for the structure.

A stone-lined drain, F197, extended north-eastwards, probably beneath the south wall of the hut; much of this feature lay outside the area of excavation. This was overlain by a thick deposit of grey/brown clay silts F202, which signalled the buildup of occupation deposits outside structure F196.

Plot B, level 1, structure F182 (figs 3.6, 3.10)
The first structure on this plot was a large post-and-wattle house, F182. The full groundplan of this structure was recovered.

Length: 6,400mm north–south, width 4,800mm.

Walls: single post-and-wattle.

Doors: opposing entrances, centrally placed on each short axis. Width of doorway: 850mm. Jambs: trapezoidal, narrow ends tapered to take rods of walls, no grooves. Alder. 200mm by 120mm. Threshold beam at northern doorway measured 1000mm by 100mm, 60mm thick-decayed. Southern jambs mostly rotted. The northern jamb, F182A, was dated by C14 in QUB (see below).

Internal uprights: plan appears as a small Type 1 house. Two uprights remain on the north side of the house, located 2,300mm from north wall, and 1,500m from side walls. A pit at the south-east quadrant of the house defines the former location of the upright here.

3.11 Plot B, structure 182, view south

Internal layout: wall benches and compartments are indicated along the eastern side of the structure by lines of stake-holes. The primary floor was of thick quarried yellow clay/silt, F186, of irregular depth, which contained many pebbles. The flooring formed a reasonably level surface, and was contained by the walls of the structure, and had contributed to the decay of the post-and-wattle walls.

The hearth F190 was set in a shallow pit in the floor, centrally placed but towards the southern end of the structure, as in all the other structures. This was up to 300mm in depth, and measured 1,000mm by 700mm. The base was an oxidized pad of clay, suggestive of a brazier. A small quantity of hazelnut shells was present in the hearth detritus.

Inside the north doorway, a regular rectangular area of flat limestone paving, F188, was placed over the primary flooring. This was bounded by laid timber planks.

A timber-planked drain, F189, extended from the west side of the hearth, set into the primary clay floor, and exited on the west side of the doorway. The drain, formed of thin oak planks set on edge, deepened to the north, and led to a small round deep sump located outside the structure.

The primary flooring was overlain by a grey organic silt, F185, which had in part retained its original structure of a brown peat-like twiggy deposit. The

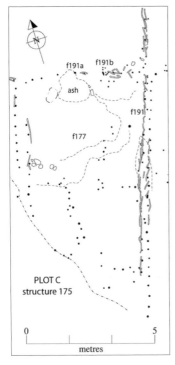

f191a f191b

ash

f191

f177

PLOT C
structure 175

0   5

metres

3.12 Plot C, level 1, structure 175

western side of the structure had been refloored with a thin, beaten clay silt, F184. The clay floor was overlain by thin ash spreads and inorganic gritty silt. The hearth was relaid at this level.

Clearance over the structure, including the removal of fragmentary upper flooring and silt layers, was numbered F181.

The upper levels of the structure, at abandonment, were cut through by an irregular linear gully type feature, F183, which had a fairly regular western edge. It was filled with inorganic gritty silt, stones, and contained pottery. It deepened to the south, and may have functioned as a drain for a later structure.

There was evidence for a pathway to the north of this structure. A compact layer of stone metalling, F199, was laid down north of the threshold of structure F182. The metalling partly overlay sloping subsoil, but it extended over the river silts F200 to the north of the site. It was flanked by the drain and sump F189 to the west. The metalling was overlain by a deposit of yellow/brown stoney clay, F198, which also functioned as a pathway external to the structure.

Plot C, level 1 (fig. 3.12)
At the earliest house level, this was a narrow plot only *c.*2,500mm in width, which was squeezed into the space between two plots of more standard width. This narrow plot overlay the layers of brushwood and wattle, later overlain by clays and stone, that suggested a crossing-point over the ditch of Phase 1. There was, however, no evidence that Plot C continued in use as a route or passage to the rear of the plots. A shallow pit, F194a, was dug into the fills of the underlying ditch of Phase 1. This measured 1,500mm north–south by 1,200mm east–west and was 300mm in depth. No finds were recovered from the pit. A thick layer of grey/brown sod, F194, was deposited over the plot, contrasting with the quarried clay floors of the structures to either side. A nail was recovered from the deposit. A spread of ash in the sod levels may indicate the former presence of a hut here. The plot boundary walls, F191, were constructed on this level. This wall was best preserved on the east side of the plot, and extended north of the wall line of the adjacent structures. However, a short length of post-and-wattle walling extended west from this line, and two

3.13 Plot D, level 1, structure 136

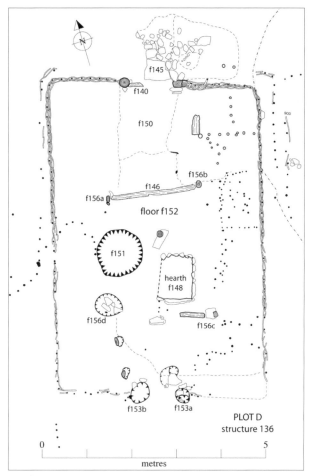

post-holes along the line of this wall suggest a threshold or entrance. The posts F191a and 191b were spaced 900mm apart from their centre points, which is the standard entrance width for this group of structures. A rectangular setting of post-holes suggested a wall bench on the east side of the enclosed area. The wall lines enclosed a flooring of thick grey sticky clay marl, F177. An oxidized area, suggestive of a hearth, was present on this surface. However, this overlay the line of the east–west walling and door-jambs. The flooring was overlain by a truncated and scrappy series of clay floors interspersed with gritty sod and silt, with frequent stones, F176. The putative structure of Plot C was overlain by structure 182, Plot B.

Plot D, level 1, structure 136 (fig. 3.13)
The first structure on this plot was a large post-and-wattle house, F136. The full groundplan of this structure was recovered.

3.14 Plot D, structure 136, view south

Length: 6,800mm north–south, width 4,600mm.

Walls: single post-and-wattle, well preserved at the northern end.

Doors: opposing entrances, centrally placed on each short axis. Width of doorway: 1,000mm. Jambs: northern (F140) both posts (alder) in the round. A threshold beam at the northern doorway was decayed, and measured 850mm in length and 150mm thick. The southern jambs were mostly rotted, but were securely indicated by round post-holes F153a and F153b.

Structural uprights: plan appears as a Type 1 house. Two uprights, F156a and F156b, remained on the north side of the house, located 2,300mm from the north wall, and 1,200mm from the side walls. A roughly-worked timber beam, F146, lay between the posts. This was up to 300mm thick, and was very decayed but had bark adhering. Differential flooring was laid to either side of the beam. The southern pair of roof supports were indicated by post-pads F156c and F156d. F156c was a single flat stone pad, with part of the base of the rotted upright *in situ*, and was placed at the end of a decayed sill-beam. The opposing post would have been placed in a shallow setting with flat stones at the base (F156d).

The walls had only slightly rounded corners. The western wall exhibited 'wailing' at the base, with long rods which bypassed every second post and looped around the base of alternate posts. Whole rods with bark were used, and the posts were evenly spaced at 200mm. The weave was a simple in-out weave, and where the rods met the jambs, the ends had rotted. There was no evidence for a groove on the jamb.

Internal layout: wall benches and/or compartments are indicated along the eastern side of the structure by lines of stake-holes.

Floors: A primary occupation horizon within the building is indicated by a deposit of charred twigs, F155, and a thin sod layer at the northern end of the building. A small unlined hearth was indicated by scorched sod and ash, located in the south part of the building beneath the later hearth. The primary floor was a thick quarried yellow/grey clay/silt, F152, of irregular depth, which contained many pebbles. The flooring formed a reasonably level surface, and was contained by the walls of the structure, contributing to their decay. A partially stone-lined rectangular hearth, F148, was laid on floor F152. This was filled with ash and charred hazelnuts. A pit, F151, located close by the hearth, was cut through the flooring. The pit measured 980mm in diameter, and was up to 700mm in depth, with overhanging sides. The fill was of sod, clay, ash and charcoal, with the bulk of the pit-fill composed of charred whole hazelnuts. The pit was probably dug to store the hazelnuts, which can be processed to increase their storage life by roasting. Hazelnuts are eaten whole or ground to produce a flour.

A rectangular compartment in the north-east corner of the house was delineated by post-holes, with evidence for decayed plank flooring or a partition.

Deposits of soft sod and organic material, interspersed with layers of charred hazelnuts, F150, were present inside the north doorway, but did not extend to the 'aisles' to either side. Additional flooring of fine gravel, F147, was laid down in the central sector of the northern part of the house.

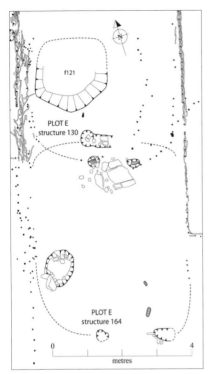

3.15 Plot E, levels 1, 2, structures 130, 164

A pathway and yard surface, F145, outside the north door of the building, was composed of large stone slabs, cobbles and gravel. This was overlain by deposits of ash, and sealed by a thick grey silt/clay soil, F141.

Plot E, levels 1 and 2 (figs 3.6, 3.15)
While the full width of this plot was recovered, there was considerable damage to the early deposits from post-medieval activity.

A probable earlier structure, F164, lay further south than the buildings of Plots A to D. This potential structure measured 4.3m in width, with a length of 5.5m, with a doorway at both ends. The doorway at the south end was centrally placed, while the possible north doorway had a stone-packed west post-hole, and stone-packed sill. A possible post-hole for an internal upright remained on the south-west side, while two posts of an aisle, along the line of the eastern jamb, were present. No flooring levels of this structure remained.

The overlying building, F130, measured 4,200mm in width, and possibly 5,500mm in length. Both jambs (ash) of the south doorway were *in situ*, and spaced 1,000mm apart. There was an external area of paving outside the door. Stake-holes along the eastern wall and post-and-wattle, F129, of the western wall line indicate a single post-and-wattle construction, with curved corners. The line of a probable aisle division was apparent on the eastern side of the structure.

No flooring levels of this structure remained. A timber-lined drain extended north-eastwards from this structure towards the northern water channel. The truncated structure was overlain by a thick deposit of uniform grey clay silt, F131.

Plot G, level 1 (figs 3.6, 3.7, 3.16)
A poorly preserved structure, F165, appears to have been the first structure on this plot. Only part of the east wall and internal compartments remained.

Structure F112 on Plot G, to the north of the earliest building, predates structure F130 on adjacent Plot F, and is probably contemporary with the earlier structure, F164, on that plot. Organic preservation of this building varied from north to south, and from east to west. The building measured 4,500mm in width by 4,800mm in length. The walls were of single post-and-wattle. Two opposing doorways were set in the short axes; post-holes (F112)

3.16 Plot F, levels 1, 2, structures 165, 112

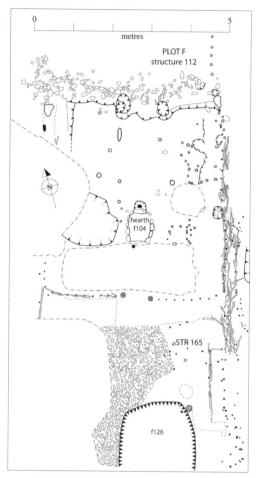

defined the limit of the primary clay floor (F109) at the north end, while the timber jambs of the southern doorway, only 600mm apart, survived. Later disturbance of the interior had cut away the floor level where internal posts may have been located. The primary floor of the structure, F122, was of thick quarried clay, with an unlined hearth set directly on the clay. A very thin lens of silt indicated an occupation layer, which was sealed by the secondary floor, F104, of thick yellow/brown quarried clay. An aisle or wall bed is indicated by a line of stake-holes on the eastern side only of the building. A sub-rectangular stone-kerbed hearth was set off centre on this clay; posts at either end of the hearth would have supported a cooking apparatus. Small fragments of burnt bone were recovered from the hearth and the thin ash and silt which overlay the floor; otherwise there were no finds.

A pathway out the back of the building led to a cess pit, F126. Primary usage of this pit is probably contemporary with this building.

Plot G, level 2 (fig. 3.7)

The building was modified, and an annex, F109, probably constructed from posts and groundbeams, was placed to the north of structure F112. The annex measured 4,000mm in width, and 2,800mm in length. It was defined by a post-hole at the north-east corner of structure F112, and a post-pad at either corner of that structure. A poorly defined earth-cut slot, F117, which contained a burnt plank, bounded the west side of floor F109, and continued northwards to the stream. Floor F109, a thick layer of yellow/brown clay, which formed the primary floor of the structure, was bounded on the northern side by an irregularly-shaped slot, probably the remains of a beam slot.

To the north of this structure, a coarse gravel formed a compacted metalled surface, F110, which sloped northwards to fill in the watercourse.

The later levels on this plot date to the early Anglo-Norman period.

Plot H

While several posts and post-holes were excavated at the earliest level in this plot, there was no apparent structure. Later levels, however, had distinct stone and sill-beam structures.

C14 DATING

Sample from fence on Phase 1 roadway

A sample of the rods (hazel) from F125, the fence along the north side of the roadway of Phase 1, was submitted for C14 dating to Queen's University, Belfast. The sample was dated twice. The first date received for F125, UBA-18679 F125 hazel twigs 831 28–32.3 0.9017 0.0031 was calibrated as follows:

68.3 (1 sigma) cal AD	1186–1201	0.214
	1205–1252	0.786
95.4 (2 sigma) cal AD	1163–1262	1.000

14C Date: 831±28 BP
AMS 13C: –32.3

This date was queried with the C14 lab, as it was apparent from the excavation that the deposits were pre-Anglo-Norman. The sample was re-run and yielded the following data (on which the lab commented that 'The result of the re-measurement on sample UBA18679 yielded a slightly older radiocarbon age that doesn't significantly disagree with our first determination but does shift the age range slightly'):

F125 UBA–18679
Radiocarbon Age BP 898 +/–23

68.3 (1 sigma) cal AD	1048–1086	0.484
	1123–1138	0.157
	1150–1181	0.358
95.4 (2 sigma) cal AD	1043–1105	0.441
	1118–1211	0.559

The C14 dating indicates a date range in the latter part of the eleventh century for the construction of the fence along the side of the road. There appears to have been little or no intervening period between the deliberate infilling of ditch F132 and the construction of buildings on top of it. This is also indicated by the closeness of the C14 dates from both levels.

Sample from door-jamb of structure F182 (Plot B, level 1)
One of the northern jambs, F182A, was dated by C14, and yielded a range of dates indicating a construction date from the late eleventh to the early twelfth century:

F182a
UBA–18680
Radiocarbon Age BP 858 +/–26
Calibration data set: intcal09.14c # Reimer et al. 2009
% area enclosed cal AD age ranges relative area under probability distribution

68.3 (1 sigma) cal AD	1166–1215	1.000
95.4 (2 sigma) cal AD	1053–1079	0.063
	1129–1131	0.001
	1153–1255	0.935

Comments:
* This standard deviation (error) includes a lab error multiplier.
** 1 sigma = square root of (sample std. dev.^2 + curve std. dev.^2)
** 2 sigma = 2 x square root of (sample std. dev.^2 + curve std. dev.^2)
where ^2 = quantity squared.
[ ] = calibrated range impinges on end of calibration data set
0* represents a 'negative' age BP
1955* or 1960* denote influence of nuclear testing C–14
Note: Cal ages and ranges are rounded to the nearest year which may be too precise in many instances. Users are advised to round results to the nearest 10 years for samples with standard deviation in the radiocarbon age greater than 50 years.

SIGNIFICANCE OF THE DATING

Preliminary evidence from the excavation indicated that the roadway of Phase 1 and the construction of the first buildings was pre-Anglo-Norman in date. However, the dating of the roadway was unclear, due to the lack of artefacts. The C14 results indicate a date in the second half of the eleventh century for the continued use of the roadway. Pottery, mainly Dublin coarsewares, was present in very small quantities in the occupation horizons of the second or third level of houses built on the site. This did not, however, indicate the earliest date for the two underlying levels. The C14 results, combined with the absence of pottery from the primary levels, suggest a date from the latter part of the eleventh century through to the first part of the twelfth century for the layout of plots and construction of the first houses at the site.

This archaeological evidence for the expansion of the late Hiberno–Norse town so far south of its original boundaries at this date, and of the formation of a suburb in this location, is of immense significance. The methodical infilling of an earlier ditch, relocation of the road further north, and laying out of plots tending to a width of 5m (the town standard) indicate the efficient action of a municipal authority. The colonization of a marginal and reclaimed block of land, close by a river, coupled with the dearth of material goods from the occupation levels, indicates that the residents were low down the social scale. The clear house plans, conforming to Hiberno–Norse Dublin Type 1 plan, suggests that the builders and occupants of the houses were in all likelihood Dubliners.

ACKNOWLEDGMENTS

The excavation team of Brian Hayden, Alan Hayden, Bella Walsh, Fergus Grant Stevenson, Augusto Vonga, Niall Colfer, and Conor McHale endured some foul weather during site work. The site and finished plans are the superb work of Conor McHale, without whom this site report would be complete chaos. Thanks to Melanie McQuade for generously supplying me with a copy of her excavation report at 103–108, The Coombe, Dublin 8; Dr Ruth Johnson and Dublin City Council for the Carbon 14 dates; and Professor Seán Duffy for his forbearance.

Finally, I would like to dedicate this paper to the memory of Dáire O'Rourke.

BIBLIOGRAPHY

Bradley, J. and King, H. n.d *Urban Archaeology Survey*, pt VIII, Dublin City. Unpublished report commissioned by the Office of Public Works. Dublin.

Doran, L. 2004 Medieval communication routes through Longford and Roscommon and their associated settlements. *Proceedings of the Royal Irish Academy* 104C, 57–80.

Hayden, A. 2002 The excavation of pre-Norman defences and houses at Werburgh Street, Dublin: a summary, In S. Duffy (ed.), *Medieval Dublin III*, 44–68. Dublin. Four Courts Press.

McQuade, M. 2005 The Coombe, 103–108. Unpublished report submitted to National Monuments Service. Dublin.

Murray, H. 1983 *Viking and early medieval buildings in Dublin*. British Archaeologial Reports, British Series 119. Oxford.

Ó Lochlainn, C. 1940 Roadways in ancient Ireland. In J. Ryan (ed.), *Féil-sgríbhinn Eóin Mhic Néill: essays and studies presented to Professor Eoin Mac Neill on the occasion of his seventieth birthday*, 465–74. Dublin. At the Sign of the Three Candles. Reprinted by Four Courts Press, Dublin, 1995.

Reimer P.J. et al. 2009 Intcal09 and Marine09 radiocarbon age calibration curves, 0–50,000 years cal BP. *Radiocarbon*, 51, 1111–50.

Simpson, L. 1997 Historical background to the Patrick Street excavations. In C. Walsh, *Archaeological excavations at Patrick, Nicholas and Winetavern Streets, Dublin*, 17–33. Tralee. Brandon.

Wallace, P.F. 1992 *The Viking Age buildings of Dublin*. Medieval Dublin Excavations 1962–81, Ser. A, vol. 1. Dublin Royal Irish Academy.

Wallace, P.F. 2000 *Garrda and airbeada*: the plot thickens in Viking Dublin. In A.P. Smyth (ed.), *Seanchas: studies in early and medieval Irish archaeology, history and literature in honour of Francis J. Byrne*, 261–74. Dublin. Four Courts Press.

Walsh, C. 1997 *Archaeological excavations at Patrick, Nicholas and Winetavern Streets, Dublin*. Tralee. Brandon.

Walsh, C. 2009 An early medieval roadway at Chancery Lane: from Duibhlinn to Áth Cliath. In S. Duffy (ed.), *Medieval Dublin IX*, 9–37. Dublin. Four Courts Press.

The topography of St Mary's Cistercian abbey and precinct, Dublin

GERALDINE STOUT

This contribution is concerned with mapping the topography of St Mary's Cistercian abbey and its precinct to the north of the city of Dublin using cartographic, historic and archaeological sources. It aims to fill the knowledge gap between the excellent 2009 paper by Bill Doran and Linda Doran, which deals mainly with the upstanding remains at Meetinghouse Lane,[1] and Fr Colmcille Ó Conbhuí's paper on the lands of St Mary's abbey published in 1962.[2] This paper provides a broader understanding of the physical legacy of this medieval abbey in the Dublin streetscape and of St Mary's contribution to the economic development of Dublin, north of the Liffey.

INTRODUCTION

An outstanding Discovery Programme monograph, *The Dublin region in the Middle Ages,* highlights how Dublin differed from other parts of Ireland in the quantity of land held by the church and religious orders and the remarkable speed of re-distribution and pace of colonization of land during the Anglo-Norman period.[3] In the north of the city and county St Mary's Cistercian abbey was the leading advocate of this. St Mary's abbey was founded initially as a daughter house of the Benedictine Order of Savigny in France in 1139.[4] The order of Savigny was united with the Cistercians in 1147 and St Mary's abbey, Dublin, was made subject initially to Combermere (Cheshire) and then in 1156 a charter granted Abbot Ranulf of Buildwas (Shropshire) the care of the abbey.[5] It functioned as an abbey for over 500 years and became the richest Cistercian house in Ireland with much of its estate in Dublin city and county. At its greatest extent, its lands amounted to over 12,000 hectares, with lands in Kildare, Louth, Meath and Westmeath, extending west into Galway,

1 Bill Doran and Linda Doran, 'St Mary's Cistercian abbey, Dublin: a ghost in the alleyways' in John Bradley, Alan Fletcher and Anngret Simms (eds), *Dublin in the medieval world: studies in honour of Howard B. Clarke* (Dublin, 2009), pp 188–201. 2 C. Ó Conbhuí, 'The lands of St Mary's abbey, Dublin', *Proceedings of the Royal Irish Academy*, 62C (1962), 21–86. 3 Margaret Murphy and Michael Potterton, *The Dublin region in the Middle Ages: settlement, land-use and economy* (Dublin, 2010), pp 76–84. 4 Aubrey Gwynn, 'The origins of St Mary's abbey, Dublin', *Journal of the Royal Society of Antiquaries of Ireland*, 79 (1949), 110–25. 5 Aubrey Gwynn and R.N. Hadcock, *Medieval religious houses: Ireland* (London,

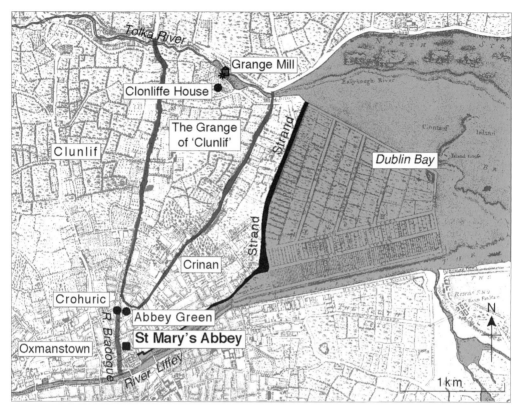

4.1 Location map of the twelfth-century grant of lands at Clunlif to St Mary's abbey,
showing the grange of Clunlif

Roscommon and Mayo and south into west Cork.[6] The nerve centre of this
vast estate was the abbey premises on the north bank of the Liffey.

This paper begins its 'journey' along the banks of the river Tolka in north
County Dublin and ends it at Meetinghouse Lane. It follows the boundaries of
the original grant of lands to the abbey at 'Clunlif', boundaries that follow the
major access routes in and out of the city. The paper goes on to explore the
natural resources that had surrounded the medieval abbey and were developed
by St Mary's. It traces the line of the abbey's precinct walls and gates; the
layout of its monastic buildings and landscaped grounds within the present
streetscape. Finally, with the aid of historical documentation and archaeological
evidence, this paper examines the cloister and conventual buildings as they
survive in the modern city.

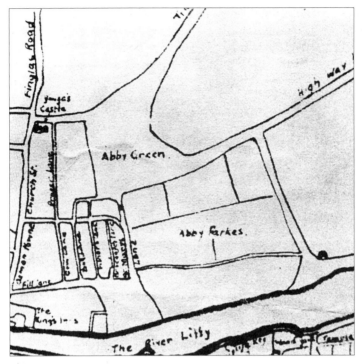

4.2 Detail of
de Gomme's
map of Dublin
(1673), showing
St Mary's
abbey and
environs

CLUNLIF

The twelfth-century abbey was located in an area known as 'Clunlif '(*Cluain
Life*, 'the meadow/pasture-land of Liffey') which is echoed in the place-name
Clonliffe Road today. The initial lands granted to the abbey amounted to an
estimated 324 to 364 hectares, and extended from the river Liffey to the river
Tolka.[7] This was a virtual island of land, defined by the sea to the east and the
river Bradogue to the west (fig. 4.1). A charter of Strongbow, dated *c*.1171–2,
confirmed a former grant to the abbey of land called 'Clonlif' which lay
between the sea and the river Tolka.[8] 'Clonlif' is mentioned in an inventory of
the abbey lands issued at around the same time by William Fitz Audelin in
King Henry II's name.[9] In 1174 another charter to St Mary's confirmed it as
part of all its possessions.[10] It is mentioned again in the famous charter of
liberties granted to the citizens of Dublin by Lord John in 1192 as one of the
boundaries of the municipal lands on the north side of the Liffey.[11]

7 Ibid., 27–32.   8 J.T. Gilbert (ed.), *Chartularies of St Mary's abbey with the register of its
church of Dunbrody and annals of Ireland*, 2 vols (London, 1884), i, p. 78.   9 Ó Conbhuí,
'The lands of St Mary's abbey', 22, 28.   10 Gilbert (ed.), *Chartularies of St Mary's abbey*, i,
p. 81.   11 Ibid., p. 267.

Disputes arose between the citizens of Dublin and the monks regarding ownership of these lands and the abbey agreed to pay rents in 1213.[12] Fortunately, these documented disputes provide place-name information from which the boundaries of their initial grant of land can be reconstructed. These lands lay outside the liberties of Dublin and included all the land between Oxmanstown and the Tolka, south to the Liffey and east to include the area called the 'Crinan' or 'Crinach' (plain by the sea) which lay along the seashore and was bordered by the mere of Clonliffe and the present-day North Strand (fig. 4.1). One of the western boundaries mentioned is 'Crohuric', where a 'gallows formerly stood'. This was located at the eastern end of North King Street, where an archaeological assessment in 1998 revealed *in situ* articulated and dis-articulated skeletons across the site.[13]

Part of this initial grant of land became a monastic farm or grange run by the lay brothers of St Mary's abbey. It was the birthplace of an abbot of St Mary's abbey, Stephen Lawless, who was in the abbey from 1429 to 1437. The boundary to this monastic grange followed the course of the river Bradoge from the abbey green running along what is today Bolton Street, Dorset Street, Drumcondra Hill in the north and Parnell Street, Summerhill and Ballybough in the south. This is a triangular block of land that has maintained its integrity to the present day and is defined by two main routes that reflect the mearing or boundary of the grange (fig. 4.1). It is well illustrated in de Gomme's map of 1673 (fig. 4.2).[14] The centre of the grange was located near the mill described in the Down Survey as the 'Grange mill'. The Civil Survey 1654–6 mentions this mill at St Mary's abbey lands and the grange of Clonliffe.[15] The 6-inch Ordnance Survey (OS) map from 1843 shows a corn mill, mill pond and mill-race on the bank of the Tolka to the east of Clonliffe College which was on this former site. A printing works occupies this location today and there is no visible trace of the mill.[16]

ABBEY GREEN

A grant of land in the vicinity of St Mary's abbey from the citizens of Dublin in 1213 contains a stipulation that a green space opposite the outer gate of the abbey should remain a common pasturage.[17] The monks were to maintain this

12 J.T. Gilbert (ed.), *Calendar of ancient records of Dublin, in the possession of the Municipal Corporation of that city*, 19 vols (Dublin, 1889–1944), i, p. 170.   13 Dermot Nelis, '189–194 King Street North, Dublin' in Isabel Bennett (ed.), *Excavations 2000: summary accounts of archaeological excavations in Ireland* (Bray, 2002), pp 88–9, 98E0088, DU018–020986–. 14 Bernard de Gomme, *The city and suburbs of Dublin from Kilmainham to Ring's End* (1673, National Maritime Museum, Greenwich, Dartmouth Collection (P49/11), reproduced by Dublin: Phoenix Maps, 1988).   15 R.C. Simington (ed.), *Civil survey 1654–1656, vol. 7: County of Dublin*, Irish Manuscripts Commission (Dublin, 1945), pp 180–1.   16 DU018– 030——.   17 Gilbert (ed.), *Calendar of ancient records of Dublin*, i, p. 248, xxxii.

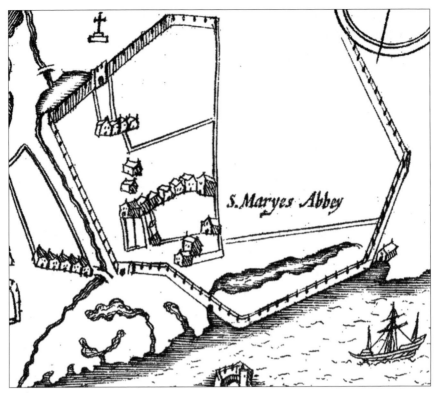

4.3 Detail of Speed's map of Dublin (1610) showing St Mary's abbey and environs.

green as a common pasture and demarcate it with crosses.[18] From the twelfth century, crosses were used to demarcate pasture; early markers may have been in timber and replaced by stone.[19] This green is mentioned again in a description of the Dublin city boundaries in 1326–7.[20] On Speed's map of 1610 there is a traditional cross on the roadway opposite the outer gate of the abbey which may be a lone survivor of the crosses which delimited the green (fig. 4.3).[21] The abbey green was located on the north side of the abbey. The *Calendar of ancient records of Dublin* records a complaint in 1603 against unfree persons pasturing their cattle on the city's commons; it was ordered that no unfree persons should pasture on Abbey Green.[22] The green survived the Dissolution because it is mentioned as late as 1639 in a renewal of a grant from Charles I.[23] It is clearly marked on de Gomme's map of 1673 (fig. 4.2).

The abbey green of St Mary's abbey originally extended to incorporate the area where Green Street now lies and the original name of the Street, 'Abbey

18 Ibid., p. 170.   19 D.H. Williams, *The Cistercians in the early Middle Ages: written to commemorate the nine hundredth anniversary of foundation of the order at Cîteaux in 1098* (Leominster, 1998).   20 Gilbert (ed.), *Calendar of ancient records of Dublin*, i, p. 158. 21 J.H. Andrews, 'The oldest map of Dublin', *Proceedings of the Royal Irish Academy*, 83C (1983), 205–37.   22 T.K. Moylan, 'The Little Green, part 1', *Dublin Historical Record*, 8, pt 3 (1946), 81–91.   23 Gilbert (ed.), *Chartularies of St Mary's abbey*, i, p. lxiii.

4.4a Detail of Rocque's map (1756) showing the   4.4b Location map of the Abbey Green
        Little Green

Green', recorded in 1568, reflects this.[24] The original extent of the green would appear to correspond with the area bounded by the modern North King Street, Halston Street, Little Britain Street, Capel Street, Parnell Street and Ryder's Row (fig. 4.4b). However, by 1756 the eastern half of the green had been built upon, reducing the area bounded by the modern King Street, Halston Street, Little Britain Street and Green Street to an area known as Little Green on Rocque's map of 1756 (fig. 4.4a).[25] It incorporates the area formerly known as the Little Green from 1727.[26] Archaeological testing at the junction of Green Street and North King Street produced evidence for medieval activity.[27]

NATURAL SETTING AND RESOURCES

The abbey was located close to the high-water shoreline of the Liffey and east of the marshy mouth of the river Bradogue (fig. 4.5).[28] The winding of Strand Street Little testifies to this former shoreline location. The river Liffey had a different physical geography durinigfhgg the medieval period than it has today. It was much wider, with many smaller streams and rivers running into it. De

24 Moylan, 'The Little Green', 83.   25 John Rocque, *Exact survey of the city and suburbs of Dublin* (Dublin, 1756).   26 Moylan, 'The Little Green, part 1'.   27 Frank Ryan, 'North King Street' in Isabel Bennett (ed.), *Excavations 1993: summary accounts of archaeological excavations in Ireland* (Bray, 1994), p. 24, 93E0104.   28 H.B. Clarke, *Medieval Dublin* (Dublin: Friends of Medieval Dublin, 1978).

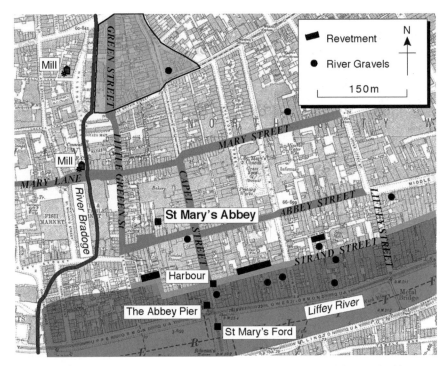

4.5 Natural setting, resources and street names in the environs of St Mary's abbey

Courcy has argued that the river between the Four Courts and the sea was originally twice its present width.[29] West of the Bradogue river was a bluff and this caused the river to deviate its course resulting in the creation of a bay beside the site of St Mary's abbey which could be used by them as a berthing post.

The location of the Liffey shoreline prior to seventeenth-century reclamation has been determined from the location of loose gravelly deposits which indicate the former presence of flowing water. It was an indented shoreline with the river flowing as far north as Abbey Street Upper and Jervis Street (fig. 4.5). Riverine deposits were revealed under seventeenth-century reclamation in 1996 at 22–23 Ormond Quay,[30] at 15 Ormond Quay in 1997,[31] and at 14 Ormond Quay/11–13 Strand Street Great in 2003.[32] Excavations at

29 J.W. de Courcy, *The Liffey in Dublin* (Dublin: Gill and Macmillan, 1996).   **30** Margaret Gowen, '22–23 Ormonde Quay, Dublin' in Isabel Bennett (ed.), *Excavations 1996: summary accounts of archaeological excavations in Ireland* (Bray, 1997), p. 30, 96E0272.   **31** Hilary Opie, '15 Ormond Quay Lower, Dublin' in Isabel Bennett (ed.), *Excavations 1997: summary accounts of archaeological excavations in Ireland* (Bray, 1998), p. 50, 97E265.   **32** Christie Baker, Teresa Bolger and Abi Cyderhall, '14 Ormond Quay/11–14 Strand Street, Dublin' in Isabel Bennett (ed.), *Excavations 2003: summary accounts of archaeological excavations in*

this last site also uncovered medieval tiles, several sherds of medieval pottery, including Dublin fine ware. It is possible that the occurrence of tiles in this riverine location was due to the removal of material for land reclamation after the demolition of St Mary's abbey in the seventeenth and eighteenth centuries. Excavations at 25–28 Great Strand Street revealed river gravels at a level of 3.30m below ground level.[33] Excavations at 43–45 Middle Abbey Street revealed gravel deposits at a level of 0.66OD.[34] Excavations at 43–44 Mary Street revealed gravels in 2000 at 2.00m below ground level.[35] River gravels were also identified during monitoring at 3–4 Capel Street.[36] This revealed natural subsoil which indicated that it lay on dry land that was subject to intermittent alluvial flooding. The site was on a narrow spur of dry land within the medieval intertidal zone along the Liffey's north edge, an alluvial deposit sandwiched between the natural subsoil and reclamation deposits. Testing at 62–63 Capel Street revealed river gravels at 2.15m below ground level.[37] Excavations at 22–24 Strand Street Great showed that there was an alluvial strand on the Liffey foreshore to the east of St Mary's abbey.[38]

The 'Pill' was an area of muddy creeks around the mouth of the river Bradogue just south-west of the abbey. De Courcy describes the Pill as 'the fretted estuary of the Bradogue river', a tidal marsh dissected by a network of creeks and channels.[39] It was waste land quite probably overflowed by high tides, and used as a berthing ground where vessels could lie at low tide upon the mud of the creeks. The whole area along the shore in this area would appear to have been river meadow. Excavations at 150–152a Capel Steet/24–28 Mary's abbey in 2003 revealed a layer of sticky grey black silt thought to be natural river deposits associated with this terrain.[40]

A fresh water supply was critical to the success of the abbey. The Cistercians were adept at channelling water into their abbeys and developing rivers for mills and fish weirs. There was probably a channel running off the river

Ireland (Bray, 2006), p. 147, 03E0964.   **33** Claire Walsh, '25–28 Strand Street Great, Dublin' in Isabel Bennett (ed.), *Excavations 2003: summary accounts of archaeological excavations in Ireland* (Bray, 2006), pp 155–6, 03E0357.   **34** Helen Kehoe, '43–45 Abbey Street, Dublin' in Isabel Bennett (ed.), *Excavations 1999: summary accounts of archaeological excavations in Ireland* (Bray, 2000), p. 59, 99E0177.   **35** Helen Kehoe, '43–44 Mary St, Dublin' in Isabel Bennett (ed.), *Excavations 2000: summary accounts of archaeological excavations in Ireland* (Bray, 2002), p. 90, 00E0083.   **36** Ruth Elliot and Judith Carroll, '3–4 Capel St Dublin' in Isabel Bennett (ed.), *Excavations 2001: summary accounts of archaeological excavations in Ireland* (Bray, 2003), pp 96–7, 01E0335.   **37** Franc Myles, '62–63 Capel Street, Dublin' in Isabel Bennett (ed.), *Excavations 2002: summary accounts of archaeological excavations in Ireland* (Bray, 2004), pp 143–4, 02E1419.   **38** Helen Kehoe, '22–24 Strand Street Great' in Isabel Bennett (ed.), *Excavations 2001: summary accounts of archaeological excavations in Ireland* (Bray, 2003), p. 113, 01E1120.   **39** De Courcy, *The Liffey in Dublin*, p. 303; J.W. de Courcy, 'The bluffs, bays and pools in the medieval Liffey at Dublin', *Irish Geography*, 33:2 (2000), 117–33.   **40** Helen Kehoe, '24–28 Mary's abbey/150–152 Capel Street, Dublin' in Isabel Bennett (ed.), *Excavations 2003: summary accounts of archaeological excavations in Ireland* (Bray, 2006), p. 141, 03E0496.

Bradogue into the south range of the abbey. The earliest depiction of the river Bradogue and the abbey is on Speed's map (fig. 4.3). It lay outside the walled precinct on the western side and there appears to have been a large mill-pond, just outside the north-west corner of the precinct wall. A large river inlet extended into the southern precinct and this might have been some sort of harbour. Speed also depicts a possible boathouse or warehouse just outside the eastern boundary wall, on a small inlet on the Liffey frontage. De Gomme's map shows Bradogue Lane east of Fishers Lane and west of the southern extension of St Mary's Lane or Arran Street East (fig. 4.2).

A Wide Streets Commission Plan by Thomas Sherard from 1795 shows a narrow channel named the river Bradogue at the rear of the properties on Boot Lane or Arran Street East and south of Mary's Lane and on an alignment with the junction of Halston Street and Mary's Lane.[41] The Bradogue flowed above ground through the site of the present-day fruit and vegetable market and the site of St Michan's church where it was 'turned, covered and arched'.[42] It ran through the Little Green, i.e., the west side of Abbey Green because in 1681 a Mr Hartstonge made an application to draw the Bradoge and the other waters in other parts of the green into one channel.[43] Halston Street is also referred to as Bradoge Street.[44] There is no visible sign of the river Bradoge today but its former presence is indicated in the curvature of Halston Street. The river Bradogue was made into a sewer below Halston Street in 1741 (fig. 4.5).

A number of stone-built millraces and watercourses have been discovered in the area of the river Bradogue including that at Balls Lane and Halston Street (fig. 4.5), which may relate to the modification of the Bradogue river.[45] Excavations revealed the demolished remains of two limestone-block-faced masonry walls of a millrace surviving just two to three courses high, 12m in length running north/south. Its base was supported with flat slabs. The millrace may have run into a sluice in the south. It had a stone-revetted bank on the east side and a ditch which was thought to relate to a man-made diversion of the river Bradoge. Another millrace running into the river Bradoge was revealed in 1992.[46] This was a 3m-wide channel running north-east to south-west with medieval finds at the base containing thirteenth- and fourteenth-century pottery (fig. 4.5).

A further inlet of the river Liffey, which ran along the line of modern Strand Street, is shown by Speed within the abbey's precinct wall (fig. 4.3). A timber revetment dating to the thirteenth century was identified in 2002 on a site to the east of Jervis Street and south of Burns Lane. This is at the eastern

41 WSC 220/1, cited in Niall McCullough, *Dublin – An urban history: the plan of the city* (Dublin, 1989).   42 Moylan, 'The Little Green, part 1', 86.   43 Ibid., 84.   44 Ibid., 86.   45 Margaret Gowen, 'Archaeological assessment of a development site at Halston Street, Ball's Lane, Dublin 7, 94E160' (unpublished report, 1994), DU018–020566. 46 Unpublished file, 92E0195, DU018–119——.

limit of the inlet and may indicate its shoreline. The revetment is thought to relate to quay and harbour activities associated with St Mary's abbey.[47] Speed's map shows an islet outside the western precinct of the abbey at the confluence of the river Liffey. The western boundary wall is relatively intact with the river Bradogue visible outside the wall, orientated north/south and feeding into the river Liffey.

In medieval times the abbey lay on an important fording point that connected the northern settlements of the city of Dublin with its more developed southern settlements (fig. 4.5). This ford was south of St Mary's abbey and stretched to the east bank of the river Poddle across the Liffey. In the fourteenth/fifteenth centuries the ford was improved from Dame's Gate on the south to St Mary's abbey on the north.[48] This ford went out of use in the fifteenth century after it was outlawed in 1455 by decree of the great council of Ireland.[49] The ford was of particular concern because it was used by raiding parties attacking the Fingal region north of the Liffey. To prevent this, the parliament at Dublin, during the abbotship of John White, ordered the erection of a wall and tower at St Mary's to control the passage of the ford and directed the amount of the expense to be levied on land in the vicinity. The abbot of St Mary's was to oversee this defence project.[50] A *c*.2m-high wall with a tower was erected around the abbey to ensure the ford was no longer used. Nevertheless, it was still functioning in 1534 when the Dublin Civic Chronicle states that Thomas Fitzgerald rode through the city with a strong company and went through Dame's Gate and over the ford onto St Mary's abbey.[51]

The abbey acquired its own harbour and quay on the Liffey by the thirteenth century as well as a less constricted harbour at Bullock in south County Dublin.[52] From these locations, the abbey traded with England and France using its own own fleet of ships.[53] St Mary's also possessed extensive fishing and shipwreck rights along the Liffey and Dublin Bay.[54] Their Liffey harbour lay in a pool at the east side of the 'Pill beyond the Water', possibly protected within the river wall shown by Speed.[55] The abbey pier was situated on the north side of the modern Grattan Bridge. A reference in 1455 mentions that the pier was to be repaired.[56]

47 Claire Walsh, 'Archaeological excavation of the Anglo-Norman waterfront at Strand Street Great, Dublin' in Seán Duffy (ed.), *Medieval Dublin V* (Dublin, 2005), pp 160–87.   **48** H.B. Clarke (ed.), *Medieval Dublin: the making of a metropolis* (Dublin, 1990).   **49** H.F. Berry (ed.), *Statute rolls of the parliament of Ireland: reign of King Henry the Sixth* (Dublin, 1910), 1455, p. 403.   **50** Philomena Connolly (ed.), *Statute rolls of the Irish parliament, Richard III–Henry VIII* (Dublin, 2002), Henry VI, 1455, p. 403.   **51** A.J. Fletcher, 'The earliest extant recension of the Dublin Chronicle' in Bradley, Fletcher and Simms (eds), *Dublin in the medieval world*, pp 390–405, at p. 405.   **52** Niall Brady, 'Dublin's maritime setting and the archaeology of its medieval harbours' in Bradley, Fletcher and Simms (eds), *Dublin in the medieval world*, pp 295–315, at p. 314.   **53** Gilbert (ed.), *Chartularies of St Mary's abbey*, ii, p. 35.   **54** Roger Stalley, *The Cistercian monasteries of Ireland* (New Haven, 1987), p. 45.   **55** De Courcy, 'The bluffs, bays and pools in the medieval Liffey'.   **56** Connolly (ed.), *Statute rolls of the Irish*

Timber revetments associated with this harbour and quayside were
uncovered at 52–56 Strand Street Great in 2002 (fig. 4.5).[57] They revealed a
timber structure *c.*30m long from a substantial waterfront revetment. It was
made from oak with blackthorn and ash. It had baseplates with plank
shuttering. This undoubtedly related to an inlet and may have represented
attempts to form a harbour, an attempt which failed because the structure was
inundated with river gravels soon after its construction. It represents the
southern side of a waterside structure, as it appears to be front-braced. This
timber revetment at the eastern margin of the precinct of St Mary's abbey may
have been a short-lived effort to form a small harbour in this long inlet in the
late twelfth–early thirteenth century.

The monks had fishing rights along the river which were granted to them
by John (then lord of Ireland) during his visit to Ireland in 1185. The rights
granted the monks the entitlement of 'having a boat on the water on the river
Liffey to fish with equal privileges to his own boat'.[58] This grant was
confirmed by John as king in 1200.[59] It also had a salmon fishery on the Liffey
in the parish of St James on Thomas Street.[60] The right of the abbey to have a
boat was contested by citizens in 1243, but the outcome favoured the abbey.
Late-medieval documents detail their practice of placing stakes and nets in the
north bank of the river to catch fish at present day Arran Quay.[61]

THE ABBEY PRECINCT

Today, the upstanding remnants of St Mary's abbey are appropriately located
north of the street known as St Mary's abbey and immediately east of
Meetinghouse Lane (fig. 4.6). The memory of its existence is preserved in the
local street names; to the north lies Little Mary Street and Mary Street, to the
east Abbey Street; to the west Mary's Lane. Arran Street East has been
included because de Gomme's map (fig. 4.2) shows that this was a southern
extension of St Mary' Lane. The former Abbey Green is preserved in Green

parliament, p. 403. **57** Walsh, 'Archaeological excavation of the Anglo-Norman
waterfront', pp 160–87, 00E0240, 2002 extension, DU018–115———. **58** Gilbert (ed.),
Chartularies of St Mary's abbey, i, p. 85; H.S. Sweetman (ed.), *Calendar of documents relating
to Ireland, 1171–1251*, vol. 1 (London, 1875), no. 903, p. 135; A.E.J. Went, 'Fisheries of the
river Liffey: notes on the Corporation fishery up to the dissolution of the monasteries',
Journal of the Royal Society of Antiquaries of Ireland, 83 (1953), 163–73, at 165. **59** Gilbert
(ed.), *Chartularies of St Mary's abbey*, i, p. 89. **60** N.B. White (ed.), *Extents of Irish
monastic possessions, 1540–1541: from manuscripts in the Public Record Office, London*, Irish
Manuscripts Commission (Dublin, 1943), p. 6. **61** Gilbert (ed.), *Chartularies of St Mary's
abbey*, ii, p. 35; Gilbert (ed.), *Calendar of ancient records of Dublin*, i, p. 175; Alan Hayden,
'Excavations of the medieval river frontage at Arran Quay, Dublin' in Seán Duffy (ed.),
Medieval Dublin V (Dublin, 2004), pp 149–242; Alan Hayden and Claire Walsh,
'Archaeological excavations at 9–14 Arran Quay, Dublin, E557' (unpublished report, 1990).

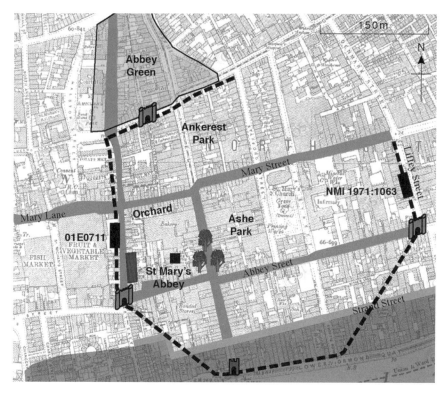

4.6 Location map of St Mary's abbey precinct, gates, gardens, orchard, parks and enclosures

Street. The abbey buildings lay close to the high-water mark of the river Liffey and its shoreline setting is suggested by Strand Street Little and Strand Street Great. These street names alone indicate a much greater footprint for the abbey than remains upstanding in Meetinghouse Lane.

Precinct walls
St Mary's abbey had a large precinct wall which has unfortunately vanished. But by combining cartographic, historic and archaeological evidence it is possible to reconstruct its layout on the ground today (fig. 4.6). Speed's map shows the upstanding remains, complete with crenellations, of the precinct wall (fig. 4.3). The northern banks of the Liffey are unchanneled and unwalled except for a small stretch where the abbey's walls follow the river edge. It was surrounded by a walled enclosure which partly followed the shoreline of the inlet known as the Pill where, as we have seen above, the monks had their own quay and harbour on the Liffey. Speed's map of this enclosure shows the surrounding polygonal precinct of the abbey building to be missing along the north-eastern side.

There were at least three phases of precinct-wall building around the abbey. The first precinct wall around St Mary's abbey was begun after 1216 when St Mary's abbey sought permission from Henry, archbishop of Dublin, to construct a wall at St Mary's abbey.[62] This was certainly constructed by 1247 when there was an agreement reached between St Mary's and Galfridus Sellarius (Geoffrey [the] Saddler) of Stratford relative to lands outside the walls.[63] In 1263 maintenance of the wall was mentioned.[64] A second phase of precinct-wall building began when the south quays were fortified in 1317. This was in reaction to the Bruce invasion which threatened the capital when the Scottish army was encamped at Castleknock. The mayor of Dublin, in fear of the city being taken, gave the order to demolish various buildings within the walls on the north side of the river to provide stone to repair and build up the city wall.[65] St Mary's abbey was also attacked by the citizens of Dublin in the same year and a tower attached to the abbey was demolished, the stones used to extend and fortify the town walls along the south quays. This secondary wall would have enclosed the inlet that runs into the southern precinct on Speed's map (fig. 4.3). The third phase of precinct-wall building involved the construction of a tower in 1455 by the boundary wall at the ford by the pier of St Mary's because this was one of the places where predators were accustomed to pass at night.[66] In 1539–40 the boundary wall and outer gates are mentioned in the monastic extents relating to the Dissolution.[67]

Historical and cartographic evidence points to at least four gates along the precinct wall, an east gate, the gate to the cemetery, the outer northern gate (with granary) and the south gate. The last two are shown on Speed's map (fig. 4.3). In 1597 the outer gate is mentioned again.[68] Lawful entrance to a monastic precinct was by means of a gateway penetrating the precinct wall. The outer north gate at St Mary's was in a typical position for Cistercian monasteries. Most gatehouses had a chamber over the entrance archway such as that at Mellifont abbey in County Louth. Where an abbey was adjacent to a large river and had its own boats for trade, another major entrance to the precinct became essential, and hence the need for the south gate. In a lease of the abbey lands to Walter Peppard in 1543 the gate near the river is mentioned.[69] In 1263 reference is made to an eastern gate.[70] This may have been located in the section of wall that had been removed by 1610 or at the junction of Abbey Street Upper and Liffey Street. Walter Peppard's lease in

---

62 Gilbert (ed.), *Chartularies of St Mary's abbey*, i, pp xxxvi, 152, 180. **63** Ibid., p. 450.
64 Gilbert (ed.), *Calendar of ancient records of Dublin*, i, p. 518. **65** Gilbert (ed.),
Chartularies of St Mary's abbey, ii, p. 44, Gilbert (ed.), *Calendar of ancient records of Dublin*,
i, p. 405. **66** Connolly (ed.), *Statute rolls of the Irish parliament*, Henry VI, pp 403, 405.
67 White (ed.), *Extents of Irish monastic possessions*, p. 1. **68** James Morrin (ed.), *Calendar
of the patent and close rolls of chancery in Ireland, of the reigns of Henry VIII, Edward VI,
Mary, and Elizabeth (1576–1602)* (Dublin, 1861–3), Elizabeth, p. 412. **69** Gilbert (ed.),
Chartularies of St Mary's abbey, ii, p. xli. **70** Gilbert (ed.), *Calendar of ancient records of
Dublin*, i, pp 140, 450.

4.7 A section of precinct wall in the Pill area (after Donnelly 1886)

1543 also mentions 'the gate of the cemetery', which may have been an internal gate north of the abbey church.[71]

A section of the precinct wall is indicated on a map of a parcel of ground situated in Oxmanstown in the suburbs of the city of Dublin formerly called 'The Pill' (fig. 4.7).[72] McCullough has also extrapolated the probable limits of the abbey precinct in the modern urban landscape using a 1756 map of the Humphrey Jervis estate (fig. 4.8).[73] In 2001 excavations at the Daisy Market off Arran Street East revealed a substantial wall of possible medieval date *c.*11m in length running north/south.[74] It overlay natural gravels in some areas and was incorporated in the basement walls. Elsewhere it was cut by the later redbrick walls. This is the only physical evidence of the precinct wall we have. The wall appears to have been incorporated into the west side of Arran Street (fig. 4.6). A National Museum file recording excavations on the site of St

71 Gilbert (ed.), *Chartularies of St Mary's abbey*, ii, p. xli.   72 P.J. Donnelly, *The remains of St Mary's abbey, Dublin: their explorations and researches, A.D. 1886* (Dublin, 1887). 73 McCullough, *Dublin – an urban history*, p. 42.   74 Emmet Stafford, 'Daisy Market, Arran Street East, Dublin' in Isabel Bennett (ed.), *Excavations 2001: summary accounts of*

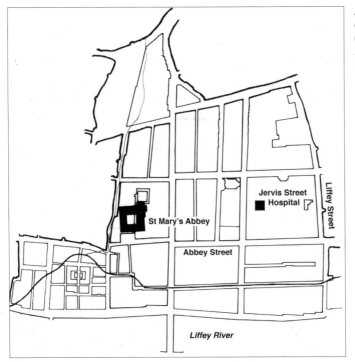

4.8 The Jervis
estate 1756
(after
McCullough
1989)

St Mary's Abbey

Jervis Street
Hospital

Liffey Street

Abbey Street

Liffey River

Mary's abbey in 1971 refers to the finding of a 'wall associated with the abbey' on the west side of Liffey Street backing onto Jervis Street hospital (fig. 4.6).[75] A further southern section of an earlier wall may have been temporarily revealed during the construction of the Luas line along Mary's Abbey Street.[76]

Within the precinct
Within the walled abbey precinct and outside the cloister and conventual buildings lay a variety of ancillary buildings, gardens, parks, orchards and woods. The former included a prison, infirmary, guesthouse, tannery, bakehouse, brewhouse and stables. It had been the ideal of the Rule of Benedict that each monastery be self-sufficient with its own watermill, bakehouse, brewhouse and gardens so that the monks would not be compelled to wander beyond its precinct walls. Speed's map (figs 4.3, 4.9) illustrates a number of these buildings within the precinct. There was a prison or gaol at St Mary's abbey. Prisons were permitted by the general chapter of 1206 and in 1229 further statutes positively encouraged their construction.[77] A feud between the monks of the grange of Portmarnock in 1277 resulted in the murder of John Comyn, lord of Kinsaley. The culprits were committed to the abbey prison.[78] On another occasion, in 1320, William Kedenor lost his sanity

archaeological excavations in Ireland (Bray, 2003), p. 95, 01E0711.   **75** NMI 1971:1063.
76 Pers. comm., Franc Myles.   **77** Stalley, *Monasteries of Ireland*, p. 174.   **78** Gilbert (ed.),

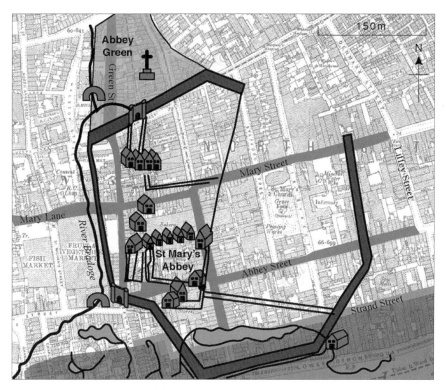

4.9 Speed's map (1610) superimposed on a street map of the area

murdered two monks. He was incarcerated for life in the abbey gaol.[79] Incarcerated monks were usually held in chains, unshaved and deprived of their habit, often surviving on a diet of bread and water.[80]

There was a guesthouse at St Mary's abbey although its precise location is unknown.[81] Hospitality and almsgiving were very important features of the Cistercian order and this may account for the presence of a granary or grain store at the outer gate of the abbey. To provide for guests, monks, lay brothers, servants, the sick and the poor at the gate, there was a brewhouse and bakehouse which produced the considerable amounts of bread and beer required. They were usually separated from the rest of the buildings because they were hazardous pursuits involving fires. These may be identified on Speed's map as those buildings south of the abbey cloister (fig. 4.3). In 1539 the convent brewhouse and bakehouse were surrendered to the crown.[82]

Within the outer court were the workshops of the tanner. In St Mary's abbey a 'tan house' is recorded as part of its possessions in 1543 in the Walter

Chartularies of St Mary's abbey, i, pp 6–7. **79** Stalley, *Monasteries of Ireland*, pp 175–6. **80** Williams, *The Cistercians in the early Middle Ages*, p. 248. **81** Gilbert (ed.), *Chartularies of St Mary's abbey*, i, pp 442, xxxvii. **82** M.C. Griffith, *Calendar of inquisitions formerly in*

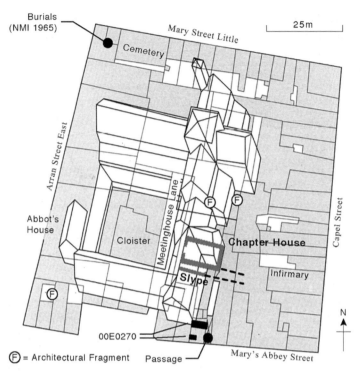

Burials (NMI 1965)

Mary Street Little

25m

Cemetery

Arran Street East

Abbot's House

Meetinghouse Lane

Cloister

(F) (F)

Chapter House

Capel Street

Infirmary

Slype

(F)

N

00E0270

(F) = Architectural Fragment   Passage

Mary's Abbey Street

4.10 Layout of cloister and conventual buildings at St Mary's abbey

Peppard lease preserved on the patent rolls.[83] This needed to be near water for the tanning pits and they probably used water from the river Bradogue and bark from the abbey's 'ashe parke' (see below). For reasons of safety, stables were also within the precincts. The stables at St Mary's abbey were next to the river side gate. In 1540 Lord Leonard Grey took a lease of the abbot's stable.[84] The patent roll of James I for 1610 contains a reference to 'the Abbott's stable, lying on the western side of the south gate, near the river Liffey, all within the precinct'.[85]

In Cistercian monasteries, the transformation of part of the cloister into a formal house for the abbot occurred all over Europe from the thirteenth century.[86] The abbot had the status of a feudal lord and lived like one. In 1540 the abbot of St Mary's had his own private houses which were soon commandeered for secular use after the Dissolution.[87] The abbot's house must have been an imposing building at St Mary's abbey as this and other buildings were leased by Lord Deputy Leonard Grey in 1540.[88] In 1541 it was described

the office of the chief remembrancer of the exchequer prepared from the Mss of the Irish record commission (Dublin, 1991), p. 78.   **83** Gilbert (ed.), *Chartularies of St Mary's abbey*, ii, p. xli.   **84** White (ed.), *Extents of Irish monastic possessions*, p. 1.   **85** Gilbert (ed.), *Chartularies of St Mary's abbey*, ii, p. lviii.   **86** Michael Thompson, *Cloister, abbot and precinct* (Stroud, 2001), p. 69.   **87** Stalley, *Monasteries of Ireland*, p. 174.   **88** White (ed.), *Extents of Irish monastic possessions*, p. 1.

as 'a mansion in the precincts called the abbot's lodging'. In 1543, in a reversion of Walter Peppard's lease, the abbot's lodging was granted to the 14th earl of Desmond.[89] By 1544 the abbot's lodgings and dormitory were considered very ruinous, and in need of repair.[90] In 1610 it is described in the patent rolls as 'A mansion or house called the Abbott's lodging, within the site of St Mary's abbey, Dublin'.[91] The stones from the 'Abbott's lodging' were later used for the construction of the wall along the strand which became Ormond Quay.[92] This mansion or abbot's lodging could be the building and garden shown to the west of the cloister on Speed's map. It is quite large and has a garden attached. There is very little room in this plot to accommodate this mansion and garden unless it was incorporated into the west range. There is a kink in the junction of Arran Street East and St Mary's abbey that corresponds to the shape of the garden.

Gardens are recorded within the precinct of Mary's abbey on the western side (fig. 4.6). A 1543 lease mentions these gardens as well as 'waste' on the west side of the monastery, and a small piece of ground called 'Shillingfoord's'.[93] The Cistercians were renowned for their skill at gardening and their meatless diet included vegetables in quantities. They lived close to the land, to their gardens, and to growing things. Their readings such as the sermons of Bernard of Clairvaux and the 'Song of Songs' are full of garden imagery and a favourite source of inspiration. For instance, in Sermon 63 Bernard compares young novices, vulnerable to temptation, to the trees of a flowering orchard when the blossoms can easily be damaged.[94] The medieval monastery was self-contained and self-sufficient; all was situated within the precinct so that the monks were not compelled to wander outside. An area within the precinct was set aside for various gardens, including a physic, herb, kitchen and ornamental gardens. Each of these had a specific location usually close to a building where these raw materials would ultimately be used.[95]

A large orchard was surrendered to the crown in 1539.[96] This lay within the abbey precinct.[97] In 1543 it is referred to as the common orchard.[98] The patent roll for 1610 has a mention of a large orchard called the 'Common Orchard' and a larger garden or orchard called 'Convent garden'.[99] The precise location of these within the precinct is unknown but they may have been near the

---

89 K.W. Nicholls (ed.), *The Irish Fiants of the Tudor sovereigns: during the reigns of Henry VIII, Edward VI, Phillip and Mary and Elizabeth I*, 4 vols (Dublin, 1994), Henry VIII, p. 386. 90 Nicholls (ed.), *The Irish Fiants of the Tudor sovereigns*, Elizabeth I, no. 6796. 91 Gilbert (ed.), *Chartularies of St Mary's abbey*, ii, p. xlviii. 92 Christine Casey, *The buildings of Ireland: Dublin: the city within the Grand Canal and Royal Canal and the Circular Road* (New Haven, 2005), p. 88. 93 Gilbert (ed.), *Chartularies of St Mary's abbey*, ii, p. xli. 94 Paul Meyvaert, 'The medieval monastic garden' in Elizabeth MacDougall (ed.), *Medieval gardens* (Washington DC, 1986), pp 25–53, see p. 49. 95 Meyvaert, 'The medieval monastic garden', pp 25–55. 96 Griffith, *Calendar of inquisitions*, Henry VIII, p. 78. 97 Ibid., Elizabeth I, p. 31. 98 Gilbert (ed.), *Chartularies of St Mary's abbey*, ii, p. xli. 99 Ibid., p. xxvii.

cemetery by the outer gate as it was customary to incorporate them into the monks' cemetery (fig. 4.6). Orchards were used to grow various types of fruits and would have been a common sight in the medieval monasteries. Most orchards were regularly laid out on a grid pattern. They were greatly valued in the Middle Ages for their blossom, and many were used as recreation grounds complete with paths, flowers and arbours. In monasteries, they were created for prayer and meditation. Apples, pears, plums, peaches, and cherries were among the fruits growing in the cemetery.[1]

In 1540 an enclosed pasture called the 'Ankerest Parke' was mentioned in the monastic extents.[2] In the following year Lord Leonard Grey took a lease of 'the anchorite park', within the precinct of 'St Mary's abbey' and an 'ashe Parke'.[3] The latter may be the garden planted with large trees east of the church that is mentioned in the 1610 patent roll of James I.[4] This refers again to the 'Anchorist's or Ankaster's Park' and locates it outside the precinct wall, north of the site of the church of St Mary's monastery, possibly in the area where the precinct wall is missing in Speed's map. Two further enclosures are mentioned in a 1552 list of features within the precinct of the abbey. These are probably the enclosed areas entitled 'Abbey Parkes' shown in de Gomme's map (fig. 4.2).

CLOISTER AND CONVENTUAL BUILDINGS

The presence today of a chapter house at Meetinghouse Lane indicates that the medieval cloister must lie to its north, south and west. The superimposition of the plan of Jerpoint abbey on the present street layout suggests that Meetinghouse Lane follows the line of the eastern cloister walk (fig. 4.10). This allows for space within the abbey precinct to the east where the infirmary was located and to the north where the cemetery lay. A lease of 1543 describes the abbey in some detail and mentions the eastern wall of the cloister.[5] The patent roll of 1610 also mentions the cloister which was described as having a ruinous tower and court in the western part.[6] Speed's map (fig. 4.3) shows a cluster of buildings arranged around an open area which must represent the cloister. This is sub-rectangular in plan, $c.75$m east/west by $c.40$m north/south. Cloisters tend to form a square in Irish Cistercian abbeys but there are at least five rectangular examples including Mellifont abbey, Co. Louth. These rectangular cloisters are a result of secondary modification. Nonetheless, it is more than likely that St Mary's abbey would have had a square cloister like that in its mother house of Buildwas, Shropshire and that it is distorted on the map. Speed's map also shows a circular turret in the south-west corner of the west range.

1 Meyvaert, 'The medieval monastic garden', pp 36, 38.   2 White (ed.), *Extents of Irish monastic possessions*, p. 1.   3 Gilbert (ed.), *Chartularies of St Mary's abbey*, ii, pp xxvii, lxxvi.
4 Ibid., ii, p. xlviii.   5 Ibid., ii, p. xli.   6 Ibid., ii, p. xlviii.

There is no definite indication of the abbey church on Speed's map even though it identifies the area as 'St Mary's abbey' (fig. 4.3). The map does identify a larger building in the north-east end of the cloister area that may be the church. Because the majority of Cistercian abbeys were built to a particular template, the abbey church is most likely to have been to the north of the chapter house. It is possible, however, to retrieve architectural detail about the abbey church from historical sources and archaeological excavation. By 1284 it had a belfry roofed with lead, a chancel, aisle, porch, vestry and dorture (dormitory) with vaults.[7] The church and belfry were roofed with lead at the expense of the archbishop of Tuam who was honourably buried in the chancel of the same church at the steps of the altar, on the left hand side.[8] In 1304 the church and monastic buildings were burnt when a fire destroyed the church and steeple of the abbey.[9] The church had a choir because when William Kedenor lost his sanity in 1320 (as noted above) he hid himself in the choir during vespers: 'He dashed into the monk's choir, flung off his clothes and stabbed two of his brothers to death, including the sacristan Thomas'. The church and buildings are mentioned in 1370.[10] By 1540 the abbey church was occupied by the Master of the King's Ordnance and 'converted into a storehouse for the king's artillery and munitions of war'.[11] A lease to Walter Peppard in 1543 provides further architectural detail in referring to the chancel and aisle of the church of the monastery.[12] The 1610 patent roll mentions a 'church porch, churchyard, dorture, vestry and cloyster, with all the vaults under the dorture, and a ruinous tower and a court in the west'.[13]

The development of this part of the city in the late seventeenth and eighteenth centuries, particularly with Georgian basements and extended cellars under the street, meant that much of the abbey remains were removed completely. In the 1880s excavations at the site of Bolands' bakery off Meetinghouse Lane were led by the famous church architect Thomas Drew, a member of the Royal Irish Academy. The results of these excavations were published in 1886, not under Drew's name, but in a volume by P.J. Donnelly.[14] The report claims that Thomas Drew had identified the south-eastern pier of the nave, the site of the cloister garth and other features pertaining to the monastic establishment.[15] A 'problematical plan' by Thomas Drew of the buildings which formed the abbey is included.[16] According to this report, 'here

7 Gilbert (ed.), *Calendar of ancient records of Dublin*, i, p. 442.   8 Walter Harris (ed. and trans.), *The works of Sir James Ware concerning Ireland revised and improved, vol. 1, containing, the history of the bishops* (Dublin, 1739), cited in Aubrey Gwynn and R.N. Hadcock, *Medieval religious houses: Ireland, with an appendix to early sites* (Dublin, 1970), p. 130.   9 Gilbert (ed.), *Chartularies of St Mary's abbey*, ii, p. 232.   10 Gilbert (ed.), *Calendar of ancient records of Dublin*, i, p. xxxiv.   11 White (ed.), *Extents of Irish monastic possessions*, p. 1.; Ailbe J. Luddy, *St Mary's abbey, Dublin* (Dublin, 1935).   12 Gilbert (ed.), *Chartularies of St Mary's abbey*, ii, p. xli.   13 Ibid., p. lvii.   14 Donnelly, *The remains of St Mary's abbey*.   15 Ibid., p. 20.   16 Ibid.

and there over a considerable space [were] masses of crumbling walls ...
varying in height from a few feet to 4 or 5 yards'.[17] Some of the original abbey
floor tiles were discovered *c*.3.50m below street level in an area where it was
conjectured that the north transept of the abbey was located. Digging where
the choir and south transept would have been, small fragments of tiles were
found and, side by side, two small vaults or graves. One of the glazed tiles
illustrated shows a church with a double aisle and steeple. Donnelly refers to a
fragment of the abbey church with doors, sills and jambs at the rear of 25 East
Arran Street.[18]

In 2000 archaeological testing by Ian Doyle at 6 St Mary's Abbey revealed
two stone walls composed of large undressed sub-rectangular blocks bonded
with medieval mortar, the north-east example running east/west and the
south-west example running north/south.[19] They appeared to extend beyond
the west and east sides of the property plot and may have formed part of the
refectory wall of the abbey. In 2003 further testing revealed a drystone
foundation running east/west, 1.10m in width. This was thought to be a
medieval wall footing. A wall standing to street height at the rear of the site also
appeared to be medieval masonry.[20] In 2002 monitoring in 3–4 Meeting House
Lane uncovered two stone architectural fragments which were similar to the
stone vault ribs in the chapter house.[21] One was a segment of an ornamental
pillar with a trefoil-shaped cross-section and the other was a vault rib.

The position today of the 'slype' (slip) south of the chapter house, which is
an original passage in the east range, suggests that the original infirmary lay to
the east of the abbey. At other abbeys such as Jerpoint in Co. Kilkenny and
Holycross, Co. Tipperary, this passage, or slip, linked the privacy of the cloister
with an open area to the east, where the infirmary was usually situated. In 1543
a patent by Henry VIII for lease to Walter Peppard confirms the location of the
infirmary beyond the east wall of the cloister.[22] In 1552 it is referred to as the
'Le Fermory' and in 1610 the grant made by James I lists among the assets of
the abbey a 'large messuage or slate house called the Fermor'.[23] Unfortunately,
it is not indicated on Speed's map of the same year. It may be a significant
coincidence that Jervis Street hospital was later located in this area.

In the 1180s Abbot Leonard of St Mary's angered local clergy by
proclaiming the spiritual advantages that would accrue if one chose to die in
the Cistercian habit and be buried in a Cistercian graveyard.[24] There are

17 Ibid., p. 19.   18 Ibid., p. 4.   19 Ian Doyle, '6 St Mary's abbey, Dublin' in Isabel Bennett
(ed.), *Excavations 2000: summary accounts of archaeological excavations in Ireland* (Dublin,
2002), p. 90, 00E0270, DU018–285——.   20 Alan Hayden, '6 St Mary's abbey, Dublin' in
Isabel Bennett (ed.), *Excavations 2003: summary accounts of archaeological excavations in
Ireland* (Bray, 2006), p. 141, 00E0270 ext, DU018–285——.   21 Elanor Larsson, '3–4
Meetinghouse Lane, Dublin' in Isabel Bennett (ed.), *Excavations 2002: summary accounts of
archaeological excavations in Ireland* (Bray, 2004), p. 151, 02E0127, DU018–020048–.
22 Gilbert (ed.), *Chartularies of St Mary's abbey*, ii, p. xli.   23 Ibid., p. lvii.   24 Aubrey

usually two areas where burials take place in a Cistercian abbey – the monastic cemetery, which normally lies to the north of the abbey church, while interments of people of high status take place in the body of the abbey church. In 1718 a corpse, apparently of a prelate in his pontificals, 'uncorrupted', was unearthed on the site while excavation was being undertaken in the ruins of the abbey.[25] He was thought to have been buried at the foot of the high altar.[26] Donnelly states that 'numerous ancient graves occurred both within and without the buildings'.[27] These were probably interments within the abbey church. The remains of a stone coffin were also found in the chapter house. Human remains were uncovered on the corner of Little Mary Street and Arran Street in 1965.[28] These were probably associated with the cemetery of St Mary's abbey. A number of the properties fronting Mary's Abbey Street today contain basements and, in at least one of them, there is evidence for earlier, probably medieval, architectural stone work incorporated in the walls (fig. 4.10). A forensic architectural survey of these properties might yield tangible evidence for the south range of the abbey.

Abbey finds

Stray finds from the abbey have turned up in the neighbourhood. The National Museum catalogue records forty-nine tiles recovered from the nineteenth-century excavations. These represented the third largest collection of floor tiles and tile fragments from Ireland.[29] Among the assemblage found at Arran Quay were a number of wasters which suggests that the tiles may have been produced locally, perhaps at St Mary's abbey itself.[30] During archaeological testing of 14 Ormond Quay/11–13 Strand Street in 2003 a compact sandy deposit produced twelve medieval tiles and several sherds of medieval pottery including Dublin fine ware.[31] One of these had a relief pattern, another one was line-incised and seven were glazed. An iron rowel spur of medieval date was found at Mary Street in 1959.[32] Excavations on the site of St Mary's abbey in 1971 produced a bronze ring.[33] Monitoring at 15 Ormond Quay Lower revealed one piece of late-medieval local Dublin ware.[34] Mary McMahon's excavation at Inns Quay produced tiles that were very similar to those found at St Mary's abbey.[35]

Gwynn, 'The origins of St Mary's abbey, Dublin', *Journal of the Royal Society of Antiquaries of Ireland*, 79 (1949), 110–25, at 124. **25** Donnelly, *The remains of St Mary's abbey*, p. 19. **26** Luddy, *St Mary's abbey*. **27** Donnelly, *The remains of St Mary's abbey*, p. 4. **28** NMI Topographical Files 23/4/1965. **29** E.S. Eames and Thomas Fanning, *Irish medieval tiles: decorated medieval paving tiles in Ireland with an inventory of sites and designs and a visual index* (Dublin, 1988), pp 63–4. **30** Hayden, 'Excavations of the medieval river frontage', pp 196–7, E557, DU018–20426—, DU018–02567—. **31** Baker, et al., '14 Ormond Quay/11–14 Strand Street', p. 147, 03E0964, DU018–115—. **32** NMI Topographical Files, 1959. **33** NMI Topographical Files 1971:1063. **34** Unpublished file, 97E265. **35** Mary McMahon, 'Archaeological excavations at the site of the Four Courts Extension, Inns Quay, Dublin', *Proceedings of the Royal Irish Academy*, 88C (1988), 271–319, see fig. 17,

CONCLUSIONS

The suburban development in the area within and without the precincts of St Mary's abbey gradually eroded the medieval site. Reuse of the stones from the abbot's lodging for the construction of the wall along the strand which became Ormond Quay was particularly damaging.[36] Many of the buildings remained intact until the late seventeenth century when the abbey was used as a quarry and redeveloped by Humphrey Jervis. In 1676 the lord mayor of Dublin used the stone from the abandoned abbey to build the first Essex Bridge. Later, the new north quays development further erased traces of its layout. The fabric of the abbey and its enclosure have now vanished almost completely, the only surviving portion of the building being the chapter house, with the adjoining passage, which is a National monument in state care. Nevertheless, St Mary's abbey has left a lasting legacy in the urban streetscape of north-city and County Dublin. The present road network evolved around the boundaries of its grange farms in north County Dublin; the street pattern and place-names preserve the location of its precinct walls, gates and topography. The importance of this area even today as a market for the agricultural produce of Fingal is a distant echo of the time when the monks of St Mary's provided Dublin with some of their garden produce. Jervis Street Hospital may reflect a tradition of care going back to the Middle Ages.

ACKNOWLEDGMENTS

I wish to thank all those who assisted me in the preparation of this paper, the OPW staff at St Mary's Abbey National Monument who provided valuable local information, the National Museum for access to their catalogue and collections, Linzi Simpson for sharing her invaluable expertise and relevant papers, Franc Myles for information on the precinct wall, my colleagues in the Archaeological Survey of Ireland and Kevin O'Brien in the OPW for helpful discussion; Matthew Stout for all the figures and reading earlier drafts and finally to Seán Duffy for asking me to prepare this paper for Medieval Dublin.

pp 296, 527.   **36** Casey, *Buildings of Ireland: Dublin*, p. 88.

Excavations at 58–59 Thomas Street/Vicar Street and 63–64 Thomas Street, Dublin 8

JUDITH CARROLL

INTRODUCTION

Two excavations were carried out on neighbouring sites in Thomas Street, Dublin 8, in 1997 and 2009. The site of the present Vicar Street Centre at nos 58 and 59 Thomas Street/Vicar Street was excavated under Licence 97E0380 during October–November 1997, while no. 63–64 Thomas Street was excavated under Licence 09E0254 during July and August 2009 (figs 5.1, 5.2). Both sites were situated on the south side of Thomas Street, opposite the parish church of Ss Augustine and John, formerly the priory and hospital of St John the Baptist of the Fratres Cruciferi which was built outside the west gate or New Gate of the city of Dublin in the late twelfth century. Evidence of leather tanning was found at both sites while iron-smelting evidence was also found at the Vicar Street site.

This report describes the excavations in their historic and archaeological context and examines the evidence for industrial sites outside the walls of Dublin in the medieval period. In the sections on the excavations, features/layers are described by 'Feature numbers' (e.g. F31) for the 1997 excavation and 'Context numbers' (e.g. C001) for the 2009 excavation as this was the way they were originally recorded.

HISTORICAL AND ARCHAEOLOGICAL BACKGROUND

Prehistoric/early medieval
The excavation sites were in the area which is proposed by Clarke (2002, 1) to be the first Dublin settlement of early medieval date, what he envisages as the proto-urban centre of Áth Cliath. Clarke locates the western extent of Áth Cliath at present St John's Lane (off Thomas Street) and its eastern side at St Audoen's church off High Street. It is suggested that two main ancient highways crossed each other in this area, the Slige Midlúachra and the Slige Cualann. The Slige Midlúachra is said to have run along present-day Francis Street, north across the ford of the hurdles (Áth Cliath) to present-day Bow Lane running northwards on the other side of the Liffey. It is said to have intersected with the main east–west trajectory, the Slige Cualann, as it ran east–west, taking in present-day Thomas Street.

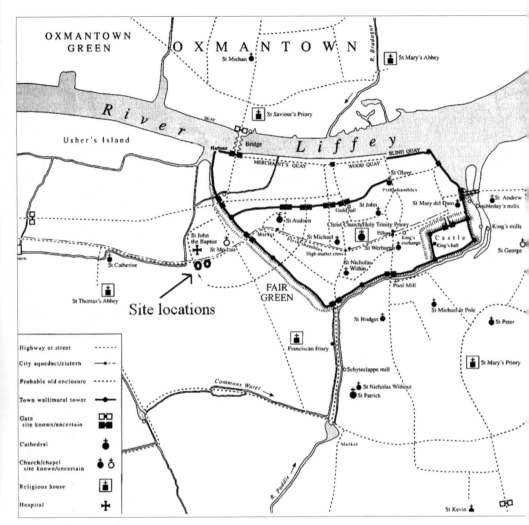

5.1 Dublin *c.*1300 with position of sites marked by arrow (after H.B. Clarke, *Dublin*, Irish Historic Towns Atlas, no. 11 (Dublin, 2002))

Later medieval and early modern

The medieval hospital of St John the Baptist, located directly to the north of the excavations described here, may have been on the site of an earlier ecclesiastical establishment. However, in the late twelfth century, it appears to have been on the curtilage of Aildred Palmer, who, along with his wife, was the founder of the hospital. Palmer had witnessed a grant about 1174 from Strongbow to Hamund Mac Turcaill, a member of the family of the recently overthrown

5.2 Thomas Street, Dublin, with positions of sites marked

Hiberno–Norse dynasty of Dublin (St John Brooks 1936, v). The couple owned substantial property in Dublin and in the country (ibid.) but took monastic vows when they set up St John's Hospital for the care of the poor and the infirm. Palmer was also known to Lorcán Ua Tuathail (St Laurence O'Toole), archbishop of Dublin, as they affixed their names to the same document. Though the precise date of the founding of the hospital is unknown, it had been established and at work for some time before 1188 when it received formal confirmation and substantial privileges from Pope Clement III.

The hospital was situated outside the West Gate (called New Gate) of the medieval city of Dublin and was bounded by Thomas Street on the south side, John's Lane on the west side, John's Street on the east, and on the north by the former Crockers' Street or Crockers' Lane. The institution was granted privileges by Clement III conformable to those granted to the Hospitallers of St John of Jerusalem, but, nevertheless, it was organized to be a house of the Canons Regular of St Augustine. At a period, not yet ascertained, the original community of canons and canonesses was converted into one of the Cruciferi or 'Crouched' (i.e., cross-bearing) friars.

The hospital appears to have been a very busy establishment into the first quarter of the thirteenth century. It maintained 155 beds in constant use at that time, but was destroyed by the war of Edward Bruce in 1317. When Bruce's army approached the city, the citizens fired the suburbs, the church and other houses of the hospital were burnt, and the stone wall of its close was levelled to the ground. Later, Edward III answered an appeal for aid, and grants were bestowed on the hospital. With the decline of English power after that period, the revenues of the hospital were diminished by the loss of distant estates and, by 1373, the number of beds had been reduced to 115 because no more could be maintained.

St John's Hospital was suppressed in 1539 under Henry VIII, its goods and chattels, vessels, jewels, ornaments, bells, superfluous buildings, utensils, household furniture being sold under Henry VIII's Commissions of 1539. The site was leased to Edmund Redman, on 27 September 1539 for twenty-one years at a rent of 43s. 4d. It was granted to Maurice, earl of Thomond, in 1544 who was succeeded by James Sedgrave in 1552 when it still had a house with beds for fifty sick men (Gwynn and Hadcock 1970, 212). During this period, the institution was probably conducted as a private charity without endowments. It functioned as a poorhouse in the seventeenth century.

Around the turn of the eighteenth century, the Augustinians rented a plot of land on the west side of the site and c.1740, a small church, 24 by 60 feet, was built and was considerably extended forty years later. The tower, the remaining fragment of the medieval hospital site, stood till about the year 1800 and was then pulled down. Subsequently, the Augustinians purchased more land on the site and in 1862 the present-day church of St Augustine and St John the Baptist was commenced.

The Thomas Street excavations in the excavation record
It is important to place excavations in the context of other excavations in the area. A very large number of archaeological testing schemes and full-scale excavations have taken place along Thomas Street and within the neighbouring streets. There are too many excavations in the area to fully summarize here, but the excavations with significant findings and industrial features in the vicinity of the sites are as follows:

1. Margaret Gowen and Linzi Simpson (Licence 95E045) carried out testing in 1995 and 1996 to the west of John's Lane. Here the trenches revealed a 3m depth of cellar rubble. Cellaring had destroyed most of the archaeological layers, but the remains of a watercourse were located, as well as black sticky layers containing cockle shell and animals bone. Two stone walls beneath the cellaring also indicated the presence of a probable mill at this point, perhaps one of the three mills owned by the hospital of the Fratres Cruciferi (Gowen 1996a; Simpson 1997).

2. At 119–121 Thomas Street, under Licence 96E280, to the west of the sites above, Edmond O'Donovan excavated a large number of medieval tanning pits dated to between 1200 and *c.*1400 (O'Donovan 2003). The finds included a substantial quantity of medieval pottery, a ring-brooch, a leather belt buckle and a decorated leather scabbard. A number of post-medieval features were recorded in overlying layers.

3. In 2003, testing commenced on a site located north of Swift's Alley and south of Thomas Street, off Francis Street, by Ciara McManus, ACS, under Licence 03E0621 (McManus 2003). Under garden soils, a silty material reminiscent of riverine or estuarine material was uncovered, indicating a possible watercourse relating to a mill. Medieval pottery and fragments of animal bone were found, as well as a series of wooden upright posts around which a deposit of brushwood came to light.

4. The sites of this report are close to (east of) the important medieval site of St Thomas's abbey. The spread-out location of the abbey has been studied by Claire Walsh in her excavations in this area. In 1995, Earl Street South was excavated by Walsh (Walsh 1996) under Licence 95E041 and this uncovered part of the precinct of St Thomas's abbey. Late in 1996 the site of a proposed development on the northern side of Earl Street South was tested. The excavator discovered the remains of an *in situ* medieval decorated tile pavement and considered part of the site of the church of the abbey to have been located here (Walsh 200b).

5. Walsh also tested nos 6–10 Hanbury Lane under Licence 98E0199 and excavations at this site took place in February 1999 (Walsh 2000a). Several medieval floor tiles were discovered, and seventeen burials were excavated, indicating 'that the entire area to the east of the abbey precinct had been used as a graveyard in the thirteenth century' (Walsh 2000b).

6. In 1995, Margaret Gowen carried out test excavations under Licence 95E110 at 29–34 Thomas Street when the remains of a possible watercourse were located (Gowen 1996b). This was identified as either a branch of the medieval watercourse known as 'Colman's Brook', which extended along Thomas Street, or the millrace of the Watte mill, located somewhere in the vicinity. In addition, the testing located the remains of a possible leather-tanning complex in the form of the remains of barrels sunk into a deep, foul-smelling organic deposit. A limited archaeological deposit, 0.2m deep, containing several timbers, was also located. This suggested that the tanning complex originally extended to the south-east.

7. At the corner of New Street South and Fumbally Lane, twelfth- to seventeenth-century tanning pits were excavated by Antoine Giacometti in New Street in 2004 under Licence 04E1286 (Giacometti 2007).

8. In 1990, Claire Walsh conducted a series of excavations under License 1990:041 in Patrick St/Nicholas St/Winetavern St, South City Ward,

Dublin (Walsh 1997). A tanning pit was found at the south end of Patrick Street, no doubt part of a larger complex.

9. At 44–49 New Row South, at the south end of Patrick Street, Georgina Scally excavated a number of pits in 1997 under Licence 96E342. These contained leather offcuts and a small quantity of leather shoe-soles (Scally 1997).

10. South of Thomas Street and west of Patrick Street, Franc Myles excavated seventeenth- and eighteenth century tanning pits at Ardee Street under Licence 03E0315 (Myles 2007).

11. At 105–109, The Coombe, Melanie McQuade excavated a number of tanning pits dated between the twelfth and the sixteenth century under Licence 03E0207 (McQuade 2007).

12. In 1993, under License 93E173, Eoin Halpin carried out excavations comprising the west side of Patrick Street as well as Dean Street and Francis Street. Results suggested that the west bank of the river Poddle was largely used as an industrial area, with tanning forming the major industry. It appears that, at the southern end of the site, the tanning was associated with the yardages to the rear of the houses along Francis Street (Halpin 1994).

The excavation record therefore attests to a very large body of evidence for industrial activity, mainly tanning for the preparation of leather, taking place outside the city walls of Dublin between the twelfth and eighteenth centuries. This was heavily concentrated to the west and south-west of the medieval city walls from Thomas Street to the Patrick Street area of the city.

THE 58–59 THOMAS STREET/VICAR STREET EXCAVATION

The site of 58–59 Thomas Street/Vicar Street was excavated in October 1997 under Licence 97E0380 during the development of the present Vicar Street Centre. The properties faced onto Thomas Street but the buildings were already demolished when archaeological monitoring began at ground level. Cellaring was found to have cut through the archaeological layers on the site, destroying, in no. 58, all but a pit which survived at the north end of the property. In no. 59, at the south-east end of this property, a small number of medieval industrial layers survived. No archaeological features survived between these two areas which are called Area 1 (no. 59) and Area 2 (no. 58).

Area 1 (fig. 5.3)
The archaeological features in this area were revealed during monitoring of the site while overburden was being removed by a machine. The area was 7.1m

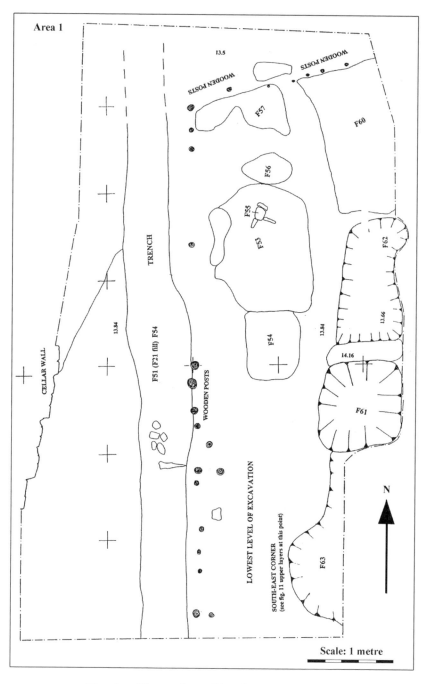

5.3 The 58–59 Thomas Street/Vicar Street excavation, Area 1

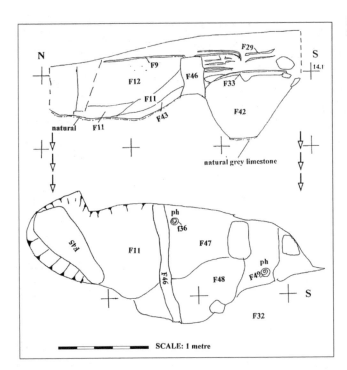

5.4 Ironworking features in Area 1

north–south and 4.4m east–west and the features in this area were found at a level of approximately 2–2.5m below ground level, apart from a narrow baulk on the east margin of no. 59 which had escaped cellaring and this produced ironworking layers F61, F63 and F63. The excavation yielded features relating to ironworking in the uppers layers, but the lower layers produced features superimposing an earlier series of wooden rectilinear pits, interpreted as tanning pits, and also a superstructure which probably related to the tanning pit complex but may also have related to the ironworking.

Ironworking

The most notable features were a furnace and two pits relating to iron smelting (figs 5.4, 5.5). The features were very disturbed and it was not possible to fully reconstruct the manner in which F62 related to F61 and the exact nature and function of F63. All the pits produced iron slag and medieval pottery. F61 produced a very large amount of iron slag.

A shallow smelting pit, F62, was approximately 1.45m in length and 0.90m in width. From the top of F46 and ash layer F9, it was roughly 0.65m in depth (fig. 3) and had a base of red oxidized clay which had been exposed to intense heat. In the pit were also found the remains of what appeared to be a large,

5.5 Ironworking features in Area 1, 58–59 Thomas Street

roughly thrown, fired clay bowl, though this did not have ironworking material adhering to it. A ceramic plug was also found in the fill of the pit cut, F62. South of this pit, clearly related to it, was another deeper pit (F61). F61 was approx. 0.90m in depth and 1.06m wide. The main fill of cut F62 was F42 which produced layers of iron waste, furnace waste, dark soil and a great deal of medieval pottery. A very large quantity of iron slag was also found in this pit, mixed with bone pottery and oyster shell.

Both features were divided (vertically) by a brown, silty organic layer (F46; see fig. 3), possibly wood (interpreted as the remains of a tanning pit), dividing the pit containing the clay smelting furnace from the slag pit at an upper level. The pits were covered with layers of ash, burnt clay and charcoal, suggesting that these features had been used and reused a number of times before being abandoned.

At a lower level to F61/F62, to its west, there were a number of clay deposits (see figs 5.6, 5.7), including F2, F3, F4 and F6, all fairly similar pale grey to orange-brown clays containing fragments of wood, charcoal and bone. A number of other layers containing burnt material, charcoal and/or fragments of iron slag included F5, F7, F8 and F10.

When these upper layers were excavated, further, more defined features associated with industrial activity were revealed (fig. 5.6). F20 was a yellow silty layer, F19 a light brown-grey silt with wood fragments; F66, a rectilinear feature of dark brown silt, covered F62. Three postholes were also found (figs

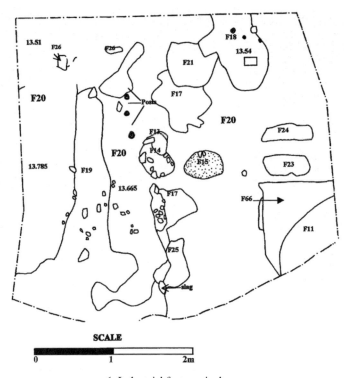

SCALE

0   1   2m

5.6 Industrial features in Area 1

5.3, 5.6). To the north of F66 are deposits F23, brown silt containing charcoal and wood fragments, and F24, red-brown clay containing wood fragments. F17 was an organic, clay deposit containing probable wood. F21, which superimposed this layer, was a dark brown gritty silt with iron slag inclusions and organic residue. F18, which appeared to partly superimpose this layer, was a red-brown organic silt containing wood fragments. F13 was a gritty burnt layer which appeared to be underlying F14, a stony deposit with fragments of slag and charcoal. F25 was a black, gritty deposit with iron fragments and slag.

Trench feature F051/F54

A linear trench (F051) was found to the west of no. 59 (fig. 5.3). This may have been a boundary division or a drain, perhaps originating in the later boundary division of the houses as all the ironworking and evidence of tanning was found in no. 59. F051 contained organic layers of grey to brown silty clay containing wood fragments (F023 and F054). It was approximately 0.50m to 0.70m in width and 0.30m in depth. Roughly 0.80m–1.20m from the west edge of the trench F51 there was a post-medieval cellar wall while there were no archaeological layers or features to the west of the trench.

5.7 Excavation of features in Area 1, 58–59 Thomas Street

Tanning pits

Underlying the ironworking pit on the east baulk, and to the east of the trench F51/F54, were a number of features cut into the natural subsoil or forming rectilinear cuts, containing wood or organic material. North of these features is a set of posts and postholes, which may have formed a rectilinear structure relating to these features. It is particularly significant that they relate directly to the north and east ends of cuts F60 and F57 (fig. 5.3). F60 was a rectilinear cut, 1.6m in length north–south and 0.92m, where exposed, east–west, running into the baulk. F57 was a brown, woody area containing wood fragments and charcoal, 1.05m east–west. This rectilinear feature is interpreted as the base of a tanning pit as is F53/F55 (fig. 5.8), a concentration of brown and grey material containing small patches of carbonized wood, orange burnt wood and charcoal. F54 was a brown soil mixed with dark carbonized wood and patches of burnt red clay, level with the surrounding silty yellow clay. F56 was a ferruginous layer about 10cm on depth. F61 was the cut of a pit containing slag to the south. F62 is the cut to the north of F61 which was the iron smelting pit described in Phase 2. This was at least partly superimposed by F11 which may have been cut into F66, a rectilinear feature of dark brown silt, 1.15m north–south and 0.91m east–west where exposed, its east side running under the baulk. F66 is also interpreted as the base of a tanning pit. F63 was the cut of a pit directly south of F61.

Other features described above (see fig. 5.6) probably also relate to the lower wood layers and rectilinear pits, including F23, brown silt containing charcoal

5.8 Bases of tanning pits found under cellaring and ironworking layers in Area 1, 58–59
Thomas Street

and wood fragments; F24, red-brown clay containing wood fragments; F17 organic, clay deposit containing probable wood. It is suggested that iron-working superimposed tanning pits sometime between the twelfth to mid-thirteenth centuries from the evidence of the pottery report (McCutcheon 1997).

Area 2

In Cutting 2, a single pit was found (figs 5.9, 5.10). At its north end, where it ran further north, towards, or under, the present main road, it was cut off by the front wall of no. 58. It was cut off by a cellar wall to the east and post-medieval disturbance to the west. There was a row of stakes on the south side of the pit. The pit was composed of a dark brown to grey, silty, organic soil (F16). The area excavated (the total area exposed by the removal of cellars) was 3.2m north–south and 4m east–west. It was approximately 0.15m–0.4m in depth and was found under rubble at a level of around 13.35 OD. A row of 12 stakes contained the fill of the pit on the south side. These, 0.02.8m–0.04m in diameter, were probably interwoven horizontally with wattle. A few pieces of wattle came to light in the pit fill. Though the fill of the pit, roughly level with the top of the stakes, was very shallow, it is probable that this may have been the original size of the pit and that it may not have been truncated by the eighteenth-century cellaring as was first thought. The tops of the stakes were

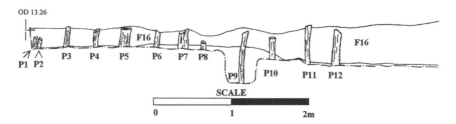

5.9 Stakes containing pit in Area 2, 58–59 Thomas Street

5.10 Excavation of pit contained by stakes in Area 2

not cleanly cut but they were all *in situ*. There may have been later pits superimposing it, but there was no evidence of these in the excavation.

The fill of the pit was F16, an homogenous dark grey-brown silty, organic clay containing moss fragments, wood, shell, iron slag, leather, animal bones and medieval pottery. The pit was sealed by superimposing layers of ash, charcoal and burnt earth.

Finds from the site
Pottery There were 234 sherds of medieval pottery from the site which have been analysed by Claire McCutcheon. The pottery, comprising Dublin-type

wares, Leinster cooking ware, Ham Green B and Saintonge green glazed ware is a standard collection for the period in Dublin. The overall assemblage, however, is early and suggests a late twelfth- to mid-thirteenth-century date for the site. There was no post-medieval pottery, except for a few sherds of seventeenth–nineteenth century pottery in the unstratified debris.

Table 1. Irish and imported medieval pottery from 58–59 Thomas St/Vicar Street, Dublin (E=early; M=mid; L=late: Report, C. McCutcheon, 1997)

Fabric type	No. of sherds	MNV	Form	Date range
Dublin-type Coarse ware	89	3	2 jugs, storage vessel	L12th–M13thC
Dublin-type ware	69	2	Jugs	13th
Dublin-type cooking ware	31	1	Cooking pot	L12th–13thC
Dublin-type fine ware	3	1	Jugs	L13th–14thC
Leinster cooking ware	8	1	Cooking pot	L12th–14thC
Ham Green B ware	5	1	Jug	L12th–M13thC
Saintonge green glazed ware	21	1	Jug	13th–14thC
Unidentified	8	1	Jug	Medieval
Totals	**234**	**11**		

Leather There was a large quantity of scrap leather from the same fill and this was examined by Dáire O'Rourke with a view to further analysis. However, this was considered by the latter to constitute scrap and would not have benefited from further analysis.

Iron Although a great deal of iron was found, there were no artefacts identified. There were a number of miscellaneous badly corroded objects and nails.

Oyster shell There was a great deal of oyster shell from the site. This shell was clearly found in stratified layers dated by the pottery to a date *circa* the thirteenth century. Much oyster shell was found among iron slag and medieval pottery in Pit F62 which was sealed by the superimposing layers of ash, charcoal and burnt earth.

THE 63–64 THOMAS STREET EXCAVATION

The excavation took place from July to August 2009 at the rear of nos 63 and 64 Thomas Street, Dublin 8 (figs 5.11, 5.12, 5.13) under Licence 09E0254. The excavation was carried out prior to mixed development of the site.

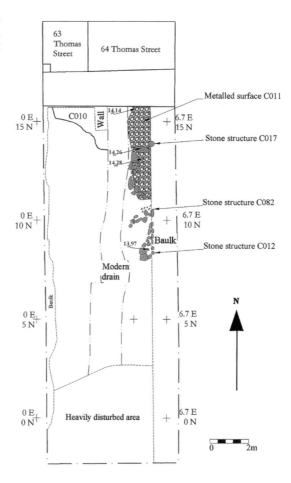

5.11 Structural layers on the north end of the site, 63–64 Thomas Street

Because of the various construction methods, the archaeological impact differed between the northern two thirds of the site and the southern third part and the site was divided into two areas: Area 1, the northern area, and Area 2, the southern area. In Area 1, it was found that there would be complete archaeological impact, but in Area 2, piling would avoid impact over most areas. Full excavation therefore took place on Area 1 with monitoring during part of some of the construction work in Area 2. Monitoring of Area 2 did not reveal archaeological layers and the following relates to medieval layers in Area 1. Archaeological layers survived throughout the northern two thirds of Area 1 and were better preserved in the north rather than in the south of this area. In the north part of Area 1, archaeological layers were located at a depth of 1m and were up to 3m in depth. In the southern half of this area, they were badly disturbed and survived at about 2m in depth while in the southern 3m of Area 1, they had been destroyed completely.

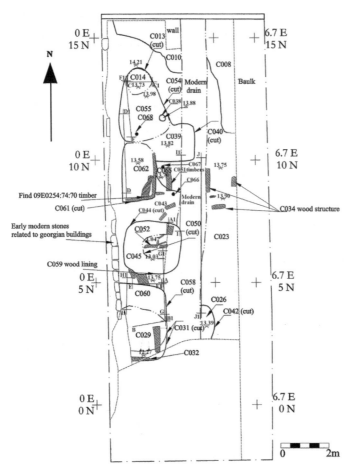

5.12 Structural layers on the north end of the site and tanning pits covering most of this area of the site, 63–64 Thomas Street

Structural remains, represented by burnt layers and wattle fragments, were found at the very north of the site only. To the south of these were a series of deep pits and composite organic layers containing medieval pottery and large planks of wood. There were nine pits, most of which recut each other, suggesting a long period of use. Wood *in situ* showed that they were wood-lined. There were both stakes of wood and flat cut planks of wood. The pits also produced medieval pottery and leather. The pits were deeply cut to a maximum depth of 3.5m below ground level, though most were no deeper than 2.7m.

There were a few post-medieval features. A pit was dug and revealed a cistern and a number of glass bottles and sherds of post-medieval pottery. A barrel pit with evidence of earlier barrels was also found on the north-west of the site in a layer superimposing the medieval layers. Otherwise, no post-medieval layers survived.

5.13 Excavation of structural features in 63–64 Thomas Street

The structural layers were probably the earliest on site and there were a number of features at the northern end of the site that either pre-dated or were contemporary with the tanning pits. These layers yielded medieval pottery that was twelfth- or thirteenth-century in date and mainly imported, while the tanning pits mainly yielded various types of Dublin local ware of thirteenth–fourteenth-century date and three sherds of seventeenth-century pottery (see Table 2).

The structural features were as follows: Cut C041 (which may have been the west side of a pit) appeared as a linear north–south-running shallow feature which was 1.8m in length and 0.44m in width and continued underneath the eastern baulk. It was 0.06m in depth. It contained a number of layers of organic, dark brown, silty clay with charcoal, wattle fragments and bone, including C020 which contained four pieces of medieval pottery and one iron bolt/nail. Above C020 was a metalled surface, C011 (fig. 5.11), which was 4.7m north/south by 1m east/west and 0.17m in depth. It comprised yellow-grey, silty clay with very closely packed stones of 0.10–0.15m in average diameter and contained nine pieces of medieval pottery

A stone structure, C017, superimposed metalled surfaces C011 and C016 (fig. 5.11). C016 was bounded by C017 which superimposed it. C016 was similar to C011 and was 2.93m north/south. It was 1.8m in width from its west edge to the east baulk which it continued under. Its stone coursing, o.o6m to o.15m in height, comprised stones ranging from o.27m x o.18m to o.38m x o.53m (fig. 5.11). One piece of medieval pottery was recovered from C16. Within the stone structure, Co17, above metalled surface Co16, was Co15, a deposit of yellow silty clay o.15m in depth.

Immediately south of Co12, the remains of a stone structure, comprising medium sized stones, was 1.5m x o.79m. Above Co11, Co12, Co16, and Co17 lay layer, Co08, a red burnt layer, which was 1.16m x 4.6m and o.35m in depth. Layer Co10, identical in composition to Co08, was located to the west of a short post-medieval brick wall projection left *in situ* at the north of the site. Co10 was 2.8m x 2m and o.2m in depth. It lay above natural clay at the west of the site just north of Pits Co40, Co54 and Co13. Layers Co08 and Co10 comprised burnt red silty clay with charcoal and wood inclusions. Seventeen sherds of medieval pottery were recovered from layer Co08 and one iron bolt. No pottery was recorded from Co10.

Tanning pits

There were eight pit features to the south of the structures and burnt layers: Co40, Co54, Co79, Co61, Co44, Co58, Co31 and Co42. The pits were lined with wood, some pieces of which still remained *in situ*. Other pieces or areas of wood lining were in decayed form and were *in situ* as layers. The remains of wooden structures given context numbers included Co66, Co67, Co68, Co34 and Co51 (fig. 5.12).

Pit Co40 Pit Co40 was a sub-rectangular pit, 2m in length east/west and 1.4m in width north/south. It was o.73m in depth. It was truncated at its western side by Pits Co54 and Co61. Pit Co40 contained decayed wooden lining, Co37, and fill, Co39.

Co37 was a compacted wood lining which lined part of the sides and part of the base of Co40 and was o.12m in depth. Co39 was the main fill of Pit Co40 and comprised yellowish-grey silty clay with lime flecks throughout. It filled pit Co40 to its wooden lining and was o.58m in depth. Co39 contained fifteen sherds of medieval pottery and a leather shoe. The wooden stake was also recovered from the fill Co39 and is likely to have collapsed in from the wood lining Co37. Above this, pit Co40 was sealed by the deposit Co63.

Pit Co61 (fig. 5.14) Pit Co61 was a sub-rectangular feature which truncated Pit Co40 at its south-west corner. It was 2.42m north/south and 1.45m east/west and 1.64m in depth. It continued underneath the limit of excavation at the west of the site and its north/south profile was visible in the baulk section face. Pit Co61 was lined with wood on its south and west sides. Organic layers contained structural wood, medieval pottery, a leather shoe and an undecorated bronze pin.

5.14 Excavation of pits Co61/Co54 in 63–64 Thomas Street

Pit Co54 (fig. 5.14) Pit Co54 was an irregularly-shaped pit which truncated Pit Co40 to its north-west and was 3m in length north/south by 1.9m east/west. Its organic fills contained twenty-one sherds of medieval pottery, a partial wooden post, five iron nails, a possible shoelace and two leather shoe parts.

Pit Co79 Pit Co79, a small pit found in the west baulk, truncated Pit Co54 on its west side and continued in underneath the western baulk. Its profile was visible in the western baulk. Co79 was 1.33m north/south by 0.44m east/west and 0.85m in depth. It contained one main fill, Co80, a dark-brown organic fill or possible wood lining, producing one piece of medieval pottery.

Pit Co13 Pit Co13 was a circular pit which truncated the northern edge of Pit Co54. Pit Co13 was 1m north/south by 1m east/west. It was 0.68m in depth. It contained a number of organic fills producing pieces of medieval pottery and worked wood.

Deposit Co63 Co63 was a yellow-grey, silty clay with small to medium angular stones. This layer superimposed and sealed pits Co40, Co13, Co54, and Co79. It was 2.9m north/south by 1.7m east/west and was 0.4m in depth. Layer Co63 contained a roof slate and two leather pieces.

Stakeholes Co66–Co68 Three stakeholes (Co66–Co68), 4mm–5mm in diameter and up to 8mm in depth, were also uncovered surrounding Pit Co61.

5.15 excavation of pit Co31 in 63–64 Thomas Street

Pit Co44 Pit Co44 was exposed as a roughly square pit, located in the west of
the excavation site but seen to continue under the west limits of the excavation.
Pit Co44 was 1.8m in depth and 2m in width east/west by 2.3m in length
north/south. It contained a wooden lining, Co52, and a number of organic
layers. Structural wood pieces show that the pit was wood lined and one piece
of wooden lining was uncovered *in situ*. It was approximately 1.5m in length
and 0.2m in width. The pit contained a number of fills and cuts, yielding wood
pieces and medieval pottery.

Pit Co58 Co58 was a sub-rectangular pit located to the south-west of the site
(fig. 5.12) and was 1.89m east/west, where it was exposed, by 0.97m
north/south. It was 0.5m in depth. The full extent of Co58 is unknown
because it continued in underneath the western limits of excavation and was
also truncated by Co31, a later pit to its south. The pit contained a number of
fills which produced medieval pottery.

Pits Co31 and Co58 Pit Co31 (fig. 5.15) was a sub-rectangular pit, 1.8m
north/south by 1.63m east/west and 1.3m in depth. Pit Co31 truncated Pit
Co58, an earlier pit to its north. It contained a number of organic fills
producing well-compacted, degraded wood fragments and some fragments of
bone and rope as well as a leather shoe and medieval pottery.

Pit Co42 Pit Co42 was a sub-circular pit which cut through the highly organic
deposit, Co23, which covered the eastern to south-eastern area of the site. Pit
Co42 was 1.4m in length, 0.6m in width but survived only 0.3m in depth.
Co42 contained one fill, Co26. Co26 was a dark grey-black, moderately
compacted, silty clay, with occasional animal bone and oyster shell inclusions.

5.16 Structural timber from tanning pits in 63–64 Thomas Street

The western edge of Pit Co42 was truncated by a modern drain and machine cut which ran the length of the site, from the northern-most limits of excavation at the 63–64 Thomas Street buildings, towards the southern most limits of the site (fig. 5.12).

Layer Co23 and wood structures Co34 and Co51 Layer Co23 covered the area east of the modern drain from where the modern trench cut through the southern edge of Co08 to the southern limits of excavation. It was a dark-brown to black soft organic soil layer comprising decayed organic material. It was 6.7m in length, 1.1m in width of excavated area (it continued in under the baulk to the east) and 0.3m in depth. Layer Co23 contained forty-nine pieces of medieval pottery, wood, oyster shell and a whetstone. Wooden structure Co34 lay above Co23 and comprised six pieces of structural wood consisting of four wooden beams (fig. 5.16) and two stakes. Co34 contained within its area one fill, Co35, which was found within the structure of Co34 and which lay above Co23. Co35 was brown, moderately compacted, silty clay with shell, wood and bone inclusions, containing twenty-two pieces of medieval pottery.

Layer Co25 was north of Co34 and was a yellow-grey silty clay deposit, visible on the east of the site. It ranged in depth from 0.1m–0.2m and lay directly above layer Co23. It was 6.7m in length by 1.1m in width. It contained twenty-four sherds of medieval ceramic which included one piece of medieval brick and one piece of medieval roof tile.

Layer Co23 appeared to be the same layer as Co65 to the west of the drain cut. A possible wooden structure, Co51, lay within Layer Co65. Co51 comprised four wooden beams, the largest of which was 1m in length, 0.07m in

5.17 Medieval pottery from 63–64 Thomas Street

depth and 0.22m in width. Above Co65 and Co51 lay the layer Coo9, a dark-brown, moderately compacted silty clay containing eleven sherds of medieval pottery.

Co43 was located in the centre of the site to the west of the modern drain which cut through the site and comprised dark reddish-brown loose peaty clay. It sealed pit Co58 and was truncated by pit Co44. It was an L-shaped deposit, containing eighteen pieces of medieval pottery.

Finds
Analysis of the pottery from Phases 1 and 2 (by Niamh Curtin) has shown that the stratified layers and features produced 276 sherds of pottery of twelfth- to fourteenth-century date with three sherds of post-medieval pottery of seventeenth-century date. A very large amount of Dublin local ware and imported pottery, in particular Ham Green and Saintonge, were present within the assemblage. It is notable that the tanning pits produced a very large amount of pottery which is dated to the thirteenth to fourteenth century, while the pottery from the layers producing evidence of structure, as well as the organic layers, produced most of the twelfth- to thirteenth-century pottery. This may suggest that the site was a habitation site in the twelfth or thirteenth century but was used for tanning from the thirteenth century onwards into the early modern period.

In the assemblage, the medieval pottery from Ireland represents 72.8% of the medieval wares. The remainder is comprised of imported pottery from Bristol, Chester, north and south-west France, Spain and Portugal and the Netherlands. The broad range of imported wares from Thomas Street reflects the wide-reaching economic activity of Dublin port in the eleventh to fourteenth centuries (Doyle 2010).

Table 2. Irish and imported medieval pottery from 63–64 Thomas Street, Dublin (prepared by Niamh Curtin) E=early; M=mid; L=late

Type	Number of sherds	MNR	MNV	Form	Origin	Date range
Irish						
Dublin-type coarse ware	20	5		jugs/jars	local	L12th–M13thC
Dublin-type ware	173	14	1	jugs/jars	local	E13th–14thC
Dublin-type cooking ware	7	2		jars	local	L12th–13thC
Leinster cooking ware	1	1		jug/jar	Ireland	12th–14thC
English						
Ham Green B	19	4		jugs	England	M12th–13thC
Ham Green undiagnostic	11	2		jugs/jars	England	E12th–13thC
Ham Green cooking ware	1	1		jar/pot	England	12th–M 13thC
Chester-type	2	2		jugs	England	13th–14thC
Bristol Redcliffe (possible)	2	1		jug	England	M13th–14thC
Continental						
Saintonge mottled green glazed ware	20	2	1	jugs/pitchers	France	13th–14thC
Saintonge green painted	1	1		jug	France	L13th–E14thC
Rouen-type	2	1		jug	France	11th–13thC
Normandy gritty ware	2	2		jug/jar	France	11th–13thC
Normandy smooth ware (possible)	1			jug/jar	France	11th–13thC
Misc. French ware, Bristol pottery yype 192	1	1		jug	France	L12th–E13thC
Glazed French medieval	5	5		jug	France	13th–14thC
Merida-type unglazed ware	2	2		jar/costrel	Spain/ Portugal	13th–17thC
Flemish redware	6	1		jug/jar	Low Countries	M13th–M14th
Totals	**276**	**47**	**2**			

Wood samples and finds

A total of seventeen wood samples were analysed (by Ellen O'Carroll) with regard to wood-species identification and woodworking evidence from the wood assemblage at 63–64 Thomas Street. The wood assemblage was excavated from a number of features which included the fill of tanning pits (C32, C36, C40, C55, C61, C50, C54, C61, C44, C40 and C52) as well as wood samples from organic silt layers (C74, C22 and C65) and the remains of a wooden structure C34. The wooden remains were comprised mainly of parts of wooden planks used to line the wooden tanning pits. Three possible stakes and two possible wooden artefacts were also identified.

The analysis indicates that there were different species consciously selected for specific uses at the site of Thomas Street. Oak was the preferred species for use as wood lining for the tanning pits as well as the wooden pin. This evidence concurs with similarly dated features from urban sites and tanning pits such as excavations at the Coombe. Two possible stakes were identified as blackthorn and one as alder. A possible alder core was also present in the assemblage. Oak and willow wood chips were also present in the assemblage. One small ash squared enigmatic wood piece was also identified and analysed from the assemblage.

The wood identified from the samples could have originated from scrub-type woodland (blackthorn) or from mixed woodlands (oak and ash) nearby. Alder and willow prefer wetter ground. Woodworking evidence, although small, points to the presence of people skilled in timber splitting techniques as well as carving and possibly turning between the twelfth and fourteenth centuries in Dublin city (O'Carroll 2010).

Leather There were numerous pieces of leather, but only three pieces which were in any way diagnostic. One was 09E0254:39:5 (fig. 5.18), a probable ankle shoe which is similar in shape and manufacture to examples of thirteenth-/ fourteenth-century date from London and appears to have a flap toggle fastener which is typical of early fourteenth-century types (Grew and de Neergaard 2001, 19–20). The sole of this shoe and find nos 09E0254:46:7 and 09E0254:55:64 (which were both mainly soles) are very similar in shape and manufacture to soles of Types 2–4 from Perth (Thomas 1987, 177–8) which are dated from the thirteenth to the fifteenth centuries.

Bronze There was one bronze pin (09E0254: 74:84), undecorated but with a curving lower shank, 11 cm in length and 0.2cm in diameter.

Iron There were several iron objects, mainly bolts and nails, but no diagnostic objects.

DISCUSSION

The two sites of this publication, close together on the south side of Thomas Street opposite the Hospital of St John the Baptist, have yielded evidence of extensive industrial activity, including leather tanning and iron smelting. They contribute to the expanding picture of medieval Dublin formed by the record of archaeological excavations in this area. This record reveals an area outside

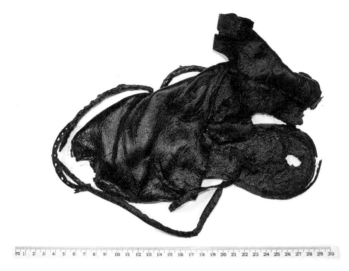

5.18 Leather shoe from 63–64 Thomas Street

the city walls of Dublin, described by Clarke as the 'western linear suburb' of Dublin (1998, 50–1), discussed also by O'Donovan (2003, 127–71), in which industries were located and concentrated.

Leather curing is a highly toxic activity, liable to contaminate water supplies. Like other industries which were toxic, noxious or in danger of causing fire – such as tanning, ironworking and pottery manufacture – the craft usually took place at a distance from urban centres. However, leather preparation required a constant supply of water as the animal skins needed to soak in vats or pits of tanning agents and lime as they were being treated. Therefore, tanning would have to be carried out in an area where a plentiful supply of water could be obtained. Ironworking, pottery making and milling would also have required regular extensive supplies of water.

In the Coombe tannery, an artificial channel was created along the northern boundary of the site in the late twelfth century. This channel would have carried water diverted from the Coombe Stream (McQuade 2007). In New Street and Patrick Street, water was most likely diverted from the Poddle and other watercourses as stated by the excavators (Halpin 1994). In the area west of St John the Baptist's Hospital, it was likely to be drawn from Coleman's Brook, which ran past St Thomas's abbey to Thomas Street, turning north at the west side of St John the Baptist's Hospital. This source may have had channels diverted to sites to the west of the hospital and may have been able to supply the tanning pits cut at a low level at 58–59 Thomas Street/Vicar Street, although it is difficult to see how it could directly supply sites more eastward such as the site at 63–64 Thomas Street.

During the excavation at 63–64 Thomas Street, it was found that the pits (in the driest part of the year, July to early August) filled immediately with groundwater as they were being excavated. Natural subsoil was only about 1.5m below ground level and the features found to the north of the site were not waterlogged, but all the pits which were cut south of the structures filled up very quickly. The pits were over 3m in maximum depth below road level at the very southern end of the complex.

Watercourses in the Thomas Street area of the city are discussed by Berry (1891) and Jackson (1949–50) in relation to historical descriptions from medieval records. An important reference on the watercourse supplying the mills of St John the Baptist's Hospital as well as the disposal of surplus water in 1458 records the lease by the city to the prior and brethren of the hospital of St John the Baptist, for a period of forty years, of 'the running water and its course … from near Crockers Barrs, passing through Thomas Street and by the hospital of St John, as far as the water mills of that hospital'. The hospital was given the right to construct a fosse from these mills to the city ditch on the south side of the bridge of Gorman's Gate (Jackson 1949–50, 19). This watercourse is plotted by Clarke on his maps of medieval Dublin (1978). Also plotted by Clarke is the city aqueduct by which water supply for the citizens of Dublin was transferred by a conduit along Thomas Street. As discussed by Berry (1891, 557), this was brought from a reservoir at James Gate which was supplied from the Dodder. This facility was set up some time between 1244 and 1254, according to Berry (ibid.), and was in use till 1775. There have been several references, however, to another water supply in the Thomas Street area of the city, the 'Glib Water', which appears to have been a free-running stream (as was Coleman's Brook) in Thomas Street.

Jackson has convincingly argued that the Glib Water was diverted from the Dodder at probably the same time that the aqueduct was constructed in the mid-thirteenth century. He proposes that it was an open stream running along Thomas Street which may have functioned to supply water to industries in the eastern Thomas Street area (Jackson 1949–50, 21–2). In 1573, the citizens of Thomas Street were ordered to 'pave the street before their houses before the same comes to the channel where the water runs or till same comes to the great pavement between both channels' as Berry shows from historical records (Berry 1891, 559).

The pits on the south side of Thomas Street were ideally placed to make use of surplus water, which would ensure constant filling of pits. Waste water and material would soak into the southward-sloping fields behind the tannery which as far as can be seen was not likely to contaminate any water supply.

Analysis of the pottery from 63–64 Thomas Street by Niamh Curtin has shown that the stratified layers and features produced 276 sherds of pottery of twelfth- to fourteenth-century date. A large amount of Dublin local ware and imported pottery, in particular Ham Green and Saintonge, was present within the assemblage. It is interesting that the tanning pits on this site produced pottery which is dated to the thirteenth–fourteenth century, while the pottery from the layers producing evidence of structure as well as the organic layers may have been earlier as they produced most of the twelfth- to thirteenth-century pottery. The tanning pits at nos 63–64, therefore, may be later than the structural/habitation layers on this site.

The 58–59 Thomas Street/Vicar Street pottery assemblage appears to accord in date with the pottery from the 'structural' layers at 63–64 Thomas Street and would seem to be earlier than the pottery from the tanning pits at the same site. Vicar Street produced pottery of twelfth- to mid-thirteenth-century date as dated by McCutcheon (1997), suggesting that the tannery may have fallen out of use at some time in the thirteenth century. Could this relate to changes in the layout of the tanneries after improvements had been made to the water supplies of Dublin in the mid-thirteenth century?

Research on tanneries found during archaeological excavation in medieval Dublin has attested to a concentration of tanning sites in the area of Thomas Street to Patrick Street, in particular, in the west and south-west of the city between the twelfth and the eighteenth centuries. Tanneries are found along Thomas Street and to the south in Patrick Street, New Street, Ardee Street and the Coombe in the medieval and early modern periods. Here they were so concentrated that an area of the Coombe is still called the Blackpits, after the dark organic waste produced by the industry. It is interesting that the tradition of tanning in these areas appears to have been continuous up to the eighteenth century and to have bridged the gap between the medieval and modern periods.

BIBLIOGRAPHY

Berry, H.F. 1891 The water supply of ancient Dublin. *Journal of the Royal Society of Antiquaries of Ireland*, 5th ser., 1:7, 557–73.

Brooks, E. St John (ed.) 1936 *Register of the Hospital of S. John the Baptist without the New Gate, Dublin*. Dublin. Irish Manuscripts Commission.

Clarke, H.B. 1978 *Dublin c.840–c.1540: the medieval town in the modern city*. Dublin. Ordnance Survey.

Clarke, H.B. 1998 *Urbs et suburbium*: beyond the walls of medieval Dublin. In C. Manning (ed.), *Dublin and beyond the Pale: studies in honour of Patrick Healy*, 45–58. Dublin. Wordwell.

Clarke, H.B. 2002 *Dublin part I, to 1610*. Irish Historic Towns Atlas no. 19. Dublin. Royal Irish Academy.

Curtin, N. 2010 The pottery from 63–64 Thomas Street, Dublin. In J. Carroll, Archaeological excavation at 63–64 Thomas Street, Dublin. Licence no. 09E0254. Unpublished report in the Department of Arts, Heritage and the Gaeltacht.

Giacometti, A. 2007 48 New Street South, Dublin. In I. Bennett (ed.), *Excavations: summary account of archaeological excavations in Ireland 2004*. Wordwell, Dublin.

Gowen, M. 1996a National College of Art and Design, Thomas St/Oliver Bond St/John's Lane/John's St, Dublin. In I. Bennett (ed.), *Excavations: summary account of archaeological excavations in Ireland 1995*. Bray. Wordwell.

Gowen, M. 1996b 29–34 Thomas St (rear), Dublin. In I. Bennett (ed.), *Excavations: summary account of archaeological excavations in Ireland 1995*. Bray. Wordwell.

Gwynn, A. and Hadcock, R.N. 1970 *Medieval religious houses, Ireland*. London. Longman.

Grew, F. and de Neergaarde, M. 1988 *Shoes and pattens: finds from medieval excavations in London*. Woodbridge. Boydell and Brewer.

Halpin, E. 1994 St Patrick's Street, Dublin. In I. Bennett (ed.), *Excavations: summary account of archaeological excavations in Ireland 1993*. Bray, Wordwell.

Jackson, V. 1949–50 The Glib Water and Coleman's Brook. *Dublin Historical Record* 11:1, 17–20.

McCutcheon, C. 1997 The pottery from Vicar Street/Thomas Street, Dublin. In J. Carroll, Archaeological excavation at Vicar Street/ nos 58–59 Thomas Street, Dublin. Licence no. 97E0380. Unpublished report in the Department of Arts, Heritage and the Gaeltacht.

McManus, C. 2007 Francis Street, Dublin. In I. Bennett (ed.), *Excavations: summary account of archaeological excavations in Ireland 2003*. Bray. Wordwell.

McQuade, M. 2007 105–109, the Coombe, Dublin. In I. Bennett (ed.), *Excavations: summary account of archaeological excavations in Ireland 2004*. Bray, Wordwell.

Myles, F. 2007 24–26 Ardee Street, Dublin. In I. Bennett (ed.), *Excavations: summary account of archaeological excavations in Ireland 2003*. Dublin. Wordwell.

O'Donovan, E. 2003 The growth and decline of a medieval suburb? Evidence from excavations at Thomas Street, Dublin. In S. Duffy (ed.), *Medieval Dublin IV, Proceedings of the Friends of Medieval Dublin Symposium 2002*, 127–71. Dublin. Four Courts Press.

Scally, G. 1997 44–49 New Row South, Dublin. In I. Bennett (ed.), *Excavations: summary account of archaeological excavations in Ireland 1998*. Bray. Wordwell.

Simpson, L. 1997 National College of Art and Design, Thomas St, Dublin. In I. Bennett (ed.), *Excavations: summary account of archaeological excavations in Ireland 1996*. Bray. Wordwell.

Simpson, L. 2000 Forty years a-digging: a preliminary synthesis of archaeological investigations in medieval Dublin, In S. Duffy (ed.), *Medieval Dublin I. Proceedings of the Friends of Medieval Dublin Symposium 1999*, 11–68. Dublin. Four Courts Press.

Thomas, C. 1987 Leather. In P. Holdsworth, *Excavations in the medieval burgh of Perth, 1979–1981*, 174–190. Society of Antiquaries of Scotland, Monograph Series vol. 5. Edinburgh.

Walsh, C. 1996 Earl Street South, Dublin. In I. Bennett (ed.), *Excavations: summary account of archaeological excavations in Ireland 1995*. Bray. Wordwell.

Walsh, C. 1998 36–37 South Earl Street, Dublin. In I. Bennett (ed.), *Excavations: summary account of archaeological excavations in Ireland 1997*. Bray. Wordwell.

Walsh, C. 1997 *Archaeological excavations at Patrick, Nicholas and Winetavern Streets, Dublin*. Dingle. Brandon Books.

Walsh, C. 2000a 6–10, Hanbury Lane, Dublin. In I. Bennett (ed.), *Excavations: summary account of archaeological excavations in Ireland 1999*. Bray. Wordwell.

Walsh, C. 2000b Archaeological excavations at the abbey of St Thomas the martyr, Dublin. In S. Duffy (ed.), *Medieval Dublin I. Proceedings of the Friends of Medieval Dublin Symposium 1999*, 185–202. Dublin. Four Courts Press.

The medieval manor of Clontarf, 1171–1540

COLM LENNON

Despite its proximity to the city, the manor of Clontarf played surprisingly little part in the history of Dublin in the late Middle Ages. After the epic events that unfolded there in 1014 and which shaped the politics of the region and the country, Clontarf appeared to relapse into relative obscurity until the Tudor and early Stuart period. Although the northern shoreline of the inner bay was technically within the franchises of Dublin, only the port of Clontarf on the periphery of the manor impinged to any extent upon municipal activity in the fourteenth and fifteenth centuries. For the rest, the district was tightly controlled from the 1170s by two powerful knightly orders, the Templars and the Hospitallers, who were the successive proprietors of Clontarf down to 1540. Under their jurisdiction, the village of Clontarf evolved, and they organized the manor and parish without any real reference to external secular or ecclesiastical authorities other than their orders' central bodies. Of course, the knights' cosmopolitan outlook encompassed commercial as well as cultural ties with the outside world. As well as sustaining a thriving manorial community at Clontarf, local agrarian and marine resources could be traded in times of surplus in the markets of the nearby city and farther afield.

This essay examines the history of the manor of Clontarf from the time of the arrival of the Anglo-Normans until the dissolution of the monasteries, with particular reference to the impact of the knightly orders upon the economy, society and culture of the district. Clontarf was a prime location for settlement, with its fertile agricultural lands, and its anchorage and harbour in close proximity to Dublin. In this favoured milieu, the Anglo-Norman feudal system was given every chance to flourish. The choice of the Knights Templar to establish social, economic and religious institutions in the area reflected their reputation as organizers of territories for their patron-rulers, even at a remove from the holy places of the Middle East where they performed their principal functions as crusaders. Under the auspices of the Knights Templar and their successors, the Knights Hospitaller, not only was the village of Clontarf nurtured, but also the links between the inhabitants and the neighbouring city of Dublin and the wider world were forged. Evidence relating to the organization of the manor of Clontarf and its productivity stems from the inquisitions and extent of the 1300s and 1540 respectively, the former made on the occasion of the trial of the Templars, and the latter taken at the time of the dissolution of the Hospitallers' preceptory at Clontarf. External factors, which caused the fall of the Templars and the entanglement of the

Hospitallers in the imbroglio of Anglo-Irish politics in the fifteenth century,
affected the proprietorship of Clontarf, but the manor remained a prized
possession for the new owners of the early modern period.

* * *

Clontarf was the subject of a royal grant within a short period of King Henry
II's seizure of control of the Anglo-Norman invasion in Ireland after 1171. The
grant, which was made by Henry to the Knights Templar at Avranches in
Normandy between 1172 and 1177, was referred to subsequently in at least
three confirmations in a little over a century. The earliest of these, dated 1199,
under King John, mentions the 'vill of Clumtorf' among a list of gifts made to
the Templars by Henry II, while the second, in a similar listing of 1226–7,
renders the place 'Clumtorp'.[1] The third reference occurs in the context of a
legal dispute involving the master of the Templars in Ireland in the 1280s,
during which he produced a charter of Henry II, which contained full details
of the order's endowment in Ireland. Included was 'a vill near Dublin called
Clemnthorp with its apputenances'.[2] That there was a community living in the
area before 1172 seems clear from the reference to a 'vill', and there was reputed
to be an old ecclesiastical centre in the district, which may have become the site
for the Templars' church.[3] It is quite possible that the burgeoning Hiberno-
Norse town of Dublin spawned an outpost in the form of a coastal station at
Clontarf after 1014 whose personnel formed themselves into a village
community, supplying the townsfolk with fish and agricultural produce.[4] While
the ethnic composition of such a putative settlement cannot be known, an

1 H.S. Sweetman (ed.), *Calendar of documents relating to Ireland, 1171–1307*, 5 vols (London,
1875–86), i, pp 13, 225.   2 Sweetman (ed.), *Cal. docs Ire*, iii, p. 329: the exact date of the
grant is uncertain but it must have been made between 1172, when Henry II was in
Avranches in Normandy, and 1177, when a reference occurs in the Christ Church deeds to
Matthew the Templar, betokening the establishment of the order in the Dublin region: M.J.
McEnery and Raymond Refaussé (eds), *Christ Church deeds* (Dublin, 2001), p. 124.
3 Modern authorities do not attribute greater antiquity to the church and parish of Clontarf
than the time of the Anglo-Norman settlement. Myles V. Ronan states that 'nothing is
known of the origin of the [early seventeenth-century] church' of Clontarf: Myles V. Ronan
(ed.), 'Royal visitation of Dublin, 1615' in *Archivium Hibernicum*, 8 (1941), 35. In their
survey of the medieval churches of County Dublin, Simms and Fagan exclude Clontarf
from the number of medieval manorial villages that had an early Christian site: Anngret
Simms and Patricia Fagan, 'Villages in County Dublin: their origins and inheritance' in
F.H. Aalen and Kevin Whelan (eds), *Dublin city and county* (Dublin, 1992), p. 86, and
Clontarf is not mentioned in a 1179 list of the churches of the Fine Gall region.   4 See
John Bradley, 'Some reflections on the problem of Scandinavian settlement in the hinterland of
Dublin during the ninth century' in John Bradley, Alan Fletcher and Anngret Simms (eds),
Dublin in the medieval world: studies in honour of Howard B. Clarke (Dublin, 2009), pp 39–62;
Mary Valente, 'Dublin's economic relations with hinterland and periphery in the later Viking
age' in Seán Duffy (ed.), *Medieval Dublin I* (Dublin, 2000), pp 69–83.

intriguing sign of possible cultural interplay between Scandinavian and Gaelic is seen in the dual form of the place-name: 'Cluain Tarbh' appears in the Irish-language sources, while 'Clumtorp', a Norse-sounding version, was apparently used in the grant of the 1170s to the Knights Templar.[5]

The choice of the Knights Templar as grantees of the strategically-placed district of Clontarf was a sign of their privileged standing in the king's entourage. Established sixty years previously to defend the crusader kingdom of Jerusalem after the first crusade, the Knights whose headquarters was at the Dome of the Rock in Jerusalem evolved into a religious order with vows and a monastic rule. Besides their main function of defending the crusader states against Moslem attack and protecting pilgrims from Europe to the Holy Land, they lived peaceably for the most part as farmers, gathering income for the effort against the infidels, and colonizing lands on behalf of secular rulers.[6] Although Clontarf was apparently already a settled district, its takeover by the Knights Templar in the 1170s assured Henry II and his successor lords of Ireland of the secure and productive management of lands there.[7] Unlike the other great knightly order which arrived in Ireland with the Anglo-Normans, the Hospitallers of St John of Jerusalem, the Knights Templar were decentralized in their national organization, the Templars having no official headquarters among their Irish houses, called commanderies or preceptories. Yet Clontarf, as the main Dublin property of the Knights Templar, had de facto enhanced status because of its proximity to the capital. The first person we can positively identify with the district is Walter, templar and master of 'Cluntarf', listed as a witness to deeds of St Mary's abbey, Dublin in 1186. Other references to personnel at Clontarf suggest that it was a key institution in the order's network and indeed in the mainstream of colonial life.[8]

Early modern maps of Clontarf give an indication of the shape of the medieval manor.[9] At the north end of a village street that led down to the sea were the principal manorial residence (or castle) and the church, situated about 150 metres apart. Although described by most modern sources as a castle from its earliest construction, the original house of the Knights may have been in reality a large fortified residence, in accordance with the normal style of Templar preceptory in Britain and Ireland. The problem in categorizing the Clontarf manor-house arises from the fact that no information about its construction survives, and most of the original building was cleared away in

5 See *Cogadh Gaedhel re Gallaibh. The war of the Gaedhil with the Gaill*, ed. J.H. Todd (London, 1867), p. 193.   **6** For a discussion of relations between the Knights and the European monarchs, see Helen Nicholson, *The Knights Templar: a new history* (Stroud, 2001), pp 160–80.   **7** Herbert Wood, 'The Templars in Ireland' in *Proceedings of the Royal Irish Academy*, 26, C (1906–7), 327–77.   **8** *Chartularies of St Mary's abbey, Dublin*, ed. J.T. Gilbert, 2 vols (London, 1884), i, pp 173, 231.   **9** For John Rocque's map of County Dublin (1760), see Paul Ferguson (ed.), *The A to Z of Georgian Dublin: John Rocque's maps of the city in 1756 and the County in 1760* (Lympne Castle, 1998), p. 26.

the reconstruction of Clontarf Castle in the 1830s.[10] The only written evidence for the medieval residence comes in the 1540 extent where it was equated to a hall and two towers, one of them probably the square 'keep' or main defensive structure of the original building, which survived in part until the nineteenth century.[11] The old, now ruinous, church at Clontarf, is the successor building to at least two others that have stood on the site, possibly stretching back to the early Christian period, but the church of the Knights Templar is the first certain ecclesiastical structure. Built about the same time as their house, the chapel building was located very close to the centre of the manor, as was the Anglo-Norman fashion. While some Templar chapels were architecturally elaborate, the church at Clontarf is likely to have been built in a plain vernacular style, similar to that of the Knights at Rincrew, Co. Waterford, for example. As well as being the chapel of the order of the Temple at Clontarf, the new church building became the place of worship for the newly formed parish of Clontarf, which was to be run by the Knights, almost independently of the archbishop of Dublin.[12]

Rocque's map of Clontarf also showed the pattern of field boundaries, probably of ancient date, spreading out from the castle/church nucleus. We see here very clearly the traces of the Knights' organization of a manor at Clontarf. Throughout their estates in Europe, they turned to agriculture to produce funds for their military activities in the east, enjoying a reputation for productive farming. Thus, by turning the district into a profitable economic unit and settled village, the Knights set the character of Clontarf. Of the original royal grant of 1,190 acres, the Knights concentrated on the development of an agrarian estate or manor of just under 400 acres. A demesne of eighty-eight acres centred on their manor-house was farmed by the Knights themselves, and the rest of the fields, comprising large and small farms, were rented out to tenants and worked by the families dwelling on the manor, who rendered labouring duties such as ploughing and reaping on the demesne lands in lieu of rent. The bulk of the manorial estate was made up of arable lands, while the balance consisted of pasture, meadow and woodland. A stand of timber, called Priorswood, survived into the early modern period, but had disappeared by the time of the 1760 survey. The cottages in the nucleated village that grew in the

10 For the context, see Margaret Murphy and Michael Potterton (eds), *The Dublin region in the Middle Ages: settlement, land-use and economy* (Dublin, 2010), pp 133, 137, 146; see also 'Clontarf Castle, County of Dublin' in *The Irish Penny Journal*, i (1840), pp 81–3; 'Clontarf Castle, Dublin' in Database of Irish Excavation Reports (www.excavations.ie/Pages/Details.php/Dublin 1715, 1994).   11 N.B. White (ed.), *Extents of Irish monastic possessions, 1540–1541*, Irish Manuscripts Commission (Dublin, 1943), p. 89.   12 Wood, 'Templars in Ireland', 334, 354; for the formation of parishes, see Adrian Empey, 'The layperson in the parish, 1169–1536' in Raymond Gillespie and W.G. Neely (eds), *The laity and the Church of Ireland, 1000–2000: 'all sorts and conditions'* (Dublin, 2002), pp 7–17; Murphy and Potterton (eds), *Dublin region in the Middle Ages*, pp 209–63; Nicholson, *Knights Templar*, p. 168.

vicinity of the manor-house housed the peasant families as well as some craft-workers and fisher folk, although the latter may have formed their own community at the shore to the east. As lords of the manor, the Knights were entitled not only to labour dues, such as reaping and sowing, but also would have received fees for use of the mill at Clontarf and for the anchoring of ships off the coastline.[13]

Of the approximately 400 acres actually farmed (excluding woodland and scrubland), 75% of the lands of the manor of Clontarf were outside the demesne of the Knights and were therefore worked by their tenants. At least a couple of large farms were formed, to judge by later references to 'Busshells Farme' and 'Whitefferme'. From an enquiry of 1308, on the occasion of the suppression of the order, we find that the bulk of the manorial territory was under the plough. Half of the fields (170.5 acres in extent) were given over to the cultivation of wheat, oats were grown on 154.5 acres, while two areas of eight acres were devoted to barley and legumes (peas and beans) respectively. As elsewhere, the Knights probably encouraged the most advanced agricultural techniques on their lands in Clontarf, including crop rotation, and crop surpluses would be sold to merchants from the neighbouring city and farther afield. The existence of a granary among the buildings near the Castle attests to the centrality of grain-growing on the manor, and the mill in Clontarf allowed for the processing of cereals in the locality. Clontarf was one of the few areas documented in the vicinity of Dublin in which barley-growing was carried out. Given the prevalence of wheat for flour and bread-making, the barley crop was probably used for malting and the brewing of beer. The oats grown at Clontarf could be turned into human foods when baked or stewed, used in the brewing of inferior ale, or given to animals as fodder. Legumes – beans and peas – were also important for human and animal consumption, and their cultivation moreover played a vital part in boosting the fertility of the soil.[14]

On the pasture and meadow lands of Clontarf, the Templars promoted animal husbandry on the demesne and manor. As Knights, they were experienced horsemen, and at Clontarf in 1308 they possessed a number of steeds. Besides the ten plough-horses ('affers'), which, along with thirty oxen, were used to pull their five ploughs, there were nine cart-horses and two pack-horses for working around the farm. The master of the order had an iron grey warhorse, worth £20, in his stable, and there were in addition four other horses,

13 Nicholson, *Knights Templar*, pp 181–7; Murphy and Potterton (eds), *Dublin region in the Middle Ages*, p. 75; J.S. Brewer and W. Bullen (eds), *Calendar of the Carew manuscripts preserved in the archiepiscopal library at Lambeth*, 6 vols (London, 1867–73), vi, p. 130; White (ed.), *Extents of Irish monastic possessions*, p. 89; see also, RIA, Haliday MS, 'Observations explanatory of a plan for a citadel at Dublin: map no 1: survey of the city of Dublin and part of the harbour, 1685' [Phillips].   **14** Gearóid Mac Niocaill, 'Documents relating to the suppression of the Templars in Ireland', *Analecta Hibernica*, 24 (1967), 188, 214, 214–15; for the context see Murphy and Potterton (eds), *Dublin region in the Middle Ages*, pp 287–324.

including a palfrey, for the use of the brothers. Apart from the beasts of burden
in the stables and behind the plough, there were herds and flocks in the
meadows and pastures. There was a cowhouse accommodating ten cows, as well
as a bull, and the fact that the larder contained four stone of cheese suggests
that the herd may have been kept for dairying purposes. Clontarf manor had a
large flock of sheep, numbering over 200 in 1308, which yielded meat and
skins, as well as wool, of which there were five stones in the storehouse. One
hundred pigs were kept on the manor, producing meat, there being twelve
sides of bacon in the larder in 1308. The produce of the land and herds thus
gave rise to domestic and commercial activities in manorial life, including
cheese-making, drying of hides, wool-gathering and preparation and cooking
of food, as well, perhaps, as brewing. In the sixteenth century, and possibly
beforehand, there was a dovecote among the complex of buildings on the
Clontarf manor-house site, where doves and pigeons were kept for eggs and
meat. References to the keeping of warrens on the lands of Clontarf and the
consumption of rabbit, especially on special occasions, date from slightly later
than the period of the Templars' tenure.[15]

There is no mention of fishing in the inquiry of 1308, but, as well as
farming the area, the Knights were doubtless involved in developing the port
of Clontarf which grew up as a satellite, coastal village on the manor. Two
members of the order, Galfridius Templarius and Henricus le Templer, were
members of the Dublin guild merchant in the mid-thirteenth century, both
presumably attached to the Clontarf preceptory, it being the only Dublin
house of the Templars. Brothers in general were entitled to become free of the
guilds in towns and engage in trade, the profits to be channelled into their
mission to the Holy Land. To facilitate this commitment, the Knights took an
interest in ports in order to build up shipping links to their principal fleets
based abroad in France and Britain. Control over the maritime reaches of the
Clontarf district was important for the order, not just for the fisheries, but also
for the dues paid by vessels putting in at the pool of Clontarf, one of the
deeper anchorages in Dublin bay, perhaps one of the 'appurtenances' of the
vill of Clontarf referred to in Henry II's grant of the 1170s. That there was a
mercantile community at Clontarf by the mid-thirteenth century is attested by
the enrolment of two merchants of Clontarf in the Dublin guild merchant,
Patricius Faber de Cluntarf in 1243–4, and Rogerus, son of Ricardus Blund de
Clontarf, in 1261–2. By the early fourteenth century, then, two communities
had grown up on the manor of the Knights, one based largely on farming and
centred on the Castle, and the other drawing its livelihood from fishing and
trade, located along the shoreline in the lea of the headland of Clontarf.[16]

15 Mac Niocaill, 'Suppression of the Templars in Ireland', 188, 214–15; for the context see
Murphy and Potterton (eds), *Dublin region in the Middle Ages*, pp 326–45. 16 Philomena
Connolly and Geoffrey Martin (eds), *The Dublin guild merchant roll, c.1190–1265* (Dublin,

By the early 1300s Clontarf had emerged as a settled and thriving manorial community centred on the Knights' castle and church, with a growing coastal hub. With their extensive freedoms from the payment of tolls at markets and fairs and tithes to the church, the Knights evidently prospered there, as the value of their preceptory at its dissolution compared favourably to the more lucrative Templar manors in England. The Knights, the fully-fledged members of the order, would have been familiar figures as they rode through the district of Clontarf, dressed in their white robes with a red cross, and sporting long beards. They differed from conventional knights in their having taken vows of poverty, chastity and obedience, and in their dedication to the defence of the Christian church. Most may have been from a noble and Anglo-Norman background, such as Robert de Pourbriggs, who was among those interrogated at the trial of 1308.[17] In addition to the lay members, there were priests or chaplains of the order who served the local church and ministered to the spiritual needs of the community as the parish of Clontarf. The Templars had the right to appoint the parish priest or rector, and they gathered in income from tithes on the manor. A curate could be hired to serve the parish, being paid a small stipend. The church appears to have been well maintained and equipped, according to the inventory of 1308. Among the liturgical books listed were a French language version of the gospels, a missal, a troper, a psalter, a manual (or guide to sacramental practice) and a gradual (a service book). The sacral vessels included two chalices of which one was gilt, and two altar vessels, one of which was silver, and there were also sacred vestments, such as chasubles, albs, amicts (or copes), stoles, maniples and girdles.[18]

Not surprisingly, given the wide-ranging privileges and exemptions enjoyed by the order, the Templars were to become the objects of jealousy on the part of religious and secular rivals. In Ireland, these generous perquisites included commercial rights such as freedom from customs levies, relief from feudal and military services, and extensive local jurisdiction over trade and justice, as well as independence of diocesan ecclesiastical supervision. Originally granted by state and church to bolster the Knights' capacity to wage war in the Holy Land, the range of privileges was eventually seen to place them at an unfair advantage *vis-à-vis* other landlords and orders, and the result was a series of cases in the courts of the land, including the dispute in the 1280s which involved a testing of their royal grants to Clontarf and all of their other manors.[19] Meanwhile, the trend of international events turned against the Templars, as the order was ousted from the Holy Land with the loss of its

1992), pp 8, 29, 80, 104; White (ed.), *Extents of Irish monastic possessions*, p. 89; Evelyn Lord, *The Knights Templar in Britain* (London, 2002), pp 119–21.   17 Wood, 'Templars in Ireland', 337, 353; Nicholson, *Knights Templar*, pp 113–36.   18 Wood, 'Templars in Ireland', 334, 354; Mac Niocaill, 'Suppression of the Templars in Ireland', 215.   19 Wood, 'Templars in Ireland', 334–6, 342; Sweetman (ed.), *Cal. docs Ire*, iii, pp 328–33; James Mills et al. (eds), *Calendar of the justiciary rolls of Ireland*, 3 vols (Dublin, 1905–56), i, p. 409.

headquarters at Acre in 1291, leaving them more vulnerable throughout Europe to the jealous claims of their religious and secular enemies. The Templars' most implacable foe was King Philip IV of France, who determined on their destruction, motivated by jealousy of their perceived wealth and resentment at their exempt status within the French church. On foot of a damning list of charges drawn up against the order, which was accused of practising heresy, idolatry, immorality and impiety, Philip ordered the arrest and imprisonment of all of the Knights in France in 1307, and, having been subjected to torture, most confessed their guilt. After a series of show trials, a number of Knights, including the master of the order, Jean de Molay, were condemned to burn at the stake for heresy. Philip put pressure on Pope Clement V, who was a Frenchman and moved the papal court to Avignon in 1309, to order the arrest and trial of the Knights Templar in territories throughout Europe.[20]

Reluctantly, King Edward II decreed that the Knights Templar in England and Ireland be rounded up in early 1309. On 3 February the Irish Knights were arrested and imprisoned in Dublin Castle, and their lands and possessions confiscated. Local juries were deputed to make inventories of properties of the Knights, including those of Clontarf, while the captive knights were subjected to a comprehensive interrogation about their beliefs and practices. The detailed listing and valuing of all the goods and estates of the order, which was drawn up, revealed that the Knights lived modestly, and were not possessed of fabulous riches, as suggested by wild rumour-mongers. In the case of Clontarf, the total value of all items, including agricultural produce and livestock, as well as books and sacral vessels, amounted to £125 17s. 7d. This rendered Clontarf the third-most valuable of the Knights' preceptories in Ireland, after Clonaul and Kilclogan.[21] Meanwhile, the interrogation of the individual Knights, who were not subjected to torture as in France, did not elicit confessions, and a trial before forty inquisitors, the vast majority of them clerics, took place in St Patrick's cathedral in 1310. In an effort to substantiate the charge that the Templars disrespected the Mass, allegations of a lack of decorum during the celebration of the liturgy at Clontarf were aired. Hugh de Lummour, a Dominican friar, claimed that, having often been at Clontarf preceptory, he witnessed William de Warecome, a Templar, turn his face to the ground at the consecration of the Mass, not caring to look at the elevated host. And William de Botiller alleged that, when he turned to exchange a kiss of peace with the brethren after the Agnus Dei, one of them refused the gesture, averring that the Templars did not care for peace. That the community at Clontarf was not particularly warlike is attested to by the presence in the inventory of the house of three swords![22]

20 Nicholson, *Knights Templar*, pp 196–226.   21 Lord, *Knights Templar in Britain*, pp 191–4; Mac Niocaill, 'Suppression of the Templars in Ireland', 188, 214–16, 224.   22 Wood,

Despite the flimsiness and unreliability of the case against the Knights Templar in Ireland and elsewhere, the order was formally dissolved by the pope in 1312, and its possessions granted to the Order of the Hospital. Among the forty inquisitors who examined the Templars in Ireland were two people bearing the epithet, 'Kilmaynan', Roger and Ralph. These were leading members of the Knights Hospitaller of St John of Jerusalem, whose Irish headquarters was at Kilmainham to the west of Dublin. Roger, whose surname was Outlaw, became prior of the order in 1315, and it was under his headship that the Irish lands and houses of the Templars were finally vested in the possession of the Hospitallers. Thus one suspects that the ambitious Roger relished the task of proving the case against the Templars, as his own order, still very much in favour with the monarchy of England, was poised to benefit from their suppression. In the case of the manor of Clontarf, however, there was a hitch: on 26 December 1310, it had been granted by the crown in fee simple to Richard de Burgh, the earl of Ulster, who was father-in-law of the earl of Cornwall, the favourite of King Edward II, and formerly the king's lieutenant in Ireland. De Burgh apparently surrendered the estate to the crown, as, by 1320, the Knights Hospitallers had got full proprietorial rights to Clontarf and the other eight former Templar preceptories in Ireland. The surviving Templars had been released from prison and were given a pension of two pence per day for the remainder of their lives.[23]

* * *

The Knights Hospitaller of St John, who took over the preceptory and manor of Clontarf as a going concern, had been founded in Jerusalem towards the end of the eleventh century, with the functions of caring for the sick and providing hospitality to pilgrims. Later, their role extended to doing battle with the Moslem armies of Mediterranean Europe and Latin Syria. The order, whose international headquarters had moved to Rhodes in 1309, was divided into sections called langues or tongues according to the language of its members, the Irish priory coming under the English langue at Clerkenwell in London. Besides providing finance for the campaigns of the Knights in the east, through the payment of responsions, or annual sums due from each priory, many western European langues transformed their duty of hospitality into the corrody or pension system, which provided long-term lodging to individuals in exchange for money or favours.[24] Like their counterpart military order, the

---

'Templars in Ireland', 350–4; Mac Niocaill, 'Suppression of the Templars in Ireland', 215. **23** Nicholson, *Knights Templar*, p. 230; Wood, 'Templars in Ireland', 352–3, 358–60, 365; Eithne Massey, *Prior Roger Outlaw of Kilmainham, 1314–41* (Dublin, 2000), p. 21. **24** See Karl Borchardt, Nikolas Jaspert and Helen Nicholson (eds), *The Hospitallers, the Mediterranean and Europe: festschrift for Anthony Luttrell* (Aldershot, 2007); Gregory O'Malley, *The Knights Hospitaller of the English langue, 1460–1565* (Oxford, 2005).

Hospitallers had been closely associated from the start with the settlement and expansion of the Anglo-Normans in Ireland. After the acquisition of the Templars' properties, the Hospitallers had seventeen houses in Ireland, with their Irish headquarters at Kilmainham. In the political sphere, the priors frequently filled some of the most important posts in the government. In the localities, the Hospitallers fostered the development of farming and village communities on their manors, and, through their priests and chaplains, ran the parish churches associated with their houses. Profits from agricultural and other economic activities contributed to the payment of responsions for the crusading goals of the order. The Hospitallers' obligation of hospitality was exercised through frankhouses in the towns, and the corrody system in their preceptories at Kilmainham and elsewhere. Through their extension of retirement facilities to some of the most prominent people in the late medieval lordship, the Hospitallers occupied an influential position in the fourteenth century.[25]

The valuable manor of Clontarf on the north side of Dublin Bay offered opportunities for the Hospitallers to consolidate their position close to the seat of the colonial government. As a thriving agricultural entity, the manor promised a profitable income in the form of produce and rentals of lands. Under the new management of the prior of Kilmainham, most of the manorial lands came to be farmed out to substantial gentry figures in the fourteenth and fifteenth centuries. The parish church retained its privilege of exemption from archiepiscopal supervision, and could be looked to for revenues and also as a means of ecclesiastical patronage. Importantly for a commercially attuned institution, the Hospital's ownership of maritime Clontarf brought with it lucrative fishing rights and also fees from vessels anchoring in the pool of Clontarf.[26] As well as a source of income from the lands of the manor with its parish rectory, and of fishery and shipping rights, the Hospitallers saw Clontarf as a place of patronage in the form of corrodies to residential pensioners of the order. While the most prestigious forms of corrody were those awarded to grandees and dignitaries at Kilmainham, most of the Clontarf corrodians, to judge by the contracts of maintenance, were of a humbler category, being free servants and tradesmen of the brothers, with occupations such as janitor, butler, carpenter and cook. These were granted dining rights at the table of the craft-workers there, and an annual gift of robes and clothing, appropriate to their stations. In addition, if they became too debilitated to attend the dining-hall, these retainers were entitled to be served a daily ration of bread and beer in their rooms, as well as adequate helpings of meat and fish from the kitchen.[27]

25 C. Litton Falkiner, 'The hospital of St John of Jerusalem in Ireland', *Proceedings of the Royal Irish Academy*, 26, C (1906–7), 275–317; O'Malley, *Knights Hospitaller*, pp 227–55. 26 Falkiner, 'Hospital of St John', 292. 27 Charles McNeill, 'The Hospitallers at Kilmainham and their guests', *Journal of the Royal Society of Antiquaries of Ireland*, 24 (1924), 15–30; *Registrum de Kilmainham, 1326–39*, ed. Charles McNeill (Dublin, 1932),

For the Knights Hospitaller, the decades after the absorption of Clontarf and the other Templar properties into their network witnessed the strengthening of the Irish priorate within the international organization. The high-profile career of Prior Roger Outlaw of Kilmainham, who also held the preceptorship of Clontarf, raised the standing of the order in Ireland, through his significant role in the government of the Irish lordship, and his adept patronage of key figures through the corrodial system down to his death in 1341. Thereafter, there may have been a period of economic and social decay due, principally, to the great cataclysm of the Black Death in the late 1340s. The plague must have affected the Dublin houses and estates of the Hospital very severely, inflicting as it did a huge rate of mortality of perhaps up to 14,000 on the city and its environs during the visitation. It was a catastrophe for the whole of the Hospitaller order from which it may have recovered only very slowly. A series of English-born priors attempted to rule the Irish institution after 1350 in adverse circumstances, thus alienating the Knights who were born in Ireland of English roots. An opportunity for the assertion of a sharpened sense of English-Irish identity came during the Great Western Schism after 1377, which divided western Christendom in two, the followers of the Rome-based popes and the adherents of the competing popes resident in Avignon. Contrary to the policy of the English langue of the Hospital, which supported the French-based pope and his approved grand master, the Irish-born Knights gave their obedience to the Roman pope who sustained an alternative grand master. After the healing of the split, the Irish priory established in 1410 the right to elect to its headship a person of Irish birth, and this position persisted as a rule until the end of the fifteenth century.[28]

The construction of a stone bridge over the Tolka in 1313, due to the benevolence of John le Decer, a former mayor of Dublin and builder of many public utilities for Dublin, established a reliable artery of communication between the village of Clontarf and the neighbouring city. The bridging of what had been 'a dangerous charge' of water allowed for agricultural and other produce to be conveyed with greater efficiency between the two locations. Contact by sea was also improved during the fourteenth and fifteenth centuries, as Clontarf harbour grew as a trading and fisheries station under the Hospitallers' jurisdiction. The Knights at Kilmainham had resorted to the law to defend their rights to fishing on the upper Liffey against the intrusion of the citizens of Dublin, and, on acquiring Clontarf preceptory, they were no doubt just as committed to protecting their fishing privileges at the estuary of the river, including the tithes of salmon. The development of a harbour at Clontarf was aided not only by the local fishing industry but also by the proximity of the deep pool of Clontarf for the anchoring of ships unable to

pp 9, 11, 26, 32, 44, 73, 84, 85, 93, 125.   28 Massey, *Prior Roger Outlaw*, pp 42–56; Charles Tipton, 'The Irish Hospitallers during the Great Schism', *R.I.A. Proc.*, 69, C (1970), 33–43.

navigate the silted-up channels of the Liffey. In 1358–9, a royal licence was issued for the export of wheat from the ports of Dublin, Dalkey and Clontarf, and by the 1370s, there was a fleet of local and visiting ships at Clontarf substantial enough to attract royal and municipal supervision. While exports continued to be licensed in the early fifteenth century, it is not clear to what extent port facilities had been developed at Clontarf. In 1416 the departing lord lieutenant of Ireland, John Talbot, embarked at Clontarf for England. During the following decades, merchants from Clontarf were engaged in trade with Chester, although their cross-channel commerce was overshadowed by that from a number of north Dublin ports including Howth and Malahide.[29]

To judge by a statute of 1455, the inhabitants of Clontarf and its Fingal hinterland were under siege from the king's 'Irish enemies' and 'English rebels', that is, the Gaelic clans and the Gaelicized English, who constantly raided the 'liege' or loyal people north of the Liffey. To prevent these attacks, a law was passed requiring that the fords along the river be suitably blocked, and that barriers be built between the city bridge and Clontarf Island, in the estuary of the river Tolka. Yet the ethnic composition of the district may not have been homogenous, as the openness of Clontarf to the sea and trading routes may have attracted settlers from a fairly wide catchment area. Certainly the bulk of the names mentioned in connection with the knightly orders are Anglo-Norman. Templars at Clontarf included the Knights Walter, Galfridius and Henricus, William de Warecombe and Robert de Pourbriggs, the chaplain, William de Botiller, and the more menial corrodians of the Hospitallers, William Geraud, William Gay, John Poytroun, Thomas Palfreyman and William de Ossyngham. Among the community of agricultural folk, fishers and traders, it is likely that there was a fusion of ethnic strains. The earliest known merchants of Clontarf were Patricius Faber (who assumed as his surname his avocation as craftsman), and Rogerus, son of Ricardus Blund (whose father's blond hair may have designated him by name). Interestingly, a Richard le Blount of Arklow petitioned for lands in Clontarf about 1320 in exchange for those he held in Killester and Raheny. Again, the composition of the fishing community is unknown, though among the names of salmon-takers at the Liffey estuary in 1473 were John Ullester and Denis Gaffney, both possibly of Gaelic origin. Not until the sixteenth century do we have definite evidence of a Gaelic element among the local population, when in the 1560s labourers employed in the quarrying of stone had names such as Rory

29 'The book of Howth' in Brewer & Bullen (eds), *Cal. Carew MSS*, vi, p. 130; A.E.J. Went, 'Fisheries of the River Liffey: notes on the corporation fishery up to the dissolution of the monasteries', *RSAI Jn.*, 83 (1953), 166–8; McEnery & Refaussé (eds), *Christ Church deeds*, no. 304, pp 91–2; Charles V. Smith, *Dalkey: society and economy in a small medieval town* (Dublin, 1996), p. 48; *Rotulorum patentium et clausorum cancellariae Hiberniae calendarium*, ed. Edward Tresham (Dublin, 1828), pp 105, 209, 212, 213; Wendy R. Childs, 'Irish merchants and seamen in later medieval England' in *Irish Historical Studies*, 32 (2000), 24.

Manchan, Donough O Schell, Art O Lennan and Connor O Bregane. They may have been recent migrants to the Dublin region from Gaelic territories, but the existence of an indigenous Irish population is confirmed in the survey of the mid-seventeenth century, when, albeit in the wake of great social upheaval, the proportion of those of English race to those of Irish on the manor of Clontarf was 57 to 43.[30]

For almost a century after 1410, the Irish Hospitallers were ruled by a series of Irish-born priors of English background, making full use of the privilege of electing natives conferred upon them at a recent chapter general.[31] Their ascendancy harmonized with the general self-reliance of the old colonial community of the emergent Pale who were anxious to assert their capability of governing the lordship during a period of weakened English rule. The interplay of institutional administration and national politics is reflected in the headship of the order of members of the leading aristocratic families – Butler, Fitzgerald and Talbot – during a fifty-year period down to 1460. While not immune from the prevailing internal factionalism which was rife among these noble families, the priors were staunch in their withstanding of outside intrusion from all quarters – church, state and international Hospital in Rhodes and England.[32] The history of the preceptory of Clontarf in the fifteenth century mirrored this pattern of increasingly vexed relations between the Kilmainham priorate and outside sources of power. As successors to the Templars in holding the rectory of Clontarf, the Knights had the rights to the tithes of the parish and also the nomination of a curate to serve the parishioners. During one of several clashes between the diocese of Dublin and the Knights Hospitallers over ecclesiastical jurisdiction, the prior of Kilmainham had, in 1367, successfully defended his full temporal and spiritual powers due to the exemption of the order's parishes, including Clontarf, from archiepiscopal visitation. But the involvement of the priors in the political struggles of the mid-fifteenth century could be detrimental to the preceptory of Clontarf and other Hospitaller houses: in 1440, as a result of Prior Thomas Fitzgerald's brothers' kidnapping of the deputy lieutenant of Ireland, Clontarf and all of the other Hospitaller properties in Ireland were seized by the crown.[33]

30 *Statutes and ordinances, and acts of the parliament of Ireland, King John to Henry V*, ed. H.F. Berry (Dublin, 1907), ii, pp 314–15; Gilbert (ed.), *Chartul. St Mary's*, i, pp 173, 231; Connolly and Martin (eds), *Dublin guild merchant roll*, pp 8, 29, 80, 104; Wood, 'Templars in Ireland', 337, 350–4; McNeill (ed.), *Registrum de Kilmainham*, pp 9, 11, 26, 32, 44, 73, 84, 85, 93, 125; Philomena Connolly, 'Irish material in the class of ancient petitions in the Public Record Office, London', *Analecta Hibernica*, 34 (1987), 12; McEnery & Refaussé (eds), *Christ Church deeds*, no. 304, p. 92; Raymond Gillespie (ed.), *The proctor's accounts of Peter Lewis, 1564–5* (Dublin, 1996), pp 50–1; R.C. Simington (ed.), *The civil survey AD1654–1656, vol. VII, county of Dublin* (Dublin, 1945), p. 176.   31 Tipton, 'Schism', 42–3.   32 O'Malley, *Knights Hospitaller*, pp 231–2, 238–42; Art Cosgrove, *Late medieval Ireland, 1370–1541* (Dublin, 1981), pp 29–46.   33 Falkiner, 'Hospital of St John', 293–4; NLI, MS 4839, 'Notes from the archives of the order of St John of Jerusalem at Valetta, 1350–1560',

Although apparently restored to its possessions soon afterwards, the order suffered dislocation in its organization in the later fifteenth century due to the political and economic imbroglio in which the priors were caught up. Because of the difficulties encountered in raising the Irish contribution to the order in Rhodes, the Irish Hospital leased out many of its estates, including Clontarf, to farmers for low rents. Thus, in 1473, Robert Dowdall, the chief justice of the common bench, was mentioned as having held the farm of the manor of Clontarf from the Hospital for a number of years. Dowdall's son, Thomas, was also granted the farm of the manor in 1484 by the prior of Kilmainham, James Keating, who was also preceptor of Clontarf. Just over half a century later, at the time of the dissolution of the religious houses in 1540, the manor and rectory of Clontarf were on lease to Thomas Plunkett, a gentleman of the Pale, who also possessed lands in Killester and Coolock. Under this lease, Plunkett would have had the right to nominate the curate to the parish church of Clontarf. It is probable that the Knights may have chosen to ally themselves through these leases with members of the Pale gentry possessed of contiguous properties in the vicinity of north Dublin. The most substantial neighbouring landlords to the manor of Clontarf in the later fifteenth century were the St Lawrences, barons of Howth, who had acquired the lands of Killester through marriage to the White family, and from whom Thomas Plunkett, a relative of the St Lawrences, held the latter estate.[34]

The contumacy of the Irish Hospitallers to both crown and langue reached a climax during the priorate of James Keating from 1459 to 1494. A political ally of the ascendant Kildare Fitzgeralds, Keating, who became preceptor of Clontarf, was removed as prior of Kilmainham in 1482 for failing to pay the Irish responsions, but was still apparently resident in Clontarf in that year. We know this because his English-born replacement, Marmaduke Lomley, recounted a frightening ordeal 'at a village called Clontarf, two miles asunder from the city of Dublin':

> Frere James [Keating] set on me with a number of people, a horseback and a foot, and there, violently putting hand on me, took me thither and kept me like a prisoner until the time that, by compulsion of dread in my life, I must have delivered as pleased him all manner of evidences, writings, bulls and letters which I brought with me into Ireland.

s.a. 1461, 1482, 1494; *Rot. pat. Hib.*, p. 262.   **34** O'Malley, *Knights Hospitaller*, pp 236–7, 242n; White (ed.), *Extents of Irish monastic possessions*, p. 89; F.E. Ball, *Howth and its owners* (Dublin, 1917), p. 54; McEnery & Refaussé (eds), *Christ Church deeds*, nos, 1191, 1250, pp 239, 252; note that Patrick White, baron of the exchequer, who is referred as a gentleman of Clontarf, was the father-in-law of Katherine, the natural daughter of the last prior of Kilmainham (and Viscount Clontarf), John Rawson: Mary Ann Lyons, 'John Rawson' in *ODNB* [http://www.oxforddnb.com/article/23199: viewed 20 April 2011].

Despite being excommunicated in 1484, Keating pursued Lomley to the point of his death in prison.[35] To Keating's defiance of the church and Hospitaller authorities was added lese-majesty in the crowning of Lambert Simnel, the Yorkist pretender to Henry VII's throne, as king of England and Ireland in Dublin in 1487. Having been pardoned for his part in that action, Keating's support for a second pretender, Perkin Warbeck, in the early 1490s, resulted in his final removal as prior, and the monarch used the opportunity of Poynings' parliament in 1494–5 to curb the autonomy of the Irish Hospitallers. Lamenting the alienation of the extensive properties of the order in Ireland by a succession of 'evil disposed priors' and their selling off of precious items and relics, including 'a piece of the holy cross', the legislators proceeded to pass a measure ensuring that in future all priors elected should be of English birth, and be 'sad, wise and discreet'.[36]

From the 1490s until its dissolution in 1540, the order of Hospitallers in Ireland, including its Clontarf preceptory, was ruled by successive English-born priors, the most notable of whom was John Rawson, who succeeded to the position in 1514. Under the management of the latter, the priory of Kilmainham was drawn into the mainstream of the Irish administration, Rawson serving in a number of state offices, including the treasurership and lord deputyship of Ireland. His successful service of King Henry VIII, however, gave rise to tensions with his superiors in Rhodes, who noted the comparative neglect of the spiritual welfare of the community of Hospitallers, membership of which had fallen to about a dozen by the 1530s.[37]

There is little evidence concerning Clontarf in the final decades of Hospitaller management. Evidently the manor and rectory were leased to laymen, who supervised the farming of the estates and the rectory of the parish. In 1540, when the order was dissolved, an enquiry into the properties at Clontarf found that Thomas Plunkett, a gentleman, held the lease for £26 13s. 4d. per annum. The main buildings of the preceptory comprised a hall, two towers, a kitchen and other farm buildings, as well as a dovecote. Of the eighty-eight acres of demesne land, eighty were devoted to arable faming, and the rest were pasture, meadow, underwood and scrub. Two designated farms, Busshells Farm and White Farm, contained 131½ acres, of which 114 were arable, and there were another 140 acres in various outfields. Besides the 360 acres of farmland, there were twenty-four wooded acres of Priorswood at Coolock. The farming village comprised twenty cottages, for which the tenants paid £4 per annum, contributed a day's sowing of crops on the demesne and presented the lord with a hen worth 3s. and 4d.[38] The manorial lord was also

35 O'Malley, *Knights Hospitaller*, pp 242–4; *Registrum Octaviani: the register of Octavian de Palatio, archbishop of Armagh, 1478–1513*, ed. Mario Sughi (Dublin, 1999), no. 185, pp 185–6. 36 O'Malley, *Knights Hospitaller*, p. 246; Falkiner, 'Hospital of St John', 304.
37 O'Malley, *Knights Hospitaller*, pp 248–51. 38 White (ed.), *Extents of Irish monastic*

entitled to a fee of 4*d*. from every ship's captain putting in and casting anchor in Clontarf Pool off the shore. Evidence of naval activity in the nearby harbour may be gleaned from references to local mariners. A dramatic encounter between two Breton ships, probably commanded by pirates, and barks of Westchester and Dublin in the port of Clontarf in 1514 resulted in many deaths, including that of Thomas Beket the elder who died of gunshot wounds. More routinely, in June 1526, merchants of Dublin were charged with illegal exportation of labourers and failure to import bows.[39]

In 1540 the preceptory of Clontarf was dissolved, and its possessions, along with those of the other Hospitaller houses, passed into the ownership of the crown. It was Prior John Rawson who was the agent for the surrender of Clontarf that brought an end to the military orders' proprietorship. As Henry VIII asserted his power over church and state in Ireland in the 1530s, Rawson had proved to be a loyal servant. The king had determined to face down the challenge of the Fitzgeralds of Kildare to his plans for reforming the Irish administration and sent a large army to defeat the uprising of 'Silken' Thomas Fitzgerald, Lord Offaly, in 1534. Despite his previous attachment to the Geraldine party in Ireland, and notwithstanding the dangers to English-born officials in Dublin, Rawson took part in the defence of the city against the Kildare attackers, and subsequently facilitated the arrest of the uncles of Thomas at Kilmainham. Rawson's loyalty to the crown ensured his acquiescence in the scheme to close all of the religious houses in the English parts of Ireland, but not before he had provided for the future of himself, his family and friends by contracting long leases of many Hospitaller estates on attractive terms. This occurred in the context of the king's religious reformation. When the dissolution finally occurred, he wangled a huge pension of 500 marks (£166 13*s*. 4*d*.) from the crown. He also gained the title Viscount Clontarf and chose to spend his last years in retirement at the north Dublin preceptory, thus underscoring the prestige of the Clontarf holding. His greatest coup, perhaps, lay in his engineering of a grant of the entire manor, with all its economic and religious perquisites to Matthew King, a royal servitor in Ireland, and husband to Rawson's niece, Eleanor. Thus the manor and estates of the Knights at Clontarf passed to a close connection of the last prior, and they remained in the King family for over a hundred years.[40]

* * *

possessions, p. 89.   **39** Alan J. Fletcher, 'The earliest extant recension of the Dublin Chronicle' in Bradley et al. (eds), *Dublin in the medieval world*, p. 400; Margaret C. Griffith (ed.), *Calendar of inquisitions formerly in the office of the chief remembrancer of the exchequer*, Irish Manuscripts Commission (Dublin, 1991), pp 15–16, 22.   **40** O'Malley, *Knights Hospitaller*, pp 252, 254–5; Lyons, 'John Rawson'.

The legacy of the military orders to Clontarf in the post-medieval period was substantial, and the manor was to become a highly-prized possession over which several prominent landholders were to contend in the early modern period. The Templars had fostered an efficient agricultural system there which was continued by the Hospitallers. Thus at the time of the dissolution of the latter, the manor had a thriving agrarian economy. Due to the maritime concerns of the Knights, there was also a busy port at Clontarf. No doubt Clontarf manor and fisheries contributed significantly to supplying the corn and fish markets of Dublin in years of local surpluses in the late medieval period. As international orders, overseas communications were important to the Knights, and shipping through the harbour appears to have increased in volume down to the earlier sixteenth century. This is suggested by the value of the farm of the anchorages of mariners putting in at Clontarf, yielding 4*d*. per skipper in 1540, by which time it was an important pool in the inner bay for larger ships unable to navigate the sand-barred harbour of Dublin, and also a harbour of transit to the English and Welsh ports. Under the auspices of the Knights, the parish of Clontarf developed in the twelfth and thirteenth centuries, and became part of the Dublin diocesan structure, although outside direct archiepiscopal jurisdiction. Finally, Clontarf was drawn into the European cultural mainstream by the Knights Templar and Hospitaller who brought with them not only the social and economic forms of organization of the Anglo-Normans but also the ideals of crusading Christendom to the northern shores of Dublin Bay.

Rivers and industry, life and death: archaeological excavations on the Coombe bypass and Cork Street realignment, Dublin

ALAN R. HAYDEN

INTRODUCTION

In the early 1990s Dublin City Council (DCC) – or Dublin Corporation as it then was – long planned to widen Cork Street and also to drive a new road through the area south of the Coombe to bypass the two right-angled turns where Cork Street met Ardee Street and it in turn met the Coombe (fig. 7.1). In 1993 archaeological test trenches were opened on the limited number of sites then in the possession of DCC and accessible for archaeological assessment (*Excavations 1993*, no. 64). From March 2000 to March 2001 further assessments were undertaken as sites became available along the route (*Excavations 2000*, no. 253; *2001*, no. 372). Eight sites, where test trenching revealed surviving features, were archaeologically excavated in 2001 in advance of the road construction (fig. 7.1). The features uncovered ranged in date from the twelfth to nineteenth centuries.

THE EXCAVATED SITES

The sites were generally excavated in a sequence from west to east (although there were some exceptions) and the description of the excavations follows this direction.

Site 1: The Coombe (figs 7.2 and 7.3)

On the south side of the Coombe modern ground level sloped upwards to the south. In the lower-lying area close to the road, mechanical clearance revealed that groundwater lay above the level of medieval deposits (fig. 7.3), probably due to the blockage of its natural flow by modern buildings on the north side of the road. This meant that hand excavation would have been both difficult and costly. As a result, the medieval deposits on the lower-lying end of the site were covered with a geotextile and the road was constructed on top of them.

The only thing of note revealed here was a line of poorly-preserved wooden water pipes that ran south from the Coombe street-front to a post-medieval well in Site 2 (see below).

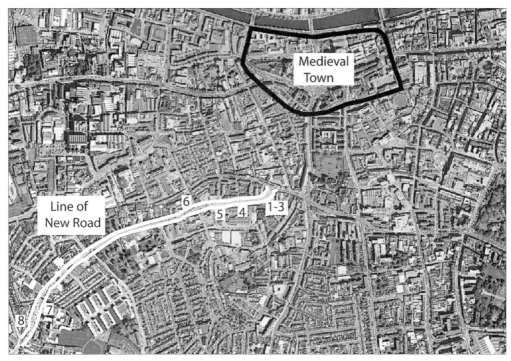

7.1 Aerial photograph (*c*.2001) showing location of roadworks and excavated areas in relation to the medieval town

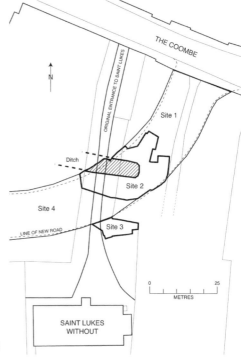

7.2 Location of Sites 1–3

7.3 Site 1, high groundwater level visible at north end of site, looking north

Site 2: The Coombe to Weavers Street (figs 7.2 and 7.4–7.6)

On the higher ground to the south, an area measuring 25m north–south by 36m east–west was hand excavated (fig. 7.4) but even here the excavation of some features deeply cut into subsoil was hampered by water inundation.

Medieval features
Ditch The earliest feature uncovered was a large counterscarp ditch (61), which ran east–west across the western half of the site (fig. 7.4). It extended westwards beyond the area of the road-take and its east end terminated about mid-way across the site. A shallow, medieval silt-filled gully (57) continued its line eastwards. The ditch measured 6m in width and up to 1.3m in depth and its basal fill consisted of compact grey-brown stony silt, which contained later twelfth-/early thirteenth-century pottery. A linear slot trench (60), possibly a palisade trench, containing a few large and small postholes, ran parallel to the ditch one metre to its south. Its east end terminated at the same point as the ditch. The slot trench measured from 0.8 to 2.0m in width at its top and was 0.3 to 0.5m in depth. It had a consistent channel, which measured about 0.75m in width at its base. The basal fill of the trench consisted of compacted grey-brown silty clay, which contained a few sherds of later twelfth-/early thirteenth-century pottery.

Grain-drying kiln and floor (figs 7.4–7.6) In the thirteenth century a keyhole-shaped grain-drying kiln (74) was built in the base of the ditch on top of its earliest fill (figs 7.4–7.6). The flue and drying chamber were stone-lined

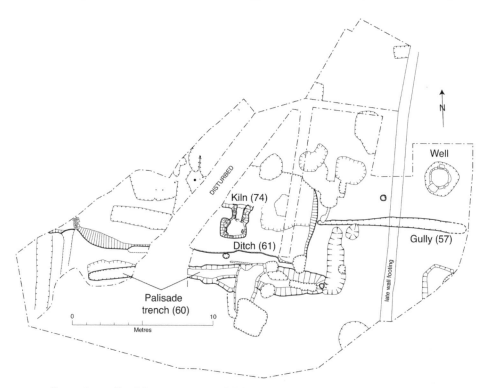

7.4 Site 2, the medieval features uncovered. The cuts and pits uncovered range in date from the later-medieval to post-medieval periods.

but only a maximum of three courses (0.4m) in height of the walling survived due to the disturbance caused by the later cultivation of the area. The drying chamber measured one metre across while the flue measured 0.45 to 0.5m in width and 1.2m in length. Originally, there may have been stone-walled returns at the outer ends of the flue, which would have retained the mound of soil that built up around the kiln but no stonework survived. The base of the flue was heavily oxidized and a thick layer of carbonized material (82) covered both it and the drying chamber. The burnt matter spread out northwards from the kiln for a distance of up to three metres.

A thin layer of soil (81), 15mm in thickness, overlay the burnt deposits emanating from the kiln. A compact clay floor (80) lay on this material north of the kiln. The floor measured 4.2m north–south by at least 3.2m east–west; its west side was truncated by modern disturbance. The floor appeared to have roughly straight edges, suggesting it may have lain inside some form of retaining structure or even a building; only a few large stones at its north-east corner survived of what might have been the enclosing wall. There were several small stakeholes in the structure and thin layers of carbonized material (77 and 75) lay on the floor.

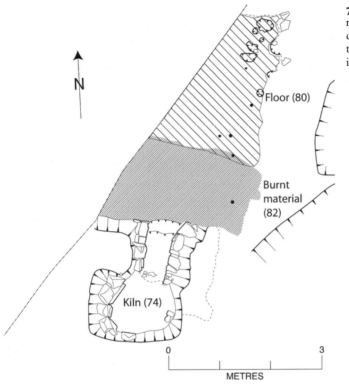

7.5 Site 2, the
medieval grain-
drying kiln and
the building to
its north

N

Floor (80)

Burnt
material
(82)

Kiln (74)

0   3

METRES

Ditch fills and cultivated soils The ditch and kiln were infilled with layers of cultivated soil (73 & 63), which were part of the base of a thick build-up of cultivated soil (64/65/67) that covered subsoil over the entire site. The cultivated soil survived to a maximum thickness of 1.5m at the northern end of the excavated area but thinned as it extended uphill to the south. No layering was obvious in it and small fragments of pottery, floor tile, animal bone, metal objects and shells were scattered evenly through it. Thirteenth-/fourteenth-century pottery occurred in its base, while there was a mixture of medieval and sixteenth-/seventeenth-century pottery in its upper levels. This is typical of similar material uncovered elsewhere in and around Dublin. The presence of medieval pottery and line-impressed floor tiles suggests that rubbish (probably largely organic in nature) from the town was being spread on the fields. Several shallow cuts and pits dug from within the cultivated material showed in subsoil across the site.

Post-medieval features (fig. 7.4)
A number of substantial pits, which contained seventeenth-century and later pottery, were cut into the surface of the cultivated soils. The exact cut level of these features was unclear due to the truncation of their tops by later

7.6 Site 2, the medieval grain-drying kiln

disturbance. The truncated 2.8m-deep base of a stone-lined well survived at the eastern side of the site. A wooden pump stick surviving in it consisted of a squared oak baulk 1.92m in length and 0.3m square in section. The top was bound with an iron band. The timber had a 100–130mm diameter round central channel. The latter was blocked with a wooden bung at the lower end of the timber and a 50mm diameter hole was bored though one side of the timber into the central channel 150mm from its lower end. The stump of a second wooden pipe, which was inserted into the upper end of the central channel, also survived. A line of wooden pipes led from the well northwards into and across Site 1. The well was infilled with rubble which contained eighteenth-/ nineteenth-century pottery. After excavation the well was left intact beneath the new roadway. It was infilled with gravel and a pipe was inserted into it leading water away into a new surface-water drain.

Site 3: The graveyard of St Luke's church (figs 7.2 & 7.7–7.9)

A small part of the north-east corner of the graveyard north of St Luke's church was excavated, as the footpath at the side of the roadway encroached on it (figs 7.2 & 7.8). Due to the higher level of the graveyard, compared to the ground to its north, the south side of the excavated area was stepped inwards, in roughly one-metre increments, as excavation progressed downwards in order to avoid the collapse of the loose graveyard soil. As a result the lowest levels of the south side of the site were not excavated.

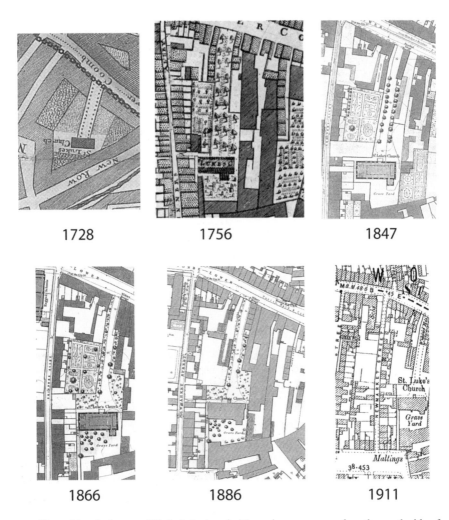

7.7 Site 3, historical maps of St Luke's church. None show a graveyard on the north side of the church.

Phase 1 – medieval cultivation
The earliest features uncovered consisted of a number of east–west-aligned cultivation furrows in subsoil beneath a covering of cultivated soil. The furrows were all roughly parallel and measured up to 100–120mm in depth and up to 200mm in width.

Phase 2 – later sixteenth / early seventeenth century
Part of a brick-walled cellar, cut into the cultivation soil, survived at the north-west corner of the site (fig. 7.8). To avoid undermining the surviving part of

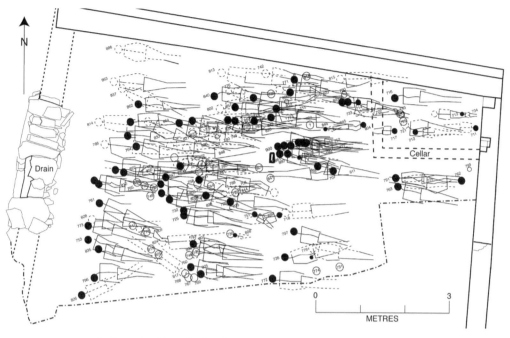

7.8 Site 3, burials and other features uncovered in St Luke's graveyard

the north wall of the graveyard, which was built over the demolished and infilled remains of the cellar with little or no foundations, the interior of the cellar was not fully excavated.

Phase 3a – early graveyard (fig. 7.8)
A deep stone-lined drain underlying the east side of a gravel pathway was revealed cutting into the medieval cultivated soil at the west side of the site. The disturbed base of the drain was also noted in Site 1. The remains of large tree stumps survived flanking the sides of the pathway. These we know from descriptions of the site were elms and they are depicted on the 1728 and 1756 maps (figs 7.48 & 7.49) on both sides of the approach road to the church from the Coombe to the south. This road predated the church and a plan from the late 1670s (fig. 7.47) shows that it originally ran right up to Newmarket. The building of St Luke's church commenced in 1714 and it was opened in 1716. Interment of burials in the graveyard continued until 1922 and the church was finally closed in 1975. The north wall and the northern end of the west wall of the graveyard were later additions, probably built sometime between 1728 and 1756 (see below). The foundation trench of the later northern graveyard wall truncated two burials (nos 813 and 815) showing that the graveyard existed before thess lengths of wall were built. Additional burial contexts (nos 810–812, 814 and 816–866) could be included in this early group as they either

Alan R. Hayden

7.9 Site 3, burial (860) associated with the only surviving grave marker

predated the two burials cut by the wall, or more tentatively, lay at a similar or lower level to the burials cut by the wall. All these burials were aligned east-west, most with head to west and all were in wooden coffins. These burials are likely to have been interred after 1716 and sometime before 1756 (see below) and, if all belong to this phase, they demonstrate how rapidly the graveyard began to fill up with burials. There was no evidence of burial north of the line of the later graveyard wall and so it would appear that the original northern boundary of the graveyard lay roughly on the same line as the later wall.

Phase 3b – later graveyard (figs 7.8 & 7.9)

The east wall of the graveyard had a vertical joint in it, four metres from its northern end. The northern four metres of this wall was a later addition and was of different construction and was narrower in width than the rest of the wall. This later section of walling was of one build with the northern wall of the graveyard. The new north wall is not shown on Brooking's map of 1728 (fig. 7.48) but is shown on Rocque's map of 1756 (fig. 7.49). The use of the graveyard continued after the construction of the new walls. The burials uncovered all lay to the east of and respected the line of the pathway leading to the church (fig. 7.8). The burials also gradually overwhelmed and hid the remains of the early brick-walled cellar. A total of 109 burial contexts (burial nos 701–809) belong to this later fully enclosed phase of the graveyard. The skulls of the latest burials lay less than 100mm below the modern ground level. All the burials were aligned east–west, most with the heads to the west but there were several laid with head to east. All appear to have been interred in coffins. Only one grave marker, a simple uninscribed block of stone was uncovered (fig. 7.9). A minimum number of 157 individuals was represented in the excavated burial contexts and by disarticulated bone. Laureen Buckley examined and recorded the human remains *in situ* and later in the laboratory. A full catalogue, description and analysis of the human remains uncovered, which is too large to reproduce here, is contained in the archive report.

Site 4: Weaver Street (fig. 7.1)

The area that was formerly Weaver Street was cleared to below the level of subsoil, probably in the 1970s or 1980s when the adjacent Corporation housing was built and nothing but modern material survived here. A 16.8m-long line of poorly preserved wooden water pipes leading from a brick-lined well to a cellar was the only thing of note that survived, as it lay well below the original ground level. Only one complete pipe (which measured 3m in length) survived. The pipes measured 100–120mm square in section and where it could be determined they were oak timbers. A pump stick was set in the well where the pipeline originated. The pump stick measured 280mm square and survived to a length of 1.05m. It had a central 100–110mm diameter bore, which was closed with a wooden bung at its base. A 100mm by 50mm rectangular hole, located in the side of the pump stick 150mm above its base, allowed water to enter the central bore. The well was backfilled in the nineteenth century.

Site 5: Brabazon Row (formerly Duck Lane and Cuckold's Row) (figs 7.10–7.13)

Between Weaver and Ardee Streets archaeological deposits and features only survived modern disturbance at the west side of the former Brabazon Row. An area measuring 24m north–south by 21m east–west was mechanically cleared and then hand excavated there (fig. 7.10). The future Brabazon Row in shown on a late 1670s plan of the development of Newmarket area (fig. 7.46) and buildings are shown on it on the 1728 and 1756 maps (figs 7.48 & 7.49). However, the earliest houses and archaeological material surviving here dated to the later eighteenth and nineteenth centuries.

Phase 1 – later eighteenth-/early nineteenth-century houses (fig. 7.11)
The earliest features uncovered consisted of three semi-basemented houses fronting onto the west side of Brabazon Row. The two southernmost buildings

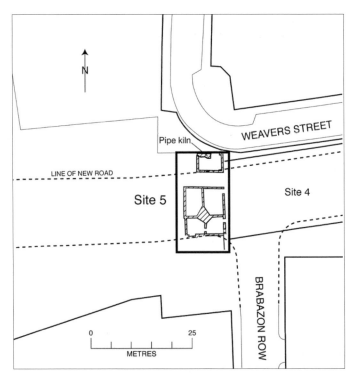

7.10 Site 5, location of excavated area, earliest surviving houses and clay-pipe kiln

(2 and 3) were built together side by side while a third (14) stood isolated from them further north. These buildings are not those shown on Rocque's map of Dublin of 1756 (fig. 7.49) but are shown on the Ordnance Survey maps of 1849 and 1866. The external walls of the houses were composed of mortar-bonded stone and brick and measured *c*.0.5m in width and stood to a maximum height of 1.46m. The front doorways of the two southernmost houses and the base of a front window of the southernmost house survived. The two southernmost houses were divided into two rooms, front and back, by an internal stone and brick wall. The dividing walls each incorporated two corner fireplaces, one in each room. The buildings were floored with beaten earth but there were small areas of stone cobbling inside the doorways of the two southernmost houses. The wall dividing the rear gardens of the two southern houses survived for a length of 4m.

Phase 2 – mid-nineteenth-century clay-pipe kiln (fig. 7.12)
After the semi-basement of the northernmost house was filled with rubble a clay-pipe kiln (15) was built inside its ruins. Clay-pipe debris was also found on the floors of the other two houses. Only a small part of the stoke pit (25) of

the kiln lay within the boundary of the excavated site. The remainder of the kiln lay under and north of the modern wall that defined the northern side of the site and so could not be excavated. The stoke pit (25) measured 1.1m in depth and was lined with mortared brick walls, all a single brick in thickness. Its base consisted of rammed clay. A thickness of 35mm of lenses of ash and clay containing clay-pipe fragments and kiln waste (26) filled the base of the stoke pit. A hard, oxidized clay floor survived on the top of this material. The east wall of the stoke pit appears to have been rebuilt (24) before this floor was inserted. The new wall was composed of a single thickness of mortared brick. Several of the bricks used were almost vitrified and covered with slag and probably came from the firing chamber of this or another kiln. The rebuilt stoke pit measured 0.75m in depth. A thickness of 100mm of pink ash accumulated in its base before it was infilled with a thick homogenous deposit (16) of grey ash, which contained clay-pipe fragments, kiln waste, slag, kiln furniture, iron nails and bricks. A

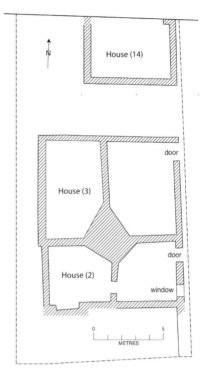

7.11 Site 5, the late eighteenth- or early nineteenth-century houses on the west side of Brabazon Row

possible fuel store lay immediately south of the stoke pit. It consisted of a sub-rectangular brick-walled pit that had a stone and brick base. It measured 1.8m in length, 0.9m in width and survived to only 200mm in depth. It was partly infilled with clay-pipe waste and ash (22) before its east wall was rebuilt, about 0.5m inside it original line. The smaller pit was finally infilled with the same material (16) used to fill the stoke pit. These two phases of usage echo those noted in the stoke pit suggesting the rebuilding of both structures may have taken place contemporaneously. A small pit (19) of uncertain function lay to the south-east of the fuel store and there was a compact clay floor (21) covered by thin deposits of soil (20 and 23) south and east of the fuel store. A brick-lined trough lay west of the old west wall of the former house that stood in this plot. The trough utilized the stump of the wall as its east side, the other three sides were of mortared brick. The trough was of rectangular shape 1.25m in length by 0.5m in width. Its west side was sloped and it measured 0.4m in depth. It did not contain clay-pipe debris but is similar to features uncovered in proximity to the clay-pipe kilns excavated at Francis Street, Dublin (Walsh, *Excavations 1997*: 132). A layer of grey soil containing clay-pipe and kiln

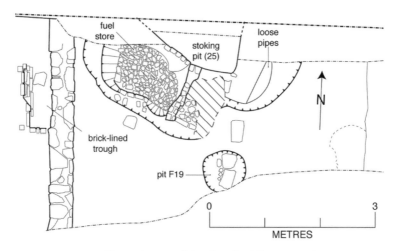

7.12 Site 5, the part of the clay-pipe kiln excavated

fragments (11) overlay the infilled kiln and much of the northern end of the site. Two residual coins of George III were found in this material. Over 4,260 intact or large fragments of clay-pipe bowls and hundreds of small bowl fragments, in addition to thousands of stem fragments, were uncovered during the excavations. Joe Norton examined the clay pipes. The pipes produced in the kiln were all of similar type with only minor variation in size. They had plain bowls, most of which had milled rims. Many were decorated on the spur with a shield copied from the Arms of Gouda (which appears on imported Dutch pipes), others with a wheel motif, a cloverleaf or a simple dot in circle. A number of nineteenth-century clay-pipe bowls, which were manufactured elsewhere, was also found among the kiln debris. Several of these were stamped and decorated and those, which were datable, were made between 1845 and 1865. This dating is consistent with the type of pipes produced in the kiln.

Phase 3 – mid- to late nineteenth-century houses (fig. 7.13)
After the kiln went out of use the remains of the houses were demolished, their semi-basements were infilled and a row of new houses was built. These houses survived very poorly and are those shown on the 1886 Ordnance Survey map. Some of the walls of the older houses were reused as footing for the walls of the new buildings. The new houses were of equal length and measured 8.5m from front to back. They were, however, of differing widths. The full width of the southernmost house did not survive but it reused the sidewalls of the previous houses on the plot. Extending northwards the next house measured 7.7m in width. Again the full width of the northernmost house was not uncovered. These houses were also divided into two rooms, front and back, by an internal wall, which in the case of the northernmost house included two back-to-back

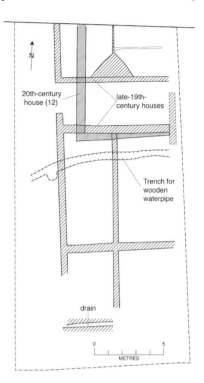

7.13 Site 5, the later nineteenth-century houses

corner fireplaces (27). Remains of floor joists and some floorboards survived in the northernmost house. An east–west aligned wooden water pipe (10) was laid beneath the central house before it was built. The backfill of its construction trench contained some clay-pipe debris. Ash and clay-pipe debris from the former kiln were also used to fill the foundation trenches (1, 7, 8 and 9) of the rear (4) and north (6) walls of the larger house.

Site 6: Ardee Street (formerly Crooked Staff) (figs 7.14–7.20)

Test trenching revealed the survival of archaeological material on the west side of Ardee Street. There, an area measuring 16m by 16m (Site 6) was mechanically cleared and then hand excavated (fig. 7.14). The main features uncovered consisted of two branches of the Abbey Stream, which crossed the site from north to south, and part of a large millpond.

Medieval river channels (figs 7.15–7.19)
A thin layer of water-deposited gravel (217) overlay subsoil suggesting that a wide and shallow stream or overflow existed here from early times. No finds were uncovered from this material. Two irregular channels cut through this deposit and crossed the site roughly from north to south (figs 7.15 & 7.16).

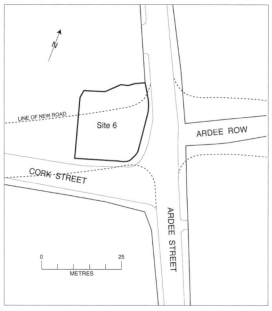

7.14 Site 6, location of excavated area

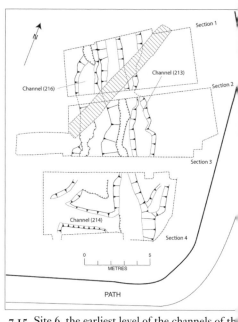

7.15 Site 6, the earliest level of the channels of th Abbey Stream

7.16 Site 6, the earliest levels of the channels of the Abbey Stream, looking south

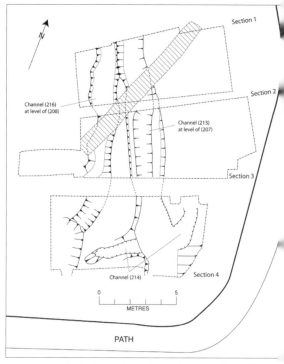

7.17 Site 6, the latest level of the channels of the Abbey Stream

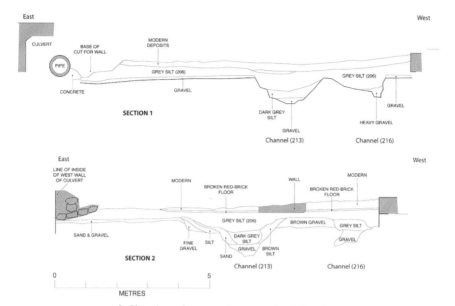

7.18 Sites 6, sections 1 and 2 across the Abbey Stream

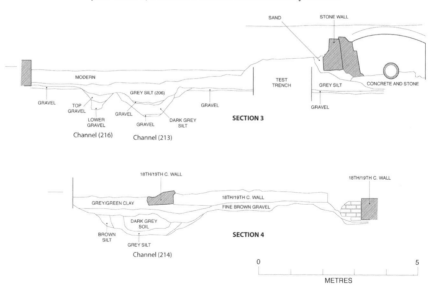

7.19 Site 6, sections 3 and 4 across the Abbey Stream

The eastern channel (213) was the larger and deeper and measured up to 4m in width and 1.3m in depth. The western channel (216) measured up to 3.5m in width and 1.2m in depth. At the south end of the site the western channel turned to the south-west and also divided into two branches (216 & 214); the eastern of the pair led into the eastern channel. The channels were unlined and filled with silt and sand. A narrow irregular channel or series of small pools

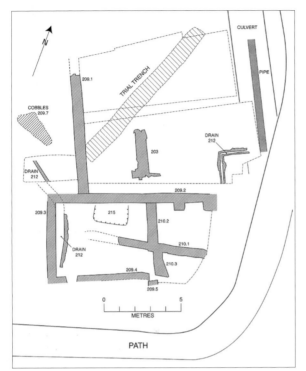

7.20 Site 6, post-medieval walls and features

survived in the base of both channels. These were filled with coarse sand and gravel. The main channels silted up and were recut by water many times over a long period. The earliest layers of silt (213, 214 and 216) in the channels contained a few sherds of medieval pottery, while the latest levels (207 and 208) (fig. 7.17) contained seventeenth-century pottery, shoes and glass. The water also frequently flooded a larger area and deposits of silt (206) up to 0.5m in thickness covered the whole site (figs 7.18 & 7.19). This larger area of water was part of a southern side of a large millpond, the north end of which, Franc Myles (2009) later excavated (fig. 7.45).

Post-medieval development (fig. 7.20)
The Abbey Stream was confined into an open-topped and stone-walled culvert at the east side of the site (201/205) in the later seventeenth century. This culvert is shown on Rocque's map of 1756 (fig. 7.49). The new culvert allowed the area west of the Abbey Stream to be developed. Layers of clay and gravel (211) were deposited to fill in the millpond and stabilize the ground. A small redbrick-walled building, of which only the west wall (203) survived was the earliest structure erected on the site (fig. 7.20). It had a floor of brick fragments in compacted clay (204) and was of late seventeenth-century date. Above this, more extensive foundations of two stone buildings (209 and 210), brick drains (202 and 212) and a cobbled yard (209.7) survived. These latter

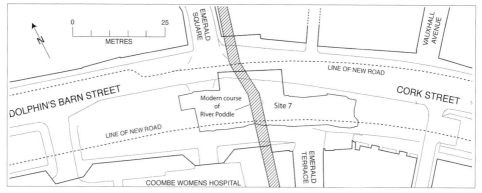

7.21 Site 7, location of excavated area

buildings correspond to those shown on Rocque's map of 1756 (fig. 7.49). Several drains led from under the buildings into the Abbey Stream culvert. At a later stage, probably in the 1820s, the river culvert was partly re-walled and roofed over with a brick vault, allowing buildings to be constructed right up to the eastern street front of the site. The remains of these modern buildings were the final features uncovered on the site. In more recent times the stream was further confined within a concrete pipe laid inside the culvert. The stream still flowed through this pipe when the site was opened for excavation and hence had survived on this site for over 800 years.

Site 7: Cork Street at Emerald Terrace (figs 7.21–7.34)

Along Cork Street subsoil generally lay but a few centimetres below the modern ground surface and no archaeological features or deposits survived until the vicinity of Emerald Terrace and the Coombe Hospital was reached. There an area measuring a maximum of 50m east–west by 12m north–south on the south side of Cork Street was mechanically cleared and hand excavated (fig. 7.21). An additional area was subsequently excavated beneath the surface of Cork Street itself after the construction of the new carriageway on the previously excavated part of the site. The area first excavated was bisected by a modern mass concrete culvert, which could not be removed as it still functioned as a sewer. Many modern services also cut through the site and as they were all still live, somewhat hampered excavation. A complex series of medieval watercourses survived on the earliest levels of the site.

Phase 1 – late twelfth-century Poddle river and millpond (figs 7.22, 7.23 & 7.25)
The earliest features uncovered consisted of the remains of a large pond and two medieval water channels (fig. 7.22). The pond (426/413) measured up to 350mm in depth and occupied all but the extreme east end of the western half of the site (fig. 7.23). Its base had a flat stony surface; the finer clay particles in

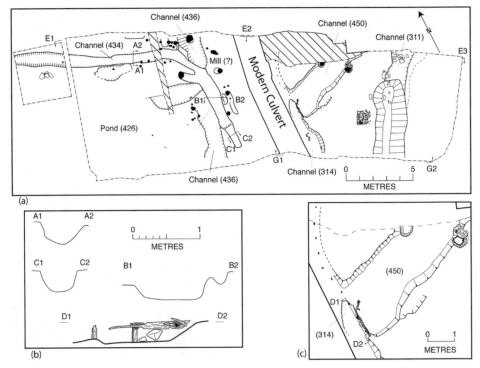

7.22 Site 7, (a) the medieval millpond, possible mill and watercourses, (b) sections of watercourses and (c) detail of timber-revetted watercourse (314)

the subsoil having been washed out leaving the stones exposed. There was a shallow north–south extending gully (436/439) in the base of the east side of the pond. It measured up to 1.2m in width and 300mm in depth. It was completely filled by a layer of light grey silt (438), which also filled much of the base of the pond to a depth of about 100mm. The silt contained a few sherds of later twelfth-/thirteenth-century pottery

Part of another watercourse (450) extending from south-west to north-east was the earliest feature revealed east of the modern mass-concrete culvert. The watercourse measured up to 2.4m in width and up to 0.7m in depth. Only a five-metre length of it survived, as it was truncated at both ends by later water channels. The base of the channel fell slightly as it extended northwards indicating the direction of the water flow. A pair of large posts, one on either side of the water channel, could have held a sluicegate. The channel was filled with grey-brown silt that contained some organic material and a few sherds of later twelfth-/thirteenth-century pottery.

Phase 2 – thirteenth-century channel and possible mill (figs 7.22, 7.24–7.26)
A steep-sided gully (434) was cut into the base of the pond and the early water channel west of the modern culvert. It ran northwards before turning to the

23 Site 7, the (434) water channel and associated postholes, possibly the remains of a mill, looking south-west

7.24 Site 7, the base of the millpond looking east. The modern concrete Poddle culvert is visible crossing the site in the background, behind the west wall of the late seventeenth-century culvert

west at the north end of the site. This channel measured 0.8 to 1m in width
and up to 0.9m in depth. A number of large postholes and stakeholes,
suggestive of a building, possibly a mill, lay on both sides of the south–north
aligned part of the water channel. Four postholes (437.1–4), regularly spaced
*c.*1.2m apart, lay on a parallel line close to the east side of the north–south
extending part of the channel. There were also traces of a shallow slot and a
number of smaller stakeholes between the larger postholes. The two central
postholes had corresponding postholes (437.5–6) on the western side of the
channel three metres away. There were also a number of smaller stakeholes on
this line and a number of further stakeholes straddled the turn of the channel
further north and west. Near the revealed west end of the channel, part of a
low drystone wall (417) lay on its north side. Grey-brown organic silt (434)
that contained many small twigs and sherds of thirteenth-century pottery filled
the north–south element of the water channel. The top of the channel, the
postholes associated with it and the pond, were then gradually infilled by layers
of silt (430/433, 427, 425, 424 and 418). There was another shallow water
channel in the top of these silt deposits at the south-west corner of the pond. A
distinctive blue-grey silt (429) filled it.

Phase 3 – later-medieval watercourses (figs 7.22 & 7.25–7.26)
Two further watercourses were constructed east of the modern culvert. The
westernmost, (314), was timber-revetted and ran from south-east to north-
northwest. Only its eastern side, which was retained by a timber revetment
(313), survived; the western side lay beneath the later concrete culvert. The
channel survived to a maximum width of 2.6m and a depth of less than
200mm. The surviving revetment consisted of small rectangular section
vertical timbers, each measuring up to 80 by 45mm across. They were spaced
0.5m apart and each was pointed and driven into the underlying subsoil to a
depth of up to 550mm. They supported, on their east side, timber planks
horizontally laid on their narrower edges. Nine of the uprights survived but
only a few fragments of the horizontally-laid planks remained in the area
where the watercourse cut through the silt fill of the earlier one. The shallow
base of the watercourse was filled with very compacted silt overlain by very
hard and compacted fine gravel. The uppermost fills consisted of soft black
highly organic silt (301 & 303), which contained post-medieval finds.
    Further to the east a second, but unlined, water channel (311) was revealed
(fig. 7.22). It ran from south to north. It continued to exist long after the
timber-revetted watercourse had gone out of use. In its final phase it flowed
into another watercourse (Phase 4) built running east–west at the north end of
the site. The junction between the two lay right at the edge of the excavated
area. The unlined watercourse measured up to 1.0m in width and 300mm in
depth and was filled with grey silt (312) that contained post-medieval
metalwork and pottery. The watercourse continued to flow across the site for a

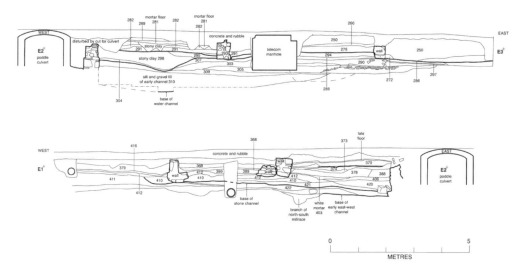

7.25 Site 7, east–west section at north end of site (see Fig. 7.22 for location)

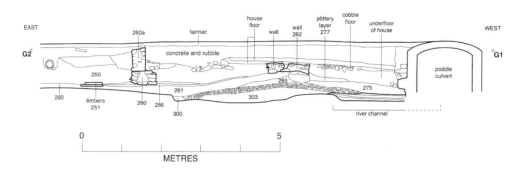

7.26 Site 7, east–west section at south end of east half of site (see Fig. 7.22 for location)

long period with its channel silting up and being recut (308, 300, 302 and 297). To its west, layers of stones, clay and brick fragments (299, 296 and 285) were thrown down to raise the ground level. These sealed the surviving top of the timber-revetted watercourse and interleaved with the layers of silt, which built up in the watercourse. At times the silt spread out over much of this area of the site showing that the stream often overflowed its banks and flooded the surrounding area.

Phase 4 – later-medieval/post-medieval watercourse (figs 7.27–7.28)
A stone-revetted watercourse (408/306) was constructed running east–west along the northern side of the site, about a half metre north of the edge of the pond (figs 7.27 & 7.28). It was uncovered on both sides of the modern concrete

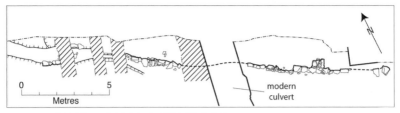

7.27 Site 7, the surviving part of the late medieval east–west-running watercourse (408)

7.28 Site 7, the surviving part of the late medieval east–west-running watercourse (408), looking east. The disturbance caused by modern services is evident

culvert. Its northern side did not survive. A drystone wall set in a 1.2m deep trench, defined its southern side. The wall, however, only survived to a maximum of two courses (0.5m) in height. It ran on a slightly curved line. A single square posthole (423), which measured 200 by 80mm across and which contained the rotted stump of a post, stood in the watercourse immediately inside the line of the wall. The watercourse deepened significantly from west to east showing the original direction of the water flow. It was gradually filled with a succession of layers of gravel, silt and sand (435, 422, 410 421 and 412) west of the modern culvert and by layers of sand, gravel and silt (310, 309, 305, 303 and 307) to its east. The uppermost layer of silt (418) filling the pond was the same deposit as the uppermost fill (412) of the east–west-running stone-lined watercourse and so the two may have finally silted up at the same time.

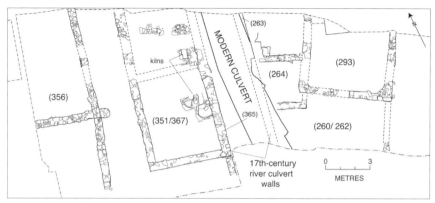

7.29 Site 7, the late seventeenth-century Poddle culvert and buildings

7.30 Site 7, the late seventeenth-century Poddle culvert beneath the old roadway; the only point where both of its sides survived.

Phase 5, level 1 – late seventeenth-century north–south river culvert and first houses (figs 7.29 & 7.30)

After the silting up of the east–west-running stone-lined watercourse a large stone-walled culvert was constructed running from south-southeast to north-northwest across the middle of the site. Its west side survived relatively intact but the later construction of the mass-concrete culvert largely removed its east side. The two sides of the culvert only survived together in the small area later

excavated beneath the roadway, as here the modern concrete culvert turned
sharply to the west. There the interior of the stone-walled culvert measured
3.6m in width and the springings of a stone arch survived over it places. The
sides of the watercourse were retained by mortar-bonded limestone rubble
walls (365 and 263a) built in deep construction trenches (432 and 304a). The
walls measured up to 0.46m in thickness and had projecting footings on both
sides. The western wall survived up to 1.0m in height above footing level. The
eastern wall only survived intact at the northern end of the site, where it stood
to a height of 0.5m above its footing. A spill of mortar (304) filled the base of
the construction trench of the eastern wall of the culvert. A coin of William
and Mary, dated 1690, was found in the rubble (298) dumped in to fill this
construction trench. The construction trench (432) of the western wall was
infilled with rubble (421) and redeposited subsoil (420). In the main area
excavated it was not possible to reveal much of the interior of the culvert due
to the presence of the later mass-concrete culvert and ESB cables.

Once the river had been constrained into its new channel the area was
developed for housing. First clay, stones, gravel and refuse containing broken
bricks and roof tiles (419, 414, 407, 406, 286, 289 290, 292, 294 and 295) were
introduced and spread out to raise the ground level on either side of the
watercourse. West of the culvert two separate stone buildings were erected.
The easternmost (351/367) of these utilized the west wall of the river culvert
as one of its side walls. The north wall of the building lay outside the area
available for excavation. The uncovered part of the building measured 10.8m
in length and 4.2m in width internally. Its external walls measured 0.5 to 0.7m
in width, survived to a maximum height of 0.5m and were composed of
roughly coursed undressed limestone blocks bonded by sandy, yellow mortar.
The mortar used was noticeably inferior to that used in the river culvert walls.
A stone wall (415), which survived as only a few mortared blocks of stone,
divided the building into two rooms, north and south. The second building
(356) was erected 2.4m to the west. The north and west walls of this structure
lay outside the excavated area. Its uncovered part measured 7m in length by
4m in width internally. Its 0.4 to 0.5m wide walls were composed of identical
masonry and mortar to that used in the walls of the other building. Thin slicks
of mortar (403, 405, 398, 399 and 416) from the construction of the two
buildings survived on the underlying levelling material all over the site. The
buildings must have had suspended floors, as there were no laid floors inside
them. None of the walls survived to a great enough height to display the offsets
that would have held the wall plates.

East of the culverted river a large detached stone building (293) was erected.
Its north wall lay outside the area available for excavation. The building
measured 5.2m in width and at least 4m in length internally. Its walls, which
varied from 0.5 to 0.6m in width, were composed of roughly coursed undressed

limestone blocks bonded by sandy yellow mortar. Inside the building, a floor composed of a thick layer of silty clay (276) capped by a thin hard layer of mortar survived. A coin of Charles II dated 1683 was found in this material. Ash (266) that spread over much of the interior of the building covered a mortar-based hearth (279) built against the centre of south wall of the structure. A hard surface was created outside and west of the building. Mortar fragments and spills (281 & 288) from the construction work covered it.

Phase 5, level 2 – dereliction, kilns and temporary buildings
The housing development does not appear to have been a great success, as the houses west of the culvert were abandoned and deposits of silt, loam and clay (404, 389, 387, 379 and 394) containing rubble and bricks were dumped all over the area west of the culvert. Three small brick- and stone-walled, coal-fired kilns (385, 386 and 402) were built amid the ruins of the house (351/367) and a well (393) was dug outside the south wall of the western house. The well measured 0.8 to 0.9m in diameter and at least 1.2m in depth. The house was then demolished and the demolition rubble (396, 400, 384 and 388) was spread over the site. A small stone-walled building was built over the remains of the northern end of the demolished house. Only its southern wall (380) and a small part of its hard clay floor (378), which was covered with ash (374), survived.

East of the river, a series of layers of silt and clay (284, 291 and 282) built up between house (293) and the river culvert before new buildings were added to the west and south sides of the house (293). A two-roomed building (264) was built to the west side of the house (293) butting up against its west wall. The north wall of the new building again lay outside the excavated area. The building measured 2.5m in width internally. The southern room measured 2.8m in length internally and the northern one measured at least 1.4m in length internally. The walls of the building, which were laid in clear trenches (287), measured 0.5m in thickness and were composed of identical stonework and mortar to that used in the earlier house. No floor level survived in the building but the mortared stone base of a fireplace remained in the south-west corner of the northern room. Another building was added to the south side of (293). A breach was made in the centre of the southern wall of (293) linking the new and old buildings. Only the footings of the east and north–west walls (260 and 262) of the new structure survived; the southern wall lay outside the area available for excavation. The walls of the new building were also of similar masonry to that used in the main house. The uneven ground inside the building was levelled by the deposition of stones, brick rubble and clay (278 and 261). The floor, however, did not survive. Construction debris (268 and 253) covered by a layer of organic refuse (275) filled the angle between the west side of the new building and the culvert to its west.

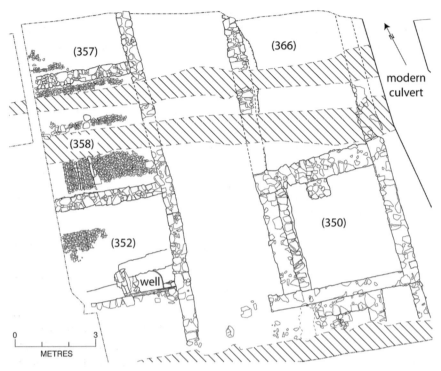

7.31 Site 7, the early eighteenth-century buildings west of the Poddle culvert

7.32 Site 7, the early eighteenth-century buildings west of the Poddle culvert, looking north-west. The gritty material between the walls is part of the extensive pottery dumps.

Phase 6 – early eighteenth-century houses (figs 7.31 & 7.32)

West of the river the temporary buildings and kilns were demolished and a layer of pottery fragments in a matrix of ash (368/256/373/445) was spread over much of the site. This layer varied in thickness from only a few millimetres to up to 300mm and was introduced clearly to raise and level the ground and improve drainage. Some 53,420 sherds of pottery were recovered from this deposit in addition to about forty fertilizer sacks of tiny fragments. The pottery was the waste from a kiln.

Three new buildings were erected over the demolished remains of the eastern building and three other small buildings replaced the western house. First a small building (350) was erected at the centre of the east side of the site. The south wall of the underlying house appears to have been reused as its south wall and the west wall of the culvert as the footing for its east wall. The excavated part of the building measured 3.8m square internally. Its west and north walls, which were laid in clear foundation trenches (354), were composed of roughly coursed undressed limestone blocks bonded with hard white mortar and they measured up to 0.8m in width. A small centrally set mortared stone buttress or firebase stood against the inner face of its north wall. The building was truncated to below its floor level by modern disturbance. The northern wall of the second new building (366) lay outside the area available for excavation but its west wall which was set in a clear foundation trench (372) was revealed. The west wall of the river culvert was also used to foot its east wall. The building also butted up against the north wall of building (350). This second building was the same width as that to its south but measured at least 6m in length internally. Remains of the floors of this building survived but only at its north end where a 60–80mm-thick layer of very compacted green clay (371) was revealed. Patches of ash lay on it. A further layer of looser clay (370) that contained pottery sherds, identical to those that immediately underlay the building, covered it. This material seems to have been introduced to further raise the floor level of the building as a hard mortar floor was laid directly on top of it. Another small structure was added to the south side of the central house. This structure was built very poorly and only a small part of it lay within the area available for excavation. It had 0.6m-wide stone walls bonded with hard white mortar. No traces of floors survived within it. A small patch of mortared stone paving (369) survived against the outside face of the west wall of building (350). It overlay the pottery rich deposits and was the only surviving part of the surface of the lane between the eastern and western lines of buildings.

The old western building was demolished and rebuilt as a row of small houses fronting onto the lane to their east. The western side of these buildings did not survive. Either two small houses or one large two-roomed building was erected at the north. The east wall of the earlier house was reused as the footing for the east wall of the structure/s. Two new east–west-aligned walls

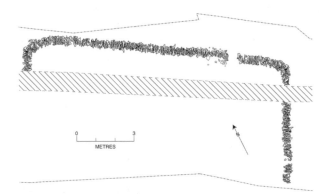

7.33 Site 7, the horn core-filled drain at the east end of the site

7.34 Site 7, detail of the horn core-filled drain. The horn cores were carefully placed in the drain in two rows with their points facing inwards.

were erected within the old building. Only the drystone footings of the two new walls (357 and 358) survived. They measured 0.5m in width and were set 4m apart. A patchy and poorly-preserved cobbled floor survived in the northernmost house or room and a well-laid cobbled floor (362) in the other. A layer of ash (361) covered the cobbles. This room/building was refloored with a layer of hard mortar (360). Another small building (352) was erected to the south. It abutted the end wall of the other two houses but had new east and south walls. The building measured 2.6m in width internally from north to south. The building was erected with its south wall partly overlying the earlier well. The top of the southern half of the well was spanned with heavy timbers, to carry the wall. Stone walls set in trenches (381, 382, 383, 395, and 377) were built around the well retaining the water in a rectangular tank. After a period the well was infilled with silt and rubble (382) and the building was floored with cobbles and a very compacted layer of clay (376). The stone-lined base of a hearth or oven (363) survived in the south-east corner of the building. East of the river culvert contemporary structures were also erected. The west wall of the southernmost building there was pulled down and a thick deposit of ash containing large quantities of pottery sherds including many wasters (277) was deposited over most of the site. The pottery was identical to the large deposits encountered at a similar level west of the culvert. A small building with a drain beneath it was erected over the remains of the eastern building. The drain (267) led into the river culvert to the west. The drain was partly timber lined with reused and poorly-preserved barrel staves. The partial remains of a short length of a second stone-lined (280) drain survived and entered the culvert close by to its north. The north-east corner of a small stone-walled building survived on top of the drain. The building appears to have abutted the culvert to the west. It was aligned at right angles to the culvert and measured 2.8m in width and at least 1.4m in length (north–south) internally. A further deposit of pottery (252), similar to the larger (277) dump, was dumped inside the building.

Horn core-filled drain (figs 7.33 & 7.34)
No pre-modern buildings survived in the area east of Emerald Terrace. Subsoil there gradually rose upwards as it extended eastwards and was less than 0.3m below modern ground level at the east end of the site. An unusual feature was uncovered in this area. This consisted of a shallow trench that described a large rectangle 14m east–west by at least 7m north–south. The trench measured less than 200mm in depth and up to 600mm in width and was filled with two rows of cattle horn cores (265/451), laid with their points facing inwards.

Phase 7 – later eighteenth-/nineteenth-century features
East of the culvert, the stump of the east wall (260) of the southern building appears to have been reused as a footing for a later building, whose north wall ran eastwards from the south-east corner of the (293) building. Little survived of its walls. Inside the building several large timber planks surrounded by sawdust (251) suggested it might have been a sawmill or carpentry workshop.

Phase 8 – modern features
The 1.8m wide, mass-concrete culvert (359) that contained the Poddle river was built in the early twentieth century; a coin of George V was found in the backfill of its construction trench. It was the final watercourse built here marking the end of an 800-year period of the construction of watercourses and

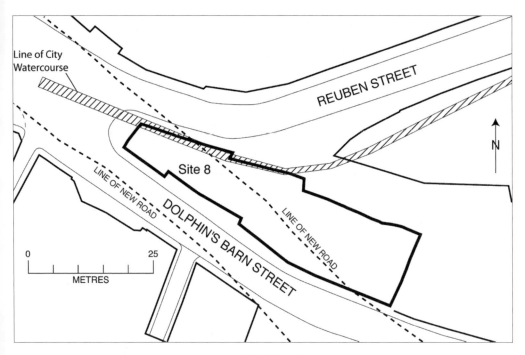

7.35 Site 8 location

millraces on the site. The remains of the floors (269 and 271) of modern
buildings, which had once stood on the site, survived east of the culvert. Such
was the degree of modern levelling that no remains of these houses survived
west of the culvert.

Site 8: Dolphin's Barn Street/Reuben Street (figs 7.35–7.43)

No archaeological features survived beneath the modern roadway over the
remainder of its line westwards. However, where it met Reuben Street, the new
roadway took in land that formerly lay north of the old road and there
archaeological features and deposits were revealed. An area measuring a
maximum of 60m east–west by 15m north–south was mechanically cleared and
hand excavated to varying degrees (fig. 7.35). The northern edge of the
excavated area was stepped in as the ground to its north lay at a much higher
level than that of the site itself. Three main phases of use of the area were
evidenced (fig. 7.36). These consisted of: (1) a silt-filled pond with two later
seventeenth-century drains in its base; (2) an extensive early eighteenth-
century tannery at the centre to the west end of the site; and (3) foundations of
houses dating from the later eighteenth century.

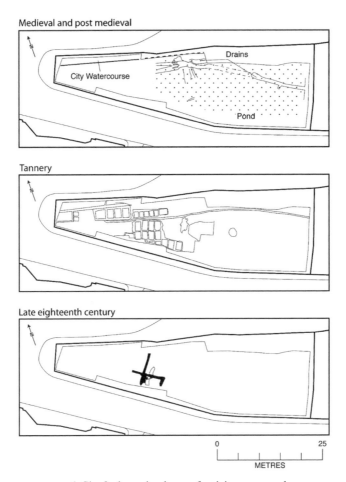

7.36 Site 8, the main phases of activity uncovered

Phase 1 – medieval features (figs 7.36 & 7.37)

The thirteenth-century city watercourse flanked the northern side of the site. However, its interior could not be excavated for safety reasons. It was defined by mortared stone walls that are likely to have been of seventeenth-century date and the excavations revealed nothing of the original medieval channel. A large hollow or pond (652) that measured up to 0.5m in depth lay at the centre of the site. It was not possible to determine whether it was of natural or man-made origin. Its western edge was uncovered but its eastern side lay outside the excavated area. Later activity truncated its southern side and its northern side lay outside the north side of the site. Two drains (649/653 and 642) survived in its base. A thin layer of organic material (631) lay in the west side of the bottom of the pond and thick layers of grey and light brown silt (635) filled it.

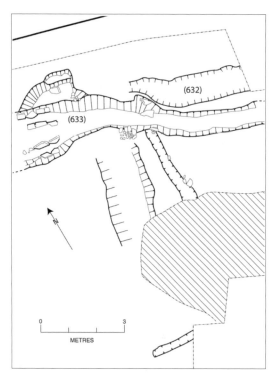

7.37 Site 8, features pre-dating the tannery at the centre north of the site

Two east–west-extending drains (632 and 633) ran along the north side of the site. The more northerly (632) only survived over a length of about 5m at the centre of the site. It measured less than 200mm in depth and 1m in width and was infilled with light brown coloured silt (628). The more southerly drain (633) survived over a much greater length. It ran right to the east end of the site. The drain consisted of two roughly parallel branches running from west to east, which joined together at the centre of the site and them ran as a single structure to the east end of the site. The channels were unlined except where they joined. There, the two branches were lined with drystone walls. Before they joined, both were about 300mm in depth and their internal channels measured 300–400mm in width. After uniting, the drain measured about 800mm in width on average and up to 500mm in depth. The very base of the drain contained gravely organic black silt. The drain was infilled with brown loam (634) and a small patch of cobbling (648) overlay its western surviving end. A number of shallow channels fed northwards into the longer drain at the centre of the site. They survived over only very short lengths due to later truncation.

Metalled surfaces at south side of site
Roughly metalled and mortar-splashed surfaces (647/619 and 645) were uncovered at the western end and centre of the site. They only intruded into the site for a distance of less than 1.5m. A band of flat stones and bricks (641)

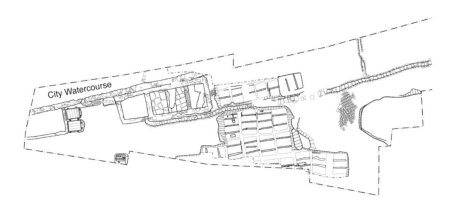

7.38 Site 8, the eighteenth-century tannery

overlay the flooring (645), and a dump of organic material and coal fragments (640) overlay the infilled pond further north. Black organic silt (618 & 646) lay on the floors.

Phase 2, level 1 – eighteenth-century tannery (figs 7.36, & 7.38–7.41)
Two mortar-bonded stone walls were next built at the north (605) and south (650) sides of the western end of the site. The lines of the walls suggested that they met west of the excavated area. Both walls petered out before they reached the centre of the site. They formed part of the boundary of a substantial early eighteenth-century tannery. The tannery consisted of a large number of stone and timber-lined tanning and de-hairing pits and a number of drains. A thick layer of redeposited subsoil (620) was dumped into the area between the walls at the very west end of the site and its surface was compacted and levelled. It formed the yard surface at this end of the tannery. A brick-sided and stone-based drain (607) led water from the adjacent city watercourse, through the northern boundary wall into the west end of four conjoined stone-lined pits, which were built as one unit against the inner side of the northern boundary wall towards the west end of the tannery. The drain was partly cut away by a later small pit (604) that had plank-lined sides secured by corner posts. Another brick-sided and stone-based drain (606) acted as an overflow leading water away from the west end of the south wall of the same pit. This drain continued eastwards beyond the end of the excavated area. It had stone-lined sides but was unlined at its base. Another brick-lined drain (647) fed into it from the north.

Stone-lined pits (fig. 7.39)
The four rectangular stone-lined pits had external mortar bonded walls varying from 0.35–0.55m in thickness. A thickness of up to 25mm of lime

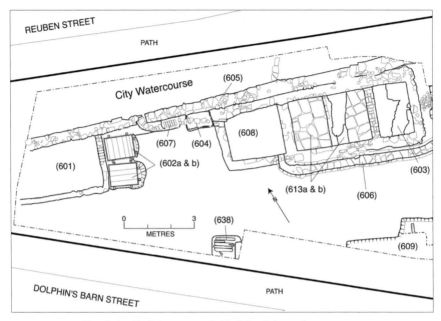

7.39 Site 8, detail of the western half of the eighteenth-century tannery

composed of a large number of very thin layers adhered to the inner faces of
the walls of the pits. The four pits had a total capacity of 14.236 cubic metres
and as evidenced by their lime fills, they were de-hairing pits. The westernmost
pit (608) measured 2.35 by 2m across and 0.95m in depth (a capacity of 4.465
cubic metres). It originally had a stone-flagged floor but this was later ripped
out. Pit (613a) measured 1.5m by 2.15m across and was 1.05m in depth
(a capacity of 3.386 cubic metres). It had a mortared stone-flagged base. The
brick wall between this pit and that (613b) to its south was robbed out to the level
of its footing. Pit (613b) measured 1.4 by 2.15m across and 1.08m in depth
(a capacity of 3.25 cubic metres). It also retained its original mortared stone-
flagged base. Pit (603) measured 2.2m by 1.5m across and 0.95m in depth
(a capacity of 3.135 cubic metres). It again had a mortared stone-flagged base.

Timber-lined pits (figs 7.40 & 7.41)
Two large trenches were dug, one on either side of the drain (606) east of the
stone-lined pits. Ranks of timber-lined tanks, separated by 100–400mm wide
baulks of redeposited subsoil were built in the two pits. Due to the
requirement to step in the sides of the excavated area for safety reasons, it was
not possible to excavate all the timber-lined tanks. However, because of the
existence of the boundary walls on the north and south sides of the tannery it
is possible to determine the original number of tanks that were present; there
were twelve north of the drain and seventeen south of it. There were two

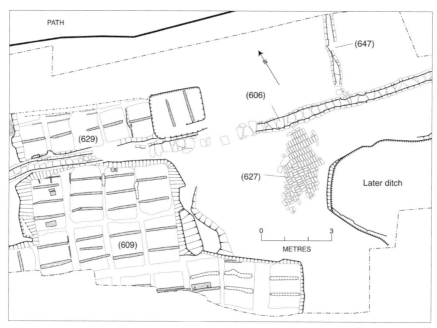

7.40 Site 8, detail of the eastern half of the eighteenth-century tannery

7.41 Site 8, the timber-lined tanning pits and brick drain in the eastern half of the tannery, looking south-east

regularly laid out and east–west-aligned rows, each containing six tanks (629) north of the drain. All or parts of eleven of these tanks were excavated. South of the drain, the tanks (609) were arranged in three east–west-aligned rows each containing four tanks. There were two additional on the south-east and three at the south-west sides of the main group. All or parts of fifteen of the original seventeen tanks were excavated. All the tanks were of rectangular shape and all but four (the two easternmost north of the drain and the two southeastern-most south of the drain, which had their long axes on east–west lines) had their long axes aligned north–south. The smaller tanks north of the drain were all roughly the same size and measured 1.3 by 1m across and were 0.8–0.9m in depth (each had a capacity of *c*.1.1 cubic metres). The two easternmost and larger tanks north of the drain measured 1.5 by 2.15m. They were also deeper than the others and measured 1.15m in depth (3.7 cubic metres each). All of the seventeen tanks south of the drain were of roughly the same size and depth and measured from 1.9 to 2.2m by 1.3 to 1.4m across and 0.8 to 0.9m in depth; a capacity of 2.295 cubic metres on average.

Only the very base of most of the tanks survived and the timbers from their sides and bases were almost totally robbed out. Traces of planks laid horizontally on their narrow sides survived at the sides of some of the tanks, and fragments of the side or base planking were uncovered in the backfill of the pits and in the foundation of the houses subsequently built over the site. One to three horizontally-laid timber runners spanning the short axis of the tanks survived set into the base of almost all of the tanks. These all had nails in them and they would have supported and joined the plank flooring of the tanks. The ground under the robbed wooden flooring in each tank was compacted and stained black. The narrow earthen baulks between the tanks survived only to a few centimetres in height at most. They were composed of redeposited subsoil that must have been packed between the tanks after they had been built. This and the regular size of the tanks show that they were pre-fabricated. The fragments of timbers that survived in the backfill of the tanks and the complete timbers uncovered in the foundations of the later house on the site show how the tanks were made. The ends of the side planking were lapped together. The bases of surviving *in situ* side planking rested on the ground at the same level as the top of the timber runners, suggesting that the base and bottom of the sides of the tanks were also lapped together. There may have been vertical bracing timbers securing the backs of the side planks together, as used in the two well preserved timber-lined tanks (602) at the west end of the site (see below), but no evidence of their presence survived. All the timbers surviving in these and the other timber-lined tanks were of oak.

Three more timber-lined tanks survived at the west end of the site (fig. 7.39), making a total of 32 timber-lined tanks within the tannery. Only the bottom planking survived of a single small tank (638) that lay partly outside the excavated area. The two perfectly preserved conjoined tanks (602a and 602b) at the west end of the tannery differed somewhat in construction from the larger group further east. Their sides and bases were not lap jointed but simply butt jointed. The floor planking of the northern of the pair spanned its short axis. In all the other tanks, including its partner, the floor planking ran parallel to the long axis of the tank. There were also two vertical bracing posts, on all but the west sides of these two tanks, securing the side planking together. These two tanks measured 0.9 by 1.2m across and 0.9m in depth (a capacity of 1.7 cubic metres). The timber lining of these tanks was coated with many thin layers of lime showing they were de-hairing pits.

Other structures
A rectangular brick- and stone-walled building (601) was erected against the northern boundary wall at the west end of the tannery (fig. 7.39). Its west wall overlay the construction trench of the conjoined wooden pits (602). Part of the building lay outside the excavated area and the revealed extent measured 4m in length by 2.3m in width externally (3.7 by 2.1m internally). No floor survived in the structure. East of the large groups of wooden tanks part of a brick floor (627) survived (fig. 7.40). Later activity heavily truncated it and its remaining part measured 3.8 by 2m across. The bricks were keyed into the sidewall of the large drain (606) to its north. A thin layer of dark grey silt (626) lay on the floor. A tiny area of stone cobbling (648) survived between the easternmost stone-lined pit and the timber-lined pits to its east.

Phase 2, level 2 – infill of pits
The four stone-lined pits in the north side of the tannery were filled with soft black noisome organic silt, which was rich in bark chips and which contained many cattle horn-cores. The two large groups of timber-lined pits were infilled with mixed deposits of redeposited subsoil (probably from the baulks between the tanks) and bark chips (612, 622, 624, 623 & 621). These deposits again contained many cattle horn-cores. A widespread layer of bricks and rubble also containing many cattle horn cores (611) overlay the remains of the tannery. The horn cores recovered from these and later deposits consisted of the cores themselves and only the very top of the skull where the horn cores were attached, the remainder of the skull must have been removed elsewhere. This suggests that the hides arrived at the tannery with the top of the skull and the horn cores still attached.

Phase 3 – later eighteenth-century houses and ditch (figs 7.36, 7.42 & 7.43)
The partial remains of the foundations (610, 630, 636 and 639) of a number of houses built over the infilled tannery were also uncovered. These houses are those shown on the Rocque's 1773 map of Dublin, which is the first to show

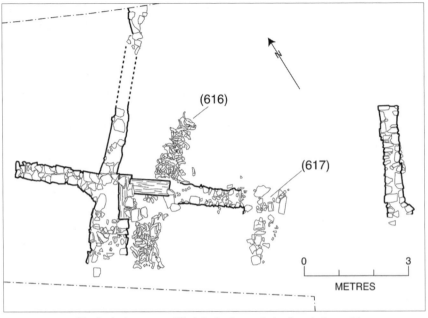

7.42 Site 8, the horn core-filled drains beneath the foundations of later eighteenth-century buildings overlying the tannery. Note the re-used timbers from the earlier tanning pits.

7.43 Site 8, horn core-filled drain (616) looking north

this area in detail. No houses were built in the eastern half of the site at this time. The houses were small in size and fronted onto the southern side of the site. Each had a small return or outshot at the rear contained within a small walled garden. Several timbers taken from the older tanning pits were reused as rafting under the foundations where they crossed the soft ground of the infilled tanning pits. Two north–south aligned drains (616 and 617), filled with cattle horn cores, underlay the foundations of the houses (figs 7.42 & 7.43). East of the houses a large ditch or pit was uncovered. It was aligned east–west and extended eastwards beyond the excavated area. It measured up to 4.5m in width, at least 6m in length and 2m in depth and was cut down into the top of bedrock. Its base was waterlogged and filled with a mixture of sand and organic material (652). The reminder was infilled with rubble and redeposited subsoil (625). These deposits contained a copper alloy token of 'Tho. Lowen, Patrick Street, Dvblin'. The ditch truncated the brick floor (627) associated with the tannery and appeared to be contemporary with the first houses built on the site but is not shown on the 1773 map.

Phase 4 – modern houses
The final deposits on the site consisted of the mass-concrete foundations of and demolition rubble from the modern houses that formerly stood on the site.

CONCLUSIONS

Given the known character and history of the area through which the road works extended, it was never envisaged that the archaeological remains that might survive would be the most spectacular, important or interesting and the archaeological excavations did not disappoint in this regard! However, the features uncovered do appear to reflect a reasonably representative slice through the history of the area.

Cork Street may have been of very ancient origin, as it supposedly roughly followed the route of the Slige Dála, the main early medieval route between Munster and the early medieval Áth Cliath. Part of an eleventh-century roadway was recently uncovered towards the east end of the Coombe (Walsh, this volume, above), however, nothing definitely of such early date was revealed during the course of the excavations for the roadworks.

The wide ditch found south of the Coombe (Site 2) was the earliest feature uncovered (fig. 7.4). Its location and the presence of the possible palisade trench on its uphill side suggest it might have had a defensive function, protecting something on the higher ground to the south. The date of the original digging of the ditch could not be determined but it was partly infilled by the later twelfth or early thirteenth century. The ditch might line up with one of the ditches associated with a street of Hiberno-Norse houses recently

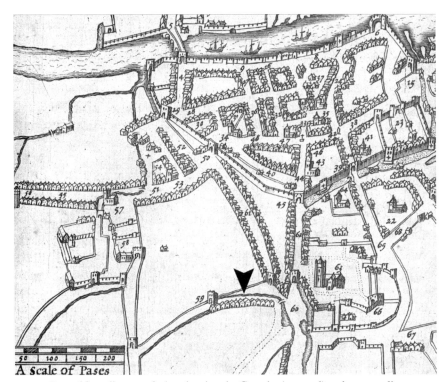

7.44 Part of Speed's map of 1610 showing the Coombe (arrowed) and surrounding area

revealed by Walsh's excavations to the east (Walsh, this volume, above) and so might also be of eleventh-century origin.

Other early features might have survived closer to the Coombe on Site 1 but due to flooding it was not possible to excavate that area. The medieval deposits there remain sealed beneath the modern roadway and are available to anyone willing in the future to undertake an exercise in underwater urban archaeology.

The eastern half of the Coombe was probably again developed for housing at some stage in the high-medieval period; Speed's map of 1610 (fig. 7.44) shows its south side lined with houses and a gateway stands midway along the street. The excavations on the new roadway only reached down to medieval levels well behind the street front and were in an area that was occupied only by fields until the end of the seventeenth century: the fields are shown on de Gomme's 1673 map (fig. 7.46). The cultivation furrows and thick deposits of cultivated soils encountered on Sites 2 and 3 attest to a long period of agriculture and are typical of such deposits found in and around the medieval town. The finds from this material show that organic waste from the town was spread on the fields as fertilizer. The thirteenth-century grain-drying kiln and the traces of an associated building (figs 7.4–7.6) found on Site 2 would not have been out of place anywhere in rural Ireland in the medieval period.

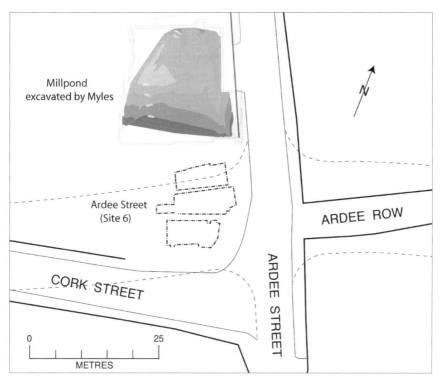

7.45 The excavated area of Site 6 in relation to the later-excavated millpond
(after Myles 2009, fig. 2)

The remainder of the area through which the roadworks extended was also
of completely rural and non-urban character in the medieval period and from
the later twelfth century much of it formed a part of the extensive estates of
St Thomas's abbey. The monks of St Thomas's undertook an ambitious
realignment and combination of the Poddle river with part of the water from
the Dodder river to bring water through their lands, probably in the main to
provide power for mills (Ronan 1927). Excavations at Patrick Street (Walsh
1997, 34–69 and 79–80) and Simpson's historical sleuthing (Simpson 1997, 25)
showed that these works were undertaken well before 1202 and possibly shortly
after the foundation of the abbey in 1177. The roadworks encountered parts of
these late twelfth-century watercourses in two places. At Ardee Street (Site 6)
the north–south-flowing Abbey Stream was revealed. It is not clear whether
the two channels excavated were the actual channels of the watercourse or
represented overflow channels. As they were completely unlined they may
represent the latter; the main channel could have lain beneath the modern
street. The Abbey Stream flowed southwards from here to where it powered a
number of mills, including the 'Red Mills', which are shown on the 1673 map
(fig. 7.46). Further west at Emerald Terrace (Site 7), the several-times-

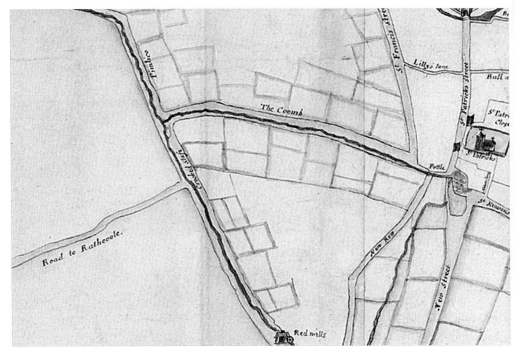

7.46 Part of the 1673 map of Dublin showing the area through which the roadworks extended. The Coombe area is still shown as fields. Note the Red Mills shown on the Abbey Stream.

realigned medieval channels of the south–north-flowing river Poddle were again encountered. There, traces were revealed of a very poorly-preserved thirteenth-century timber revetment constraining one of the channels. Better-preserved timber revetments were previously excavated further downstream along the sides of the western branch of the river where it was diverted down both sides of Patrick Street (Walsh 1997).

In the mid-thirteenth century the city authorities also got in on the act of diverting rivers and a third of the waters from the combined Poddle/Dodder system were diverted at the 'Tongue' in Mount Argus and conveyed in a new watercourse, skirting around the land of St Thomas's abbey to a large basin near St John's Church (Simpson 1997, 22). Part of this city watercourse was also uncovered at the very western end of the roadway at Dolphin's Barn (Site 8), an area previously known as the 'Back of the Pipes'. However, due to safety considerations it was not possible, nor indeed necessary, to excavate the interior of the watercourse itself here, as it was to be preserved beneath the roadway. Part of the watercourse was later excavated during the private development of the adjacent area to the east and north of the site (*Excavations 2004*, no. 583).

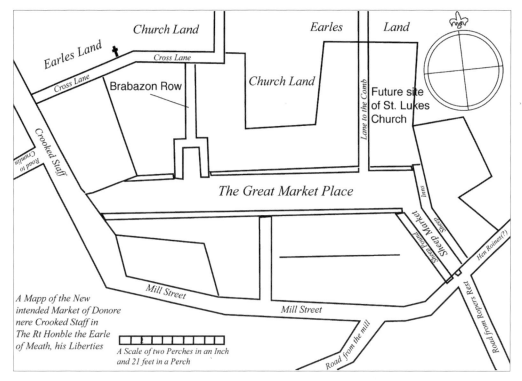

7.47 Tracing of a 1670s plan for the development of the Newmarket Area. Note 'lane to the Coom' on future site of St Luke's church and site of future Brabazon Row.

Substantial ponds were also revealed at the three sections of the medieval watercourses crossed by the recent roadworks. That at Ardee Street formed part of the large millpond subsequently excavated by Franc Myles (Myles 2009) (fig. 7.45). The pond at Emerald Terrace (Site 7) may also have been a millpond and the gullies and postholes found in it (figs 22–4) might even have been part of a medieval mill or structures associated with one. While the locations of a number of the mills on these watercourses are known, the only definite one excavated to date was the 'Shyteclappe Mill' on Patrick Street (Walsh 1997, 30–59). It is not clear what function the early pond at Dolphin's Barn (Site 8) fulfilled.

In the medieval period these watercourses also provided water for other industries, such as tanning and cloth dying, but the excavations along the roadway did not reveal any evidence of these. However, an extensive medieval tannery was later excavated north of the roadway and just to the east of Ardee Street at 48 New Street (*Excavations 2004*, no. 546) and the remains of other medieval tanneries have also been revealed close to the Poddle on Patrick Street (Walsh 1997, 39–41; *Excavations 1991*, no. 39). In 1545, after the Dissolution,

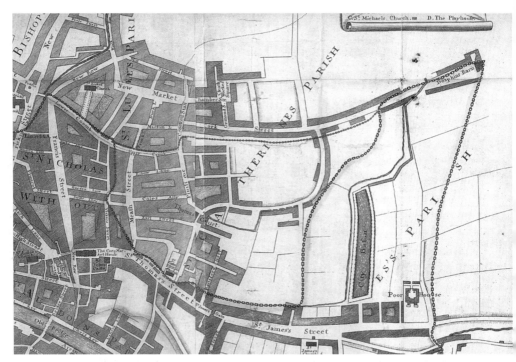

7.48 Part of Brooking's map of 1728 showing the area through which the roadworks extended

the lands of St Thomas's passed to William Brabazon, the ancestor of the earls of Meath, who continued to hold extensive properties in the area for many centuries. While some parts of the estate further north and closer to Thomas Street were developed quite early, the area through which the roadway extended retained its rural character until the later seventeenth or eighteenth centuries.

Dublin began to expand in the seventeenth century and the pace and extent of development increased greatly after the Restoration. The eastern end of the area through which the roadway ran began to be overtaken by the expanding city at the end of the seventeenth century. A plan dating to the mid-1670s (fig. 7.47) shows the intended layout of the Newmarket area – the earl of Meath had obtained a royal patent for a twice-weekly agricultural market at Newmarket in 1674 – which included part of the area through which the eastern end of the roadway ran. The rapid pace of the development in the area is well illustrated by a comparison between the 1673, 1728 and 1756 maps (figs 7.46, 7.48–7.49). The old watercourses were also constrained at this time, presumably to prevent flooding, make better use of their waters and allow the development of areas adjacent to them. The Poddle at Emerald Terrace (Site 7) was channelled between stone walls in the 1690s and buildings were erected along its sides. These seventeenth- and early eighteenth-century buildings are

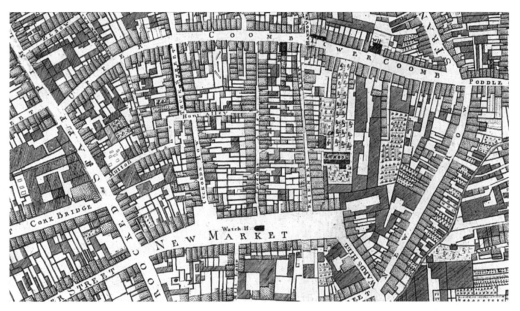

7.49 Part of Rocque's map of 1756 showing the area from the Coombe to Ardee Street, through which the roadworks extended

not shown on any maps. Brooking's 1728 map (fig. 7.48) shows the site as developed but the first map of the area showing individual buildings was only published by Rocque in 1773, well after they had been demolished. At Ardee Street (Site 6) the Abbey Stream was also confined between stone walls in the later seventeenth century, just before the area was developed. The culvert and the second earliest buildings found on the site are shown on Rocque's map of 1756 (fig. 7.49). The river here was re-channelled again in the eighteenth century, this time in a stone- and brick-walled and brick-vaulted underground culvert. This may have been an attempt at least partly to keep the waters clean (Simpson 2007, 32). The first houses may have been built on Brabazon Row (Site 5) by the 1690s (Peter Walsh, pers. comm.) and both Brooking's map of 1728 and Rocque's of 1756 (figs 7.48 & 7.49) show buildings on the street. However, these houses did not survive; the earliest buildings uncovered there were of later eighteenth-century or early nineteenth-century date (see below).

Seventeenth- to nineteenth-century walls, pits and a cellar were also revealed in the area excavated south of the Coombe (Sites 2 and 3). The remains of eighteenth- or nineteenth-century wells, wooden pump sticks and water pipes providing water to houses, were also uncovered in several places in that area (Sites 2, 4 and 5). The negative consequences of building on floodplains and close to rivers, well attested in modern times in this country, were also revealed at Emerald Terrace (Site 7). The late seventeenth-century houses erected there rapidly fell into decay, probably because of flooding and

7.50 One of the eighteenth-century tanneries excavated at Old Kilmainham, looking south.
The river Camac is in the foreground.

several kilns and temporary structures were erected in the shelter of their
ruins. However, the area was soon redeveloped and new housing was built in
the early eighteenth century after the ground level had been raised further.
The material used to consolidate the ground consisted of the waste from an
early eighteenth-century pottery manufactory and is one of the largest, if not
the largest, concentration of pottery found in the city to date.

The old watercourses flowing through the area still provided water and
power for many industries. They also helped to attract an influx of Huguenots
and others associated with the distilling, tanning and cloth industries to the
area in the latter part of the seventeenth century. The number of these
industries known in the area in the early eighteenth century is illustrated on a
map compiled by Lennon (2008, fig. 4). Excavations have also revealed several
seventeenth- to nineteenth-century tanneries on Cork Street (*Excavations
2004*, no. 530; 2005, nos 247 and 608). The substantial early eighteenth-
century tannery revealed at Dolphin's Barn (Site 8) is a good example of these
water-dependent industries. It again escaped early mapping. Brooking's 1728
map simply shows the site as developed and Rocque's detailed map of 1756
does not cover this area. Rocque's later map of 1773 was the first to show
individual structures here but only shows the houses erected on top of the

7.51 The late nineteenth-century tannery excavated at Marrowbone Lane

infilled tannery. When it was excavated, this was the largest tannery yet uncovered in the city. However, in subsequent years other large tanneries have been unearthed, for example, at Kilmainham (fig. 7.50), a series of substantial tanneries dating from the seventeenth to nineteenth centuries (*Excavations 2004*, no. 567; 2005, no. 500), James Street, several substantial nineteenth-century tanneries (*Excavations 2003*, no. 541) and Marrowbone Lane (fig. 51), a late nineteenth-century tannery (*Excavations 2005*, no. 453). The features uncovered on all these sites are closely paralleled at the Dolphin's Barn tannery: the form, layout and construction of the tanning pits, the use of drains from nearby watercourses to fill the pits and the use of oak chips (probably provided by bark mills) to provide the tannin. The form and layout of these tanneries is even echoed by some still in use today, for example, those in the well-known leather-producing city of Fez in Morocco.

Many of the excavated tanneries contained substantial quantities of cattle horn cores and the large number that accumulated is highlighted at Emerald Terrace and Dolphin's Barn where they were used to create drains. As is well represented here and also in Britain in medieval and post-medieval times, skins were usually delivered to the tanner with the horns and hooves attached. Late-medieval illustrations also show hides brought to tanneries with the front of the animal's skull and the horn cores still attached (fig. 7.52).

7.52 Late and post-medieval woodcuts showing tanners at work. Note the skulls and horn cores still attached to some of the pelts.

A new parish, St Luke's, was created by act of Parliament (26 Anne 21) in 1707 to cater for the growing Protestant population of the area. Building of the new parish church, close to Newmarket, began in 1714 and it was opened in 1716. The church was accessed up a long elm tree-lined avenue (figs 7.7, 7.48 & 7.49), which followed an earlier laneway laid out probably in the later 1670s. The lane is shown on the plan of the proposed development of the Newmarket area (fig. 7.47). A recently compiled conservation plan for the Church (Shaffrey et al., undated) contains a comprehensive analysis of the history and architecture of the church. The graveyard was in use for burial from 1713 to 1922 and the church finally closed its doors to worship in 1975. The graveyard associated with the church is shown on all maps from 1728 onwards as lying only to the south of the church. However, an 1818 drawing (reproduced in Costello 1989, 203) clearly shows that there were also graves on the north side of the church; upright gravestones are depicted on this side of the church, but none survived there when the excavations were undertaken.

The density of burial encountered in the small part of the graveyard excavated came as a surprise, as the area lay well away from the church and on its north side. Despite the fact that only two thirds of the volume of the area opened was excavated to subsoil, a minimum number of 157 interments was uncovered. Allowing for a third more in the unexcavated part of the opened area yields a possible total of approximately 235 burials or a density of a little over six burials per square metre. The uppermost burials lay only 100mm below modern ground level, which accords with the shallow depth at which burials were noted east and west of the church in test pits excavated by Myles (*Excavations 2001*, no. 373). All the burials uncovered were aligned east–west with the majority being interred with the head to the west facing east. Remains of coffins, in the form of decayed wood or iron nails survived around the vast majority of the burials but only one grave marker (an undecorated and uninscribed stone) was found. The human remains constitute one of the best-preserved samples of its date yet uncovered in Dublin and so are of considerable interest.

The burial register for St Luke's from 1716 onwards survives and a study of the burials represented in it compared with the statistics derived from the excavated burials might make an interesting future undertaking. The trades of many of those buried are mentioned in the earlier part of the register and demonstrate the association of many of the parishioners with the cloth and hide trades that were developing in the area. The trade of the deceased is also recorded on some of the memorials in the church, which include a 'cloathier' and 'silk manufacturer'. The Reverend Theophilius Broca, a minister of St Luke's, was apparently also a keen supporter of the developing silk industry in the 1740s. However, the decline of the silk industry in the area in the 1770s and the weaving industry in general left the area impoverished. By 1792, for example, it is recorded that 5,000 weavers in the area were unemployed (Whitelaw et al. 1818, 982) and St Luke's was then regarded as the poorest parish in Dublin. This decline may perhaps also be illustrated by the construction of the mid-nineteenth-century clay-pipe kiln in the ruins of former houses on Brabazon Row (Site 5). Unfortunately, most of the actual kiln lay outside the road-take and the pipes produced were undecorated and all of the same type. The kiln was probably operated by one of the Casey brothers (Joe Norton, pers. comm.) who also had a number of kilns on Francis Street, some of which have been revealed by excavation (*Excavations 1997*, no. 132). Perhaps, some of the products of the Brabazon Row kiln may even have been used by those buried in the graveyard of St Luke's, as 35% of the males and one of the older females buried there had notches, caused by smoking clay pipes, in their teeth.

The construction of the new roadway in 2001–2 marked the beginning of the redevelopment of this run-down part of the town, which today is almost unrecognizable compared to a little over a decade ago. However, the medieval rivers still survive; both the *c.*800-year-old diverted river Poddle and Abbey Stream still flow through the area, although now largely hidden below ground. These rivers provided the power and water for the area in the medieval period, were highly influential in the shaping of its development in the late

seventeenth century and today provide one of the few surviving physical links
with its medieval past.

ACKNOWLEDGMENTS

The work was entirely funded by Dublin City Council. I would specially like to
thank Sally Redmond (the DCC engineer who directed the road works) and
Andy Halpin and Ruth Johnson (successive DCC City Archaeologists) for
their help and support. Much praise is due to Conor McHale, who undertook
all the on-site surveying and produced the final plans. I am also indebted to
Laureen Buckley for her work with the human remains from St Luke's, Joe
Norton for his work on the clay pipes and Rosanne Meenan for her analysis of
the pottery. Thanks also to the multinational excavation crews. The excavation
assistants were Brian Hayden, Niall Colfer, Jose Carrascosa and Simon
Gannon. The excavators were John Barrett, Jack Bates, Nora Bermingham,
Cathy Byrne, Dave Carr, Jose Luis Centelles, Duncan Clarke, Charlotte
Comyns, Nico Contatore, Wilf Dell, Deane di Millions, Raoul Empey,
Raphael Estefanis, Peter Ferguson, Pedro Pablo Garcon de Hernandez,
Jasmine Godwin, Paul Grace, Steve Harte, Hans Heckel, Barry Hurley, John
Kelly, Kurt Kyck, Simon Manahan, Carol Martin, Aideen McDermott, Barry
Molloy, Eva Neukirchen, Stan Queally, Juan Raccionero, Skadi Schulz, Jane
Stradwick, Enda Sweeney, Pierce Walsh and John Whelan.

BIBLIOGRAPHY

Costello, P. 1989 *Dublin Churches*. Dublin. Gill & Macmillan.
Excavations 1986[-] = I. Bennett (ed.), *Excavations 1986[-]: summary accounts of
        archaeological excavations in Ireland*. Dublin and Bray. Wordwell.
Lennon, C. 2008 *Dublin Part II, 1610 to 1756*. Irish Historic Towns Atlas, *no. 19*. Dublin.
        Royal Irish Academy.
Myles, F. 2009 Archaeological excavations at the millpond of St Thomas's abbey, Dublin. In
        S. Duffy (ed.), *Medieval Dublin IX: Proceedings of the Friends of medieval Dublin
        Symposium 2007*, 183–212. Dublin. Four Courts Press.
Ronan, M.V. 1927 The Poddle River and its branches. *Journal of the Royal Society of
        Archaeologists of Ireland* 57, 39–46.
Shaffrey, M. et al. undated *St Luke's Conservation Plan*. Dublin. Dublin City Council.
Simpson, L. 1997 Historical background to the Patrick Street Excavation, in C. Walsh (ed.),
        Archaeological excavations at Patrick, Nicholas and Winetavern Streets, Dublin, 17–33.
        Dingle. Brandon Books.
Walsh, C. 1997 *Archaeological excavations at Patrick, Nicholas and Winetavern Streets, Dublin*.
        Dingle. Brandon Books.
Whitelaw, J., Walsh, R. and Warburton, J. 1818 *The history of Dublin*. London. Cadell &
        Davies.

Excavations at 23–27 Stephen Street Lower, Dublin

ROSANNE MEENAN

INTRODUCTION

Excavations were carried out over a three-week period in June 1992. The clients were Mr Patrick Sexton and Mr Oliver McCormack of Mullingar who had received planning permission to construct a four-storey building along the street frontage comprising retail units with car parking at the rear. The site fronts on to Stephen St Lower which forms part of a curving street plan which, it has been suggested (e.g., Clarke 1990, 61–3), may retain the ground plan of an early Christian monastic enclosure, possibly encircling St Stephen's or St Peter's churches, the latter known to have been in existence before the arrival of the Anglo-Normans (Coughlan 2003, 16). Stephen St Lower forms part of the northern boundary of the possible enclosure.

Archaeological excavations in the last twenty years have produced some evidence for enclosing ditches in the northern sector of this possible enclosure. Excavations by Coughlan (2003) and Ó Néill (2004) produced arcs of ditches, both curving in such a direction as to suggest they formed two parts of an enclosure that may have enclosed St Peter's church; it would have lain to the west, south and south-east (Coughlan 2003, 15) of the 23–27 Stephen St Lower excavation site and would have been much smaller than the enclosure of which Stephen St Lower formed part as suggested by Clarke. The section excavated by Ó Néill produced a piece of eleventh-century roof tile in the ditch fill (Ó Néill, 78). Hayden, excavating in 1991 on the east side of Digges Lane, found no evidence for a ditch along the Stephen St Lower frontage; there were no finds or features pre-dating the twelfth century (Hayden and Buckley 2002, 172). Therefore, it is evident that further work still needs to be carried out to establish if the modern street plan reflects the outline of an early medieval feature. In particular the footprint of the street itself needs to be investigated as the majority of the excavation described above has been located inside the line of the street plan. Traces of an enclosing feature, if it ever existed, may survive under the surface of Stephen St Lower itself.

THE SITE

The site had been previously tested when the presence of what appeared to be either a large pit or a ditch was uncovered, the fill of which had produced

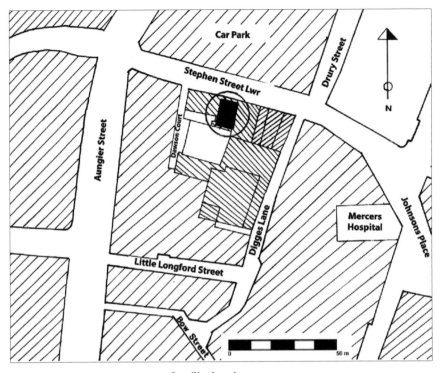

8.1 Site location map

medieval and early post-medieval potsherds along with charcoal and cockle shells. It was obvious that there was survival of archaeological material on the site. The client was therefore required to fully excavate the site which was located along the street frontage with access from the west side via Dawson Court. The facades of the buildings fronting the street were still standing when the excavation took place. The edge of the cutting on the street frontage was brought in one metre from the facade so that the standing walls would not be undermined. The site measured 16.5m (N/S) x 10.5m (E/W). The dimensions were laid down in the planning permission. The area to be excavated was covered with overburden deriving from the demolition of the buildings and shops that had stood on the site. It was removed by mechanical digger leaving a layer of brick and other building rubble over the area to be excavated. It was clear that there had been basements under the houses and that the space occupied by the basements was filled with demolition rubble. The basements ranged in depth from 1.5 to 2.8m below street level.

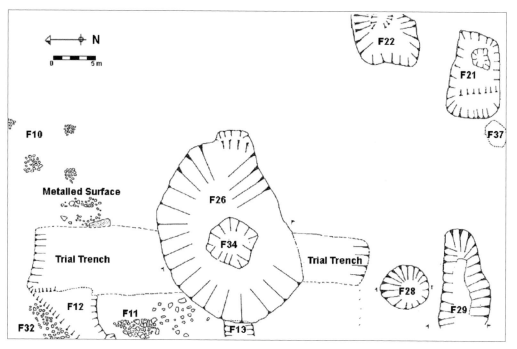

8.2 Plan of Phase 1 features

THE EXCAVATION

Two broad phases of activity on the site were identified. The earlier (phase 1) indicated medieval and early post-medieval activity while the second phase involved the construction of the brick and stone houses on the site.

Phase 1

Phase 1 comprised pits of varying sizes which were cut into the natural boulder clay and which were medieval and/or early post-medieval in date. They varied in size and depth and their function was not clear.

The largest feature on the site was a large pit (F26). It measured 4.7 x 2.9m and was 1.9m deep. The sides were cut almost vertically into the boulder clay and the fill comprised redeposited boulder clay. The bottom of the pit (F34) narrowed considerably and was dug another 1.1m deeper through the subsoil. The fill included shell and charcoal and 381 sherds of medieval pottery comprising Leinster cooking ware, Ham Green, Saintonge and three fabric types of Dublin-type ware. A piece of floor tile with two-colour decoration was recovered; it can be paralleled at Christ Church Dublin (Eames and Fanning 1988, 81, T69) and dates to the thirteenth century (ibid., 23). It was probably

8.3 Floor tile from pit 26 and base of candlestick from pit 22

associated with St Stephen's church; floor tile was also found on Hayden's excavation (Buckley and Hayden 2002, 172). The bottom layer of fill produced large sherds of a green-glazed Dublin-type ware pot. Some of the animal bone from this feature showed a high incidence of gnawing and erosion suggesting that they had been lying around the surface before deposition. The potsherds, on the other hand, did not show such evidence.

Another pit (F22) was located along the eastern side of the site and the uppermost 0.2m had been removed during trial trenching. In plan it measured approx. 1.60m x 1.50m and the sides were almost vertical. Its maximum depth was 0.8m. There were two distinct elements within the fill, the uppermost comprising a grey/green silty clay and the lower layer comprising very organic material with visible plant remains.

Four sherds of pottery were retrieved from the fill of pit F22. Two of the sherds featured black glaze, one of which was probably the base of a candlestick and the other a jug handle; the other two sherds represented a bowl or jar rim and a body sherd of glazed red earthenware. This assemblage probably dated to the mid- to late seventeenth century, based on the form of the candlestick. There was one piece of hand-made brick. A fragment of textile was also recovered from this pit. Heckett (unpublished specialist report) described it as plain tabby-woven wool lacking any trace of sewing or selvedges. She compared it with other pieces of textile in Ireland such as the Dungiven costume (late sixteenth/early seventeenth century) and the clothing from Tawnmore, Co. Sligo, dating to the mid-seventeenth century. The piece of textile was also submitted for testing to investigate whether it was dyed or not. No traces of dye could be recovered.

Collins (unpublished specialist report) carried out an environmental report on the pit (F22) fill in which food remains were found including cockle and mussel shell fragments, fish bones, animal bone and hazelnut shells. They were very fragmentary, suggesting that they had been lying around on the surface before being swept into the pit. There were also charred grains of oat, wheat and possibly rye along with blackberry and grape – grape is not found in deposits that are earlier than the thirteenth century. The plant remains were all indicative of disturbed conditions; grassland species indicating undisturbed conditions were not present in the assemblage. Seeds of bell heather were also present. Collins suggested that they could either have been grown in the area as a decorative plant or otherwise come into the town with the heather that had been collected for use in the home such as insulation or rope making. Hemlock was abundant in the organic level of the pit – this favours damp places such as river banks, hedges and roadsides and may have been growing in damp waste ground near the pit. There is also the possibility that it was being used medicinally as, although very poisonous, it was used as a pain reliever and as a sedative.

In summary it appears that this sixteenth- to seventeenth-century pit was used to dispose of occupation debris as typical cesspit material was not present. Food remains were present but not abundant and it appears likely that the material was lying around and being trodden on before it was dumped in the pit. Interestingly however, the animal bone was exceptionally well-preserved and was probably deposited into the pit shortly after use.

Another nearby pit (F21) was sub-rectangular in plan, 2.10m (E/W) x 1.10m (N/S), 0.9m deep. It produced a large quantity of cockle shells and twelve sherds of locally manufactured pottery and a piece of Saintonge ware.

One fragment of whale bone was found in the fill of this pit (F21). McCarthy (unpublished specialist report) identified no obvious butchery marks but recognized blunt instrument marks on the vertebrae. She quoted the reference from Warburton, Whitelaw and Walsh (1818) to a school of whales which went aground in the mouth of the Dodder in 1331 and which were killed and butchered by the poor of Dublin. Permission had to be sought to slaughter whales and dolphins as they were considered royal fish.

Pit F28 was a small circular pit which produced a small amount of medieval pottery but was unusual in that the west wall and base of the pit had been hardened as if vitrified although there was no sign of burning. The fill produced very dark wet silty material with a small amount of charcoal at the base with fragments of unworked timber.

Feature F29 was a shallow trench or gully the terminal of which was exposed in the middle of the trench but it continued under the west baulk. There were no finds.

Function of the pits
The function of the pits was not clear. They had different shapes and depths and the nature of the fills varied although there was little organic material in any of them apart from pit F22. Bone and shells in the content of the fill suggested food waste. The pottery assemblage was mixed in date. There was no evidence that there had been structures surrounding any of them or that they had been enclosed.

Other evidence for medieval activity comprised scattered patches of metalling (F11). These were concentrated in the north-west corner of the site and although they had been disturbed by the excavation of the trial trench, it would be fair to assume that they had all formed part of the same feature. The metalling consisted of rounded or slightly irregular pebbles set into the boulder clay; it was cut by a shallow gully (F12) the fill of which produced local and imported medieval pottery.

Phase 2
This phase was represented by eighteenth-/nineteenth-century building activity. If there had been activity on the site between the period when the pits were dug and the house building, no evidence for it was found. The cellars for the houses that fronted onto Stephen St had been dug to a depth of 1.5 to 2.8m below the present street level and so it is possible that they had removed any archaeological stratigraphy that had survived there. When building the houses, particularly sound foundations would have been required on those parts where the pits were encountered. Two sets of timbers were exposed lying horizontally in an east–west alignment over the top of F26. A narrow trench was dug to receive them and there were stones lying on top of them.

SUMMARY

There was no evidence on the site for early medieval activity, that is, features associated with a pre-Anglo-Norman ecclesiastical foundation. The pits were the only evidence for medieval activity on the site. It was not possible to date them closely as the pottery that they contained was mixed in date. There was no evidence for structures and there was no evidence for enclosing ditches. Cellars of later houses may have destroyed surviving remnants of sixteenth- and seventeenth-century material apart from one pit which contained sixteenth- to seventeenth-century pottery and fabric. The remains of the later houses were represented by horizontal timbers laid down over areas of soft ground.

Recent excavation (see above) has not yielded sufficient archaeological material to confirm the existence for the monastic enclosure as suggested by

Clarke. To clarify the issue, more research needs to be carried out, both to further investigate the possible enclosure uncovered by Coughlan and Ó Néill to the west and to establish whether there are archaeological remains under Stephen St Lower itself.

BIBLIOGRAPHY

Buckley, L. and Hayden, A. 2002 Excavations at St Stephen's leper hospital, Dublin: a summary account and an analysis of burials. In S. Duffy (ed.), *Medieval Dublin III*, 151–94. Dublin. Four Courts Press.

Clarke, H.B. 1990 *Medieval Dublin: the making of a metropolis*. Dublin. Irish Academic Press.

Collins, B. 1993 Environmental samples from 23–27 Stephen St Lower, Dublin. Unpublished report.

Coughlan, T. 2003 Excavations at the medieval cemetery of St Peter's church, Dublin. In S. Duffy (ed.), *Medieval Dublin IV*, 11–39. Dublin. Four Courts Press.

Eames, E.S. and Fanning, T. 1988 *Irish medieval tiles*. Dublin. Royal Irish Academy.

Heckett, E.W. 1993 Textile from 23–27 Stephen St Lower, Dublin. Unpublished report.

McCarthy, M. 1993 Faunal report from St Stephen St Lower Dublin. Unpublished report.

Ó Néill, J. 2004 Excavations at Longford Street Little: an archaeological approach to Dubh Linn. In S. Duffy (ed.), *Medieval Dublin V*, 73–90. Dublin. Four Courts Press.

Warburton, J., Whitelaw, J. and Walsh, R. 1818 *History of the city of Dublin*. London.

The sheriff of Dublin in the fourteenth century

ÁINE FOLEY

In his article on the sheriffs of Cork, published more than a century ago, Henry Berry stated that 'no systematic list of the ancient sheriffs of any Irish county has yet appeared'.[1] More than a century later the list he compiled of the sheriffs of Cork at the end of his article is one of the only detailed catalogues of medieval Irish sheriffs so far published. The Appendix below will attempt to rectify this deficiency for County Dublin at least, by documenting the men who held this office throughout the late medieval period. The majority of those men who were appointed sheriffs may have appeared relatively unimportant and left little impression in the sources individually, but as a group, they were arguably the adhesive that held the Lordship together. In their hands, the apparatus of local government was sturdy enough to survive the difficulties that marked the fourteenth century.

The lack of research carried out on the sheriff of Dublin is remarkable considering how pervasive this officer is in the surviving records. The sheriff was the principal royal official within the shire administration and he served as a vital conduit between the crown and the county community. In the thirteenth century, men who had no connection with County Dublin frequently held this office, but by the middle of the fourteenth century, it was the preserve of members of the local elite. Increasingly, its holders came from the most politically prominent families of the county. These officers were primarily responsible for collecting the king's revenue, and were in charge of the judicial and military activities within the county. They were substantially responsible for the financial wellbeing of the crown, as well as being the nearest thing the community had to a police force. The focus will be on the officeholder rather than the office itself and its various functions – the sheriff, at least from the last quarter of the thirteenth century, was chosen from the leading members of local gentry society and can therefore offer much information on this social group.

THE THIRTEENTH-CENTURY SHERIFF

The office of sheriff was introduced from England in the aftermath of the Anglo-Norman invasion of Ireland. The existence of a county court in Dublin

1 Henry F. Berry, 'Sheriffs of the County Cork: Henry III to 1660', *Journal of the Royal Society of Antiquaries of Ireland*, 5th series, 35:1 (1905), 40.

in the 1190s would suggest that there was certainly a sheriff of Dublin by this time, as one institution was synonymous with the other.[2] Initially, just like in England, many of those who served as sheriffs of Dublin had close associations with the crown. The first known sheriff of Dublin, who held office *c.*1202, was Henry of Braybrooke, whose father Robert had risen from obscurity to become sheriff of Bedfordshire and Buckinghamshire, Northamptonshire, and Rutland. Henry himself subsequently served as sheriff of Bedfordshire and Buckinghamshire, before falling out with King John when he sided with the barons.[3] Geoffrey Luttrell, who was sheriff of Dublin in 1212, was another close associate of King John whose main landed interests were in Yorkshire and not Ireland.[4] Hence, just like in England in this period, most sheriffs in charge of County Dublin were not locals, but in fact were royal officials or intimates of the king.

A letter from the bishop of Waterford dated to 1281 complained about these men who were imported from England to serve as sheriff. He maintained that, because they had no property in Ireland, once they left it was not possible to bring errant sheriffs to justice. The bishop went on to describe these sheriffs as being malicious and causing conflict between the English settlers in Ireland and their friends in England. He accused two sheriffs, Henry and William Pycot, of receiving money for which they did not answer.[5] A statute from 1293 complained that sheriffs were often appointed using the great seal of England and consequently were less obedient to the exchequer of Ireland. In future, it was ordered that the treasurer and barons of the exchequer would appoint them. While it appears that most sheriffs from Dublin and counties closest to the central administration were appointed in the Dublin exchequer, a high number of sheriffs from counties like Kerry, Cork and Limerick continued to be appointed under the great seal of England.[6] This may simply have been because it was as easy to get to London from south-west Ireland as it was to travel to the exchequer in Dublin. Evidently, appointing men who had no loyalty to the Dublin exchequer or did not have any local interests or sympathy with the county community was proving problematic. It may even be the case that men like the Pycots considered themselves to be above the law because they almost certainly left the country once their term in office was completed.

2 *Calendar of documents relating to Ireland, 1171–1307*, ed. H.S. Sweetman, 5 vols (London, 1875–86) [hereafter *CDI*], i, no. 116; Gerard McGrath, 'The shiring of Ireland and the 1297 parliament' in James Lydon (ed.), *Law and disorder in thirteenth-century Ireland: the Dublin parliament of 1297* (Dublin, 1997), p. 109; Judith A. Green, *The government of England under Henry I* (Cambridge, 1989), p. 119.   3 George Garnett, 'Braybrooke, Henry of (*d.* 1234)', *Oxford Dictionary of National Biography*, Oxford, 2004; online edn, Sept. 2010 [http://www.oxforddnb.com/view/article/3300, accessed 18 May 2011].   4 Robert W. Dunning, 'Luttrell family (*per. c.*1200–1428)', *Oxford Dictionary of National Biography* (Oxford, 2004) [http://www.oxforddnb.com/view/article/54529, accessed 18 May 2011].   5 *CDI*, ii, no. 1881.   6 John de Athy (sheriff of Limerick) was made sheriff of Kerry in 1312 under the great seal of England, *Calendar of the fine rolls* [...], *1272–[1509]*, 22 vols

The shift towards choosing locals as sheriffs in the latter half of the thirteenth century reflected trends occurring across the Irish Sea. Sheriffs had existed in England as far back as the Anglo-Saxon period; however, they became much more powerful and influential in the aftermath of the conquest.[7] By the mid-thirteenth century, the king and his officials were concerned that these sheriffs were growing much too powerful. Indeed, this may have been the motivation behind removing royal lands from the control of the sheriff.[8] Some English historians have proposed a theory that this transfer of control of the king's demesne to keepers, which coincided with the shift towards locals holding the office of sheriff, resulted in the decline of the office of sheriff in England. Certainly, in the first half of the twentieth century, many historians considered this shift to be symptomatic of a decline of this office in England, though this view has been modified somewhat in more recent scholarship.[9] Of course, from the perspective of central administration, there may have been a decline since those close to the crown no longer had a monopoly on the office – but the county communities who now dominated this office would probably have viewed it differently.

In Dublin, the trend towards employing members of prominent families of the county as sheriff was underway by 1274 with the election of Hugh de Cruise. He came from a long-established family who held lands in north County Dublin and, from 1275 until 1284, he served as king's serjeant for County Dublin.[10] This office became a hereditary one within the family and, on occasion, they were described as the chief serjeants of Leinster. The Cruise family continued to hold this office until the early years of the seventeenth century. Moreover, they also served as chief serjeants of Louth for much of the medieval period.[11] On 6 February 1279, Hugh was granted the royal manors of Newcastle Lyons, Saggart and Crumlin for twelve years.[12] The 1270s had been a particularly turbulent decade for those living in this locality. It was at this time that the English started to lead expeditions into the Dublin and Wicklow mountains in order to subdue the Irish. The focus of these expeditions was Glenmalure,[13] although it is clear that the threat was felt much closer to Dublin

(London, 1911–62) [hereafter *CFR*], *1308–19*, p. 151 and again in 1313, ibid., p. 163. William de Caunteton was made sheriff of Cork in 1309 under the great seal of England, ibid., p. 51. Richard de Clare was made sheriff of Limerick in 1309 under the English great seal, ibid., p. 42. John de Athy, who had previously served as sheriff, was made sheriff in 1310 under the same seal, ibid., p. 55 and again in 1312, p. 135.   **7** Astin Lane Poole, *Domesday to Magna Carta* (Oxford, 1951), pp 387–8.   **8** Robert S. Hoyt, *The royal demesne in English constitutional history: 1066–1272* (New York, 1950), pp 156–7.   **9** Richard Gorski, *The fourteenth-century sheriff* (Suffolk, 2003), pp 1–4.   **10** Philomena Connolly (ed.), *Irish exchequer payments, 1270–1446* (Dublin, 1998), p. 104; Margaret Murphy and Michael Potterton, *The Dublin region in the Middle Ages* (Dublin, 2010), p. 87.   **11** A.J. Otway-Ruthven, 'Anglo-Irish shire government in the thirteenth century' in Peter Crooks (ed.), *Government, war and society in medieval Ireland: essays by Edmund Curtis, A.J. Otway-Ruthven and James Lydon* (Dublin, 2008), p. 136.   **12** *CDI*, ii, no. 1528.   **13** *Chartularies of St Mary's abbey, Dublin*

too. The decision to grant these manors to Hugh de Cruise, with his combined experience as sheriff and chief serjeant was therefore an eminently sensible one. The Cruise family served as sheriffs of Dublin many times throughout the medieval period.[14]

Members of other prominent local families also served as sheriff during this period. In 1260, Robert de Clahull held this office.[15] His family had obtained the lands of Taney and Dundrum by the end of the twelfth century and Robert himself held Ballyfermot in south Dublin and Balrothery in the northern part of the county.[16] Robert's son Thomas died without issue but one of his daughter's Nichola married a future sheriff of Dublin, Wolfran de Barnewell. This family would later inherit de Clahull's property in Ballyfermot and Balrothery and go on to produce several generations of sheriffs of the county. Later in the thirteenth century, Geoffrey de Clahull served as sheriff of Dublin but this family's interests gradually shifted to County Kerry, where he also served as sheriff on at least two occasions. Though the main line of the Clahull family no longer had any discernible presence in County Dublin, through intermarriage with other prominent families, Robert's descendants continued to serve in this office for many centuries to come.

THE 1297 PARLIAMENT

The 1297 parliament brought significant changes for the sheriff of Dublin and resulted in a considerable amount of reorganization in terms of his responsibilities. For example, the ordinances passed at this parliament removed many of the duties formerly associated with this office. This may support the

[hereafter *CStM*], ed. J.T. Gilbert, 2 vols (RS, London, 1884), ii, p. 318, refers to an expedition which occurred in 1274 and ibid., no. 1389 mentions another expedition which took place two years later; see also James Lydon, 'Medieval Wicklow – "A land of war"' in Ken Hannigan and William Nolan (eds), *Wicklow: history and society: interdisciplinary essays on the history of an Irish county* (Dublin, 1994), pp 151–89. **14** See Appendix. **15** *Reports of the deputy keeper of the public records in Ireland* (Dublin, 1869–) [hereafter *DKR*], vol. 35 (1903), pp 39, 43–4; *Register of the abbey of St Thomas the Martyr, Dublin*, ed. J.T. Gilbert (RS, London, 1889), p. 200. Robert was possibly a descendant of John de Clahull, one of Strongbow's followers who was granted lands near Leighlin on the river Barrow: Giraldus Cambrensis, *Expugnatio Hibernica:the conquest of Ireland*, ed. A.B. Scott and F.X. Martin (Dublin, 1978), p. 195. Robert held lands in Balrothery: see Peter Crooks (ed.), *A Calendar of Irish Chancery Letters, c.1244–1509* (online edition, Dublin, 2012), available at http://chancery.tcd.ic/ [hereafter CIRCLE], PR 11 Edw. II, §16. According to http://thepeerage.com/p29952.htm#i299516 Robert de Clahull married Isolde de Courcy – her parents (Patrick de Courcy and Nesta) died in the mid-thirteenth century – so her husband is a contemporary of the sheriff and is possibly the same individual – they had no issue. Robert must have subsequently remarried or had issue from a previous marriage because his heir is mentioned in various chancery letters: CIRCLE, PR 11 Edw. II, §§16, 56, 117, CIRCLE, CR 20 Edw. II, §168. **16** F.E. Ball, *The history of the County Dublin*, 6 vols (Dublin, 1902–20), iv, pp 101–2.

notion that the office of sheriff in Ireland, much like its counterpart in England, was experiencing something of a decline. However, it is far more likely that the apparatus of local government simply outgrew the office of sheriff. The thirteenth century was a time when the government of English Ireland, in regard to both central and local administration, expanded enormously. As the sheriff's responsibilities increased, the tasks associated with the office would have become virtually impossible for one man to manage by himself. Before 1297, the sheriff of Dublin was not only responsible for the county as we would recognize it today, because it also included much of the modern county of Wicklow; he was also responsible for the de Verdon lands of Meath, the cross-lands (church lands) of the rest of Leinster as well as far-flung Ulster. Additionally, it appears that the sheriff of Dublin often held the office of constable of Dublin Castle during the thirteenth century. In 1245, for example, Simon Murdagh held both offices.[17] The sheriff was also accountable for the lands belonging to the king in Dublin, which will be investigated below.

The solution to the overburdened sheriff in the wake of the 1297 parliament was to create new offices and officials. Kildare acquired its own sheriff shortly before this parliament was summoned and in its aftermath County Meath was created out of Theobald de Verdun's share of the liberty of Meath, acquiring its own county court located in Kells. The existence of a county court should have meant that Meath also procured its own sheriff but the sheriff of Dublin continued to act as sheriff of this new county for a further five years. From this point on, however, although sheriffs of Dublin occasionally served as sheriff of Meath, the offices were never again held jointly. During the fourteenth century, the administrations of both counties were always distinct and separate. Conversely, the sheriff of Dublin was still involved in the administration of the liberty of Ulster after this date, proving that statutes passed in parliament were not necessarily always enforced.

Up to the end of the thirteenth century, the sheriff of Dublin was also responsible for the crown lands located in the hinterland of Dublin. At the time of the invasion, it would seem that the crown intended on retaining most of the land around Dublin. By 1235, however, Henry III decided to let most of the royal demesne out to farm, keeping just Crumlin, Newcastle Lyons, Esker and Saggart in his own hands.[18] As well as the financial, judicial and adminis-trative organization of these manors, the sheriff was also responsible for their defence. These duties became the responsibility of the seneschal of the royal demesne from the beginning of the fourteenth century at the very latest.[19] The office of seneschal, like that of the sheriff, had military functions and

---

17 Also spelled Murydach and Muridac: *Calendar of the patent rolls* [...], *1232–[1509]*, 53 vols (PRO, London, 1911) [hereafter *CPR*], *1367–70*, pp 123–4; he also served as constable of the Dublin Castle because on 16 Nov. 1245 he was ordered to deliver the castle and county to John fitz Geoffrey, the Justiciar: *CDI*, i, no. 2792.   18 *CDI*, i, no. 2254.   19 Áine Foley, 'Crown and community on the royal manors of the Liffey Valley' (PhD, University of

considering the strategic importance of the royal manors to the overall defence of Dublin it made sense creating an officer with similar powers whose duties would be specifically focussed in this area. The sheriff, however, was not completely excluded from the administration of the royal demesne. He had the duty of seizing the property of any keepers or farmers who failed to pay their revenues into the exchequer and he could also be called upon to hold inquests.[20]

SHRIEVAL CORRUPTION

Central government was not only concerned that the sheriff was overburdened with responsibility, it also appears to have had very little trust in the men who held the office. This, at least, is the distinct impression given by earlier statutes passed in 1285. One ordinance claimed that in the past sheriffs imprisoned those who committed relatively minor crimes, while frequently allowing serious offenders and notorious felons to go free. It appears that these officers often released prisoners when it was to their own financial benefit, even if it was to the detriment of the community at large. However, they kept their enemies and those who could not pay their fines in prison. This is an indication that the office of sheriff was often open to corruption. It would seem that sheriffs sometimes used their position to help friends as well as settling personal scores. The ordinance threatened to imprison sheriffs involved in these practices. Another statute from the same year ordered that no sheriff could take any reward in relation to his office apart from the fees paid to him by the king. This also implies that the office could be open to corruption. The punishment for profiting from the office was to be fined twice the amount of the reward they received. There is not a lot of evidence of corruption and extortion committed by the sheriff of Dublin. The sheriff had a chamber in Dublin Castle and his proximity to central government – at least when it was based in Dublin – was undoubtedly a powerful incentive not to misbehave.

The further away one got from Dublin the more likely it was that sheriffs would be involved in corruption and an examination of the justiciary rolls from the turn of the fourteenth century confirms the notion that the sheriffs of far-flung counties like Limerick and Kerry were particularly notorious individuals. In 1295, for example, Richard de Cantelup was accused of cutting off the limbs of Thomas Obrochan during his tenure as sheriff of Kerry. Thomas had been apprehended for the death of Ralph de Cantelup, undoubtedly a relative of the sheriff, and Richard decided to take matters into his own hands rather than going through official channels.[21] He was clearly

Dublin, 2010), pp 111–37.   **20** Ibid., p. 95; Gorski, *The fourteenth-century sheriff*, p. 2.
21 *Calendar of the justiciary rolls of Ireland*, ed. J. Mills et al., 3 vols (Dublin, 1905–56) [hereafter *CJR*], *1295–1303*, p. 25.

using the office to settle personal scores. The behaviour of his successor Nicholas de Sampford was more typical of the kind of corruption committed by sheriffs. On 6 September 1295, for example, he was charged with releasing a certain Peter son of John from prison on the payment of two marks.[22] This was just the tip of the iceberg and at the same court session in Tralee, he was accused of taking cattle, sheep, horses, money and other items from several different individuals. The sheriff claimed to have returned some of these items and asserted that other items were presented to him as gifts, while claiming that the rest were handed over for the king's use and were not in his possession at all. Nicholas's excuses, by and large, appear to have been accepted by the jury, but in the same year Roger de Lesse, sheriff of Limerick, was jailed for – among other acts of misconduct – confiscating livestock belonging to Margery Goer. He defended himself by saying that taking her cattle was an act of 'gentleness', maintaining that some of his predecessors would have taken much more severe action and imprisoned her.[23]

It would be a mistake to focus too much on misconduct committed by various sheriffs. There are no sources as full as the justiciary rolls for the rest of the fourteenth century – the published version of these rolls ends in 1314 – so it is impossible to quantify how common this corruption was. Certainly, judging by this source for this short period, the sheriff of Dublin did not appear to have the same opportunities for corruption enjoyed by his counterparts elsewhere in Ireland. There is no doubt that even in Dublin the office of sheriff offered its holder the opportunity for extortion and it is possible that some individuals were more capable than others of covering up evidence of corruption. Judging by the multiple examples of men deeply in debt after their term as sheriff, however, one has to wonder how many took advantage of the office in this manner.

SOCIAL STATUS AND FINANCIAL LIABILITY

The men who held the office of sheriff of County Dublin were usually significant landholders within the county. The St Lawrence family of Howth held it on many occasions, for example, as did the Talbots of Malahide and the Tyrel family of Castleknock. All these families held their lands in chief from the king. In the late twelfth century the lands surrounding the city of Dublin were divided into small knights' fees. In theory, the men who held these fees were expected to bear arms in order to defend the city of Dublin, although by the fourteenth century they were simply expected to pay towards the defence of the city rather than do military service themselves. Many, however, continued to be involved in its defence, most tangibly through the office of

22 Ibid., p. 53.   23 Ibid., p. 41.

sheriff. As can be seen from the list in the Appendix below the same surnames appear repeatedly. The majority of those who served as sheriff of Dublin came from the families who held lands in chief from the king either in Dublin or in nearby Meath and Kildare. It is remarkable how many families whose members served as sheriff in the fourteenth century came from this small group. What is even more extraordinary is how they still had a monopoly over this office two centuries later.

The sheriffs of Dublin were mostly drawn from this small pool, but occasionally individuals who did not hold their lands in chief attained this office. Adam de Crumlin was one of these men. His family established itself in the locality during the early thirteenth century and may in fact have being among the first wave of English settlers in the aftermath of the invasion. Though they did not hold land in chief from the king their parcels of lands scattered across the county added up to a substantial landholding – most of these lands were held on the royal manors or on lands belonging to the archbishop of Dublin. They also had a history of being involved in county administration: Adam's father Thomas, for example, served as a tax collector towards the end of the thirteenth century.

Adam's involvement with the office of sheriff of Dublin dated back to at least 1290 when he served as clerk to the sheriff.[24] In 1299, Adam became sheriff and, just like other Dublin sheriffs serving in this period, he was sheriff of Meath too:[25] Adam being named as sheriff in judicial cases held in Meath while he served as sheriff of Dublin confirms this.[26] In 1304, a memoranda roll entry records that he was appointed sheriff of Meath again although on this occasion he held this office for just a month.[27] Luke de Belynges replaced him as sheriff in Meath and as John Comyn was sheriff of Dublin in this same year, it would appear that by this date the same individual no longer held these offices at the same time.[28]

Even if the sheriff of Dublin was no longer responsible for Meath, it is clear that his resources were stretched to the limit. Adam's stint as sheriff of Dublin suggests that an administrative career could prove not only time-consuming but also very expensive. Moreover, this is probably why the office was usually confined to the county elite. In fact, at the end of the thirteenth century, several men, including Adam, served as sheriff and each of their terms must have been very brief. Though at least one of them – Geoffrey Harold – originated from one of the main families of County Dublin, it is possible that he and the other men who served at the end of the thirteenth century were of lesser social status. The officials of the exchequer may have hoped that these men would be easier to control. Their terms of office came after the 1297 parliament and it is entirely possible that their appointments were associated

---

24 *CDI*, ii, no. 598.   25 Otway-Ruthven, 'Anglo-Irish shire government', p. 124.   26 *CJR, 1295–1303*, p. 283.   27 NAI, EX 2/1, 109; *CJR, 1305–1307*, p. 1.   28 NAI, EX 2/1, p. 77.

with the reforms implemented in its wake. The fact that each of these men
only served in office for a matter of weeks or months at most would imply that
they did not have the financial means to carry out the duties of sheriff. In
contrast, the terms of office of sheriffs serving in the early fourteenth century
appear to have been for longer periods. Moreover, most of them came from the
more important families in the county.

Certainly, the financial pressures placed on the sheriff were considerable
and Adam de Crumlin may not have had the means necessary to carry out the
tasks associated with the office. Robert le Blund of Tallaght took him to court
on at least two occasions seeking £6 5s. owed to him but each time the then
sheriff claimed that Adam did not have the means to pay this back because all
his goods had been taken to pay debts owed to the king.[29] There is some truth
in this because, in 1304, 38½ acres of wheat and 29 acres of oats at Crumlin
were taken from Adam to satisfy debts owed to the king.[30] However, the court
did not accept that Adam could not pay Robert le Blund and pressure was put
on the sheriff to make Adam satisfy this debt. It established that, although all
of Adam's lands in Crumlin were indeed in the king's hand, he also had rents
from property in the city and held lands from the archbishop of Dublin. It was
ordered that Robert le Blund be paid from these rents.[31] It is clear that the
sheriff was reluctant to extract this money from Adam. He was undoubtedly
keenly aware that a year or two down the road another sheriff might have the
awkward duty of confiscating his property in order to pay debts acquired while
on the job.

There are multiple examples of ex-sheriffs owing arrears on their accounts.
Some of these debts were still outstanding long after their deaths, which meant
that the duty fell on their descendants to pay these arrears. Adam de Crumlin
still owed money three decades after his term as sheriff – and long after his
death – underlining the pitfalls of this office.[32] Alternatively, it might demonstrate
the reluctance of subsequent sheriffs to call in these debts. In any case, some
individuals were very unwilling to be saddled with the responsibilities of this
office; in 1304, Gerard Cokerel refused to take the oath as sheriff of Dublin
and was fined 40s. He was ordered to take office on three subsequent occasions
but refused each time. His stubbornness earned him additional fines, which
grew increasingly larger, proving that those avoiding this office were just as
likely to incur debt as those willing to take it on.[33] Though the source suggests
Cokerel did not want to be sheriff, it may in fact be the case that he was not
available to hold office. On 25 June 1303, a letter of protection was issued to a

29 *CJR, 1305–1307*, p. 22.   30 NAI EX 2/1, p. 174.   31 *CJR, 1305–1307*, p. 199.
32 *DKR*, vol. 45, p. 24; NAI, EX 8/4, p. 999; Richard de Crumlin is named as Adam's heir
in the memoranda rolls for 1309–10 so he may have been deceased by this time.   33 NAI,
EX 2/1 p. 120; J.T. Gilbert (ed.), *Historic and municipal documents of Ireland, AD1172–1320*
(RS, London, 1870), pp 528–9.

Guido Cokerel while he was away on the king's service in Scotland and it is entirely possible that this was the same individual.[34]

Considering not only these financial liabilities but also taking into account how time-consuming this office was it would be reasonable to assume that most men would wish to avoid it. This, however, does not seem to have been the case. So what were the attractions of this office? The sheriff received a fee, which in 1300 was about £10 per annum. Taking into consideration that the sheriff had to pay his staff out of this relatively small sum, it is unlikely the job was sought for financial gain, or at least not for legitimate financial gain. The prestige of the office must have been a lure to some men and could serve as a stepping stone to other – potentially more profitable – administrative offices. In the 1290s David de Offinton who had previously served as sheriff of Dublin became a baron of the exchequer.[35] Other sheriffs were rewarded with the custody of lands belonging to the crown. John Garget who served as both mayor and sheriff of Dublin in 1273–4 was granted lands in Saggart in 1278 and ex-sheriff Henry de Gorham held Chapelizod and Newcastle MacKinegan.[36] Adam de Crumlin did not go on to hold higher office and the explanation could be that he died not long after his term as sheriff. In 1309, Adam's heir Richard is mentioned in the sources and Adam himself is conspicuous by his absence from the records after this date.[37] In fact, Adam was the only member of his family to serve as sheriff and this suggests they died out or declined in fortunes during the course of the fourteenth century.

THE COUNTY COMMUNITY AND THE COUNTY COURT

In spite of this example of a relatively minor landholder like Adam de Crumlin holding the office of sheriff the evidence demonstrates that in Dublin a small tightly-knit oligarchy dominated the office of sheriff in the fourteenth century, which will be explored in an investigation into the county community and the county court. There has been much debate, particularly among historians of medieval England, about the validity of the county community. For example, in her study of Warwickshire, Christine Carpenter expressed some misgivings about using the county as the basis for her study and argued that 'most counties had very little existence as political and social units until the later sixteenth century'. Other historians, like John Maddicott, trace the origins of the shire community in England back to the tenth century. He argued that in the fourteenth century 'the variety of the court's functions, part social, part

34 CIRCLE, PR 31 Edw. 1, §22.   35 Connolly (ed.), *Exchequer payments*, pp 74, 123, 127, 129, 134, 137.   36 *Calendar of Archbishop Alen's register, c.1172–1534*, ed. Charles McNeill (Dublin, 1950), p. 146; *DKR*, vol. 36, p. 25; *CDI*, ii, nos 1496, 1425, 1760.   37 NAI, EX 2/2, p. 434.

judicial, part administrative, part political, brought together all the constituent parts of local society'.[38] In English Ireland, the county communities were essential in terms of ensuring the survival of an English identity here, particularly in the area that would later encapsulate the Pale, but also to a lesser extent areas dominated by Anglo-Irish magnates. Brendan Smith has investigated the county community in Louth and Ciarán Parker has looked at Waterford but it is important that similar studies are done for other counties to help expand our knowledge of gentry communities elsewhere in Ireland.[39]

We must also question how useful the county is as a basis for local study. Both Dublin and Louth had strong county communities, but for very different reasons. Smith believes the 'primacy of the county' existed in Louth by the 1330s. It developed through the 'prompting of the crown' and the removal of 'its traditional magnate families and the demands of war. It has also come about through rebellion and mass violence'.[40] Dublin did not have these traditional magnate families – much of the land was held by the church or the crown in the thirteenth century and the knights' fees here were small in comparison to the rest of the colony.

In Ireland as in England, the landed elite of the county were obliged to attend the county court on a regular basis and these gatherings helped define the county community and gave it a voice. One of the most important roles of the sheriff was the administration of this county court. The first reference to a county court in Dublin appears before 1200; therefore, as noted above, the office of sheriff was established by this date and indeed had probably been in existence for quite some time.[41] It was essentially the sheriff's duty to ensure that all parties involved in a court case appeared on the appointed day. He also presided over the court and was responsible for the appointment and summoning of jurors. Aside from these financial and judicial aspects of his office, the sheriff was also in charge of maintaining castles and gaols in his county and, by extension, he was accountable for prisoners until they were summoned to court.[42]

A detailed account survives of an election that took place in the county court in 1375 to appoint representatives to go to Westminster on Edward III's orders and it provides a revealing window into the workings of the county court and community.[43] William Windsor, governor and keeper of Ireland,

38 J.R. Maddicott, 'The county community and the making of public opinion in fourteenth-century England', *Trans. Royal Hist. Soc.*, 5th series, 161:28 (1978), 30.   39 For example, Ciarán Parker, 'The politics and society of County Waterford in the thirteenth and fourteenth centuries' (PhD, University of Dublin, 1992) and Brendan Smith, *Colonisation and conquest in medieval Ireland: the English of Louth, 1170–1330* (Cambridge, 1999). 40 Brendan Smith, 'A county community in early fourteenth-century Ireland: the case of Louth', *English Historical Review*, 108:428 (July 1993), 587.   41 *CDI*, i, no. 116. 42 Otway-Ruthven, 'Anglo-Irish shire government', p. 130.   43 'Documents relating to the elections in the county court of Dublin, 1375–6' in M.V. Clarke, 'William of Windsor in Ireland, 1369–76' in L.S. Sutherland and May McKisack (eds), *Fourteenth century studies by*

tried to interfere in the functions of the county court by having Nicholas Houth [St Laurence] and William FitzWilliam elected to go to England. The purpose of sending these men over to England was undoubtedly to put pressure on the county community to grant subsidies to Windsor. Here is a list of the 44 men who elected them:[44]

Schedule with the names of the forty-four electors of Nicholas Houth* and William FitzWilliam.*[45]

William Youglon, prior St Mary's Abbey	Thomas Staunton
Henry Michelle*	Prior de Holmpatrick
William FitzEustace	Robert Holywod**
William Rodiard	Nicholas Cowlok
John Gerveys	William White de Borondistone**
John Haselbery	Richard Glandhary
Patrick Carmardyn	Robert Kysshok
John Walsh	Walter Rath
Richard Milys	John FitzWilliam**
Michael Darcy	Roger Belynges de Rogerestoun
Richard Tyrelle**	William FitzWilliam*
Hugo FitzWilliam**	Nicholas Snyterby
Roger Tyrell**	Nicholas Lympt
John Belynges de Balyloghe	Reginald Bernevalle**
John Beg	Thomas Tyrell**
John Belynges de Belynges	Robert Gale
Hugo Byrmyngham	Richard Venerous
William Boltham	John Kedy
Reginald Blakebourne	Richard Forneys
Robert Cadell*	John Bristow
Richard Bernard	Reginald Lovelle
Ralph Prodom	Robert Bernevalle**

A second group of men, just twenty in total, elected Nicholas Houth and Richard White – it appears that they did not want William FitzWilliam representing the county because he was an associate of the controversial chief governor of Ireland, William Windsor, and potentially would not have served

M.V. Clarke (Oxford, 1937), pp 237–41 (I have not standardized the spelling of names from these lists); CIRCLE, PR 50 Edw. III, §4. For an account of the circumstances surrounding the summoning of this county court, see Peter Crooks, 'Negotiating authority in a colonial capital: Dublin and the Windsor Crisis, 1369–78' in Seán Duffy (ed.), *Medieval Dublin IX* (Dublin, 2009), pp 131–51. **44** Those listed with one asterisk beside their name served as sheriff at some point and those marked with two asterisks were family members of sheriffs. **45** Many of these names occur on the petition for a new election: Clarke, 'William of

the best interests of the county. Though the second list is shorter, there are a greater number of men who served as sheriff or were family members of sheriffs:

Schedule with the names of the twenty electors of Nicholas Houth* and Richard White**:

Prior St Trinity, Dublin	Nicholas White**
Nicholas Houth*	John Tryveus
John Fynglas**	Thomas Botyller*
Richard White de Kyllestyr**	Robert Wellys
Richard Cruise de Kylsalghan**	John Houthe**
John Cruise*	Thomas Houthe**
Laurence Wodeloke**	John Talbot de Mayn**
Richard FitzRoberti Cruise**	Richard Talbot*
William Seriaunt	Richard Netervyll**
Robert Geffrey	Richard Cruise, junior**

A patent letter dated 26 March 1376 reveals that the sheriff, who is unnamed but is probably Reginald Talbot, considered the men represented in this second list to be the 'better magnates and commons of the county'.[46] The implication here is that the social make-up of the county court was quite diverse and included men of different social ranks, with those families who controlled the office of sheriff at the top. Richard White's election in place of William FitzWilliam did cause some resentment in the county court and a complaint was sent to the king from some individuals declaring that they had not agreed to this election. William Windsor and the Irish council, perhaps unsurprisingly, described those from the longer list who elected William FitzWilliam as the better and more sufficient persons in the county. The county was ordered to accept William FitzWilliam, but they did not do so. Moreover, the fact that the sheriff backed the candidate not supported by the crown's representative indicates that his loyalties lay squarely with his own community, or at least the factions within this community that represented the shrieval class.

The list includes many men who never served in the office of sheriff, but even so, they were important members of the county community. Though members of the Serjeant family never served as sheriff – and most of their interests lay within the city of Dublin – they contributed to the defence of the county.[47] In 1403, for example, Thomas Serjeant was a keeper of the peace

Windsor', p. 237.   **46** CIRCLE, PR 50 Edw. III, §4.   **47** For the family, see Charles Smith, 'Patricians in medieval Dublin: the career of the Sargent family' in Seán Duffy (ed.), *Medieval Dublin XI* (Dublin, 2011), pp 219–28.

along with Thomas Houth (who is also on the list), and they were commissioned to defend the marches. Thomas Serjeant was the nephew of Robert Tyrel, baron of Castleknock, and through him inherited several parcels of land and many of his tenants shared the same surnames as sheriffs of Dublin including the Oweyns, Cruises, Tyrells and Luttrells.[48]

An examination of the records reveals that all these men were closely connected through kinship, marriage and landed interests. Chancery letters, for example, highlight some of these affiliations. In 1303, Guido Cokerel, who is probably the same person as Gerard Cokerel who refused to accept the office of sheriff, appointed John Locard, possibly a relative of a recent sheriff of Dublin Richard Locard, his attorney while he went to Scotland.[49] In 1377, the incumbent sheriff of Dublin William FitzWilliam and former sheriff Henry Michell served on an inquisition together.[50] The close connections among the shrieval elite of County Dublin are highlighted in 1382 when six men who had either served as sheriff or who would subsequently serve in this office were appointed keepers of the peace for County Dublin.[51] This is not to suggest that interactions were always positive: in 1382 FitzWilliam was ordered to arrest former sheriff Reginald Talbot, who appeared to be fleeing the jurisdiction, possibly because he owed the king money that had not been accounted for in the exchequer.[52] Notably, Talbot may have been the sheriff who previously tried to block FitzWilliam's election to represent the county before the king. If this is the case, there probably was very little love lost between them.

The fact that the office of sheriff was usually granted to an important landowner from the locality suggests that the crown was generally willing to accommodate local interests and local men. Of course, crown policy changed according to whoever was sitting on the throne. An examination of the Statutes reveals that in 1331, during the reign of Edward III, the county community were given the right to elect their own sheriff, although this was revoked in 1391 during the reign of Richard II.[53] Richard put the responsibility of appointing sheriffs into the hands of the chancellor, treasurer and chief baron of the exchequer. Richard clearly wanted greater government control over the choice of sheriff. It is difficult to say if Richard's decree had any great effect in Ireland because the sheriffs for the five-year period following this parliament have not been identified by this present writer, but William Ardern who served in 1396 might have been an outsider because it is the only time this surname appears among the list of sheriffs.[54] Logically, if sheriffs were elected by the community at this time it is far more likely that they would have chosen a local.

48 CIRCLE, PR 9 Hen. IV §37. 49 CIRCLE, PR 31 Edw. I, §28. 50 CIRCLE, CR 51 Edw. III, §11. 51 In 1382, Richard Talbot, Nicholas Howth, William FitzWilliam, Thomas Maureward, John Cruise and Reginald Talbot became keepers of the peace for County Dublin: CIRCLE, PR 5 Ric. II, §206. 52 CIRCLE, PR 5 Ric. II, §198. 53 *Statutes and ordinances and acts of the parliament of Ireland, King John to Henry V*, ed. H.F. Berry (Dublin, 1907), pp 325, 493. 54 John D'Alton, *The history of the County Dublin* (Dublin, 1838), p. 47.

We must be cautious about putting too much reliance on acts of parliament. Though the county communities were given the right to elect their own sheriffs on more than one occasion during the fourteenth century the evidence would suggest that elections never continued for very long and sheriffs were usually appointed by the exchequer – this practice closely parallels what was going on in England at this time. On the other hand, evidence of sheriffs being appointed in the exchequer is not proof that elections in the county court did not occur. It may be the case that when a sheriff was appointed by the exchequer it was simply a confirmation of an election that had already taken place in the county court. Certainly, the county community must have had some input into the choice of sheriff. If the exchequer picked an individual with no standing or influence in the locality, it is not likely that he would have lasted very long. Clearly, the needs of the crown had to be balanced with the needs of the community. The community who resisted the interference of William Windsor in their county court would not have tolerated a sheriff who was not of their choosing. It is possible that they avoided holding elections because they feared that they would be held liable for any debts or transgressions committed by the sheriff during his term of office.

CONCLUSION

The appendix of this article furnishes evidence of how the leading gentry families in County Dublin dominated the office of sheriff. This was not true of everywhere in Ireland. In Waterford, for example, magnates and their followers, including several men who came from the city of Waterford, dominated the office. Here, the county community was weakened significantly by strong lordship. On the other hand, powerful magnates never served as sheriff in Dublin and it was very rare for men from the city of Dublin to serve as sheriff. In fact only on three occasions did an individual serve as both mayor of the city and sheriff of the county – during the thirteenth century Peter Abraham and John Garget served in both offices and later in the early fifteenth century Walter Tyrel served as both mayor and sheriff concurrently.[55] Compared with Waterford, the county community in Dublin appears to have been much more independent and not under the influence of magnate power, at least not obviously so. This was due, no doubt, in no small part to County Dublin's proximity to the central administration and the fact that, certainly during the fourteenth century, it did not have a resident magnate.

However, even in places like Waterford county communities existed, albeit under the control of a powerful lord. These nobles were anxious that they or

55 See Appendix; these are the only examples I have been able to find of men who held both offices.

one of their followers held the office of sheriff to enable them to manipulate the apparatus of county administration to their own advantage. A resident magnate may not have controlled the county community in Dublin, but this did not mean it was any more pliable to royal administration. The sheriff may have been a crown official but he always had to balance the needs of the administration with those of the locality. He may have had to answer to the king, but he also had to answer to his own community.

APPENDIX: SHERIFFS OF DUBLIN 1202–1485[56]

Name	Tenure	Name	Tenure
Henry de Braybrook	$c.$1202–6[57]	Simon Murdagh	$c.$1245[64]
Geoffrey Luttrell	1212[58]–13[59]	Walter de Gateleye	$c.$1247[65]
Richard le Corner	$c.$1220[60]	William the Clerk	1254–5[66]
John Travers	1228[61]	Peter Abraham	1256–7[67]
Meyler de Cursun	1228–9[62]	Ralph de Euere	1258[68]
Hugh de Leg'	1232–7[63]	Robert de Clahull	1260–61[69]

56 Though the article is mainly concerned with the fourteenth-century sheriff, this list will catalogue all sheriffs of Dublin between 1202, when the first known sheriff was recorded, up to 1485. The author intends on constructing similar inventories for the all the counties and liberties of Ireland and would welcome any amendments or additions to this list. Where possible, spelling has been standardized.   **57** *Christ Church deeds*, ed. M.J. McEnery and Raymond Refaussé (Dublin, 2001), no. 16, p. 39; *DKR*, vol. 20, p. 39; *CStM*, i, p. 77; Braybrook also served as sheriff in England, see D.A. Carpenter, 'The decline of the curial sheriff in England 1194–1258', *EHR*, 91:358 (Jan., 1976), 9.   **58** O. Davies and D.B. Quinn, 'The Irish pipe roll of 14 John', *Ulster Journal of Archaeology*, 3rd ser., 4, supp. (Jul. 1941), 7.   **59** Sir John T. and Lady Gilbert (eds), *Calendar of ancient records of Dublin* [hereafter *CARD*], 19 vols (Dublin, 1889–1944), i, p. 170; *Reg. St Thomas*, pp 17, 23, 283; *CStM*, i, p. 249.   **60** *CStM*, i, p. 119; *CDI*, i, no. 768. This sheriff is possibly related to William de la Corner, bishop of Meath: B.R. Kemp, 'Corner, William de la (*d.* 1291)', *Oxford Dictionary of National Biography*, [http://www.oxforddnb.com/view/article/95179, accessed 18 May 2011]. Avicia de la Corner, the founder and first prioress of the priory of the Holy Trinity at Lismullen, county Meath, may have been another relative: Murphy & Potterton (eds), *The Dublin region*, p. 256.   **61** *DKR*, vol. 35, p. 21; *Reg. St Thomas*, p. 35; John Travers is Geoffrey de Marisco's nephew: see *CDI*, i, p. 314. The Travers family later held the manor of Monkstown: Murphy & Potterton (eds), *The Dublin region*, p. 104. They were also prominent landholders in the northern part of Fingal: Ball, *History of the County Dublin*, vi, p. 51.   **62** *DKR*, vol. 35, p. 30; *CStM*, i, p. 129.   **63** *DKR*, vol. 35, p. 34; *CStM*, i, p. 37.   **64** This name is also spelled Murydach and Muridac: *CPR 1367–70*, pp 123–4; he also served as constable of the Dublin Castle and on 16 Nov. 1245 he was ordered to deliver the castle and county to John fitz Geoffrey, the justiciar: *CDI*, i, no. 2792.   **65** *Christ Church deeds*, no. 58; *DKR*, vol. 20 p. 46.   **66** 'The Book of Howth' in J.S. Brewer et al. (eds), *Calendar of the Carew manuscripts preserved in the archiepiscopal library at Lambeth, 1515–74*, 6 vols (London, 1867–73), v, p. 432.   **67** *CARD*, i, p. 101. Abraham also served as mayor of the city of Dublin.   **68** During Easter term 42 Hen. III [1258] Ralph was paid £18 13s. 4d. to freight ships with grain to Gascony, NLI, [Harris] MS 1, p. 220v; CIRCLE, Hen. III, §14.   **69** *DKR*, vol. 35, pp 39, 43–4; *Reg. St Thomas*, p. 200. Robert was possibly a

Name	Tenure	Name	Tenure
Ralph de Oure	1267[70]	Henry de Gorham	*c.*1 Nov. 1278–
Robert de Thurleby	1270–73[71]		Easter 1279[77]
Henry de Gorham	1 May 1272–	Robert de Thurleby	*ante* 1279[78]
	1 May 1273[72]	David de Offinton	*c.*1279–82[79]
John Garget	1273–4[73]	Wolfran de Barnewall	*c.*1281–4[80]
Hugh de Cruise	*ante* 1274[74]	Thomas de Isham	*c.*1286[81]
Geoffrey de Clahull	*ante* 1274[75]	Milo de Cruise	1287[82]
David de Offinton	*c.*1277[76]	Thomas de Isham	1288[83]

descendant of John de Clahull, one of Strongbow's barons, who according to Giraldus held a castle near Leighlin: Giraldus Cambrensis, *Expugnatio Hibernica* (Dublin, 1978), p. 195. This family held Dundrum and Taney after the invasion: Ball, *A history of the County Dublin*, ii, p. 66. A Robert Clahull, who may have been the sheriff, or his son, held lands in Ballyfermot and Balrothery: Ball, *History of the County Dublin*, iv, p. 101; James Grace of Kilkenny, *Annales Hiberniae*, ed. Richard Butler (Dublin, 1842), p. 60; CIRCLE, PR 11 Edw. II, §§16, 56, 117; CR 20 Edw. II, §§122, 168; a Robert de Clahull, who was a contemporary of the sheriff married Isolde, daughter of Patrick and Nesta de Courcy, http://thepeerage.com/ p29952.htm#i299516.   **70** On 29 Oct. 1267 Ralph de Oure was serving as sheriff, probably the same individual as Ralph de Euere who previously served as sheriff, *Calendar of ancient deeds and muniments preserved in the Pembroke Estate Office, Dublin* (Dublin, 1891), p. 4.   **71** *CDI*, ii, nos 889, 1053, 1577; *DKR*, vol. 36, p. 25. **72** *DKR*, vol. 36, pp 25, 45. Gorham held the manor of Chapelizod: *CDI*, ii, no. 1760. **73** Garget is named as mayor and sheriff of Dublin: *Alen's register*, p. 146. Garget had custody of Saggart in 1278: *CDI*, ii no. 1496; *DKR*, vol. 36, p. 27.   **74** *DKR*, vol. 36, p. 45. He was king's serjeant of County Dublin from Michaelmas 1275 until Michaelmas 1284: CIRCLE, CR 13 Edw. I, §4. The Cruise family held the office of chief serjeant of Dublin by hereditary title throughout the late medieval period and they held lands in Naul in chief from the king: Murphy & Potterton (eds), *The Dublin region*, p. 93.   **75** *DKR*, vol. 36, p. 45. Geoffrey de Clohuile was sheriff of Kerry in 1265: Michael C. O'Laughlin, *Families of County Kerry, Ireland* (n.p., 2000), p. 38. He was made sheriff of Kerry again in 1284 under the great seal of England: *CFR 1272–1307*, p. 201.   **76** *Pembroke deeds*, p. 10.   **77** *DKR*, vol. 36, p. 42, he owed 70s. 8d. profit of county from feast of St Martin [11 Nov., 1278] 6 Edw. I until the following Easter.   **78** *CDI*, ii, no. 1763, Thurleby served as sheriff between 1270–3 but this seems to refer to a subsequent term.   **79** He was constable of Newcastle McKinegan at the time he served as sheriff and later served as a baron of the exchequer: Connolly (ed.), *Exchequer payments*, pp 74, 123, 127, 129, 134, 137; *CDI*, ii, no. 1614, *CDI*, iii, no. 169.   **80** *CDI*, ii, nos 1577, 1814. He paid various debts of the county into the Exchequer on 17 May 1281: Connolly (ed.), *Exchequer payments*, p. 103; *DKR*, vol. 36, p. 69. He was also responsible for conducting Robert le Poer from Ireland to the king in Wales, in 1284, during which time he appears to have been still sheriff: *CDI*, ii, nos 2257, 2310, *CDI*, iii, no. 169, CIRCLE, CR 12 Edw. I, §37. The Barnewall family held lands in Drimnagh, Terenure, Ballyfermot, Bremore, Balrothery and Balbriggan in the medieval period and would serve as sheriff on multiple occasions: Ball, *History of Dublin*, iv, pp 125–8.   **81** *CDI*, iii, nos 215, 271.   **82** He was sheriff by Easter 1287 at latest (*DKR*, vol. 37, p. 29); on 5 February 1288 he paid the profits of the county into the Exchequer (*CDI*, iii, no. 361), and was still sheriff on 1 July 1288 (*CDI*, iii, no. 403). See also *DKR*, vol. 37, p. 39. **83** *Registrum prioratus Omnium Sanctorum juxta Dublin* [hereafter *Reg. All Hallows*], ed. Richard Butler (Dublin, 1845), p. 60. Isham (spelled Hysham in this source) witnessed a deed on 28 October 1288, and is described as sheriff of Dublin; presumably he was serving a subsequent term as sheriff.

Name	Tenure	Name	Tenure
Richard Teling	*ante* 1290[84]	Adam Carmarthen	*c.*1298[92]
Ralph Bagot	1290–91[85]	Adam de Crumlin	*ante* 1299[93]
Richard Teling	1291[86]	Geoffrey Harold	*ante* 1299[94]
Richard Locard	*ante* 1292[87]	John Tuyt	*ante* 1299[95]
John Wodeloke	*ante* 1292[88]	Nicholas Nettervile	*ante* 1299[96]
Richard de Exeter	*ante* 1295[89]	Thomas de Isham	*c.*1299[97]
John Wodeloke	1295[90]	Riryth FitzJohn	*c.*1300[98]
Richard Taaffe	1297[91]	Richard de Exon	*ante* 1302[99]

84 *CDI*, iii, no. 780; *CFR 1272–1307*, p. 309.   **85** *DKR*, vol. 37, pp 44–5, paid the profits of the county between All Saints 18 Edw. I [1290] until Tuesday after St Patrick 19 Edw. I [1291]. The Bagot [or Bagod] family held Baggotrath near Dublin: Murphy & Potterton (eds), *The Dublin region*, p. 431.   **86** He appears to have served as sheriff both before and after Ralph Bagot's term: *CDI*, iii, no. 884. Teling was accused of concealing the chattels of felons when he was sheriff of Dublin: *CFR 1272–1307*, p. 309.   **87** *CDI*, iii, no. 1148. On 8 June 1290 Locard was in prison charged with trespasses of the king's money and other trespasses: *CPR 1281–1292*, p. 403, see also *CDI*, iii, p. 340. Locard held lands in Bothercolyn (south of Tallaght) that had previously belonged to Walter de Bodenham: ibid., pp 144, 149, 253–4, 296–8. He also held the manor of Kilsallaghan in north County Dublin in chief; Robert de Bree, sometime mayor of Dublin, held lands of him here: *Papers by Command*, vol. 42 (London, 1907), p. 22.   **88** *CDI*, iii, no. 1148. Wodelock was also constable of Dublin Castle: CIRCLE, CR 25 Edw. I §11.   **89** *CDI*, iv, no. 226. He was a justice of the common bench in 1302: H.G. Richardson and G.O. Sayles (eds), *The administration of Ireland, 1172–1377* (IMC, Dublin, 1963), p. 130. And he served as constable of Roscommon Castle in 1305: CIRCLE, CR 33 Edw. I, §§ 22, 23. He may have been related to Richard de Exeter who served as a justice itinerant in 1259 and deputy justiciar in 1270, Richardson & Sayles (eds), *Admin. Ire.*, pp 81, 136–7.   **90** He served as sheriff before 1292 appears to have been sheriff again in 1295: *CJR, 1295–1303*, pp 8, 66; *CDI*, iv, no. 264.   **91** *Stat. John to Hen. V*, pp 194*n*, 197, 261; *CJR, 1295–1303*, p. 99. Taaffe was sheriff of Meath sometime before 1308: NAI EX 2/1, p. 370. He held the manors of Liscartan and Callanstown in county Meath: CIRCLE, PR 8 Ric. II, §70. In 1284, Nicholas Taaffe, possibly a relative, was justice of the Dublin bench: CIRCLE, CR 12 Edw. I, §31. The Taaffes were one of the most prominent families in Meath until the male line died out at the end of the fourteenth century: Murphy & Potterton (eds), *The Dublin region*, p. 99.   **92** *CDI*, iv, nos 550, 613.   **93** *CJR, 1295–1303*, pp 261, 364; *DKR*, vol. 20, p. 66; *DKR*, vol. 38, p. 51; in 1304 made sheriff of Meath, just for a month (*CDI*, iv, no. 658), had previously served as clerk to the sheriff in 1290 (*CDI*, iii, no. 830).   **94** *DKR*, vol. 38, p. 51. Harold was dead by 1305 when his widow is mentioned in a close letter: CIRCLE, CR 33 Edw. I, §9. The Harold family held lands in Whitechurch and Haroldsgrange: Murphy & Potterton (eds), *The Dublin region*, p. 90.   **95** *DKR*, vol. 38, p. 51. The Tuyt family were one of the major landholding families in county Meath: Murphy & Potterton (eds), *The Dublin region*, p. 99.   **96** *DKR*, vol. 38, p. 51; *CJR, 1295–1303*, p. 438. He held the manor of Balygarth in Co. Meath: CIRCLE, PR 7 Hen. IV, §112.   **97** He previously served as sheriff in the 1280s and appears in the exchequer accounts for 1299: *CDI*, iv, nos 658, 705.   **98** *DKR*, vol. 38, pp 60–61. He held the manors of Clogheran and Balybren, County Dublin: see CIRCLE, PR 9 Ric. II, §158. See CIRCLE, CR 27 Edw. I, §22 for an assize of *novel disseisin* on four carucates of land in Clonmethan called Oldtown which also appears to have been held by this family. He served as a justice of the common bench in 1319: Richardson & Sayles, *Admin. Ire.*, pp 154–5.   **99** *CDI*, iv, no. 129; *CDI*, v, no. 72; *DKR*, vol. 37, p. 52; NAI, RC 8/2, p. 323. He held land in chief called Dervy (CIRCLE, CR 18

Name	Tenure	Name	Tenure
Adam de Hollywood	*ante* 1302[1]	Thomas de Rathlawe	*c.*1306–7[10]
John Wodeloke	1302[2]	Thomas de Cantewell	1307[11]
David le Maryner	*c.*1302[3]	Richard de Costentin	1307–8[12]
Adam de Hollywood	*c.*1303[4]	Geoffrey le Bret	*ante* 1309[13]
Gilbert le Blound	*ante* 1304[5]	Thomas de Rathlawe	1309–10[14]
John Comyn	1304[6]	John Oweyn	1310–11[15]
Gerard Cokeral	1304[7]	Geoffrey de Brandewode	*c.*1311–12[16]
Luke de Belinges	*c.*1304–5[8]	John Deerpatrick	1312[17]
Gilbert le Blound	1305[9]	William de la Felde	1313–14[18]

Edw. III, §210), possibly Darver in Co. Louth.   1 *CDI*, v, no. 72. Adam and his wife Clarice granted lands in Clogher to the archbishop of Armagh in 1293: Paul Dryburgh and Brendan Smith (eds), *Inquisitions and extents of medieval Ireland*, List & Index Society (Kew, 2007), nos 91, 102. Hollywoodrath in Mulhuddart, north County Dublin, was probably named after this family: Ball, *History of the County Dublin*, vi, pp 38–9.   2 D'Alton, *County Dublin*, p. 609; *CJR*, *1295–1303*, p. 409; *CDI*, v, no. 58.   3 *CJR*, *1295–1303*, p. 375, described as sheriff of Dublin on 13 May 1302; he was serving as sheriff of Kildare in 1310 (NAI, RC 8/5, p. 510).   4 NAI, RC 8/2, p. 307; see also RC 8/1, p. 277; RC 8/2, p. 329.   5 In 1304 he was described as former sheriff of Dublin (ibid., p. 305). He held lands in Callan, Co. Kilkenny: Dryburgh & Smith (eds), *Inquisitions and extents*, no. 154.   6 NAI EX 2/1, p. 77; NAI, RC 8/1, p. 284; NAI, RC 8/5, pp 669–70; NAI, RC 8/9, p. 105.   7 NAI EX 2/1, p. 120 [never actually sheriff: 'Girido Cokerel was commanded to take the oath as sheriff of Dublin. He said he did not wish to be sheriff. Therefore in mercy, assessed at 40s. On successive commands and refusals the mercy was successfully assessed at 100s.; £10; £20.'] It is possible that Cokerel was not able to assume the office of sheriff because he was fighting in Scotland at the time, on 25 June 1303 a letter of protection was issued to a Guido Cokerel and this may be the same individual: CIRCLE, PR 31 Edw. 1, §22. His wife Leticia held lands in dower in Castleknock: CIRCLE, CR 2 Edw. II, §60.   8 Accounted for the profits of the country between the 14 September 32 Edw. I [1304] until 7 Dec. 34 Edw. I [1305]: *DKR*, vol. 38, pp 98–100. The placename Belinstown in north Dublin may have been derived from this family: Murphy & Potterton (eds), *The Dublin region*, p. 184.   9 *Stat. John to Hen. V.*, pp 479–80; NAI, EX 2/1, p. 131; *DKR*, vol. 38, pp 98–100; *CJR*, *1305–1309*, p. 479; NAI, RC 8/12, p. 382; RC 8/2, p. 474.   10 *CJR*, *1308–1314*, pp 153–4.   11 NAI EX 2/1, p. 202. He held lands in Tipperary: Dryburgh & B. Smith, *Inquisitions and extents*, nos 273, 278, 282, 283.   12 *CJR*, *1308–1314*, pp 29–30; NAI, EX 2/1, p. 210; NAI, RC 8/10, pp 196–7, 575, 807–8; *DKR*, vol. 39, pp 21, 52–3; Richard Costentin held the manor of Balyrothery while the heir of Robert Clahull (possibly the former sheriff) was underage: CIRCLE, PR 11 Edw. II, §16. See also Dryburgh & Smith (eds), *Inquisitions and extents*, no. 14. In the late twelfth century this family held this manor: TNA, C132/14; Murphy & Potterton (eds), *The Dublin region*, p. 230.   13 NAI, EX 2/3, p. 638; CIRCLE, CR 24 Edw. I §10. This family held the manor of Rathfarnham: Murphy & Potterton (eds), *The Dublin region*, p. 89. Geoffrey le Bret held lands in Knocklyon: CIRCLE, PR 11 Edw. II §191. He also had property in Naul in north Dublin and Tipperary: Dryburgh & Smith (eds), *Inquisitions and extents*, nos 85, 163.   14 NAI, EX 2/1, pp 475–8, 485–6; *CJR*, *1308–1314*, p. 144.   15 NAI, RC 8/5, pp 669–70; *DKR*, vol. 39, p. 47. The Oweyn family held Rowlagh, Co. Dublin, in chief of the king, they also held land in Blanchardstown from the Tyrel family and Coldcut, which was part of the royal manor of Saggart: CIRCLE, CR 4 Ric. II, §32.   16 NAI, RC 8/6, p. 1.   17 *CJR*, *1308–1314*, p. 286; NAI, RC 8/7, pp 92–3; RC 8/9, p. 594.   18 NAI, RC 8/9, pp 384–5; RC 8/10, pp 415–16; RC 8/12, pp 154–5; *DKR*, vol. 39, pp 52–3. Fieldstown in county Meath was probably named after this family: Murphy & Potterton (eds),

Name	Tenure	Name	Tenure
Robert Clahull	*ante* 1315[19]	Philip le Bret	*c.*1327[31]
Adam de Howth		John de Balygodman	*c.*1327[32]
[St Lawrence]	*ante* 1315–16[20]	Philip le Bret	1329[33]
Simon FitzRichard	*ante* 1315–16[21]	Robert Sturmyn	1329–30[34]
Richard Talbot [of Malahide]	1315[22]	William de Finglas	1330[35]
Riryth FitzJohn	1315[23]	Richard Deerpatrick	*ante* 1331[36]
Simon de Feypo	*ante* 1316[24]	John Cruise [of Naul]	*ante* 1331[37]
Philip de Rathlawe	*ante* 1317[25]	Richard Talbot [of Feltrim]	*ante* 1331[38]
Geoffrey de Brandewode	1317[26]	Walter de la Hyde	1331[39]
Riryth FitzJohn	1317–18[27]	Richard Deerpatrick	*c.*1332[40]
Geoffrey de Brandewode	*c.*1319–24[28]	Peter Harold	*c.*1333[41]
John le Bret	1324–6[29]	Hugh Tyrell	*c.*1333[42]
William de Finglas	*c.*1327[30]		

The Dublin region, p. 184. **19** NAI, RC 8/10, pp 466, 575. **20** *DKR*, vol. 39, pp 52–3; NAI, RC 8/10, pp 806–7. **21** *DKR*, vol. 39, pp 52–3. Simon FitzRichard held a part of the manor of Maynooth during the minority of the heir of the earl of Kildare: *CFR 1327–37*, pp 271, 304. He also held lands of the archbishop of Dublin in Lusk: TNA, C 143/82. He subsequently served as a justice of the common bench, a justice of the justiciar's bench and a king's pleader: Richardson & Sayles (eds), *Admin. Ire.*, pp 156, 170, 176–7. **22** NAI, RC 8/10, pp 411, 806–7; D'Alton, *County Dublin*, pp 191–2; *DKR*, vol. 39, pp 69–70. The Talbot family held Malahide throughout the late medieval period. **23** Appointed on the 9 Sept. 1315, NAI, RC 8/10, p. 765. **24** *DKR*, vol. 39, pp 69–70, 71; NAI, RC 8/10, pp 531–2, 589, 743–4, 806–7. Simon de Feypo held lands in Santry: CIRCLE, CR 30 Edw. I, §1; NAI, RC 7/7, p. 508; Murphy & Potterton (eds), *The Dublin region*, p. 93. **25** NAI, RC 8/12, p. 348. **26** Ibid., p. 217, his name is misspelled Warnewood in this source. **27** *DKR*, vol. 42, p. 54. He arrested John Pecock, prior of Christ Church on either 18 Jan. or 17 May 1317: H.J. Lawlor, 'A calendar of the Liber Niger and Liber Albus of Christ Church, Dublin', *Proceedings of the Royal Irish Academy*, 27, C (1908–9), no. 1; *CStM*, i, p. 261. He had served as sheriff of Meath during the reign of Edward I (*CPR 1317–21*, p. 344) and was named as sheriff of Meath again in 1317 (NAI, RC 8/12, pp 56–7). **28** CIRCLE, PR 13 Edw. II, §57; *DKR*, vol. 42, pp 29–30, 54; NAI, RC 8/12, p. 541; RC 8/13, pp 1, 335, 510; RC 8/14, p. 1. **29** *DKR*, vol. 42, p. 54. John le Bret of Tulok was sheriff in 19 Edw. II: RC 8/14, pp 597, 638. Geoffrey le Bret held lands in the vicinity of Taney and Rathfarnham: *Alen's reg.*, pp 8, 86, 295, 303. He also received seisin of land in Colagh (in the barony of Talbotstown in modern-day in Wicklow): *Alen's reg.*, p. 168. **30** *DKR*, vol. 43, pp 32–4, he accounted at the Exchequer for the first year of Edward III's reign. On 13 October 1334, he was described as former sheriff of Dublin: NAI, RC 8/18, pp 287–8. As well as holding lands on the manor of Finglas from the archbishop of Dublin, this family held Dunbro, located in the parish of St Margaret, as well as Dunsoghly in the same parish: Ball, *A history of the County Dublin*, vi, pp 58–9. **31** *DKR*, vol. 43, pp 32–4, he accounted at the exchequer for the first year of Edward III's reign: *DKR*, vol. 44, 1912, p. 21. **32** *DKR*, vol. 43, pp 32–4, he accounted at the exchequer between the first and fourth years of Edward III's reign. **33** NAI, RC 8/15, pp 377, 425. **34** *DKR*, vol. 43, p. 34. **35** NAI, RC 8/15, p. 541. **36** *DKR*, vol. 44, pp 18–22. **37** Ibid., pp 18–22. **38** Ibid., pp 18–22. **39** *DKR*, vol. 43, pp 58–9; accounted in the exchequer for Michaelmas term 5 Edw. III (NAI, RC 8/16, p. 1; NAI, RC 8/16, p. 22). **40** *DKR*, vol. 44, pp 18–22. **41** Ibid., pp 18–22. **42** Ibid., pp 18–22. On 3 March 1335 Tyrell owed £7 16s. 4d. arrears of his account from the time he was sheriff: NAI, RC 8/18, p. 418. Hugh held one carucate of land in Knocklyon of Geoffrey le Bret, a previous sheriff of Dublin: CIRCLE, PR 11 Edw. II, §191. The Tyrell family were established in Castleknock by the late twelfth century: Murphy &

Name	Tenure	Name	Tenure
Walter de la Hyde	c.1334[43]	Rithery fitz Rithery	c.1337[52]
Wolfran de Barnewall	c.1334[44]	Geoffrey de Brandewode	c.1339–40[53]
John de Balygodman	c.1334[45]	Nicholas Abbot	1339–40[54]
Richard Deerpatrick	1334[46]	Maurice Roleg'	1341–2[55]
John Michel de Kyllegh	1335[47]	John de Cruise	1342[56]
Adam Talbot	1336[48]	Nicholas Abbot	c.1342[57]
Wolfran de Barnewall	c.1337[49]	Adam Talbot	1342–3[58]
William Comyn	c.1337–8[50]	John Haket	ante 1344[59]
Gilbert Travers	c.1337[51]	Wolfran de Barnewall	c.1344[60]

Potterton (eds), *The Dublin region*, p. 93. **43** He is referred to as sheriff of Dublin in a memoranda roll entry dating to 1334, NAI, RC 8/18, p. 453. He held the lands of Ballymadun, Dunshaughlin and Moyglare, TNA, C135/75. The Delahide family were major landholders in Meath: Murphy & Potterton (eds), *The Dublin region*, p. 99. **44** Accounted for his term as sheriff in the Exchequer between 1332 and 1335, *DKR*, vol. 44, pp 18–22; on 22 Dec. 1334 he was described as former sheriff of Dublin, NAI, RC 8/18, pp 422–3. **45** Letter dated 22 Dec. 1334 describes how he was appointed sheriff but could not come to the Exchequer to take his oath because he was on expedition with the justiciar John Darcy, he probably served as sheriff around 1334, which coincides with Darcy's term of office, NAI, RC 8/18, pp 422–3, CIRCLE, CR 8 Edw. III, §176. **46** *DKR*, vol. 44, pp 18–22; accounted in the Ex. for Michaelmas term 8 Edw. III, NAI, RC 8/18, p. 269. **47** Accounted in the Exchequer for Easter term 9 Edw. III, NAI, RC 8/18, p. 491; On 12 May 1343 he was described as former sheriff of Dublin, NAI, RC 8/22, p. 484, also known as John, son of Michael Kyllgh. Kyllegh might be Killeigh in Co. Meath: Murphy & Potterton (eds), *The Dublin region*, p. 101. **48** D'Alton, *County Dublin*, p. 47. **49** *DKR*, vol. 45, p. 24. Barnewall also served before 1334 (see above), and he certainly served for subsequent terms as he is named as sheriff of Dublin in July 1337: *DKR*, vol. 43, p. 102. **50** *DKR*, vol. 45, p. 24. In Feb. 1337 he was described as sheriff: *The account roll of the priory of the Holy Trinity, Dublin, 1337–1346*, ed. James Mills (Dublin, 1891; repr. 1996), pp 7–8. He accounted in the exchequer for Michaelmas term 1338 (12 Edw. III): NAI, RC 8/21, p. 1. He also accounted for Easter term 1339 (13 Edw. III): NAI, RC 8/21, p. 186. William Comyn held lands in chief in Balgriffin, Co. Dublin: CIRCLE, PR 20 Edw. III, §33. **51** *DKR*, vol. 45, p. 24. **52** Ibid., p. 24; He was granted wardship of Richard Talbot's lands in Malahide on 7 July 1329, Talbot had previously served as sheriff of Dublin in 1315: *CFR 1327–37*, p. 140; CIRCLE, CR 3 Edw. III, §2. **53** *DKR*, vol. 47, p. 23. **54** Accounted for Michaelmas term 13 Edw. III (NAI, RC 8/21, p. 333); accounted for Easter term 14 Edw. III (RC 8/22, p. 173, see also RC 8/23, pp 95–96, 207). Abbot held lands in Kilmacridok, Co. Kildare in chief: Dryburgh & Smith (eds), *Inquisitions and extents*, no. 317. The pitfalls of being sheriff are revealed in 1355 when John Butler was accused of burning Abbot's houses: CIRCLE, PR 29 Edw. III §44. **55** *DKR*, vol. 47, 1915, p. 52. This surname is unusual, and may indicate where he comes from – perhaps Rowlagh in south Dublin. **56** Accounted for Michaelmas term 16 Edw. III: NAI, RC 8/22, p. 1. **57** *DKR*, vol. 53, p. 31. **58** Connolly (ed.), *Exchequer payments*, p. 413; CIRCLE, CR 18 Edw. III, §§32, 38; *DKR*, vol. 53, p. 17; NAI, RC 8/22, p. 589 and accounted in the exchequer at Michaelmas term 1343 (RC 8/22, p. 616); in a memoranda roll from 18–19 Edw. III [c.1344–5] he was described as former sheriff (RC 8/23, p. 74). **59** *Account roll of Holy Trinity*, p. 76. In 1330 Haket went on expedition with the justiciar against the O'Byrnes in the Leinster mountains: CIRCLE, CR 3 Edw. III, §14. **60** Accounted at the exchequer c.1344–5 [18–19 Edw. III] (NAI, RC 8/23, p. 336); referred to as sheriff in a court case that dates to on or before 1344 (CIRCLE, CR 18 Edw. III, §68; see also *DKR*, 54, p. 21); in a memoranda roll from 18–19 Edw. III [c.1344–5]

Name	Tenure	Name	Tenure
Michael Montgomery	c.1344[61]	William Comyn	1355–6[70]
Fromund le Brun	1345–8[62]	Robert Cadell	1355–6[71]
Adam Talbot	1349[63]	Nicholas de Houth	
Henry Michel	1350[64]	[St Lawrence]	c.1356–8[72]
Nicholas Abbot	1351–2[65]	Richard Butler	1359–60[73]
Francis Oweyn	1352[66]	William Comyn	1361[74]
Nicholas Abbot	1353[67]	John Cruise	1362–3[75]
David Tyrel	c.1353–61[68]	Simon Cruise	1364–8[76]
Robert Cadell	1354–5[69]		

he was described as former sheriff (RC 8/23, pp 3, 7, 209, 331). **61** Montgomery succeeded Barnewall in the office on 15 Dec. 1344 (NAI, RC 8/23, pp 394–5; *DKR*, vol. 54, p. 21; *Account roll of Holy Trinity*, p. 83); accounted in the exchequer for Easter term 1345 (NAI, RC 8/23, p. 161). **62** Ibid., pp 439, 580, 691; RC 8/24, pp 1, 401; Connolly (ed.) *Exchequer payments*, p. 422; he was sheriff at some point during Ralph Ufford's term as justiciar (1344–6): RC 8/24, p. 129; *DKR*, vol. 54, p. 21; *CPR 1348–50*, p. 143. Brun was probably related to his namesake who served as chancellor in the previous century: Richardson & Sayles (eds), *Admin. Ire.*, p. 92. **63** NAI, RC 8/24, pp 574, 703, 750; RC 8/25, p. 93. **64** Was sheriff of Dublin during Michaelmas term 24 Edw. III [1350]: NAI, RC 8/25, pp 224–6. He is mentioned in a chancery letter dated 28 July 1359: NAI, RC 8/27, pp 474–7; CIRCLE, CR 33 Edw. III, §166, which confirms that his term of office was 1350–51. In a chancery letter dating to 25 October 1352 he is described as former sheriff: NAI, RC 8/26, pp 502–3; see also RC 8/25, p. 55. In 1362 he became king's attorney and in 1376 he was appointed a baron of the exchequer: Richardson & Sayles (eds), *Admin. Ire.*, pp 114, 180–1. **65** NAI, RC 8/25, pp 242, 299, 599. **66** NAI, RC 8/26, pp 1, 110–11, 274; RC 8/28, pp 67–8; CIRCLE, CR 27 Edw. III, §1. **67** Appointed in February 1353: NAI, RC 8/26, p. 120; see also ibid., 142, 260. **68** Joseph Henry Tyrrell, *A genealogical history of the Tyrrells* (Twickenham, 1904), p. 67. **69** NAI, RC 8/26, pp 441, 525, 617; RC 8/27, p. 1; NAI, 999/275/4; CIRCLE, PR 29 Edw. III, §§29, 132, 133; D'Alton, *County Dublin*, p. 47. He held lands in the Naul. **70** CIRCLE, PR 29 Edw. III, §108, he is also appointed escheator for Dublin. In the same year he was appointed sheriff he was also appointed captain of the ward of Tallaght: CIRCLE, PR 29 Edw. III, §34. **71** CIRCLE, PR 29 Edw. III, §§132, 133. **72** NAI, RC 8/26, p. 311, RC 8/27, p. 215; Connolly (ed.), *Exchequer payments*, p. 483. His term was completed by 14 February 1359: NAI, RC 8/27, pp 297, 414. In 1382, he became a keeper of the peace for County Dublin: CIRCLE, PR 5 Ric. II, §206. **73** CIRCLE, CR 34 Edw. III, §12, NAI, RC 8/27, pp 436, 483, 597–8. Butler had previously served as sheriff of Waterford: CIRCLE, CR 24 Edw. III, §1. **74** On 7 April 1361, on the order of the king, Comyn and 17 others came to the exchequer where he was chosen to be both sheriff and escheator of Dublin – Comyn had previously served in both offices: NAI, RC 8/27, p. 509. He accounted for Michaelmas term 35 Edw. III [1361] as both sheriff and escheator: RC 8/28, p. 1. Comyn held lands in chief in Balgriffin: CIRCLE, PR 20 Edw. III, §33. **75** NAI, RC 8/28, pp 99, 171, 303, 360–1, CIRCLE, CR 37 Edw. III, §15. He served as deputy escheator in 1369: Richardson & Sayles, *Admin. Ire.*, p. 129. In 1382, he became a keeper of the peace for County Dublin: CIRCLE, PR 5 Ric. II, §206. He held the manor of the Naul in north Co. Dublin: CIRCLE, CR 29 Edw. III, §136. **76** On 20 January 1364 he was sworn in as sheriff: NAI, RC 8/28, p. 361; see also ibid., pp 375, 447, 570, 577, 686; RC 8/29, pp 5, 267, 403; RC 8/30, pp 1, 78, 79; *The register of Milo Sweteman, archbishop of Armagh 1361–1380*, ed. Brendan Smith (IMC, Dublin, 1996), no. 26. In 1366, he was escheator in County Dublin: CIRCLE, PR 40 Edw. III, §12. Simon was the son of Robert Cruise, chief serjeant of County Dublin, an office he held by right of his ancestor Henry

Name	Tenure	Name	Tenure
William FitzWilliam	1373–5[77]	Richard Talbot	1386–8[83]
Reginald Talbot	1375[78]	William Ardern	1396[84]
William FitzWilliam	1377[79]	William FitzWilliam	1396–7[85]
Reginald Talbot	ante 1380[80]	Thomas Butler	1397[86]
Thomas Maureward	ante 1380[81]	Thomas Maureward	1399–1402[87]
William FitzWilliam	1382[82]	John Deerpatrick	1403[88]

Tyrel: CIRCLE, CR 40 Edw. III, §§5, 40. There is some evidence of a close relationship between these two families. Robert Cruise held land in Mulhuddart from the Tyrel family: Ball, *History of the County Dublin*, vi, p. 39.   77 NAI, RC 8/30, pp 116, 121, 560–61; RC 8/31, pp 58, 310–16; Connolly (ed.), *Exchequer payments*, p. 531; COA, PH 15170, p. 204. In 1382 FitzWilliam was escheator of Ireland: *DKR*, vol. 20, p. 84. In 1375, he was constable of Wicklow Castle, an office he held for the next decade: CIRCLE, CR 49 Edw. III, §38; CR 51 Edw. III, §§4, 25, 36; CR 1 Ric. II, §6; CR 2 Ric. II, §43; PR 5 Ric. II, §142; CR 6 Ric. II, §§55, 89; CR 7 Ric. II, §§22, 36; PR 9 Ric. II, §§33, 34; PR 10 Ric. II, §§157, 259. In 1382, he became a keeper of the peace for County Dublin: CIRCLE, PR 5 Ric. II, §206. On 20 September 1385, he was appointed keeper of the great seal of Ireland: CIRCLE, PR 9 Ric. II, §26. The FitzWilliam family were major landholders in south County Dublin and by the fifteenth century held the manors of Merrion, Thorncastle, Dundrum and Baggotrath: Ball, *History of the County Dublin*, ii, p. 2.   78 Was sheriff in Michaelmas term 1375; however, William FitzWilliam accounted for this term (NAI, RC 8/32, pp 1, 46); Talbot accounted for Easter term 1376 (RC 8/32, p. 50). In 1382, he became a keeper of the peace for County Dublin (CIRCLE, PR 5 Ric. II, §206).   79 CIRCLE, CR 51 Edw. III, §11.   80 D'Alton, *County Dublin*, pp 47, 200; on 15 Jan. 1382 he was described as former sheriff in an Irish patent letter and William FitzWilliam who was then sheriff was ordered to arrest him for attempting to go overseas, even though he owed various debts and accounts to the exchequer: CIRCLE, PR 5 Ric. II, §198. In NAI, RC 8/33 [*c.*1380], p. 137, he is described as former sheriff.   81 NAI, RC 8/33, p.145; *Rotulorum patentium et clausorum cancellariae Hiberniae calendarium, Hen. II–Hen. VII*, ed. E. Tresham (Dublin, 1828), p. 165. In 1382, he became a keeper of the peace for County Dublin: CIRCLE, PR 5 Ric. II, §206. The Maureward family held the manor of Skreen, Co. Meath, in chief: TNA, E 28/36/39.   82 Was appointed sheriff on 13 Jan. 1382: CIRCLE, PR 5 Ric. II, §42. And is described as sheriff on 15 Jan.: CIRCLE, PR 5 Ric. II, §198.   83 CIRCLE, PR 10 Ric. II, §§ 222, 227, 237; D'Alton, *County Dublin*, pp 47, 201. In 1382, he became a keeper of the peace for County Dublin: CIRCLE, PR 5 Ric. II, §206.   84 D'Alton, *County Dublin*, p. 47.   85 On 27 April 1396 he was appointed sheriff of Dublin, during pleasure: *Pembroke deeds*, no. 85; see also NAI, RC 8/33, p. 175.   86 On 21 Oct. 1397 [21 Ric. II] he was made sheriff, NAI, RC 8/33, pp 178–9. Previously, on 22 October 1386, he was appointed as a keeper of the peace in County Dublin: CIRCLE, PR 10 Ric. II, §195. He held the manor of Dunboyne, Co. Meath by right of his wife Sinolda le Petit: Murphy & Potterton (eds), *The Dublin region*, p. 99.   87 He was sheriff in 1399: D'Alton, *County Dublin*, p. 29. On 3 May 1400 he was appointed sheriff during pleasure: CIRCLE, PR 1 Hen. IV, §61. He was still sheriff in 1402: D'Alton, *County Dublin*, p. 29. On 1 June 1402 he was appointed to assess a subsidy of the county in his capacity as sheriff, he was also made a keeper of the peace: CIRCLE, PR 3 Hen. IV, §249. See also CIRCLE, PR 3 Hen. IV, §§227, 235.   88 On 19 March 1403 he was named as sheriff: Lawlor, 'Cal. Liber Albus of Christ Church', no. 38 (p. 21). Deerpatrick was killed in 1410 while on expedition with Thomas Butler, prior of Kilmainham, deputy keeper of Ireland against the O'Byrnes in the Dublin mountains: Walter Harris, *The history and antiquities of the city of Dublin* (Dublin, 1766), pp 276–7.

Name	Tenure	Name	Tenure
Thomas Cruise	c.1403–4[89]	John Talbot	1423[99]
John FitzMaurice	1404–6[90]	Sir Walter Tyrell	1425[1]
Robert White	1407[91]	Sir Robert Hollywood	1426–7[2]
Thomas Cruise	1408[92]	William FitzWilliam	c.1429[3]
Walter Tyrell	1408–14[93]	Nicholas Hollywood	c.1435–6[4]
Thomas Tyrell	1414[94]	Thomas de la Feld	1440[5]
Walter Tyrell	1416[95]	Robert Bathe, knight	
John Barret clerk, sub-sheriff	1416[96]	[of Laundeyeston]	1446[6]
John Talbot	1416–18[97]	Christopher St Lawrence	1449[7]
Walter Tyrell	1418–23[98]		

89 Thomas was the son of former sheriff Simon Cruise, he served as sheriff before 7 July 1404: *CPR 1401–5*, p. 406. In 1425 Thomas son of Simon Cruise was chief serjeant of the king in County Dublin: CIRCLE, PR 3 Hen. VI, §132.   90 He was appointed sheriff, during pleasure, on 7 July 1404: *CPR 1401–5*, p. 406. Still sheriff in 1406: D'Alton, *County Dublin*, p. 47. He had previously served as sheriff of Kildare: CIRCLE, PR 16 Ric. II, §11. He was pardoned the debts of both these counties on 1 April 1407: CIRCLE, PR 8 Hen. IV, §67.   91 NAI, RC 8/33, p. 188. The White family held the manor of Killester before it passed to the St Lawrence family of Howth. In 1423–4 White was appointed a justice and keeper of the peace in County Dublin: CIRCLE, PR 2 Hen. VI, §35.   92 NAI, RC 8/33, p. 191. He was appointed sheriff again in Michaelmas term 8 Hen. IV: ibid., p. 193.   93 Was named as sheriff on 20 Aug. 1408: CIRCLE, PR 9 Hen. IV, §33; see also D'Alton, *County Dublin*, p. 29; CIRCLE, PR 10 Hen. IV, §201; NAI, RC 8/34, p. 2, RC 8/35, p. 1.   94 NAI, RC 8/34, p. 12. In RC 8/35, p. 8 it says Walter Tyrell accounted for this term, so it is possible that Thomas is a scribal error.   95 NAI, RC 8/36, pp 5, 25, 566; in 1416 he was mayor of Dublin, ibid., p. 617.   96 Described as subsheriff for Walter Tyrell in Michaelmas term 1416: RC 8/36, p. 613. He also served as bailiff for the city of Dublin during Walter Tyrell's term as mayor.   97 NAI, RC 8/36, pp 28–9; RC 8/37, pp, 5, 16. John was the son of previous sheriff Reginald Talbot. He was still sheriff on 14 February 1418: CIRCLE, PR 6 Hen. V, §14.   98 D'Alton, *County Dublin*, p. 29; *Christ Church deeds*, no. 275, p. 87. NAI, RC 8/38, pp 3, 11; RC 8/39, pp 212, 215; RC 8/40, p. 254.   99 He was appointed on 25 Oct. 1423, NAI, RC 8/40, p. 258. In the following year on 24 March he was granted the manor of Drinan, which is located close to Kinsaley in north Co. Dublin: ibid., pp 263, 267.   1 CIRCLE, PR 3 Hen. VI, §§117, 130, 132; D'Alton, *County Dublin*, p. 47.   2 Became sheriff at some point before 24 Oct. 1426 (CIRCLE, CR 5 Hen. VI, §17), in fact his term of office may have been completed by this date; in D'Alton, *County Dublin*, p. 47 the date of his term of office is given as 1427, it is possible that this is a subsequent term. Robert was dead by 12 September 1430: CIRCLE, PR 9 Hen. VI, §38.   3 *Statute rolls of the parliament of Ireland, reign of King Henry the sixth*, ed. H.F. Berry (Dublin, 1910), p. 37, he was sheriff at the same time that Sir John Sutton served as deputy lieutenant.   4 Appointed after 6 Oct. 1435: CIRCLE, CR 14 Hen. VI, §26; Connolly (ed.), *Exchequer payments*, p. 574. Nicholas was the son of Christopher Hollywood and brother (and heir male) of previous sheriff Robert, on 22 December 1434 he was granted custody of two-thirds of the manor of Artane: CIRCLE, PR 13 Hen. VI, §34.   5 In a patent letter dated 6 February 1440 he is named as sheriff of Dublin: *COD*, iii, no. 135, p. 120.   6 *COD*, iii, no. 165, p. 162; on 29 April 1448 he was described as former sheriff: *Dowdall deeds*, no. 448. The Bathe family were major landowners in County Meath, but they did establish themselves in Dublin by the mid-sixteenth century when they acquired the lands of Drumcondra: Ball, *History of the County Dublin*, vi, p. 158.   7 NAI, M 2653, pp 138–9; CIRCLE PR 27 Hen. VI, §2. St Lawrence was named as usher on the Irish treasurer's account for Michaelmas 1431 to 27

Name	Tenure	Name	Tenure
Robert Bathe	1450[8]	John Barnewall	
Robert St Lawrence	c.1456[9]	[of Drimnagh]	*ante* 1470[15]
Robert Burnell, knight	*ante* 1459[10]	John Talbot	1473[16]
Richard Maureward, knight	1459[11]	John Talbot	c.1481[17]
Michael Trevers, gentleman,		Richard Cadell de Morton	1484[18]
sub-sheriff	c.1460[12]	Thomas Luttrell	
Robert Burnell	1465–6[13]	[of Luttrellstown]	1484–5[19]
James Blakeney [of Harristown]	1466[14]		

May 1436, TNA (PRO), E 364/73, m. B. In 1461, he was appointed a justice of the peace for County Dublin: CIRCLE, PR 1 Edw. I, §76.   **8** *Stat. Hen. VI*, pp 292, 705.   **9** *Stat. Rolls Hen. VI*, p. 465, he was sheriff at the time James, earl of Ormond served as deputy lieutenant, he appears to have served for one year, not during pleasure: J. Elrington Ball, *The judges in Ireland, 1221–1921*, 2 vols (London, 1926), i, p. 186. In 1462 Robert became Lord Howth.   **10** *Stat. Rolls Hen. VI*, p. 609, statute dates to 1459 and it describes Burnell as a former sheriff of Dublin. He also served as mayor of Dublin in 1450, 1454 and 1461: see *CARD*, i, pp 273, 282, 310. In 1461, he was appointed a justice of the peace for County Dublin: CIRCLE, PR 1 Edw. I, §76. He held lands in Balgriffin: CIRCLE, PR 15 Hen. VII, §1. Burnell married Margaret, daughter of previous sheriff Robert Hollywood sometime before 21 December 1440: CIRCLE, CR 19 Hen. VI, §13.   **11** *Stat. Rolls Hen. VI*, p. 605. Richard Maureward was baron of Skreen.   **12** *Stat. Rolls Hen. VI*, p. 755.   **13** NAI, RC 8/41, pp 24, 52–3; CIRCLE, CR 5 Edw. IV §2.   **14** Appointed sheriff 11 October 1466, NAI, RC 8/41, p. 32; see also ibid., p. 30. Harristown is located north of Finglas.   **15** Described as former sheriff of Dublin on 12 December 1470, RC 8/41, pp 213–14. Entry on p. 243 suggests that he was sheriff in 1468 and perhaps up to Easter term 1470.   **16** *Statute rolls of the parliament of Ireland, twelfth and thirteenth to the twenty-first and twenty-second years of the reign of King Edward the fourth*, ed. J.F. Morrissey (Dublin, 1939), pt 2, p. 138.   **17** *Stat. Rolls Edw. IV*, pt 2, p. 876.   **18** He was appointed on 12 Dec. 2 Ric. III: NAI, RC 8/33, p. 409.   **19** Ibid., p. 392.

Manuscript sources for the history of medieval Dublin in Trinity College Library, Dublin

ELLEN O'FLAHERTY

Many records have arrived at the Manuscripts & Archives Research Library (M&ARL) of Trinity College Library as a result of a conscious collecting policy of material associated with the College and its members. However, it appears that there was a less deliberate strategy employed in the acquisition of the manuscripts and documents that serve as sources for the history of medieval Dublin, and this fact is borne out in the variety of such documents available.

These important records are cared for by the staff of the M&ARL (formerly the Manuscripts Department), while repair and preservation work is carried out by the Preservation and Conservation Department. Together these two departments ensure that all archival documents are stored in the best possible conditions, and that they may be available for consultation (within reason) by all those with a genuine research interest. The digital imaging of part of the manuscript collection has been begun by TCD Library's Digital Resources and Imaging Service (DRIS), and it is hoped that one day all of M&ARL's collections, including those which cast some light on the history of Dublin city and county in medieval times, may be available in digital format.

It would be impossible to describe here in adequate detail each manuscript or document relating to the period and location in question, and so for the purposes of this survey a number of documents have been selected and these are divided loosely into three categories: first, collections of legal documents, including leases, deeds, grants, agreements and testamentary records (of both a secular and ecclesiastical nature); second, manuscripts produced by or for individual religious institutions (serving both administrative and sacred functions); and third, other miscellaneous documents and manuscripts, which do not fit into the other two categories, and which include annals and collections of historical writings.

* * *

Within the first category, the first collection to be discussed is TCD MS 1477, which is a collection of deeds relating to the parish of St John the Evangelist (also known as the parish of St John of Bothestrete) in the city of Dublin. This area includes the land surrounding the church of SS Michael and John, as well as streets such as Fishamble Street and Winetavern Street. These documents were lodged in Trinity College by the prebendary and churchwardens of the parish in the mid-nineteenth century, and the collection consists of 203 vellum deeds (many with seals attached), including leases, wills, grants, licences and appointments. These deeds were accompanied by an abstract of the contents of the documents (TCD MS 1477a). The documents range in date from *c.*1230 right up to the early eighteenth century. All are handwritten, and most – but not all – are in Latin. An introduction to the collection, with a calendar containing transcriptions or translations of each document, is available in a contribution by John L. Robinson and E.C.R. Armstrong to the *Proceedings of the Royal Irish Academy* in the early twentieth century.[1] The basis of the entire collection is TCD MS 1477/110, which is the will of John Lytill, a citizen of Dublin, who died in 1434 (fig. 10.1). By this deed he bequeaths his holdings in various Dublin parishes to the chapel of the Blessed Virgin Mary in the parish church of St John, and directs that his title-deeds be preserved among the deeds of that chapel. The collection provides an account of these properties over a certain period of time (before and after his death), including the various owners of the holdings, and the transactions in which they were involved. The documents provide evidence for the study of the history of the parish and its parishioners, the geography and topography of certain areas within and without the medieval city of Dublin, as well as links between the parish and the cathedral church of the Holy Trinity (Christ Church cathedral), and other religious houses in the city. The deeds deal with property within the bounds of the parish, as well as property outside the city walls, including land and dwellings in Oxmantown, a suburb on the north bank of the river Liffey. Extracts from the English translations of the Latin deeds and transcriptions of those in English by Robinson give an idea of the kind of transactions recorded by the deeds, and the areas and people involved:

> Richard called 'le Vineterer' & Robert de Yoaule, executors of the will of Richard formerly Inn-Keeper of Henry le Mareschal, convey to the said Henry a tenement in the Street of the Fishers, Parish of St Olave, Dublin, in breadth, facing the King's Way, 34 feet from the tenement of the Abbess & Convent 'del Hoggis' on the east to the land which was Henry Baret's on the west ... (fig. 10.2)[2]

> John de Capelis called le Boteler & Dyonisea his wife grant to William de Berdyffeld & Katherine his wife a piece of land in Oxmantown ... (fig. 10.3)[3]

1 J.L. Robinson and E.C.R. Armstrong, 'On the ancient deeds of the parish of St John, Dublin, preserved in the Library of Trinity College', *Proceedings of the Royal Irish Academy*, 33, C (1916/17), 175–224. 2 Translation from the Latin of TCD MS 1477/4 (1299); Robinson and Armstrong, 'On the ancient deeds', 180. 3 Translation from the Latin of TCD MS 1477/8 (1301); Robinson and Armstrong, 'On the ancient deeds', 181.

10.1 MS 1477/110: the will of John Lytill, a citizen of Dublin, who died in 1434

As well as providing material for the study of property transactions in medieval Dublin, these deeds also give us a glimpse into the life of the parish and its parishioners. They refer to streets such as Winetavern Street, Fishamble Street and Francis Street, and to buildings and landmarks such as Christ Church, the convent of Mary del Hogges, the King's mill, St Andrew's cemetery, and the gate of St Mary del Dam. Property types include houses, shops, 'tenements', 'messuages', and plots of land. The names and descriptions

10.2 MS 1477/4 (1299): conveyance by Richard called 'le Vineterer' and Robert de Yoaule, executors of the will of Richard, formerly Inn-Keeper of Henry le Mareschal, of a tenement in Fishamble Street

10.3 1477/8 (1301): John de Capelis called
le Boteler and Dyonisea his wife grant to
William de Berdyffeld and Katherine his
wife a piece of land in Oxmantown

of those involved give some idea of the general character of the landowning
classes, and of their origin and occupations: Henry le Mareschal, John le
Whyte, Elena Bretonn, Roger de Notyngham, John de Bristoll, 'gentleman',
'knight', 'fisher', 'taillour', 'sadeler', and so forth.

Those deeds originally in English are a valuable source for the study of the
late middle English or chancery standard which was in use in administrative
circles in Dublin during the period in question. An examination of the
nomenclature applied to the streets and areas involved reveals that there was
no discernible uniformity in spellings or designations. Oxmantown, for
example, is referred to variously as 'Oustmanton', 'Oxmanton', 'Ostmantown'
and 'Oxemaneston'; Fishamble Street is called the 'Street of the Fishers',
'Fishamelstrete', and '*Vico Pistarie*'; and what is now Christchurch Place has
been designated 'Bothestrete', 'Bowstret' and 'Bovestret'.

This collection, hitherto in a fragile state, has recently been carefully
conserved by the Preservation and Conservation Department; a special folder
has been constructed for each deed, which precludes the need for unnecessary
handling of the documents, and ensures their preservation.

Another collection of deeds relating to medieval Dublin is TCD MS 1207.
This is a collection of around 320 documents on vellum, some with seals
attached. Like TCD MS 1477 most of the documents are in Latin, and the rest
are in English. They were presented to Trinity College by John Stearne, the

then vice-chancellor, in the early 1700s, and they consist mainly of grants, leases and wills, and relate to property not just in Dublin city but also to land in more outlying areas in County Dublin. They range in date from 1246 to 1671. A calendar of some of the documents in this collection is available over six contributions by J.G. Smyly to Trinity College's journal, *Hermathena*, from 1945 to 1949. The numbering of deeds in Smyly's catalogue differs from the current references, and this can lead to some confusion over identification of particular documents.[4]

Ninety of the deeds in this collection belong to the Ashburn or Essebourne family, who had land and property in Dublin city, as well as in Kilmainham, Rathcoole and Swords. Another group of documents from this collection is known as the Passavant papers and relate to the Meonis family, and further deeds relate to the Stanyhurst family, some of whose members were prominent citizens of Dublin in the late medieval period. The remainder of the deeds are miscellaneous in nature and relate to other Dublin families and individuals. Other types of documents include copies of papal bulls, royal letters patent, declarations and petitions.

The property-related deeds involve several types of transactions, including grants of land from citizen to citizen, from the mayor and corporation of Dublin to individual citizens, and from religious houses to individual citizens. Property types include houses, tenements, messuages, and acres. The following is an extract from English translation an undated deed:

> John Britte of Rathfernan [Rathfarnham] assigns to John Passauant the guardianship and marriage of John, son and heir of Richard Harrold, and of all the lands and tenements which the aforesaid Richard held of him near Temelog [Templeogue] for the annual service of one pair of spurs.[5]

This is an example of an assignment of land relatively far away from the city of Dublin. Many of the properties referred to in these documents, however, were within the city walls, as can be seen from the following, dating from 1290, which describes a piece of land given from one couple to another for a token annual rent:

> William de Bristoll and his wife Juliana give as a wedding present to Thomas le Blound and Matilda his wife a messuage, which they had bought from William le Taylur situated between the messuages of Unfrid le Taylur and of William le Loungtayllur, extending in length from the road which is called Botestrete to another road which is called

---

4 J.G. Smyly, 'Old Latin deeds in the Library of Trinity College', *Hermathena*, 66, 69, 70, 71, 72, 74 (1945–9). An annotated copy of the bound version is available for consultation in the Manuscripts & Archives Research Library reading room.   5 Translation from the Latin of Deed 77 [*c*.1362]; Smyly, 'Old Latin deeds', *Hermathena* (now TCD MS 1207/136).

Krokerestrete for the annual payment of one rose at the feast of St John the Baptist … (fig. 10.4)[6]

The various wills in the collection date from between 1280 and 1691 and feature, among others, members of the families which dominate the collection, for example:

Testamentum et inventarium bonorum Gillanae de Meonis civitatis Dublinenses viduae.[7]

Testamentum et inventarium bonorum omnium Ricardi Stanyhurst olim majoris Dublinensis.[8]

Among those documents in English is the following that relates to property in Winetavern Street and Skinners Row, and the area now known as Darndale:

Be hit knowen to all men Þt I Richard Allen notary wrotet my hand a dede apon Þe towre & Þe hall wt thaportenances in Þe Wynetauern-strete & an orchard called Dernedale & ii meses in the Skynnerewe in Þe Citte of Diuelin in Þe name of sir Thomas Moyow chapelyn to John Hegham for terme of his lyve …[9]

The names of streets and areas that feature in this collection of documents are also worthy of note, for example, 'Rathfernan' (Rathfarnham), 'Rathcoule' (Rathcoole), 'Kilmaynan' (Kilmainham) and 'Temelog' (Templeogue); as well as 'Botestrete', 'Krokerstrete', 'Wynetauern-strete', '*Vicus Tabernariorum*' (Winetavern Street) and '*Vicus ovium*' (Sheep Street, now corrupted to Ship Street).

The final collection of deeds in this category differs from the other two collections in that it is in the form of a volume of transcriptions. This is TCD MS 552, which is the register of wills and inventories of the diocese of Dublin during the period 1457 to 1483 when Michael Tregury and John Walton were archbishops of Dublin. The volume itself contains sixty-three paper leaves, including transcriptions of documents in Latin, most of which are wills and inventories. The collection also contains some ecclesiastical-related documents. It is not known how the volume ended up in the Library of Trinity College. It was published by H.F. Berry for the Royal Society of Antiquaries of Ireland in the 1890s, which included translations of the text of the documents into

6 Translation from the Latin of Deed 6 (1290); Smyly, 'Old Latin deeds', *Hermathena* (now TCD MS 1207/65).   7 TCD MS 1207/128 (1348) (Smyly's Deed 69).   8 TCD MS 1207/258 (1501) (Smyly's Deed 199).   9 Transcription of Deed 168 (*c*.1470); Smyly, 'Old Latin deeds', *Hermathena* (now TCD MS 1207/227).

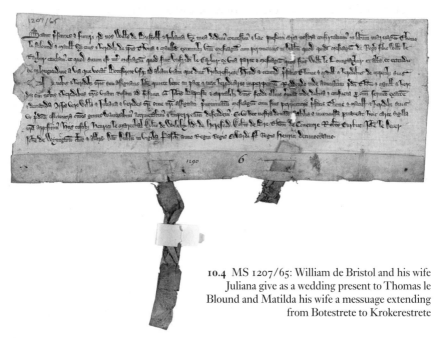

10.4 MS 1207/65: William de Bristol and his wife
Juliana give as a wedding present to Thomas le
Bround and Matilda his wife a messuage extending
from Botestrete to Krokerestrete

English.[10] Fifty-eight of the eighty-five documents in the volume are wills and
inventories, many belonging to farmers residing in the outlying districts of
County Dublin (mostly in Fingal), in areas such as Balrothery, Balscaddan,
Ballymadun, Mulhuddart, Gracedieu, Lusk, Swords, Finglas, Howth, Malahide,
Santry and Glasnevin. Some hailed from south and west Dublin, including
areas such as Newcastle Lyons, Esker, Clondalkin, Tallaght and Crumlin.
Some of the testamentary documents belonged to citizens of the city of
Dublin, including merchants and other well-to-do inhabitants. The will and
inventory of Archbishop Tregury himself, dating from 1471, is also included,
as is that of Archbishop Walton. The former follows a recognizable format: the
inventory lists the goods and property of the testator, as well as debts owed by
him; the will itself begins with the Latin words, whose English equivalent is 'In
the name of God, Amen. I — being sound of mind though weak in body … '.
This first part also deals with the appointment of executors and the proving of
the document before an official of the metropolitan court. The contents of the
inventories give a good indication of the type of goods and property belonging
to the testators, and of their status and lifestyle. Those of farmers refer to
livestock, crops, farming equipment and the price of land. Other objects
bequeathed include household goods, such as furniture and kitchen equipment
(pans, brass pots, skillets, bowls, basins and blankets) as well as fine clothes,
jewellery and ornaments. The text reflects contemporary social traditions: the
importance of religion and faith, burial customs, and the status of women.

Recipients of bequests include relatives of the testator, as well as the church, individual churches and religious houses, individual clergy, the poor, apprentices and servants of the testator, and religious and secular guilds. The names of testators reflect the ethnic origin of the better-off citizens, and sometimes their occupations. Names include Thomas Herford; Agnes Broun; Richard Boys, merchant, of Coventry; Robert Pecocke of Howth; John Hay of Santry; John Hamlet of Balrothery; Ellen Stiward; Peter the Smith; and Hugh Galyane, citizen of the city of Dublin.

This collection is an important one, not least because it is apparently the only official collection of fifteenth-century wills in existence in Ireland, and because relatively few documents of a testamentary nature from the period before the sixteenth century have survived. Another section of the volume contains official records of visitations made to several religious houses (including the priory of All Hallows) and communities in Dublin and its neighbourhood in 1468 by Archbishop Tregury and other high-ranking church officials. The names of all the members of the community are given in each case; lists such as these could be of assistance in the research of specific churches and religious houses during that period. The last section contains records of twenty-four sentences of excommunication – during the period April to May 1478 – pronounced against various citizens for the offence of contumacy (contempt of the authority of an ecclesiastical court). Such sentences were in Latin, and followed the same basic formula. The English translations of formulaic introductions to two of them are as follows:

> In the name of God, Amen. In these writings, justice intervening, we excommunicate Henry Russell, of Malahide, on account of his contumacy ...[11]

> In the name of God, Amen. In these writings, we suspend from the divine offices the parish curates of Rathmichael and Killiney, on account of their contumacy ...[12]

Other documents transcribed include appeals to the Holy See, marriage dispensations and judgments, and fragments of sentences by apostolic delegates. These are of value in the study of – among other subjects – the relations between Rome and the church in Ireland in the medieval period.

* * *

The second category of documents includes those that were produced by or for individual religious houses in Dublin city or nearby areas, and which give

10 H.F. Berry (ed.), *Register of wills and inventories of the diocese of Dublin in the time of Archbishops Tregury and Walton, 1457–1483, from the original manuscript in the library of Trinity College, Dublin*, RSAI (Dublin, 1898).   11 Ibid., p. 180.   12 Ibid.

10.5 MS 525, fos 46v–47r: extract from the register of the priory of All Hallows

some insight into the operations of these communities and, at times, the daily lives of their members. TCD MS 525 is the register of the priory of All Hallows (fig. 10.5). It was on the lands of this house that Trinity College was founded, around sixty years after the dissolution of the monasteries by King Henry VIII. The priory itself was established by Diarmait Mac Murchada in 1166 for Augustinian canons, and was later a victim of the process of the dissolution of the monasteries, becoming the property of the mayor and corporation of Dublin in 1538. The register is a small volume consisting of vellum leaves. The handwriting is secretary hand, with some Anglicana letter forms. The ornamentation consists of blue initials with red flourishes. It contains transcriptions of documents relating to the house itself and was put together in the fifteenth century. There are also some notes made in the sixteenth century throughout the text. The original documents, however, date from between the twelfth and fifteenth centuries, and consist of papal bulls, royal confirmations, legal documents regarding property in Dublin city, and grants of land in other parts of Ireland. In Richard Butler's edition of the documents in the volume, he provides a brief history of the priory and the

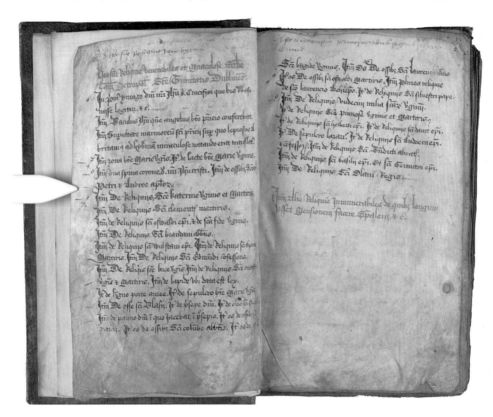

10.6 MS 576, fos 1v–2r: extract from the Book of Obits and Martyrology of Christ Church cathedral, Dublin

composition of the register.[13] Some relevant documents from other sources, including the Dublin City Archives, are also included in this work.

The papal bulls were issued by various popes, including Gregory IX, Urban III and Innocent IV. They confirm spiritual and temporal rights, property, privileges and immunities of the house. The royal documents include confirmations of rights and properties, and were issued by Edward II and Richard II, with references to the confirmations of Henry II. Throughout these documents are references to familiar areas, such as Baldoyle ('Baledubgall'), Glendalough ('Glindellacha'), and Donnybrook ('Donenachbroc'). The spellings of these and other places vary throughout the documents, and could be used, as could the other documents already referred to, as a source for the study of place-names and their evolution. It is also interesting to note the perceived geographical position of the priory according to various documents in the register, including *de Dublin, in orientale parte Dublin* and *iuxta Dublin*. This

13 Richard Butler (ed.), *Registrum prioratus omnium sanctorum juxta Dublin* (Dublin, 1845).

variance serves to emphasize the shift in the perception of the centre of the city
during and since the medieval period. As in the previous documents there are
many examples of names of citizens, including men with names such as Robert
le Decer, William de Bristol, Henry Tyrell and Theobald Walter, who were
involved in transactions with the priory, and who could be said to represent a
certain well-off stratum of Dublin society in the medieval period.

The second volume associated with a religious house is TCD MS 576, the
Book of Obits and Martyrology of Christ Church cathedral, Dublin (fig. 10.6).
This volume, which originally belonged to the latter cathedral, actually
contains two manuscripts bound together: a fifteenth-century book of obits
and a thirteenth-century martyrology. J.H. Todd, in his introduction to J.C.
Crosthwaite's edition of the text of the two documents, asserts that they should
be treated as two separate documents.[14] Both were written on vellum, entirely
in Latin, and were in use in Christ Church (the church of the Holy Trinity)
until the mid-sixteenth century. Holy Trinity was founded *c.*1030 by Bishop
Dúnán (Donatus) and the Hiberno-Norse king of Dublin Sitric 'Silkenbeard',
and was developed in the second half of the twelfth century by the then
archbishop of Dublin Lorcán Ó Tuathail (Laurence O'Toole) as a priory of
Augustinian canons. The volume belonged to the collection of Archbishop
Ussher, and may have been presented to Trinity College by King Charles II. It is
also thought that it was probably the work of Thomas Fyche, the sub-prior of
Holy Trinity, as it bears similarities to an early sixteenth-century register from
the same institution – the *Liber Albus* – which contains an ascription to Fyche.[15]

The first part – the book of obits – is fifty folios in length. It contains a list
of names of those for whose souls prayers were to be offered by members of the
community. The names of over 1000 individuals are recorded. The entries are
in various hands and date from the between the fifteenth and sixteenth
centuries. Todd claims that many entries are copied from older documents.
Names include those of individuals who were connected to the cathedral –
bishops, abbots, priors, cathedral officers, canons and brothers – as well as lay
people, including members of the confraternity. Also listed were prominent
state and municipal officeholders, archbishops, and priors of other religious
houses. Included is a record of the death of a mayor of Dublin, John Savage,
who died in 1499, as well as other prominent citizens of the city and the
country. In this way the Book of Obits is a source for dating important events
in the history of the city and the country at large. Caution must be exercised,
however, as Todd claims that there are many errors of fact and spelling in the
text. At the beginning is a list of relics that were to be found in Christ Church
in the medieval period, including a speaking crucifix, the staff of St Patrick
(*Bachall Íosa*), and a marble altar stone.

14 James Henthorn Todd, Introduction to John Clare Crosthwaite, *The Book of Obits and
Martyrology of the cathedral church of the Holy Trinity, commonly called Christ Church, Dublin*

There is agreement that the Martyrology – which follows the Book of Obits – is an earlier document than the latter. However, Raymond Refaussé asserts that it dates from the thirteenth century,[16] while Todd contended that it was 'not written before the end of the fourteenth, or beginning of the fifteenth century'.[17] It is written in a large bold hand, and is a register of Christian saints and martyrs. Among the feasts included are those of St Laurence O'Toole, patron saint of Dublin, and Saint Michan, and various other saints associated with the diocese of Dublin, such as St Fintan of Howth and St Begnet of Dalkey. The Martyrology is preceded by a calendar of holy days and an Easter table, and followed by some texts, including short lessons to be recited in the Chapter, and part of the Rule of St Augustine.

The third volume in this category of manuscripts produced by or for religious houses in Dublin in the Middle Ages is TCD MS 97, *Varia de Vita Monastica*, a thirteenth- to fourteenth-century manuscript from the abbey of St Thomas in Dublin. It is written in Latin on vellum, and has 274 folios. It contains various sections, including a calendar of holy days, a *doctrina tabularum*, regulations for members of the house, the rules of St Benedict and St Francis, and a transcription of a papal document, issued by Gregory IX. Being a Dublin manuscript, there are naturally various references to the city and environs throughout the text. These include an arrangement between St Thomas's abbey, St Mary's abbey and two Dublin citizens, Philip Bermengham and James Aylmer, for prayers to be said for the souls of deceased relatives in exchange for money for the repair of the monastic church of St Thomas; a fire in Dublin in 1283; and a list of saints, including some connected with Dublin, such as St Laurence O'Toole and St Audoen. On the last page is a reference to the last abbot of the abbey, Henry Duff. This document is therefore a source for the study of the religious house to which it belonged, and the relations that house had with other institutions in Dublin, as well as a source of information on a certain section of Dublin secular society.

Another manuscript associated with one of Dublin's religious houses is contained within TCD MS 175: the annals of St Mary's abbey. The abbey – part of which still exists (see Stout's essay in this volume, above) – was situated on the north side of the Liffey, roughly at the present-day intersection of Abbey St and Capel St. The manuscript is discussed by John T. Gilbert in his preface to a work on the chartularies of St Mary's abbey.[18] It is thought to have been written in the fifteenth century by Thomas Case, a cleric of the church of St Werburgh the Virgin, and subsequently bound with other writings of the

(Dublin, 1844), p. v. **15** Raymond Refaussé and Colm Lennon (eds), *The registers of Christ Church cathedral, Dublin* (Dublin, 1998). **16** Raymond Refaussé, 'Administration and rubrication: the Christ Church Psalter in context', *Irish Arts Review*, 21:2 (Summer, 2004), 102. **17** Todd, Introduction to *The Book of Obits and Martyrology*, p. xli. **18** John T. Gilbert (ed.), *Chartularies of St Mary's Abbey, Dublin, with the register of its house at Dunbrody, and annals of Ireland*, vol. II (London, 1884).

10.7 MS 1282, fo. 43v: extract from the Annals of Ulster

period, including the Lives of Irish saints. It is written in Latin, on vellum, and was in Trinity College Library by the latter part of the seventeenth century, when James Ware had access to it.[19] There is no title at the beginning, and the text begins with the birth of Christ, and passes relatively quickly through the first one thousand years AD. It refers to important dates in the civil and ecclesiastical history of Britain and Ireland, such as 1066 and 1169. Gilbert notes the similarity of certain entries to those in the *Liber Niger* of the cathedral church of the Holy Trinity.[20] There is much information relating specifically to Dublin and to the abbey itself, to its relationship with the church authorities, and to other religious houses. It records important events such as the founding of St Mary's abbey in 1139, the death of one of its abbots (Leonard), as well as other important incidents relating to Dublin:

> MCXXIL Obiit Samuel, quartus Episcopus Dublin.[21]
>
> Eodem anno [MCLXX] civitas Dublin per Comitem Ricardum et suos capta est.[22]
>
> Eodem anno [MCCIV], obiit pie memorie Leonardus, Abbas Domus Beate Marie, juxta Dubliniam.[23]

This manuscript of the annals merits study as a document with a unique perspective on the history of the religious house to which it belonged, and to the city of Dublin and its environs.

* * *

The third category of manuscripts is rather more heterogeneous than the two previous groups. These documents are grouped together simply because they do not fit into either of the above categories, but among their subjects is the common – and relevant – theme of Dublin in the Middle Ages. Included in this group are three volumes of miscellaneous collections of writings regarding Ireland in the medieval period. They date from the fifteenth to the seventeenth centuries, but the later compilations refer to the preceding centuries, and there are numerous references to Dublin throughout.

TCD MS 578 – 'Miscellanea de rebus Hibernicis ab Usserio collecta' – contains such eclectic items as a transcription of an extract from the register of St Thomas's abbey in Dublin, a list of the mayors of Dublin in the time of King Edward I, a list of bishops of Dublin, and a calendar of the obits of residents of Lusk. MS 591 – 'Collectanea de rebus Hibernicis' – is a collection of writings on Ireland from the fifteenth and sixteenth centuries, and contains

---

19 Ibid., p. xci. 20 Ibid., p. cxii. 21 TCD MS 175, fo. 5v. 22 TCD MS 175, fo. 8v. 23 TCD MS 175, fo. 11r.

10.8 MS 1209/7: Speed's 1610 map of the 'Countie of Leinster', with plan of the city of Dublin in its top right-hand corner, from the collection of almost seventy maps, also known as the Hardiman Atlas what Raymond Gillespie refers to as 'the most complete urban chronicle for Dublin', which covers the period 1408 to 1576, and which may have been written by a merchant from the city.[24] Another similar document is TCD MS 804, 'Miscellanea de rebus Hibernicis'. This volume contains a description of the extent of several counties, including Meath, Dublin and Louth, as well as a register of the members of the priory of All Hallows, whose register (TCD MS 525) has already been described. Also included is 'The Case of St Mary's Abbey and diverse other lands in Ireland, granted by ye late King James to John Wakeman', and 'Annales Monasterii B. Mariae Virginis Dub.'[25]

A manuscript about which much has already been written, but which is not immediately associated with Dublin, is TCD MS 1282, also known as the Annals of Ulster (fig. 10.7). It was compiled in the fifteenth and sixteenth centuries, partly by the scribe Ruaidhri Ó Luinín. It was written on vellum and contains 116 folios, and covers the period AD431–1540. It differs from the other manuscripts referred to already in that it was written beyond the Pale, and in that most of it is written in Irish, the vernacular language. For these reasons it could be said to give an alternative perspective on the events of the period in question. In relation to Dublin, it records the arrival of 'Amlaiph & Imhar' to the city in 870; a 'great leprosy' that came upon the foreigners in Dublin, and a 'bloody flux' in 950; in 1171 the arrival of Henry II; and other similar events.

The last document to be discussed is also one familiar to students of the history of medieval Ireland: John Speed's 1610 map of the 'Countie of Leinster', with a large inset plan of the city of Dublin in its top right-hand corner. It is from the collection of almost seventy maps, also known as the Hardiman Atlas, named after their first cataloguer James Hardiman (fig. 10.8). The set arrived in Trinity College in the late eighteenth century. The main image (of the province of Leinster) is filled with place-names, including those of the various suburbs of Dublin referred to in the deeds of collections such as TCD MSS 1207 and 1477, including 'Fyngal', 'Kilmanan', 'Cromlyn' and 'Malahedert'. The map of Dublin gives a good idea of the layout and extent of the walled city during the medieval period. With the aid of a numbered key, the major streets, buildings and other landmarks are easily identifiable; they include High Street, St Francis Street, Trinity College, Christ Church, Dublin Castle, and the one and only bridge over the Liffey at that time. Many of these places are those that are referenced in the manuscripts and other documents already discussed. It can be observed how the layout of modern Dublin is still rooted in that of the medieval city, and how many of the names of streets and landmarks have been retained (with slight alterations in spellings).

---

24 Raymond Gillespie, 'Dubliners view themselves: the Dublin city chronicles' in Seán Duffy (ed.), *Medieval Dublin VIII* (Dublin, 2008), p. 214.   **25** For a list of the contents of this and other manuscripts referred to in this article, see T.K. Abbott, *Catalogue of the manuscripts in the library of Trinity College Dublin* (Dublin, 1900).

Much work has already been done in the translation, transcription and description of many of these documents; there is, however, still room for more study of these and others, in order to provide a clearer picture of Dublin in the medieval period. While the digitization and description of such manuscripts aids their dissemination by means of the internet and other technologies, nothing can be taken away from the evidential value of the originals, or replace their intrinsic value as primary sources for the history of medieval Dublin.